Masterworks of
Latin American
Short Fiction

MASTERWORKS OF LATIN AMERICAN SHORT FICTION

Eight Novellas

Edited by Cass Canfield, Jr.

Introduction by Ilan Stavans

Icon Editions
An Imprint of HarperCollins*Publishers*

Grateful acknowledgment is made for permission to reprint the following:

"Innocent Eréndira" from *Innocent Eréndira and Other Stories* by Gabriel García Márquez, translated by Gregory Rabassa. English translation copyright © 1978 by Harper & Row. Reprinted by permission of HarperCollins Publishers.

"Miss Florence's Trunk" from *True and False Romances* by Ana Lydia Vega, translated by Andrew Hurley. Copyright © 1994 by Ana Lydia Vega. English translation copyright © 1994 by Ana Lydia Vega and Andrew Hurley. Reprinted by permission of Serpent's Tail Press, London.

"I Heard Her Sing" from *Three Trapped Tigers* by Guillermo Cabrera Infante, translated by D. Gardner, S. J. Levine, and G. C. Infante. Copyright © 1965 by Guillermo Cabrera Infante. English translation copyright © 1971 by Harper & Row. Reprinted by permission of HarperCollins Publishers.

"The Snow of the Admiral" from *Maqroll: Three Novellas* by Alvaro Mutis, translated by Edith Grossman. Copyright © 1986 by Alvaro Mutis. English translation copyright © 1992 by Edith Grossman. Reprinted by permission of HarperCollins Publishers.

"The Road to Santiago" from *The War of Time* by Alejo Carpentier, translated by Frances Partridge. Copyright © 1970 by Victor Gollancz, Ltd. Reprinted by permission of Warren W. Cook, agent for Andrea Esteban Carpentier, Mount Kisco, New York.

"The Pursuer" from *End of the Game and Other Stories* by Julio Cortázar, translated by Paul Blackburn. Copyright © 1967 by Random House, Inc. Reprinted by permission of Pantheon Books, a division of Random House, Inc., New York.

"My Uncle, the Jaguar" from *Estas Estórias* by João Guimarães Rosa. Copyright © 1985 by the heirs of João Guimarães Rosa. English translation copyright © 1996 by Giovanni Pontiero. Reprinted by permission of Livraria Jose Olympia Editoria, Rio de Janeiro.

"The Daisy Dolls" from *Piano Stories* by Felisberto Hernández. Copyright © 1993 by the heirs of Felisberto Hernández. English translation copyright © 1993 by Luis Harss. Reprinted by permission of Marsilio Publishers, New York.

HarperCollins books may be purchased for educational, business, or sales promotional use. For information please write: Special Markets Department, HarperCollins Publishers, Inc., 10 East 53rd Street, New York, NY 10022.

Designed by Nina Gaskin

ISBN 0-06-431502-9

96 97 98 99 00 ❖/HC 10 9 8 7 6 5 4 3 2

CONTENTS

PREFACE

THE AIM OF THIS ANTHOLOGY IS FOR THE READER TO EXPERIENCE THE work of a number of major Latin American writers in selections of sufficient length to give a real appreciation of each writer. The novella has been masterfully used in Latin American literature, as Ilan Stavans points out in his introduction, and this allows longer selections from each writer than in most anthologies. To keep the volume to a reasonable length and price only eight novellas could be included. So obviously important Latin American writers, men and women, are missing, some simply because they didn't write novellas at all. But I hope the novellas included show the richness and variety of modern Latin American literature and offer diverse examples of style, tone, theme and subject.

Over the years I have learned a good deal about Latin American writers and writing from the following people some of whom I've been privileged to publish. To all of them my thanks and gratitude: Carmen Balcells, Guillermo Cabrera Infante, Thomas Colchie, John A. Coleman, Carlos Fuentes, Gabriel García Márquez, Edith Grossman, Luis Harss, Suzanne Jill Levine, Alvaro Mutis, Gregory Rabassa, Alastair Reid, Barbara Probst Solomon, Ilan Stavans, Mario Vargas Llosa. I am particularly grateful to two friends and authors—Ilan Stavans for his help and support and thoughtful introduction and Alvaro Mutis for his enthusiasm and advice.

CASS CANFIELD, JR.

INTRODUCTION

EDMUND WILSON, IN A SECTION CALLED "CURRENT CLICHÉS AND Solecisms" originally published in *The New Yorker* and later included in his collection of essays, *The Bit Between My Teeth*, discussed terms whose common usage he was uncomfortable with. One of them was the word *novella*. He wrote: "It is true that we do not have in English any single word for the narrative that is longer than a short story but not so long as a novel. But why go so far afield for it? Saintsbury and Henry James were in the habit of using *nouvelle*, and this seems to me better than *novella*, for which I have a special dislike because I think it was introduced by the American *Story* magazine and was an ignorant affectation." Wilson's discomfort gives the impression of being purely personal, his own animosity against a certain word sound or verbal texture; but being at odds as to how to call what the *Oxford English Dictionary* describes as "a short fictitious prose tale published as a complete book" is in fact a common malaise. Nobody is quite sure how to address it. Should one call it a "short novel" or "long story"? Should one choose the German wording, *novelle*, instead of the French *nouvelle*? Or should one resort, as Merriam-Webster does, to the vile diminutive *novelette*?

The more one reflects on Wilson's uneasiness, the clearer it becomes that the status of novellas in the United States and England is shaky at best. Magazine editors, confused as they are about its potential, are leery of granting them too much space in their periodicals; and publishers normally don't package them as a complete book, accompanying them instead with shorter stories to make a heftier and more salable volume. No wonder readers have so much trouble visualizing the novella as anything other than a hybrid—a sheer abstraction. But one need only invoke Joseph Conrad's *Heart of Darkness*, Melville's *Bartleby the Scrivener*, and Henry James's *Daisy Miller*, not to mention others equally famous, to realize how fecund and industrious this form has been. James himself, a master of the form and one of its most serious theoreticians, reflected on its purpose and limitation in several of his prefaces to the New York Edition of his work. His argument is that novellas can be successful when matched with a "perfect theme," a subject neither too long so as to spill the matter over, nor too limiting so as to cut its breath short. Its creator is like a trapeze artist: "a single spill," says James, a careless wrong move can make it, in the expert eyes of the knowing, a major embarrassment. A novella (or to use the term he preferred, *nouvelle*) requires, as he put it, a "foreshortening," an attitude of straps and buckles. James also complains that people in the literary business look down at it as an "awkward" form, "unacceptable," in an eternal state of "editorial disfavor." In his preface to *Daisy Miller* he describes how he wanted "to ride the *nouvelle* down-town, to prance and curve and caracole with it there—that would have been the true ecstasy."

But while the novella remains amorphous among English speakers, it is cultivated with unequal intensity in other cultures. It has reached a high esteem in Russia and Europe, for instance, as well as in the Latin American orbit, where, marked by its Iberian ancestry, it is embraced wholeheartedly and without vacillation. Indeed, ever since its debut, in 1832, under the title of *Don Catrín de la Fachenda: His Life and Occurrences*, penned by "the Mexican thinker," José Joaquin Fernández de Lizardi (whom Katherine Anne Porter translated into English) the novella south of the Rio Grande has been candidly experimented upon and reflected about by writers of different ideological and artistic persuasions. Some, like the Mexican *femme de lettres* Rosario Castellanos, have even called it "the region's preeminent literary vessel"; others, such as the Uruguayan novelist and critic Mario Benedetti, author of *The Truce*, in a famous 1953 essay compared it in stature to the other favorite prose forms, the novel and short story, and described the novella as a "*tranche de vie*, full of details, antecedents, and consequences." This is not to say, of course, that the Spanish lexicon is more clear-cut, less ambivalent than the English. We seem incapable of making our minds up as to which term to use: Is it *relato, noveleta, novelita, novela breve,* or *novela corta*? Happily, this discrepancy has had little effect. The upheavals in Latin America in the last two hundred years have been quite positive for the novella: many dozens are printed and reprinted annually in book form, and they enjoy enormous prestige and high respect.

Largely as a result of the belletristic boom of the late sixties and seventies, personified by Gabriel García Márquez, Guillermo Cabrera

Infante, José Donoso, Julio Cortázar, Carlos Fuentes, Mario Vargas Llosa, and others, that brought the region to the Western cultural banquet, international readers have been educated—and have thus come to expect—voluptuousness and excess as a pair of constants in its literary output. Known as *la generación del boom*, these writers, whom John Updike described as capable of "writing with magical lucidity along the thin edge where objective fact and subjective myth merge," created an enchanting, mysterious portrait of Latin America, a land forgotten by God, visited by epidemics of insomnia and rainstorms of butterflies, where prostitutes are visionaries and colonels become allegories. They were all native, middle- and upper-middle-class men (women like Isabel Allende and Laura Esquivel entered the international literary scene much later), rebellious, influenced by the left-wing rhetoric of the early fifties, who sought exile in Europe and learned to appreciate the region's contrast and contradictions from afar. They experimented on all fronts, stylistically and formally, and while the world recognizes them as masters of the novel and the short story, the novella was among their favorite literary forms, one with which they reached astonishing heights. Indeed such was their creative revolution that they managed to spill a bit of the international attention they were receiving to many precursors known only within their linguistic boundaries, thus creating their own literary genealogy: João Guimarães Rosa, Miguel Angel Asturias, Graciliano Ramos, Horacio Quiroga, María Luisa Bombal, Felisberto Hernández, and Juan Rulfo, among other predecessors, many of them masters of the novella as well, began to be read globally, expanding the horizon of Latin American letters and offering a fiesta of artistic possibilities few suspected possible in the Southern Hemisphere.

The actual reasons that catapulted *la generación del boom* into stardom are still hotly debated. Some see them as a sheer marketing product orchestrated in Barcelona by powerful agents and publishers. Others claim they were the antidote to the decaying European novel. What's unquestionable is that, just as the second half of the nineteenth century belongs to Russian classics like Chehkov, Gogol, Tolstoi, and Dostoevski, these writers belong to the golden age of Latin American letters. The image they sold of the hemisphere as an exotic land, full of lust and magic, was enthusiastically endorsed in Europe and the United States. But their vision has also been put to question by their successors, who argue that Latin America is much more than a land of radical ideologies, power thirst, and sexual arousal. While applauding the immense talent of the old guard, the new generation had also accused them of representing the region as a racial monolith, a Banana Republic allergic to civilized democratic debate and akin to hallucinatory escapes. Minorities in their work are invariably portrayed as freaks, women are instinctual by nature and have superficial intellects, the military is a body politic beyond redemption, and morality is both proverbial and malleable. Mempo Giardinelli, an Argentine born in 1947 and the recipient of the prestigious Romulo Gallegos award for his novel *Holy Office of Memory*, a writer who came of age under the shadow of the boom, argues that "these masters left us memorable works, they opened the way, they conceived our continent in an audacious, original way, and they became our modern classics." But despite their greatness, their books "no longer explain contemporary Latin America," and it is therefore not valid to go on thinking about the region in the terms they articulated.

This change of gear is obviously the result of a generation break: the young are forced to overcome, to push aside the influence of their forebears in order to gain momentum and move into the spotlight; and they need to do so by articulating a rival vision, a refreshing look into what surrounds them and what their role as intellectuals ought to be in a continent afflicted by fragile democracies, social unbalance, and political extremism. The gap is made perfectly clear as one follows the transformation undergone in the region by the way writers understand fiction in general, and the novella in particular. Alejo Carpentier, for instance, because of his exposure to surrealism in Paris in the twenties and thirties, enjoyed saying that "incongruity and paradox were at the heart of Latin American life," that the Continent is known as a space where "everything is outsized and disproportionate: towering mountains and waterfalls, endless plains, impenetrable jungles," and "an anarchic urban spread [overlying] breathless virgin expanses." In his eyes, the literature coming from this habitat needed to reflect such profusion by accentuating colors and human polarities, by portraying dreams as mammoth utopias and its sites and citizens as extravagant, prodigal, and lavish. Carpentier, who was born in 1904, has been applauded for his long novels, such as *Explosion in a Cathedral* and *The Rite of Spring*, bravura performances and admirable baroque constructions professing the philosophy of "more is more" and "dreaming of swallowing the globe entire"; he also excelled in the short story, which he approached as an opportunity to condense, but not sacrifice, his excessive style, and which he envisioned as an intellectual genre, perplexing, obtuse, to be assembled with startling craftsmanship. However, it is in his many novellas, such as *The Road to Santiago*, *Manhunt*, and *Concierto Barroco*, where he was at once parsimonious and extravagant, where he arguably reached some of his most inspired artistic moments by intertwining race, history, and myth, and where his theory of composition can best be understood. He managed to re-create the inner life of a character, all the while striving to create an overall effect. In fact, it is fair to claim, as several literary critics do, that throughout his career Carpentier articulated a vision of the novella as a well-centered, self-contained "medium-size" system of signs that differs from others provided by Western culture in that it reflects the relation between history and narrative unique to Latin America.

Something similar ought to be said about many other boom members, from Cortázar to García Márquez. For all their flamboyant excess in megafictions like *Hopscotch* and *One Hundred Years of Solitude*, for all the precision they display in their magisterial short stories, Latin American fiction during the boom after World War II often found its perfect balance in the novella. And this applies to their forerunners and progeny as well, which testifies, once again, to the incredible vitality of the genre. In fact, I cannot think of a single writer of relevance who didn't, at some point in his life, take a deep breath and plunge into this most challenging literary form. Even Borges, known for his personal caution against novel writing and in general for psychological fiction ("where all things are plausible"), tried his luck in *The Congress*, a failed *nouvelle* published in a noncommercial edition in 1971 and unquestionably his most extensive narrative. In this work, which had been zigzagging in his mind since 1945, Borges returned to the concept of secret societies displayed in "Tlön, Uqbar, Orbis Tertius."

But each generation offers a distinctive world view, a collective notion of life and death unlike those that come before and after. Think of Esteban Echeverría's semi-essayistic *The Slaughterhouse*, Machado de Assis's *The Alienist*, Sallarué's *The Negro Christ*, Fuentes's *Aura*, Bombal's *The Shrouded Woman*; García Márquez's *No One Writes the Colonel*, and *Chronicle of a Death Foretold*; Augusto Roa Bastos's *Kurupi*, Ernesto Sábato's *The Outsider*, João Guimarães Rosa's *The Opportunity of Augusto Matraca*, Antonio Skármeta's *Burning Patience*, Juan Carlos Onetti's *The Pit*, José Donoso's *The Closed Door*, Vargas Llosa's *The Cubs*, José María Arguedas's *Amor Mundo*, Adolfo Bioy Casares's *The Invention of Morel*, Reinaldo Arenas's *Old Rosa*, and Elena Poniatowska's *Dear Diego*. This is clearly a very limited list of novellas of various lengths. It excludes many other memorable ones,

most significantly the eight *chef d'oeuvres* in this volume. What makes
them attractive is not only their individual beauty, their distinctive
mood and joie de vivre, but the overall aggregated effect they deliver.
They are prime examples covering a vast stylistic and thematic territory
and offering a taste of what each artistic generation strives to accomplish within the borders of the genre: Hernández, Carpentier, and
Guimarães Rosa date to the preboom era and their novellas are medita-
tions on time, memory, and the fragile borderline where dreams and
reality intertwine; the entries by García Márquez, Guillermo Cabrera
Infante, and Cortázar, all technically innovative, are models of the mas-
tery the boom generation was capable of; Alvaro Mutis navigates his
own Conradian route, polishing a fanciful narrative about exile in the
most universal way possible; and Ana Lydia Vega's novella is a stellar
case of what the post-boom generation has accomplished, a study of the
effects of race and nationalism in Puerto Rico at the end of the nineteenth century that serves as a telescope to understand what the island
has become today. In many ways Latin American letters, up until *la generación del boom*, was a male-dominated affair, and Vega is a first-rate
representative of the massive entrance of extraordinarily talented
women to the canon that occurred in the eighties.

Reading novellas is like savoring a plentiful main dish without the
risk of indigestion. Each of these eight narratives offer a map of its creator's mind, allowing the reader to enjoy their talents in full. Some random clues might be helpful before the reading begins. Cortázar has
stated that the source of the novella's power is its inner tension. The
higher the tension the better it transmits the writer's pulsations. "What
the exact method of transmitting this pulsation is, I can't say," he told
the critic Luis Harss, "but in any case it depends on the ruthless execution." As a rule in Cortázar's work, the tension in a story is apparent
even before it begins, but in *The Pursuer*, published in 1959, which was
inspired by the lives of jazz saxophonist Charlie Parker and writer Dylan
Thomas, the tension is inside: it begins at the beginning and continues
to grow as the narrative develops. Cortázar published numerous stories
in the fifties, and by the time he began working on this novella, he felt
he had exhausted the form: he wanted to go beyond, to turn their extension and scope upside down. "By then I was fully aware of the dangerous perfection of the storyteller who reaches a certain level of achieve-
ment and stays at that same level forever, without moving on. I was a
bit sick and tired of how well my stories turned out." He looked for a
more ambitious theme, "an existential problem, a human problem," . . .

"something a lot closer to me." Only four years later, at age 49, he would produce *Hopscotch*, his magnum opus, so *The Pursuer* served as the overpass, a leap of faith, a step forward, a new frontier.

Its enchantments are many and multifaceted. The Argentine plays modernist tricks with different views of the same event. He puts forth a provocative view of the parasitic relationship between art and criticism by establishing that a biographer distorts a biographee's life as much as the biographee acts out variations of himself so that the biographer will "improve" him, making him immortal in the eyes of society. In a sense, the theme of the double, ubiquitous in Cortázar, colors the entire novella, linking it to Carpentier's *The Road to Santiago*. The two writers couldn't have been more different. Carpentier, a myth maker, frequented the novella at different stages in his life. He thought of the archetypal Latin American man as an "ever present, overshadowing figure in a telluric background, at once redundant and multiple." His main point "is the age-old struggle for survival and renewal," since "we citizens of the ridiculously called Third World are at once young and old." Thus he believed the artist who dreams of re-creating this man "must be at once a miniaturist and a muralist, a moralist and a minstrel, a sociologist and a poet." And that's precisely his goal in *The Road to Santiago*, probably the most ambitious of Latin America's novellas and certainly among Carpentier's most accomplished works.

Published in 1958, it was originally translated into English as *The Highroad of Saint James*. While doing research for a history of Cuban music in an old chronicle of Havana, Carpentier came across the name of Juan de Amberes. As he explained in a note in the newspaper *El Nacional*, Amberes "played the drum when a ship was sighted," and it suddenly occurred to him to write "an imaginary biography of this character who left no further trace of his existence." He artfully uses the pre-Columbian concept of cyclical time, rearticulated and orientalized by Nietzsche as "The Myth of Eternal Return," to recount the conquest of the New World from a European perspective. Set in Flanders, France, Spain, and Cuba, Carpentier imagines the double life of a prototypical Indiano: Juan de Amberes/Juan Romero. They meet at the Burgos Fair in the sixteenth century: one travels to Cuba in search of fortune; the other remains in Europe. In the end, the double meets its counterpart as the journey is about to repeat itself. As in Borges's short story, "The Garden of Forking Paths," the two Juans are not only their own double but, more accurately, different versions of themselves: their past and future cohabiting. What's extraordinary is that, fooled by

Carpentier's baroque style, the reader gets the feeling the novella has magnified itself tremendously, that extension has been swapped by depth.

From the Latin American writer's point of view, a novella is a most challenging endeavor, a trial of will and muscle. It requires the meticulousness, the mathematical approach of a short story, each word sitting in its right place so as to carry the plot's overall effect; but it also needs the panoramic appetite and ardor of a novel, its wider cry and spell, to be properly effective. Parsimonious by nature and perhaps even avaricious, a story succeeds by subtraction; its beauty is in its smallness, its delicate balance between brevity and scope. The novel, on the other hand, is an anything-goes, hodgepodge genre whose main principle is addition: anything can be pushed in and between its covers, as long as it finds a suitable justification, a *raison d'etre*. García Márquez uses the verb "to add" to describe the novel: "the building of a wall by *adding* one brick after another," whereas the short story, in his view, is exemplified the verb "to eliminate": "the art of eliminating, of emptying a container." But the novella is far less flexible—"the middle ground," in García Márquez's words, "an addition by way of subtraction."

These theoretical reflections are put into practice by García Márquez in *Innocent Eréndira*, published in 1972, when he was 44, and whose complete, endearing title is *The Incredible and Sad Tale of Innocent Eréndira and Her Heartless Grandmother*. As in the case of Carpentier's novella, it also emits mythical echoes. It revolves around the fable of the merciless matron whose daughter, having committed a crime against the family, has to purify her sins by means of more sinful behavior. Eréndira is forced to submit to masses of men to pay back the destruction of her grandmother's possessions, which she accidentally provoked. As the plot unravels, the theme of love, running through the entire oeuvre of the Colombian writer, becomes the leitmotiv. García Márquez's universe is ornate; his characters, while highly political, are not clichés of political rhetoric; his prose, as V. S. Pritchett once remarked, "is plain, exact, subtle and springy and easily leaps into the comical and the exuberant." What's compelling in this case, at least to me, is his choice of genres: García Márquez, who was awarded the Nobel Prize for Literature in 1982, has his share of distinguished novellas but, could Eréndira's plight have acquired the shape of a short story? After all, his short stories are as abundant and all-encompassing as his novellas. And yet, the answer must be negative: both the overall suspense and the protagonist's transformation keep *Innocent Eréndira* together; they allow for a certain beat, a certain rhythm to his tragedy that would otherwise be lost.

Alvaro Mutis, an itinerant traveler, a dilettante and a fellow Colombian (five years older than García Márquez), is equally obsessed by rhythm, but of a very different kind. He has spent most of his writing life re-creating the adventures of Maqroll the Gaviero, also a devoted voyager—the word *gaviero* is Spanish for mast-man or lookout. While his debut dates back to when Mutis was in his twenties, he began to pop up as poetic hero and has experienced multiple transformations (including Mutis's collection of poems, *Summa de Maqroll El Gaviero: 1948–1970*). His evasive presence recalls Kurtz in *Heart of Darkness*. Very little is known about his origin and past. He is described as "a born anarchist who pretends not to know that about himself, or to ignore it." He is a Quixotic dreamer, an eternal wanderer, and a Byronic hero: melancholic, defiant, brooding on some mysterious,unforgiving sin of the past.

Maqroll appears in seven of Mutis's novellas: in some his role is that of a protagonist, while in others he has a cameo appearance; but none of these novellas depends on the others in content and chronology, which means that they can be read as autonomous and self-sufficient tales. *The Snow of the Admiral*, the most famous, was published in 1973 and is a sideboard of Mutis's style: while showing absolutely no interest in politics, it delivers a poignant portrait of Latin America, albeit one seen from a distance. Mutis is the most Europeanized, the most detached, of modern Latin American novelists, as is clear in the way he explores the region's nature and idiosyncrasy. He evidently owes more to Jules Verne, Emilio Salgari, Conrad, and Graham Greene than to any of his contemporaries. He is above all a storyteller, a master of creating mood, atmosphere, place and circumstance.

We find João Guimarães Rosa, intrigued by the dichotomy of primitivism versus civilization permeating Latin America since the arrival of Europeans on the mainland in 1498, at the opposite side of the spectrum; his mounting monologue *My Uncle, the Jaguar* couldn't exemplify this fixation of his any better. His literature is pure stream of consciousness in the Joycean sense: language dances free, unabated, across time and space zones (as Luis Harss put it, "in him outer scope is inner range"), re-creating the eternal conflict between man and nature, between progress and barbarism. Some writers, in spite of their talents, have the misfortune of having been born in the wrong time and place. In the case of Guimarães Rosa time is of little consequence, but not place. (His birth was in 1908, into the generation of Octavio Paz, Carpentier, and Asturias, and he died just as *la generación del boom* was gaining momentum—in 1967, a turning point in Latin American letters, the year Editorial Sudamericana brought out García Márquez's *One Hundred Years of Solitude* in Buenos Aires and Asturias was awarded the Nobel Prize for Literature in Stockholm). The fact that he comes from Brazil, which, while being the largest and most populated of all Latin American countries, is also linguistically and culturally isolated, has obscured his work, which is devoted to exploring the human complexities of the sertão. Guimarães Rosa managed to overcome this isolation by means of his polyglotism—aside from Portuguese, he knew German, Spanish, English, Italian, Swedish, Serbo-Croatian, and Russian—and by using fiction as both a microscope and a telescope to understand Brazilian society. As in the novel-as-mural, exemplified by his most memorable opus, *The Devil to Pay in the Backlands* (in Portuguese, *Grande Sertão: Veredas*), he believed the challenge in Brazilian literature was "to be inclusive and exclusive, to strive for the universal and the particular." This he found most daunting to achieve in the novella, which he cultivated extensively, as in *Corpo de Baile*, composed of seven short narratives, and in *Estas estórias*, consisting of nine (one of which is *My Uncle, the Jaguar*). Notice the fashion in which his fabulous display of language and his encyclopedic knowledge are neutralized by a Chekhovian attitude to character: Guimarães Rosa turns the speaker into a unsanctimonious storyteller, at once map and compass to Brazil's modern hardships.

Ana Lydia Vega, born in 1946, is perhaps the least known of the eight writers in this volume, but *Miss Florence's Trunk*, published in 1991 and included in *True and False Romances*, a volume of assortments, should serve both as an introduction to her work and as a reminder of the ghosts and obsessions that the post-boom writers are concerned with. Vega has always been concerned with the hallucinatory line separating fiction from reality. She has coined the paradoxical term of "false chronicle" to describe untrue firsthand testimony, and her novella exemplifies her quest. Reminiscent of the work of E. M. Forster and Charlotte Brontë, *Miss Florence's Trunk* is an old-fashioned narrative using letters, diaries, and first-person accounts to revive the sexual, patriotic, and racial tension that populated the Caribbean between 1858 and the dawn of the Spanish-American War. Her female narrator and protagonist, Miss Florence Jane, is a British tutor of French to the grandson of the inventor Samuel Morse. She is a timid beauty, a reader of the Brontë sisters and George Sand, working for Morse's daughter (who actually lived in Arroyo, Puerto Rico, for forty years). As the plot unravels, the reader witnesses the disparity between the Europeanized aristocracy and black slaves, between extroverted male slave owners and their submissive, introverted wives, between Western knowledge and aboriginal ways of healing, such as *curandería*, all in the microcosm of a large estate named La Enriqueta. Vega is a seasoned post modernist, always ready to experiment by subverting literary traditions and using pastiches of genre fiction, such as the thriller and the historical romance, and *Miss Florence's Trunk* is no exception: its characters fall victim to hysterical outbursts, nostalgic drives, and suicidal attempts, mixing history and fiction to allow for a reflection on Puerto Rican's past and present. One ought to remember that Samuel Morse, who in the novella is seen installing the first telegraphic system in Puerto Rico, was known as an anti-abolitionist: a clear sign of what Latin American often inherits from abroad—technology and regressive politics.

What makes Ana Lydia Vega an undisputed leader of the post-boom generation is her strong feminist voice. While her female characters are passive and obedient, the fashion in which she portrays them, as folks to be pitied, is ideologically charged; she might be realistic, but she isn't pamphleteering. Also, Vega has a strong interest in using memory as a laboratory to investigate Hispanic idiosyncrasy and has strived to find in her work ways to abandon the cartoonish legacy of magical realism. These two are essential characteristics of the literary generation that came of age while García Márquez, Vargas Llosa, and their pals wined and dined around the world: they are interested in political violence, denunciation of dictatorship, and testimonial writing, but in an irreverent, disruptive manner; they are still akin to *lo fantastico*, but enjoy pop culture and like satire and farce to tone their imagination.

All in all, Latin Americans in their novellas enjoy paying tribute to Cervantes, and to a lesser extent to other medieval and golden age precursors, such as *Lazarillo de Tormes*, *Amadís de Gaula*, and *Tirant lo Blanc*. One senses the ghost of Cervantes meddling in Maqroll's affairs, as one does in most of what Cabrera Infante, the Cuban émigré, writes. Linguistic brio, but accompanied by humor and a critique of frivolity, an aspect often missing in Guimarães Rosa, is one of Cabrera Infante's easy-to-recognize specialties. But his parodic approach to high- and low-brow culture and his baroque style are equally recognizable in *I Heard Her Sing*—his 1965 novella, which Cortázar loved (it is known in Spanish as *Ella cantaba boleros*). This narrative is ingeniously cut into eight sequential pieces and interspersed throughout his masterpiece, *Three Trapped Tigers*, his hidden tribute to Cervantes's "Impertinent Curiosity"—a tale-within-a-tale. His attempt is to re-create the verbosity and nightlife of Havana in 1958, *el inframundo*, as Fidel Castro is about to stage his coup. Cabrera Infante uses language as narrative, creating characters and events through dialogue that becomes a portrait of Cuban society. But his portrait is quite different from Ana Lydia Vega's: while hers is a rural overview, his palpitates with the rhymes of the inner city; while she investigates the demons obsessing the mind of a female stranger, an intellectual as well as a porcelain beauty, in Puerto Rican society, he approaches the female body as an object of lust and adoration. The central theme of *I Heard Her Sing*, as in Cortázar's *The Pursuer*, is the chase: Codac, a photojournalist, wants to preserve the memory of La Estrella, a mulatto who has just died and whose singing and dancing exemplifies Cuban Bolero. Lionel Trilling liked to say that "all prose fiction is a variation of the theme of Don Quixote: the link between dream and reality," and, much like Cortázar's novella, Cabrera Infante's openly addresses the foggy limit between the two: in the carnivalesque world of Codac and La Estrella, honesty and histrionics, objectivity and hallucination, are hard to separate.

I have saved for last my own personal favorite among these novellas: Felisberto Hernández's *The Daisy Dolls*, published in 1949, a macabre view of bourgeois decadence and the impact of the Industrial Revolution. Hernández approached the novella as an excuse to dissect our innermost delusions and anxieties; thus, his is not a style that reaches out but one that insists on digging in. The Latin America of his imagination isn't a natural but a mental landscape, a view of the many complexes of its citizens. The central theme of *The Daisy Dolls*, a house isolated from humanity, is not original, but in his hand it acquires an astonishing effect. A peculiar couple lives surrounded by full-sized dolls, treating them as daughters. But the dolls soon ignite erotic needs, and extramarital love as well as incest become central themes. Hernández's novella is a critique of capitalist society, particularly its cult of fetishism. In this setting isolation turns into lunacy; but lunacy, when seen in the abstract, is nothing but normality. An ontological chase is, once again, the main concern. Like the characters of Cortázar, Cabrera Infante, and Carpentier, those of Hernández are in pursuit of an evasive utopia, a universe where dreams follow their own rules. Hernández once masterfully summarized his whimsical views on art and artistic creation as follows: "At a given moment," he wrote, "I think a plant is about to be born in some corner of me . . . I must take care that it does not occupy too much space or try to be beautiful or intense, helping it to become only what it was meant to be."

If Guimarães Rosa had the misfortune to be born into the wrong linguistic and national sphere, Hernández, another urban dweller, strikes me as a bizarre case of literary obscurity: he has talents not unlike Kafka's; his vision, particularly in his masterful novellas (they include *The Stray Horse* and *In the Times of Clemente Colling*), rivals anything written by Bruno Schulz; and his surrealist twists equal Cortázar's early stories. Why then is he eclipsed? As consolation, one must cherish the fact that Hernández remains the property of a small number of initiated readers, and the longer he remains in obscurity, the more his followers can enjoy their collective secret. Among them is García Márquez, who claims that "if I hadn't read [Hernández's] stories in 1950, I wouldn't be the writer I am today," since "he taught me that the most haunting mysteries are those of everyday life." Equally, Italo Calvino, another of the *iniciados,* calls him "an irregular," eluding classification and labeling, "unmistakable on any page on which one might randomly open one of his books."

Every anthology creates its own double, a volume of everything it leaves out. Behind these eight novellas, many other accomplished ones prance and curve and caracole into unforeseen stratospheres. But these examples are a showcase of the way in which the continent strives to define itself. At the verge of the next millennium, the legacy of Latin America in the twentieth century is unequivocal: the region has little to offer in political terms, but much to deliver when it comes to the imagination. The struggle between authenticity and foreign influence, between the old and the new, is as vivid as ever. Generations come and go, each proposing a different thesis on where the continent should go and a different interpretations of where it's coming from. Each speaks of destruction and redemption, of death and rebirth, but in terms particular to the time and place they were produced. Because of the nature of the region, these views always have had incredible urgency in fiction. When metamorphosed into novels and stories, they say more about the abysmal state of its citizens than any eloquent political speech. And they do so particularly well in the novella, a genre melodious and hypnotizing, perfectly designed for modern sensibilities: at once brief and detailed, incisive yet light hearted, an ideal form in a land where people either cannot read or have no time to do so. Even when its concerns are apolitical, the Latin American novella is an unruly artifact par excellence: it blossoms by suggesting rather than accusing, by hiding rather than revealing.

These eight novellas are displays of "the trapeze art" Henry James talked about, the technique of straps and buckles needed to control the beast. They are careful in their foreshortening, attentive to the single spill that can mess it all up, and they thrive in redefining and subverting the immense possibilities of the genre—precisely because they are the product of a milieu considerably more comfortable with "riding the novella all around," as James would put it, than its English-speaking counterpart. No apologies are offered, no editorial explanations: they are showcases of what in-depth fiction but with preconceived restraint, politically motivated yet savvy in its dealings with censorship, can accomplish. In a land where writers are speakers of the unspeakable, readers have embraced the novella form in full as free spirited and self-sufficient, brave and uncompromising, because it is what Latin America always longs for: a mirror unsimplified, an honest exhibition of its complexities, a map to its identity.

ILAN STAVANS

MASTERWORKS OF LATIN AMERICAN SHORT FICTION

The Incredible and Sad Tale of Innocent Eréndira and Her Heartless Grandmother

by Gabriel García Márquez

translated by Gregory Rabassa

ERÉNDIRA WAS BATHING HER GRANDMOTHER WHEN THE WIND OF HER misfortune began to blow. The enormous mansion of moonlike concrete lost in the solitude of the desert trembled down to its foundations with the first attack. But Eréndira and her grandmother were used to the risks of the wild nature there, and in the bathroom decorated with a series of peacocks and childish mosaics of Roman baths they scarcely paid any attention to the caliber of the wind.

The grandmother, naked and huge in the marble tub, looked like a handsome white whale. The granddaughter had just turned fourteen and was languid, soft-boned, and too meek for her age. With a parsimony that had something like sacred rigor about it, she was bathing her grandmother with water in which purifying herbs and aromatic leaves had been boiled, the latter clinging to the succulent back, the flowing metal-colored hair, and the powerful shoulders which were so mercilessly tattooed as to put sailors to shame.

"Last night I dreamt I was expecting a letter," the grandmother said.

Eréndira, who never spoke except when it was unavoidable, asked:

"What day was it in the dream?"

"Thursday."

"Then it was a letter with bad news," Eréndira said, "but it will never arrive."

When she had finished bathing her grandmother, she took her to her bedroom. The grandmother was so fat that she could only walk by leaning on her granddaughter's shoulder or on a staff that looked like a bishop's crosier, but even during her most difficult efforts the power of an antiquated grandeur was evident. In the bedroom, which had been furnished with an excessive and somewhat demented taste, like the whole house, Eréndira needed two more hours to get her grandmother ready. She untangled her hair strand by strand, perfumed and combed it, put an equatorially flowered dress on her, put talcum powder on her face, bright red lipstick on her mouth, rouge on her cheeks, musk on her eyelids, and mother-of-pearl polish on her nails, and when she had her decked out like a larger than life-size doll, she led her to an artificial garden with suffocating flowers that were like the ones on the dress, seated her in a large chair that had the foundation and the pedigree of a throne, and left her listening to elusive records on a phonograph that had a speaker like a megaphone.

While the grandmother floated through the swamps of the past, Eréndira busied herself sweeping the house, which was dark and motley, with bizarre furniture and statues of invented Caesars, chandeliers of teardrops and alabaster angels, a gilded piano, and numerous clocks of unthinkable sizes and shapes. There was a cistern in the courtyard for the storage of water carried over many years from distant springs on the backs of Indians, and hitched to a ring on the cistern wall was a broken-down ostrich, the only feathered creature who could survive the torment of that accursed climate. The house was far away from everything, in the heart of the desert, next to a settlement with miserable and burning streets where the goats committed suicide from desolation when the wind of misfortune blew.

That incomprehensible refuge had been built by the grandmother's husband, a legendary smuggler whose name was Amadís, by whom she had a son whose name was also Amadís and who was Eréndira's father. No one knew either the origins or the motivations of that family. The best known version in the language of the Indians was that Amadís the father had rescued his beautiful wife from a house of prostitution in the Antilles, where he had killed a man in a knife fight, and that he had transplanted her forever in the impunity of the desert. When the Amadíses died, one of melancholy fevers and the other riddled with bullets in a fight over a woman, the grandmother buried their bodies in the courtyard, sent away the fourteen barefoot servant girls, and continued ruminating on her dreams of grandeur in the shadows of the furtive house, thanks to the sacrifices of the bastard granddaughter whom she had reared since birth.

Eréndira needed six hours just to set and wind the clocks. The day when her misfortune began she didn't have to do that because the clocks had enough winding left to last until the next morning, but on the other hand, she had to bathe and overdress her grandmother, scrub the floors, cook lunch, and polish the crystalware. Around eleven o'clock, when she was changing the water in the ostrich's bowl and watering the desert weeds around the twin graves of the Amadíses, she had to fight off the anger of the wind, which had become unbearable, but she didn't have the slightest feeling that it was the wind of her misfortune. At twelve o'clock she was wiping the last champagne glasses when she caught the smell of broth and had to perform the miracle of running to the kitchen without leaving a disaster of Venetian glass in her wake.

She just managed to take the pot off the stove as it was beginning to boil over. Then she put on a stew she had already prepared and took advantage of a chance to sit down and rest on a stool in the kitchen. She closed her eyes, opened them again with an unfatigued expression, and began pouring the soup into the tureen. She was working as she slept.

The grandmother had sat down alone at the head of a banquet table with silver candlesticks set for twelve people. She shook her little bell and Eréndira arrived almost immediately with the steaming tureen. As Eréndira was serving the soup, her grandmother noticed the somnambulist look and passed her hand in front of her eyes as if wiping an invisible pane of glass. The girl didn't see the hand. The grandmother followed her with her look and when Eréndira turned to go back to the kitchen, she shouted at her:

"Eréndira!"

Having been awakened all of a sudden, the girl dropped the tureen onto the rug.

"That's all right, child," the grandmother said to her with assuring tenderness. "You fell asleep while you were walking about again."

"My body has that habit," Eréndira said by way of an excuse.

Still hazy with sleep, she picked up the tureen, and tried to clean the stain on the rug.

"Leave it," her grandmother dissuaded her. "You can wash it this afternoon."

So in addition to her regular afternoon chores, Eréndira had to wash the dining room rug, and she took advantage of her presence at the washtub to do Monday's laundry as well, while the wind went around the house looking for a way in. She had so much to do that night came upon her without her realizing it, and when she put the dining room rug back in its place it was time to go to bed.

The grandmother had been fooling around on the piano all afternoon, singing the songs of her times to herself in a falsetto, and she had stains of musk and tears on her eyelids. But when she lay down on her bed in her muslin nightgown, the bitterness of fond memories returned.

"Take advantage of tomorrow to wash the living room rug too," she told Eréndira. "It hasn't seen the sun since the days of all the noise."

"Yes, Grandmother," the girl answered.

She picked up a feather fan and began to fan the implacable matron, who recited the list of nighttime orders to her as she sank into sleep.

"Iron all the clothes before you go to bed so you can sleep with a clear conscience."

"Yes, Grandmother."

"Check the clothes closets carefully, because moths get hungrier on windy nights."

"Yes, Grandmother."

"With the time you have left, take the flowers out into the courtyard so they can get a breath of air."

"Yes, Grandmother."

"And feed the ostrich."

She had fallen asleep but she was still giving orders, for it was from her that the granddaughter had inherited the ability to be alive still while sleeping. Eréndira left the room without making any noise and did the final chores of the night, still replying to the sleeping grandmother's orders.

"Give the graves some water."

"Yes, Grandmother."

"And if the Amadíses arrive, tell them not to come in," the grandmother said, "because Porfirio Galán's gang is waiting to kill them."

Eréndira didn't answer her any more because she knew that the grandmother was getting lost in her delirium, but she didn't miss a single order. When she finished checking the window bolts and put out the last lights, she took a candlestick from the dining room and lighted her way to her bedroom as the pauses in the wind were filled with the peaceful and enormous breathing of her sleeping grandmother.

Her room was also luxurious, but not so much as her grandmother's, and it was piled high with the rag dolls and wind-up animals of her recent childhood. Overcome by the barbarous chores of the day, Eréndira didn't have the strength to get undressed and she put the candlestick on the night table and fell onto the bed. A short while later the wind of her misfortune came into the bedroom like a pack of hounds and knocked the candle over against the curtain.

At dawn, when the wind finally stopped, a few thick and scattered drops of rain began to fall, putting out the last embers and hardening the smoking ashes of the mansion. The people in the village, Indians for the most part, tried to rescue the remains of the disaster: the charred corpse of the ostrich, the frame of the gilded piano, the torso of a statue. The grandmother was contemplating the residue of her fortune with an impenetrable depression. Eréndira, sitting between the two graves of the Amadíses, had stopped weeping. When the grandmother was convinced that very few things remained intact among the ruins, she looked at her granddaughter with sincere pity.

"My poor child," she sighed. "Life won't be long enough for you to pay me back for this mishap."

She began to pay it back that very day, beneath the noise of the rain, when she was taken to the village storekeeper, a skinny and premature widower who was quite well known in the desert for the good price he paid for virginity. As the grandmother waited undauntedly, the widower examined Eréndira with scientific austerity: he considered the strength of her thighs, the size of her breasts, the diameter of her hips. He didn't say a word until he had some calculation of what she was worth.

"She's still quite immature," he said then. "She has the teats of a bitch."

Then he had her get on a scale to prove his decision with figures. Eréndira weighed ninety pounds.

"She isn't worth more than a hundred pesos," the widower said.

The grandmother was scandalized.

"A hundred pesos for a girl who's completely new!" she almost shouted. "No, sir, that shows a great lack of respect for virtue on your part."

"I'll make it a hundred and fifty," the widower said.

"This girl caused me damages amounting to more than a million pesos," the grandmother said. "At this rate she'll need two hundred years to pay me back."

"You're lucky that the only good feature she has is her age," the widower said.

The storm threatened to knock the house down, and there were so many leaks in the roof that it was raining almost as much inside as out. The grandmother felt all alone in a world of disaster.

"Just raise it to three hundred," she said.

"Two hundred and fifty."

Finally they agreed on two hundred and twenty pesos in cash and some provisions. The grandmother then signaled Eréndira to go with the widower and he led her by the hand to the back room as if he were taking her to school.

"I'll wait for you here," the grandmother said.

"Yes, Grandmother," said Eréndira.

The back room was a kind of shed with four brick columns, a roof of rotted palm leaves, and an adobe wall three feet high, through which outdoor disturbances got into the building. Placed on top of the adobe wall were pots with cacti and other plants of aridity. Hanging between two columns and flapping like the free sail of a drifting sloop was a faded hammock. Over the whistle of the storm and the lash of the water one could hear distant shouts, the howling of far-off animals, the cries of a shipwreck.

When Eréndira and the widower went into the shed they had to hold on so as not to be knocked down by a gust of rain which left them soaked. Their voices could not be heard but their movements became clear in the roar of the squall. At the widower's first attempt, Eréndira shouted something inaudible and tried to get away. The widower answered her without any voice, twisted her arm by the wrist, and dragged her to the hammock. She fought him off with a scratch on the face and shouted in silence again, but he replied with a solemn slap which lifted her off the ground and suspended her in the air for an instant with her long Medusa hair floating in space. He grabbed her about the waist before she touched ground again, flung her into the hammock with a brutal heave, and held her down with his knees. Eréndira then succumbed to terror, lost consciousness, and remained as if fascinated by the moonbeams from a fish that was floating through the storm air, while the widower undressed her, tearing off her clothes with a methodical clawing, as if he were pulling up grass, scattering them with great tugs of color that waved like streamers and went off with the wind.

When there was no other man left in the village who could pay anything for Eréndira's love, her grandmother put her on a truck to go where the smugglers were. They made the trip on the back of the truck in the open, among sacks of rice and buckets of lard and what had been left by the fire: the headboard of the viceregal bed, a warrior angel, the scorched throne, and other pieces of useless junk. In a trunk with two crosses painted in broad strokes they carried the bones of the Amadíses.

The grandmother protected herself from the sun with a tattered umbrella and it was hard for her to breathe because of the torment of sweat and dust, but even in that unhappy state she kept control of her dignity. Behind the pile of cans and sacks of rice Eréndira paid for the trip and the cartage by making love for twenty pesos a turn with the truck's loader. At first her system of defense was the same as she had used against the widower's attack, but the loader's approach was different, slow and wise, and he ended up taming her with tenderness. So when they reached the first town after a deadly journey, Eréndira and the loader were relaxing from good love behind the parapet of cargo. The driver shouted to the grandmother:

"Here's where the world begins."

The grandmother observed with disbelief the miserable and solitary streets of a town somewhat larger but just as sad as the one they had abandoned.

"It doesn't look like it to me," she said.

"It's mission country," the driver said.

"I'm not interested in charity, I'm interested in smugglers," said the grandmother.

Listening to the dialogue from behind the load, Eréndira dug into a sack of rice with her finger. Suddenly she found a string, pulled on it, and drew out a necklace of genuine pearls. She looked at it amazed, holding it between her fingers like a dead snake, while the driver answered her grandmother:

"Don't be daydreaming, ma'am. There's no such thing as smugglers."

"Of course not," the grandmother said. "I've got your word for it."

"Try to find one and you'll see," the driver bantered. "Everybody talks about them, but no one's ever seen one."

The loader realized that Eréndira had pulled out the necklace and hastened to take it away from her and stick it back into the sack of rice. The grandmother, who had decided to stay in spite of the poverty of the town, then called to her granddaughter to help her out of the truck. Eréndira said good-bye to the loader with a kiss that was hurried but spontaneous and true.

The grandmother waited, sitting on her throne in the middle of the street, until they finished unloading the goods. The last item was the trunk with the remains of the Amadíses.

"This thing weighs as much as a dead man," said the driver, laughing.

"There are two of them," the grandmother said, "so treat them with the proper respect."

"I bet they're marble statutes." The driver laughed again.

He put the trunk with bones down carelessly among the singed furniture and held out his open hand to the grandmother.

"Fifty pesos," he said.

"Your slave has already paid on the right-hand side."

The driver looked at his helper with surprise and the latter made an affirmative sign. The driver then went back to the cab, where a woman in mourning was riding, in her arms a baby who was crying from the heat. The loader, quite sure of himself, told the grandmother:

"Eréndira is coming with me, if it's all right by you. My intentions are honorable."

The girl intervened, surprised:

"I didn't say anything!"

"The idea was all mine," the loader said.

The grandmother looked him up and down, not to make him feel small but trying to measure the true size of his guts.

"It's all right by me," she told him, "provided you pay me what I lost because of her carelessness. It's eight hundred seventy-two thousand three hundred fifteen pesos, less the four hundred and twenty which she's already paid me, making it eight hundred seventy-one thousand eight hundred ninety-five."

The truck started up.

"Believe me, I'd give you that pile of money if I had it," the loader said seriously. "The girl is worth it."

The grandmother was pleased with the boy's decision.

"Well, then, come back when you have it, son," she answered in a sympathetic tone. "But you'd better go now, because if we figure out accounts again you'll end up owing me ten pesos."

The loader jumped onto the back of the truck and it went off. From there he waved good-bye to Eréndira, but she was still so surprised that she didn't answer him.

In the same vacant lot where the truck had left them, Eréndira and her grandmother improvised a shelter to live in from sheets of zinc and the remains of Oriental rugs. They laid two mats on the ground and slept as well as they had in the mansion until the sun opened holes in the ceiling and burned their faces.

Just the opposite of what normally happened, it was the grandmother who busied herself that morning fixing up Eréndira. She made up her face in the style of sepulchral beauty that had been the vogue in her youth and touched her up with artificial fingernails and an organdy bow that looked like a butterfly on her head.

"You look awful," she admitted, "but it's better that way: men are quite stupid when it comes to female matters."

Long before they saw them they both recognized the sound of two mules walking on the flint of the desert. At a command from her grand-mother, Eréndira lay down on the mat the way an amateur actress might have done at the moment when the curtain was about to go up. Leaning on her bishop's crosier, the grandmother went out of the shel-ter and sat down on the throne to wait for the mules to pass.

The mailman was coming. He was only twenty years old, but his work had aged him, and he was wearing a khaki uniform, leggings, a pith helmet, and had a military pistol on his cartridge belt. He was rid-ing a good mule and leading by the halter another, more timeworn one, on whom the canvas mailbags were piled.

As he passed by the grandmother he saluted her and kept on going, but she signaled him to look inside the shelter. The man stopped and saw Eréndira lying on the mat in her posthumous make-up and wearing a purple-trimmed dress.

"Do you like it?" the grandmother asked.

The mailman hadn't understood until then what the proposition was.

"It doesn't look bad to someone who's been on a diet," he said, smil-ing.

"Fifty pesos," the grandmother said.

"Boy, you're asking a mint!" he said. "I can eat for a whole month on that."

"Don't be a tightwad," the grandmother said. "The airmail pays even better than being a priest."

"I'm the domestic mail," the man said. "The airmail man travels in a pickup truck."

"In any case, love is just as important as eating," the grandmother said.

"But it doesn't feed you."

The grandmother realized that a man who lived from what other people were waiting for had more than enough time for bargaining.

"How much have you got?" she asked him.

The mailman dismounted, took some chewed-up bills from his pocket, and showed them to the grandmother. She snatched them up all together with a rapid hand just as if they had been a ball.

"I'll lower the price for you," she said, "but on one condition: that you spread the word all around."

"All the way to the other side of the world," the mailman said. "That's what I'm for."

Eréndira, who had been unable to blink, then took off her artificial eyelashes and moved to one side of the mat to make room for the chance boyfriend. As soon as he was in the shelter, the grandmother closed the entrance with an energetic tug on the sliding curtain.

It was an effective deal. Taken by the words of the mailman, men came from very far away to become acquainted with the newness of Eréndira. Behind the men came gambling tables and food stands, and behind them all came a photographer on a bicycle, who, across from the encampment, set up a camera with a mourning sleeve on a tripod and a backdrop of a lake with listless swans.

The grandmother, fanning herself on her throne, seemed alien to her own bazaar. The only thing that interested her was keeping order in the line of customers who were waiting their turn and checking the exact amount of money they paid in advance to go in to Eréndira. At first she had been so strict that she refused a good customer because he was five pesos short. But with the passage of months she was assimilating the lessons of reality and she ended up letting people in who completed their payment with religious medals, family relics, wedding rings, and anything her bite could prove was bona-fide gold even if it didn't shine.

After a long stay in that first town, the grandmother had sufficient money to buy a donkey, and she went off into the desert in search of places more propitious for the payment of the debt. She traveled on a litter that had been improvised on top of the donkey and she was protected from the motionless sun by the half-spoked umbrella that Eréndira held over her head. Behind them walked four Indian bearers with the remnants of the encampment: the sleeping mats, the restored throne, the alabaster angel, and the trunks with the remains of the Amadíses. The photographer followed the caravan on his bicycle, but never catching up, as if he were going to a different festival.

Six months had passed since the fire when the grandmother was able to get a complete picture of the business.

"If things go on like this," she told Eréndira, "you will have paid me the debt inside of eight years, seven months, and eleven days."

She went back over her calculations with her eyes closed, fumbling with the seeds she was taking out of a cord pouch where she also kept the money, and she corrected herself:

"All that, of course, not counting the pay and board of the Indians and other minor expenses."

Eréndira, who was keeping in step with the donkey, bowed down by the heat and dust, did not reproach her grandmother for her figures, but she had to hold back her tears.

"I've got ground glass in my bones," she said.

"Try to sleep."

"Yes, Grandmother."

She closed her eyes, took in a deep breath of scorching air, and went on walking in her sleep.

A small truck loaded with cages appeared, frightening goats in the dust of the horizon, and the clamor of the birds was like a splash of cool water for the Sunday torpor of San Miguel del Desierto. At the wheel was a corpulent Dutch farmer, his skin splintered by the outdoors, and with a squirrel-colored mustache he had inherited from some great-grandfather. His son Ulises, who was riding in the other seat, was a gilded adolescent with lonely maritime eyes and with the appearance of a furtive angel. The Dutchman noticed a tent in front of which all the soldiers of the local garrison were awaiting their turn. They were sitting on the ground, drinking out of the same bottle, which passed from mouth to mouth, and they had almond branches on their heads as if camouflaged for combat. The Dutchman asked in his language:

"What the devil can they be selling there?"

"A woman," his son answered quite naturally. "Her name is Eréndira."

"How do you know?"

"Everybody in the desert knows," Ulises answered.

The Dutchman stopped at the small hotel in town and got out. Ulises stayed in the truck. With agile fingers he opened a briefcase that his father had left on the seat, took out a roll of bills, put several in his pocket, and left everything just the way it had been. That night, while his father was asleep, he climbed out the hotel window and went to stand in line in front of Eréndira's tent.

The festivities were at their height. The drunken recruits were dancing by themselves so as not to waste the free music, and the photographer was taking nighttime pictures with magnesium papers. As she watched over her business, the grandmother counted the bank notes in her lap, dividing them into equal piles and arranging them in a basket. There were only twelve soldiers at that time, but the evening line had grown with civilian customers. Ulises was the last one.

It was the turn of a soldier with a woeful appearance. The grandmother not only blocked his way but avoided contact with his money.

"No, son," she told him. "You couldn't go in for all the gold in the world. You bring bad luck."

The soldier, who wasn't from those parts, was puzzled.

"What do you mean?"

"You bring down the evil shadows," the grandmother said. "A person only has to look at your face."

She waved him off with her hand, but without touching him, and made way for the next soldier.

"Go right in, handsome," she told him good-naturedly, "but don't take too long, your country needs you."

The soldier went in but he came right out again because Eréndira wanted to talk to her grandmother. She hung the basket of money on her arm and went into the tent, which wasn't very roomy, but which was neat and clean. In the back, on an army cot, Eréndira was unable to repress the trembling in her body, and she was in sorry shape, all dirty with soldier sweat.

"Grandmother," she sobbed, "I'm dying."

The grandmother felt her forehead and when she saw she had no fever, she tried to console her.

"There are only ten soldiers left," she said.

Eréndira began to weep with the shrieks of a frightened animal. The grandmother realized then that she had gone beyond the limits of horror and, stroking her head, she helped her calm down.

"The trouble is that you're weak," she told her. "Come on, don't cry any more, take a bath in sage water to get your blood back into shape."

She left the tent when Eréndira was calmer and she gave the soldier waiting his money back. "That's all for today," she told him. "Come back tomorrow and I'll give you the first place in line." Then she shouted to those lined up:

"That's all, boys. Tomorrow morning at nine."

Soldiers and civilians broke ranks with shouts of protest. The grandmother confronted them, in a good mood but brandishing the devastating crosier in earnest.

"You're an inconsiderate bunch of slobs!" she shouted. "What do you think the girl is made of, iron? I'd like to see you in her place. You perverts! You shitty bums!"

The men answered her with even cruder insults, but she ended up controlling the revolt and stood guard with her staff until they took away the snack tables and dismantled the gambling stands. She was about to go back into the tent when she saw Ulises, as large as life, all by himself in the dark and empty space where the line of men had been before. He had an unreal aura about him and he seemed to be visible in the shadows because of the very glow of his beauty.

"You," the grandmother asked him. "What happened to your wings?"

"The one who had wings was my grandfather," Ulises answered in his natural way, "but nobody believed it."

The grandmother examined him again with fascination. "Well, I do," she said. "Put them on and come back tomorrow." She went into the tent and left Ulises burning where he stood.

Eréndira felt better after her bath. She had put on a short, lace-trimmed slip and she was drying her hair before going to bed, but she was still making an effort to hold back her tears. Her grandmother was asleep.

Behind Eréndira's bed, very slowly, Ulises' head appeared. She saw the anxious and diaphanous eyes, but before saying anything she rubbed her head with the towel in order to prove that it wasn't an illusion. When Ulises blinked for the first time, Eréndira asked him in a very low voice:

"Who are you?"

Ulises showed himself down to his shoulders. "My name is Ulises," he said. He showed her the bills he had stolen and added:

"I've got money."

Eréndira put her hands on the bed, brought her face close to that of Ulises, and went on talking to him as if in a kindergarten game.

"You were supposed to get in line," she told him.

"I waited all night long," Ulises said.

"Well, now you have to wait until tomorrow," Eréndira said. "I feel as if someone had been beating me on the kidneys."

At that instant the grandmother began to talk in her sleep.

"It's going on twenty years since it rained last," she said. "It was such a terrible storm that the rain was all mixed in with sea water, and the next morning the house was full of fish and snails and your grandfather Amadís, may he rest in peace, saw a glowing manta ray floating through the air."

Ulises hid behind the bed again. Eréndira showed an amused smile.

"Take it easy," she told him. "She always acts kind of crazy when she's asleep, but not even an earthquake can wake her up."

Ulises reappeared. Eréndira looked at him with a smile that was naughty and even a little affectionate and took the soiled sheet off the mattress.

"Come," she said. "Help me change the sheet."

Then Ulises came from behind the bed and took one end of the sheet. Since the sheet was much larger than the mattress, they had to fold it several times. With every fold Ulises drew closer to Eréndira.

"I was going crazy wanting to see you," he suddenly said. "Everybody says you're very pretty and they're right."

"But I'm going to die," Eréndira said.

"My mother says that people who die in the desert don't go to heaven but to the sea," Ulises said.

Eréndira put the dirty sheet aside and covered the mattress with another, which was clean and ironed.

"I never saw the sea," she said.

"It's like the desert but with water," said Ulises.

"Then you can't walk on it."

"My father knew a man who could," Ulises said, "but that was a long time ago."

Eréndira was fascinated but she wanted to sleep.

"If you come very early tomorrow you can be first in line," she said.

"I'm leaving with my father at dawn," said Ulises.

"Won't you be coming back this way?"

"Who can tell?" Ulises said. "We just happened along now because we got lost on the road to the border."

Eréndira looked thoughtfully at her sleeping grandmother.

"All right," she decided. "Give me the money."

Ulises gave it to her. Eréndira lay down on the bed but he remained trembling where he was: at the decisive moment his determination had weakened. Eréndira took him by the hand to hurry him up and only then did she notice his tribulation. She was familiar with that fear.

"Is it the first time?" she asked him.

Ulises didn't answer but he smiled in desolation. Eréndira became a different person.

"Breathe slowly," she told him. "That's the way it always is the first time. Afterwards you won't even notice."

She laid him down beside her and while she was taking his clothes off she was calming him maternally.

"What's your name?"

"Ulises."

"That's a gringo name," Eréndira said.

"No, a sailor name."

Eréndira uncovered his chest, gave a few little orphan kisses, sniffed him.

"It's like you were made of gold all over," she said, "but you smell of flowers."

"It must be the oranges," Ulises said.

Calmer now, he gave a smile of complicity.

"We carry a lot of birds along to throw people off the track," he added, "but what we're doing is smuggling a load of oranges across the border."

"Oranges aren't contraband," Eréndira said.

"These are," said Ulises. "Each one is worth fifty thousand pesos."

Eréndira laughed for the first time in a long while.

"What I like about you," she said, "is the serious way you make up nonsense."

She had become spontaneous and talkative again, as if Ulises' innocence had changed not only her mood but her character. The grandmother, such a short distance away from misfortune, was still talking in her sleep.

"Around those times, at the beginning of March, they brought you home," she said. "You looked like a lizard wrapped in cotton. Amadís, your father, who was young and handsome, was so happy that afternoon that he sent for twenty carts loaded with flowers and arrived strewing them along the street until the whole village was gold with flowers like the sea."

She ranted on with great shouts and with a stubborn passion for several hours. But Ulises couldn't hear her because Eréndira had loved him so much and so truthfully that she loved him again for half price while her grandmother was raving and kept on loving him for nothing until dawn.

A group of missionaries holding up their crucifixes stood shoulder to shoulder in the middle of the desert. A wind as fierce as the wind of misfortune shook their burlap habits and their rough beards and they were barely able to stand on their feet. Behind them was the mission, a colonial pile of stone with a tiny belfry on top of the harsh whitewashed walls.

The youngest missionary, who was in charge of the group, pointed to a natural crack in the glazed clay ground.

"You shall not pass beyond this line!" he shouted.

The four Indian bearers carrying the grandmother in a litter made of boards stopped when they heard the shout. Even though she was uncomfortable sitting on the planks of the litter and her spirit was dulled by the dust and sweat of the desert, the grandmother maintained her haughtiness intact. Eréndira was on foot. Behind the litter came a file of eight Indians carrying the baggage and at the very end the photographer on his bicycle.

"The desert doesn't belong to anyone," the grandmother said.

"It belongs to God," the missionary said, "and you are violating his sacred laws with your filthy business."

The grandmother then recognized the missionary's peninsular usage and diction and avoided a head-on confrontation so as not to break her head against his intransigence. She went back to being herself.

"I don't understand your mysteries, son."

The missionary pointed at Eréndira.

"That child is underage."

"But she's my granddaughter."

"So much the worse," the missionary replied. "Put her under our care willingly or we'll have to seek recourse in other ways."

The grandmother had not expected them to go so far.

"All right, if that's how it is." She surrendered in fear. "But sooner or later I'll pass, you'll see."

Three days after the encounter with the missionaries, the grandmother and Eréndira were sleeping in a village near the mission when a group of stealthy, mute bodies, creeping along like an infantry patrol, slipped into the tent. They were six Indian novices, strong and young, their rough cloth habits seeming to glow in the moonlight. Without making a sound they cloaked Eréndira in a mosquito netting, picked her up without waking her, and carried her off wrapped like a large, fragile fish caught in a lunar net.

There were no means left untried by the grandmother in an attempt to rescue her granddaughter from the protection of the missionaries. Only when they had all failed, from the most direct to the most devious, did she turn to the civil authority, which was vested in a military man. She found him in the courtyard of his home, his chest bare, shooting with an army rifle at a dark and solitary cloud in the burning sky. He was trying to perforate it to bring on rain, and his shots were furious and useless, but he did take the necessary time out to listen to the grandmother.

"I can't do anything," he explained to her when he had heard her out. "The priesties, according to the concordat, have the right to keep the girl until she comes of age. Or until she gets married."

"Then why do they have you here as mayor?" the grandmother asked.

"To make it rain," was the mayor's answer.

Then, seeing that the cloud had moved out of range, he interrupted his official duties and gave his full attention to the grandmother.

"What you need is someone with a lot of weight who will vouch for you," he told her. "Someone who can swear to your moral standing and your good behavior in a signed letter. Do you know Senator Onésimo Sánchez?"

Sitting under the naked sun on a stool that was too narrow for her astral buttocks, the grandmother answered with a solemn rage:

"I'm just a poor woman all alone in the vastness of the desert."

The mayor, his right eye twisted from the heat, looked at her with pity.

"Then don't waste your time, ma'am," he said. "You'll rot in hell."

She didn't rot, of course. She set up her tent across from the mission and sat down to think, like a solitary warrior besieging a fortified city. The wandering photographer, who knew her quite well, loaded his gear onto the carrier of his bicycle and was ready to leave all alone when he saw her in the full sun with her eyes fixed on the mission.

"Let's see who gets tired first," the grandmother said, "they or I."

"They've been here for three hundred years and they can still take it," the photographer said. "I'm leaving."

Only then did the grandmother notice the loaded bicycle.

"Where are you going?"

"Wherever the wind takes me," the photographer said, and he left. "It's a big world."

The grandmother sighed.

"Not as big as you think, you ingrate."

But she didn't move her head in spite of her anger so as not to lose sight of the mission. She didn't move it for many, many days of mineral heat, for many, many nights of wild winds, for all the time she was meditating and no one came out of the mission. The Indians built a lean-to of palm leaves beside the tent and hung their hammocks there, but the grandmother stood watch until very late, nodding on her throne and chewing the uncooked grain in her pouch with the invincible laziness of a resting ox.

One night a convoy of slow covered trucks passed very close to her and the only lights they carried were wreaths of colored bulbs which gave them the ghostly size of sleep-walking altars. The grandmother recognized them at once because they were just like the trucks of the Amadíses. The last truck in the convoy slowed, stopped, and a man got out of the cab to adjust something in back. He looked like a replica of the Amadíses, wearing a hat with a turned-up brim, high boots, two crossed cartridge belts across his chest, an army rifle, and two pistols. Overcome by an irresistible temptation, the grandmother called to the man.

"Don't you know who I am?" she asked him.

The man lighted her pitilessly with a flashlight. For an instant he studied the face worn out by vigil, the eyes dim from fatigue, the withered hair of the woman who, even at her age, in her sorry state, and with that crude light on her face, could have said that she had been the most beautiful woman in the world. When he examined her enough to be sure that he had never seen her before, he turned out the light.

"The only thing I know for sure is that you're not the Virgin of Perpetual Help."

"Quite the contrary," the grandmother said with a very sweet voice. "I'm the Lady."

The man put his hand to his pistol out of pure instinct.

"What lady?"

"Big Amadís's."

"Then you're not of this world," he said, tense. "What is it you want?"

"For you to help me rescue my grandmother, Big Amadís's granddaughter, the daughter of our son Amadís, held captive in that mission."

The man overcame his fear.

"You knocked on the wrong door," he said. "If you think we're about to get mixed up in God's affairs, you're not the one you say you are, you never knew the Amadíses, and you haven't got the whoriest notion of what smuggling's all about."

Early that morning the grandmother slept less than before. She lay awake pondering things, wrapped in a wool blanket while the early hour got her memory all mixed up and the repressed raving struggled to get out even though she was awake, and she had to tighten her heart with her hand so as not to be suffocated by the memory of a house by the sea with great red flowers where she had been happy. She remained that way until the mission bell rang and the first lights went on in the windows and the desert became saturated with the smell of the hot bread of matins. Only then did she abandon her fatigue, tricked by the illusion that Eréndira had got up and was looking for a way to escape and come back to her.

Eréndira, however, had not lost a single night's sleep since they had taken her to the mission. They had cut her hair with pruning shears until her head was like a brush, they put a hermit's rough cassock on her and gave her a bucket of whitewash and a broom so that she could whitewash the stairs every time someone went up or down. It was mule work because there was an incessant coming and going of muddied missionaries and novice carriers, but Eréndira felt as if every day were Sunday after the fearsome galley that had been her bed. Besides, she wasn't the only one worn out at night, because that mission was dedicated to fighting not against the devil but against the desert. Eréndira had seen the Indian novices bulldogging cows in the barn in order to milk them, jumping up and down on planks for days on end in order to press cheese, helping a goat through a difficult birth. She had seen them sweat like tanned stevedores hauling water from the cistern, watering by hand a bold garden that other novices cultivated with hoes in order to plant vegetables in the flintstone of the desert. She had seen the earthly inferno of the ovens for baking bread and the rooms for ironing clothes. She had seen a nun chase a pig through the courtyard, slide along holding the runaway animal by the ears, and roll in a mud puddle without letting go until two novices in leather aprons helped her get it under control and one of them cut its throat with a butcher knife as they all became covered with blood and mire. In the isolation ward of the infirmary she had seen tubercular nuns in their nightgown shrouds, waiting for God's last command as they embroidered bridal sheets on the terraces while the men preached in the desert. Eréndira was living in her shadows and discovering other forms of beauty and horror that she had never imagined in the narrow world of her bed, but neither the coarsest nor the most persuasive of the novices had managed to get her to say a word since they had taken her to the mission. One morning, while she was preparing the whitewash in her bucket, she heard string music that was like a light even more diaphanous than the light of the desert. Captivated by the miracle, she peeped into an immense and empty salon with bare walls and large windows through which the dazzling June light poured in and remained still, and in the center of the room she saw a very beautiful nun whom she had never seen before playing an Easter oratorio on the clavichord. Eréndira listened to the music without blinking, her heart hanging by a thread, until the lunch bell rang. After eating, while she whitewashed the stairs with her reed brush, she waited until all the novices had finished going up and coming down, and she was alone, with no one to hear her, and then she spoke for the first time since she had entered the mission.

"I'm happy," she said.

So that put an end to the hopes the grandmother had that Eréndira would run away to rejoin her, but she maintained her granite siege without having made any decision until Pentecost. During that time the missionaries were combing the desert in search of pregnant concubines in order to get them married. They traveled all the way to the most remote settlements in a broken-down truck with four well-armed soldiers and a chest of cheap cloth. The most difficult part of that Indian hunt was to convince the women, who defended themselves against divine grace with the truthful argument that men, sleeping in their hammocks with legs spread, felt they had the right to demand much heavier work from legitimate wives than from concubines. It was necessary to seduce them with trickery, dissolving the will of God in the syrup of their own language so that it would seem less harsh to them, but even the most crafty of them ended up being convinced by a pair of flashy earrings. The men, on the other hand, once the women's acceptance had been obtained, were routed out of their hammocks with rifle butts, bound, and hauled away in the back of the truck to be married by force.

For several days the grandmother saw the little truck loaded with pregnant Indian women heading for the mission, but she failed to recognize her opportunity. She recognized it on Pentecost Sunday itself, when she heard the rockets and the ringing of the bells and saw the miserable and merry crowd that was going to the festival, and she saw that among the crowds there were pregnant women with the veil and crown of a bride holding the arms of their casual mates, whom they would legitimize in the collective wedding.

Among the last in the procession a boy passed, innocent of heart, with gourd-cut Indian hair and dressed in rags, carrying an Easter candle with a silk bow in his hand. The grandmother called him over.

"Tell me something, son," she asked with her smoothest voice. "What part do you have in this affair?"

The boy felt intimidated by the candle and it was hard for him to close his mouth because of his donkey teeth.

"The priests are going to give me my first communion," he said.

"How much did they pay you?"

"Five pesos."

The grandmother took a roll of bills from her pouch and the boy looked at them with surprise.

"I'm going to give you twenty," the grandmother said. "Not for you to make your first communion, but for you to get married."

"Who to?"

"My granddaughter."

So Eréndira was married in the courtyard of the mission in her hermit's cassock and a silk shawl that the novices gave her, and without even knowing the name of the groom her grandmother had bought for her. With uncertain hope she withstood the torment of kneeling on the saltpeter ground, the goat-hair stink of the two hundred pregnant brides, the punishment of the Epistle of Saint Paul hammered out in Latin under the motionless and burning sun, because the missionaries had found no way to oppose the wile of that unforeseen marriage, but had given her a promise as a last attempt to keep her in the mission. Nevertheless, after the ceremony in the presence of the apostolic prefect, the military mayor who shot at the clouds, her recent husband, and her impassive grandmother, Eréndira found herself once more under the spell that had dominated her since birth. When they asked her what her free, true, and definitive will was, she didn't even give a sigh of hesitation.

"I want to leave," she said. And she clarified things by pointing at her husband. "But not with him, with my grandmother."

Ulises had wasted a whole afternoon trying to steal an orange from his father's grove, because the older man wouldn't take his eyes off him while they were pruning the sick trees, and his mother kept watch from the house. So he gave up his plan, for that day at least, and grudgingly helped his father until they had pruned the last orange trees.

The extensive grove was quiet and hidden, and the wooden house with a tin roof had copper grating over the windows and a large porch set on pilings, with primitive plants bearing intense flowers. Ulises' mother was on the porch sitting back in a Viennese rocking chair with smoked leaves on her temples to relieve her headache, and her full-blooded-Indian look followed her son like a beam of invisible light to the most remote corners of the orange grove. She was quite beautiful, much younger than her husband, and not only did she still wear the garb of her tribe, but she knew the most ancient secrets of her blood.

When Ulises returned to the house with the pruning tools, his mother asked him for her four o'clock medicine, which was on a nearby table. As soon as he touched them, the glass and the bottle changed color. Then, out of pure play, he touched a glass pitcher that was on the table beside some tumblers and the pitcher also turned blue. His mother observed him while she was taking her medicine and when she was sure that it was not a delirium of her pain, she asked him in the Guajiro Indian language:

"How long has that been happening to you?"

"Ever since we came back from the desert," Ulises said, also in Guajiro. "It only happens with glass things."

In order to demonstrate, one after the other he touched the glasses that were on the table and they all turned different colors.

"Those things happen only because of love," his mother said. "Who is it?"

Ulises didn't answer. His father, who couldn't understand the Guajiro language, was passing by the porch at that moment with a cluster of oranges.

"What are you two talking about?" he asked Ulises in Dutch.

"Nothing special," Ulises answered.

Ulises' mother didn't know any Dutch. When her husband went into the house, she asked her son in Guajiro:

"What did he say?"

"Nothing special," Ulises answered.

He lost sight of his father when he went into the house, but he saw him again through a window of the office. The mother waited until she was alone with Ulises and then repeated:

"Tell me who it is."

"It's nobody," Ulises said.

He answered without paying attention because he was hanging on his father's movements in the office. He had seen him put the oranges on top of the safe when he worked out the combination. But while he was keeping an eye on his father, his mother was keeping an eye on him.

"You haven't eaten any bread for a long time," she observed.

"I don't like it."

The mother's face suddenly took on an unaccustomed liveliness. "That's a lie," she said. "It's because you're lovesick and people who are lovesick can't eat bread." Her voice, like her eyes, had passed from entreaty to threat.

"It would be better if you told me who it was," she said, "or I'll make you take some purifying baths."

In the office the Dutchman opened the safe, put the oranges inside, and closed the armored door. Ulises moved away from the window then and answered his mother impatiently.

"I already told you there wasn't anyone," he said. "If you don't believe me, ask Papa."

The Dutchman appeared in the office doorway lighting his sailor's pipe and carrying his threadbare Bible under his arm. His wife asked him in Spanish:

"Who did you meet in the desert?"

"Nobody," her husband answered, a little in the clouds. "If you don't believe me, ask Ulises."

He sat down at the end of the hall and sucked on his pipe until the tobacco was used up. Then he opened the Bible at random and recited spot passages for almost two hours in flowing and ringing Dutch.

At midnight Ulises was still thinking with such intensity that he couldn't sleep. He rolled about in his hammock for another hour, trying to overcome the pain of memories until the very pain gave him the strength he needed to make a decision. Then he put on his cowboy pants, his plaid shirt, and his riding boots, jumped through the window, and fled from the house in the truck loaded with birds. As he went through the groves he picked the three ripe oranges he had been unable to steal that afternoon.

He traveled across the desert for the rest of the night and at dawn he asked in towns and villages about the whereabouts of Eréndira, but no one could tell him. Finally they informed him that she was traveling in the electoral campaign retinue of Senator Onésimo Sánchez and that on that day he was probably in Nueva Castilla. He didn't find him there but in the next town and Eréndira was no longer with him, for the grandmother had managed to get the senator to vouch for her morality in a letter written in his own hand, and with it she was going about opening the most tightly barred doors in the desert. On the third day he came across the domestic mailman and the latter told him what direction to follow.

"They're heading toward the sea," he said, "and you'd better hurry because the goddamned old woman plans to cross over to the island of Aruba."

Following that direction, after half a day's journey Ulises spotted the broad, stained tent that the grandmother had bought from a bankrupt circus. The wandering photographer had come back to her, convinced that the world was really not as large as he had thought, and he had set up his idyllic backdrops near the tent. A band of brass-blowers was captivating Eréndira's clientele with a taciturn waltz.

Ulises waited for his turn to go in, and the first thing that caught his attention was the order and cleanliness of the inside of the tent. The grandmother's bed had recovered its viceregal splendor, the statue of the angel was in its place beside the funerary trunk of the Amadáses, and in addition, there was a pewter bathtub with lion's feet. Lying on her new canopied bed, Eréndira was naked and placid, irradiating a childlike glow under the light that filtered through the tent. She was sleeping with her eyes open. Ulises stopped beside her, the oranges in his hand, and he noticed that she was looking at him without seeing him. Then he passed his hand over her eyes and called her by the name he had invented when he wanted to think about her:

"Arídnere."

Eréndira woke up. She felt naked in front of Ulises, let out a squeak, and covered herself with the sheet up to her neck.

"Don't look at me," she said. "I'm horrible."

"You're the color of an orange all over," Ulises said. He raised the fruits to her eyes so that she could compare. "Look."

Eréndira uncovered her eyes and saw that indeed the oranges did have her color.

"I don't want you to stay now," she said.

"I only came to show you this," Ulises said. "Look here."

He broke open an orange with his nails, split it in two with his hands, and showed Eréndira what was inside: stuck in the heart of the fruit was a genuine diamond.

"These are the oranges we take across the border," he said.

"But they're living oranges!" Eréndira exclaimed.

"Of course." Ulises smiled. "My father grows them."

Eréndira couldn't believe it. She uncovered her face, took the diamond in her fingers and contemplated it with surprise.

"With three like these we can take a trip around the world," Ulises said.

Eréndira gave him back the diamond with a look of disappointment. Ulises went on:

"Besides, I've got a pickup truck," he said. "And besides that . . . Look!"

From underneath his shirt he took an ancient pistol.

"I can't leave for ten years," Eréndira said.

"You'll leave," Ulises said. "Tonight, when the white whale falls asleep, I'll be outside there calling like an owl."

He made such a true imitation of the call of an owl that Eréndira's eyes smiled for the first time.

"It's my grandmother," she said.

"The owl?"

"The whale."

They both laughed at the mistake, but Eréndira picked up the thread again.

"No one can leave for anywhere without her grandmother's permission."

"There's no reason to say anything."

"She'll find out in any case," Eréndira said. "She can dream things."

"When she starts to dream that you're leaving we'll already be across the border. We'll cross over like smugglers," Ulises said.

Grasping the pistol with the confidence of a movie gunfighter, he imitated the sounds of the shots to excite Eréndira with his audacity. She didn't say yes or no, but her eyes gave a sigh and she sent Ulises away with a kiss. Ulises, touched, whispered:

"Tomorrow we'll be watching the ships go by."

That night, a little after seven o'clock, Eréndira was combing her grandmother's hair when the wind of her misfortune blew again. In the shelter of the tent were the Indian bearers and the leader of the brass band, waiting to be paid. The grandmother finished counting out the bills on a chest she had within reach, and after consulting a ledger she paid the oldest of the Indians.

"Here you are," she told him. "Twenty pesos for the week, less eight for meals, less three for water, less fifty cents on account for the new shirts, that's eight fifty. Count it."

The oldest Indian counted the money and they all withdrew with a bow.

"Thank you, white lady."

Next came the leader of the band. The grandmother consulted her ledger and turned to the photographer, who was trying to repair the bellows of his camera with wads of gutta-percha.

"What's it going to be?" she asked him. "Will you or won't you pay a quarter of the cost of the music?"

The photographer didn't even raise his head to answer.

"Music doesn't come out in pictures."

"But it makes people want to have their pictures taken," the grandmother answered.

"On the contrary," said the photographer. "It reminds them of the dead and then they come out in the picture with their eyes closed."

The bandleader intervened.

"What makes them close their eyes isn't the music," he said. "It's the lightning you make taking pictures at night."

"It's the music," the photographer insisted.

The grandmother put an end to the dispute. "Don't be a cheap-skate," she said to the photographer. "Look how well things have been going for Senator Onésimo Sánchez and it's thanks to the musicians he has along." Then, in a harsh tone, she concluded:

"So pay what you ought to or go follow your fortune by yourself. It's not right for that poor child to carry the whole burden of expenses."

"I'll follow my fortune by myself," the photographer said. "After all, an artist is what I am."

The grandmother shrugged her shoulders and took care of the musician. She handed him a bundle of bills that matched the figure written in her ledger.

"Two hundred and fifty-four numbers," she told him. "At fifty cents apiece, plus thirty-two on Sundays and holidays at sixty cents apiece, that's one hundred fifty-six twenty."

The musician wouldn't accept the money.

"It's one hundred eighty-two forty," he said. "Waltzes cost more."

"Why is that?"

"Because they're sadder," the musician said.

The grandmother made him take the money.

"Well, this week you'll play us two happy numbers for each waltz I owe you for and we'll be even."

The musician didn't understand the grandmother's logic, but he accepted the figures while he unraveled the tangle. At that moment the fearsome wind threatened to uproot the tent, and in the silence that it left in its wake, outside, clear and gloomy, the call of an owl was heard.

Eréndira didn't know what to do to disguise her upset. She closed the chest with the money and hid it under the bed, but the grand-mother recognized the fear in her hand when she gave her the key. "Don't be frightened," she told her. "There are always owls on windy nights." Still she didn't seem so convinced when she saw the photographer go out with the camera on his back.

"Wait till tomorrow if you'd like," she told him. "Death is on the loose tonight."

The photographer had also noticed the call of the owl, but he didn't change his intentions.

"Stay, son," the grandmother insisted. "Even if it's just because of the liking I have for you."

"But I won't pay for the music," the photographer said.

"Oh, no," the grandmother said. "Not that."

"You see?" the photographer said. "You've got no love for anybody."

The grandmother grew pale with rage.

"Then beat it!" she said. "You lowlife!"

She felt so outraged that she was still venting her rage on him while Eréndira helped her go to bed. "Son of an evil mother," she muttered. "What does that bastard know about anyone else's heart?" Eréndira paid no attention to her, because the owl was calling her with tenacious insistence during the pauses in the wind and she was tormented by uncertainty. The grandmother finally went to bed with the same ritual that had been *de rigueur* in the ancient mansion, and while her granddaughter fanned her she overcame her anger and once more breathed her sterile breath.

"You have to get up early," she said then, "so you can boil the infusion for my bath before the people get here."

"Yes, Grandmother."

"With the time you have left, wash the Indians' dirty laundry and that way we'll have something else to take off their pay next week."

"Yes, Grandmother," Eréndira said.

"And sleep slowly so that you won't get tired, because tomorrow is Thursday, the longest day of the week."

"Yes, Grandmother."

"And feed the ostrich."

"Yes, Grandmother," Eréndira said.

She left the fan at the head of the bed and lighted two altar candles in front of the chest with their dead. The grandmother, asleep now, was lagging behind with her orders.

"Don't forget to light the candles for the Amadíses."

"Yes, Grandmother."

Eréndira knew then that she wouldn't wake up, because she had begun to rave. She heard the wind barking about the tent, but she didn't recognize it as the wind of her misfortune that time either. She looked out into the night until the owl called again and her instinct for freedom in the end prevailed over her grandmother's spell.

She hadn't taken five steps outside the tent when she came across the photographer, who was lashing his equipment to the carrier of his bicycle. His accomplice's smile calmed her down.

"I don't know anything," the photographer said, "I haven't seen anything, and I won't pay for the music."

He took his leave with a blessing for all. Then Eréndira ran toward the desert, having decided once and for all, and she was swallowed up in the shadows of the wind where the owl was calling.

That time the grandmother went to the civil authorities at once. The commandant of the local detachment leaped out of his hammock at six in the morning when she put the senator's letter before his eyes. Ulises' father was waiting at the door.

"How in hell do you expect me to know what it says!" the commandant shouted. "I can't read."

"It's a letter of recommendation from Senator Onésimo Sánchez," the grandmother said.

Without further questions, the commandant took down a rifle he had near his hammock and began to shout orders to his men. Five minutes later they were all in a military truck flying toward the border against a contrary wind that had erased all trace of the fugitives. The commandant rode in the front seat beside the driver. In back were the Dutchman and the grandmother, with an armed policeman on each running board.

Close to town they stopped a convoy of trucks covered with waterproof canvases. Several men who were riding concealed in the rear raised the canvas and aimed at the small vehicle with machine guns and army rifles. The commandant asked the driver of the first truck how far back they had passed a farm truck loaded with birds.

The driver started up before he answered.

"We're not stool pigeons," he said indignantly, "we're smugglers."

The commandant saw the sooty barrels of the machine guns pass close to his eyes and he raised his arms and smiled.

"At least," he shouted at them, "you could have the decency not to go around in broad daylight."

The last truck had a sign on its rear bumper: I THINK OF YOU, ERÉNDIRA.

The wind became drier as they headed north and the sun was fiercer than the wind. It was hard to breathe because of the heat and dust inside the closed-in truck.

The grandmother was the first to spot the photographer: he was pedaling along in the same direction in which they were flying, with no protection against the sun except for a handkerchief tied around his head.

"There he is." She pointed. "He was their accomplice, the lowlife."

The commandant ordered one of the policemen on the running board to take charge of the photographer.

"Grab him and wait for us here," he said. "We'll be right back."

The policeman jumped off the running board and shouted twice for the photographer to halt. The photographer didn't hear him because of the wind blowing in the opposite direction. When the truck went on, the grandmother made an enigmatic gesture to him, but he confused it with a greeting, smiled, and waved. He didn't hear the shot. He flipped into the air and fell dead on top of his bicycle, his head blown apart by a rifle bullet, and he never knew where it came from.

Before noon they began to see feathers. They were passing by in the wind and they were feathers from young birds. The Dutchman recognized them because they were from his birds, plucked out by the wind. The driver changed direction, pushed the gas pedal to the floor, and in half an hour they could make out the pickup truck on the horizon.

When Ulises saw the military vehicle appear in the rearview mirror, he made an effort to increase the distance between them, but the motor couldn't do any better. They had traveled with no sleep and were done in from fatigue and thirst. Eréndira, who was dozing on Ulises' shoulder, woke up in fright. She saw the truck that was about to overtake them and with innocent determination she took the pistol from the glove compartment.

"It's no good," Ulises said. "It used to belong to Sir Francis Drake."

She pounded it several times and threw it out the window. The military patrol passed the broken-down truck loaded with birds plucked by the wind, turned sharply, and cut it off.

It was around that time that I came to know them, their moment of greatest splendor, but I wouldn't look into the details of their lives until many years later when Rafael Escalona, in a song, revealed the terrible ending of the drama and I thought it would be good to tell the tale. I was traveling about selling encyclopedias and medical books in the province of Riohacha. Álvaro Cepeda Samudio, who was also traveling in the region, selling beer-cooling equipment, took me through the desert towns in his truck with the intention of talking to me about something and we talked so much about nothing and drank so much beer that without knowing when or where we crossed the entire desert and reached the border. There was the tent of wandering love under hanging canvas signs: ERÉNDIRA IS BEST; LEAVE AND COME BACK— ERÉNDIRA WAITS FOR YOU; THERE'S NO LIFE WITHOUT ERÉNDIRA. The endless wavy line composed of men of diverse races and ranks looked like a snake with human vertebrae dozing through vacant lots and squares, through gaudy bazaars and noisy marketplaces, coming out of the streets of that city, which was noisy with passing merchants. Every street was a public gambling den, every house a saloon, every doorway a refuge for fugitives. The many undecipherable songs and the shouted offerings of wares formed a single roar of panic in the hallucinating heat.

Among the throng of men without a country and sharpers was Blacamán the Good, up on a table and asking for a real serpent in order to test an antidote of his invention on his own flesh. There was the woman who had been changed into a spider for having disobeyed her parents, who would let herself be touched for fifty cents so that people would see there was no trick, and she would answer questions of those who might care to ask about her misfortune. There was an envoy from the eternal life who announced the imminent coming of the fearsome astral bat, whose burning brimstone breath would overturn the order of nature and bring the mysteries of the sea to the surface.

The one restful backwater was the red-light district, reached only by the embers of the urban din. Women from the four quadrants of the nautical rose yawned with boredom in the abandoned cabarets. They had slept their siestas sitting up, unawakened by people who wanted them, and they were still waiting for the astral bat under the fans that spun on the ceilings. Suddenly one of them got up and went to a balcony with pots of pansies that overlooked the street. Down there the row of Eréndira's suitors was passing.

"Come on," the woman shouted at them. "What's that one got that we don't have?"

"A letter from a senator," someone shouted.

Attracted by the shouts and the laughter, other women came out onto the balcony.

"The line's been like that for days," one of them said. "Just imagine, fifty pesos apiece."

The one who had come out first made a decision:

"Well, I'm going to go find out what jewel that seven-month baby has got."

"Me too," another said. "It'll be better than sitting here warming our chairs for free."

On the way others joined them and when they got to Eréndira's tent they made up a rowdy procession. They went in without any announcement, used pillows to chase away the man they found spending himself as best he could for his money, and they picked up Eréndira's bed and carried it out into the street like a litter.

"This is an outrage!" the grandmother shouted. "You pack of traitors, you bandits!" And then, turning to the men in line: "And you, you sissies, where do you keep your balls, letting this attack against a poor defenseless child go on? Damned fags!"

She kept on shouting as far as her voice would carry, distributing whacks with her crosier against all who came within reach, but her rage was inaudible amongst the shouts and mocking whistles of the crowd.

Eréndira couldn't escape the ridicule because she was prevented by the dog chain that the grandmother used to hitch her to a slat of the bed ever since she had tried to run away. But they didn't harm her. They exhibited her on the canopied altar along the noisiest streets like the allegorical passage of the enchained penitent and finally they set her down like a catafalque in the center of the main square. Eréndira was all coiled up, her face hidden, but not weeping, and she stayed that way under the terrible sun in the square, biting with shame and rage at the dog chain of her evil destiny until someone was charitable enough to cover her with a shirt.

That was the only time I saw them, but I found out that they had stayed in that border town under the protection of the public forces until the grandmother's chests were bursting and then they left the desert and headed toward the sea. Never had such opulence been seen gathered together in that realm of poor people. It was a procession of ox-drawn carts on which cheap replicas of the paraphernalia lost in the disaster of the mansion were piled, not just the imperial busts and rare clocks, but also a secondhand piano and a Victrola with a crank and the records of nostalgia. A team of Indians took care of the cargo and a band of musicians announced their triumphal arrival in the villages.

The grandmother traveled on a litter with paper wreaths, chomping on the grains in her pouch, in the shadow of a church canopy. Her monumental size had increased, because under her blouse she was wearing a vest of sailcloth in which she kept the gold bars the way one keeps cartridges in a bandoleer. Eréndira was beside her, dressed in gaudy fabrics and with trinkets hanging, but with the dog chain still on her ankle.

"You've got no reason to complain," her grandmother had said to her when they left the border town. "You've got the clothes of a queen, a luxurious bed, a musical band of your own, and fourteen Indians at your service. Don't you think that's splendid?"

"Yes, Grandmother."

"When you no longer have me," the grandmother went on, "you won't be left to the mercy of men because you'll have your own home in an important city. You'll be free and happy."

It was a new and unforeseen vision of the future. On the other hand, she no longer spoke about the original debt, whose details had become twisted and whose installments had grown as the costs of the business became more complicated. Still Eréndira didn't let slip any sigh that would have given a person a glimpse of her thoughts. She submitted in silence to the torture of the bed in the saltpeter pits, in the torpor of the lakeside towns, in the lunar craters of the talcum mines, while her grandmother sang the vision of the future to her as if she were reading cards. One afternoon, as they came out of an oppressive canyon, they noticed a wind of ancient laurels and they caught snatches of Jamaica conversations and felt an urge to live and a knot in their hearts. They had reached the sea.

"There it is," the grandmother said, breathing in the glassy light of the Caribbean after half a lifetime of exile. "Don't you like it?"

"Yes, Grandmother."

They pitched the tent there. The grandmother spent the night talking without dreaming and sometimes she mixed up her nostalgia with clairvoyance of the future. She slept later than usual and awoke relaxed by the sound of the sea. Nevertheless, when Eréndira was bathing her she again made predictions of the future and it was such a feverish clairvoyance that it seemed like the delirium of a vigil.

"You'll be a noble lady," she told her. "A lady of quality, venerated by those under your protection and favored and honored by the highest authorities. Ships' captains will send you postcards from every port in the world."

Eréndira wasn't listening to her. The warm water perfumed with oregano was pouring into the bathtub through a tube fed from outside. Eréndira picked it up in a gourd, impenetrable, not even breathing, and poured it over her grandmother with one hand while she soaped her with the other.

"The prestige of your house will fly from mouth to mouth from the string of the Antilles to the realm of Holland," the grandmother was saying. "And it will be more important than the presidential palace, because the affairs of government will be discussed there and the fate of the nation will be decided."

Suddenly the water in the tube stopped. Eréndira left the tent to find out what was going on and saw the Indian in charge of pouring water into the tube chopping wood by the kitchen.

"It ran out," the Indian said. "We have to cool more water."

Eréndira went to the stove, where there was another large pot with aromatic herbs boiling. She wrapped her hands in a cloth and saw that she could lift the pot without the help of the Indian.

"You can go," she told him. "I'll pour the water."

She waited until the Indian had left the kitchen. Then she took the boiling pot off the stove, lifted it with great effort to the height of the tube, and was about to pour the deadly water into the conduit to the bathtub when the grandmother shouted from inside the tent:

"Eréndira!"

It was as if she had seen. The grandmother, frightened by the shout, repented at the last minute.

"Coming, Grandmother," she said. "I'm cooling off the water."

That night she lay thinking until quite late while her grandmother sang in her sleep, wearing the golden vest. Eréndira looked at her from her bed with intense eyes that in the shadows resembled those of a cat. Then she went to bed like a person who had drowned, her arms on her breast and her eyes open, and she called with all the strength of her inner voice:

"Ulises!"

Ulises woke up suddenly in the house on the orange plantation. He had heard Eréndira's voice so clearly that he was looking for her in the shadows of the room. After an instant of reflection, he made a bundle of his clothing and shoes and left the bedroom. He had crossed the porch when his father's voice surprised him:

"Where are you going?"

Ulises saw him blue in the moonlight.

"Into the world," he answered.

"This time I won't stop you," the Dutchman said. "But I warn you of one thing: wherever you go your father's curse will follow you."

"So be it," said Ulises.

Surprised and even a little proud of his son's resolution, the Dutchman followed him through the orange grove with a look that slowly began to smile. His wife was behind him with her beautiful Indian woman's way of standing. The Dutchman spoke when Ulises closed the gate.

"He'll be back," he said, "beaten down by life, sooner than you think."

"You're so stupid," she sighed. "He'll never come back."

On that occasion Ulises didn't have to ask anyone where Eréndira was. He crossed the desert hiding in passing trucks, stealing to eat and sleep and stealing many times for the pure pleasure of the risk until he found the tent in another seaside town which the glass buildings gave the look of an illuminated city and where resounded the nocturnal farewells of ships weighing anchor for the island of Aruba. Eréndira was asleep chained to the slat and in the same position of a drowned person on the beach from which she had called him. Ulises stood looking at her for a long time without waking her up, but he looked at her with such intensity that Eréndira awoke. Then they kissed in the darkness, caressed each other slowly, got undressed wearily, with a silent tenderness and a hidden happiness that was more than ever like love.

At the other end of the tent the sleeping grandmother gave a monumental turn and began to rant.

"That was during the time the Greek ship arrived," she said. "It was a crew of madmen who made the women happy and didn't pay them with money but with sponges, living sponges that later on walked about the houses moaning like patients in a hospital and making the children cry so that they could drink the tears."

She made a subterranean movement and sat up in bed.

"That was when he arrived, my God," she shouted, "stronger, taller, and much more of a man than Amadís."

Ulises, who until then had not paid any attention to the raving, tried to hide when he saw the grandmother sitting up in bed. Eréndira calmed him.

"Take it easy," she told him. "Every time she gets to that part she sits up in bed, but she doesn't wake up."

Ulises leaned on her shoulder.

"I was singing with the sailors that night and I thought it was an earthquake," the grandmother went on. "They all must have thought the same thing because they ran away shouting, dying with laughter, and only he remained under the starsong canopy. I remember as if it had been yesterday that I was singing the song that everyone was singing those days. Even the parrots in the courtyard sang it."

Flat as a mat, as one can sing only in dreams, she sang the lines of her bitterness:

> Lord, oh, Lord, give me back the innocence I had
> So I can feel his love all over again from the start.

Only then did Ulises become interested in the grandmother's nostalgia.

"There he was," she was saying, "with a macaw on his shoulder and a cannibal-killing blunderbuss, the way Guatarral arrived in the Guianas, and I felt his breath of death when he stood opposite me and said: 'I've been around the world a thousand times and seen women of every nation, so I can tell you on good authority that you are the haughtiest and the most obliging, the most beautiful woman on earth.'"

She lay down again and sobbed on her pillow. Ulises and Eréndira remained silent for a long time, rocked in the shadows by the sleeping old woman's great breathing. Suddenly Eréndira, without the slightest quiver in her voice, asked:

"Would you dare to kill her?"

Taken by surprise, Ulises didn't know what to answer.

"Who knows," he said. "Would you dare?"

"I can't," Eréndira said. "She's my grandmother."

Then Ulises looked once more at the enormous sleeping body as if measuring its quantity of life and decided:

"For you I'd be capable of anything."

Ulises bought a pound of rat poison, mixed it with whipped cream and raspberry jam, and poured that fatal cream into a piece of pastry from which he had removed the original filling. Then he put some thicker cream on top, smoothing it with a spoon until there was no trace of his sinister maneuver, and he completed the trick with seventy-two little pink candles.

The grandmother sat up on her throne waving her threatening crosier when she saw him come into the tent with the birthday cake.

"You brazen devil!" she shouted. "How dare you set foot in this place?"

Ulises hid behind his angel face.

"I've come to ask your forgiveness," he said, "on this day, your birthday."

Disarmed by his lie, which had hit its mark, the grandmother had the table set as if for a wedding feast. She sat Ulises down on her right while Eréndira served them, and after blowing out the candles with one devastating gust, she cut the cake into two equal parts. She served Ulises.

"A man who knows how to get himself forgiven has earned half of heaven," she said. "I give you the first piece, which is the piece of happiness."

"I don't like sweet things," he said. "You take it."

The grandmother offered Eréndira a piece of cake. She took it into the kitchen and threw it in the garbage.

The grandmother ate the rest all by herself. She put whole pieces into her mouth and swallowed them without chewing, moaning with delight and looking at Ulises from the limbo of her pleasure. When there was no more on her plate she also ate what Ulises had turned down. While she was chewing the last bit, with her fingers she picked up the crumbs from the tablecloth and put them into her mouth.

She had eaten enough arsenic to exterminate a whole generation of rats. And yet she played the piano and sang until midnight, went to bed happy, and was able to have a normal sleep. The only thing new was a rocklike scratch in her breathing.

Eréndira and Ulises kept watch over her from the other bed, and they were only waiting for her death rattle. But the voice was as alive as ever when she began to rave.

"I went crazy, my God, I went crazy!" she shouted. "I put two bars on the bedroom door so he couldn't get in; I put the dresser and table against the door and the chairs on the table, and all he had to do was give a little knock with his ring for the defenses to fall apart, the chairs to fall off the table by themselves, the table and dresser to separate by themselves, the bars to move out of their slots by themselves."

Eréndira and Ulises looked at her with growing surprise as the delirium became more profound and dramatic and the voice more intimate.

"I felt I was going to die, soaked in the sweat of fear, begging inside for the door to open without opening, for him to enter without entering, for him never to go away but never to come back either so I wouldn't have to kill him!"

She went on repeating her drama for several hours, even the most intimate details, as if she had lived it again in her dream. A little before dawn she rolled over in bed with a movement of seismic accommodation and the voice broke with the imminence of sobs.

"I warned him and he laughed," she shouted. "I warned him again and he laughed again, until he opened his eyes in terror, saying, 'Agh, queen! Agh, queen!' and his voice wasn't coming out of his mouth but through the cut the knife had made in his throat."

Ulises, terrified at the grandmother's fearful evocation, grabbed Eréndira's hand.

"Murdering old woman!" he exclaimed.

Eréndira didn't pay any attention to him because at that instant dawn began to break. The clocks struck five.

"Go!" Eréndira said. "She's going to wake up now."

"She's got more life in her than an elephant," Ulises exclaimed. "It can't be!"

Eréndira cut him with a knifing look.

"The whole trouble," she said, "is that you're no good at all for killing anybody."

Ulises was so affected by the crudeness of the reproach that he left the tent. Eréndira kept on looking at the sleeping grandmother with her secret hate, with the rage of her frustration, as the sun rose and the bird air awakened. Then the grandmother opened her eyes and looked at her with a placid smile.

"God be with you, child."

The only noticeable change was a beginning of disorder in the daily routine. It was Wednesday, but the grandmother wanted to put on a Sunday dress, decided that Eréndira would receive no customers before eleven o'clock, and asked her to paint her nails garnet and give her a pontifical coiffure.

"I never had so much of an urge to have my picture taken," she exclaimed.

Eréndira began to comb her grandmother's hair, but as she drew the comb through the tangles a clump of hair remained between the teeth. She showed it to her grandmother in alarm. The grandmother examined it, pulled on another clump with her fingers, and another bush of hair was left in her hand. She threw it on the ground, tried again and pulled out a larger lock. Then she began to pull her hair with both hands, dying with laughter, throwing the handfuls into the air with an incomprehensible jubilation until her head looked like a peeled coconut.

Eréndira had no more news of Ulises until two weeks later when she caught the call of the owl outside the tent. The grandmother had begun to play the piano and was so absorbed in her nostalgia that she was unaware of reality. She had a wig of radiant feathers on her head.

Eréndira answered the call and only then did she notice the wick that came out of the piano and went on through the underbrush and was lost in the darkness. She ran to where Ulises was, hid next to him among the bushes, and with tight hearts they both watched the little blue flame that crept along the wick, crossed the dark space, and went into the tent.

"Cover your ears," Ulises said.

They both did, without any need, for there was no explosion. The tent lighted up inside with a radiant glow, burst in silence, and disappeared in a whirlwind of wet powder. When Eréndira dared enter, thinking that her grandmother was dead, she found her with her wig singed and her nightshirt in tatters, but more alive than ever, trying to put out the fire with a blanket.

Ulises slipped away under the protection of the shouts of the Indians, who didn't know what to do, confused by the grandmother's contradictory orders. When they finally managed to conquer the flames and get rid of the smoke, they were looking at a shipwreck.

"It's like the work of the evil one," the grandmother said. "Pianos don't explode just like that."

She made all kinds of conjectures to establish the causes of the new disaster, but Eréndira's evasions and her impassive attitude ended up confusing her. She couldn't find the slightest crack in her granddaughter's behavior, nor did she consider the existence of Ulises. She was awake until dawn, threading suppositions together and calculating the loss. She slept little and poorly. On the following morning, when Eréndira took the vest with the gold bars off her grandmother, she found fire blisters on her shoulders and raw flesh on her breast. "I had good reason to be turning over in my sleep," she said as Eréndira put egg whites on the burns. "And besides, I had a strange dream." She made an effort at concentration to evoke the image until it was as clear in her memory as in the dream.

"It was a peacock in a white hammock," she said.

Eréndira was surprised but she immediately assumed her everyday expression once more.

"It's a good sign," she lied. "Peacocks in dreams are animals with long lives."

"May God hear you," the grandmother said, "because we're back where we started. We have to begin all over again."

Eréndira didn't change her expression. She went out of the tent with the plate of compresses and left her grandmother with her torso soaked in egg white and her skull daubed with mustard. She was putting more egg whites into the plate under the palm shelter that served as a kitchen when she saw Ulises' eyes appear behind the stove as she had seen them the first time behind her bed. She wasn't startled, but told him in a weary voice:

"The only thing you've managed to do is increase my debt."

Ulises' eyes clouded over with anxiety. He was motionless, looking at Eréndira in silence, watching her crack the eggs with a fixed expression of absolute disdain, as if he didn't exist. After a moment the eyes moved, looked over the things in the kitchen, the hanging pots, the strings of annatto, the carving knife. Ulises stood up, still not saying anything, went in under the shelter, and took down the knife.

Eréndira didn't look at him again, but when Ulises left the shelter she told him in a very low voice:

"Be careful, because she's already had a warning of death. She dreamed about a peacock in a white hammock."

The grandmother saw Ulises come in with the knife, and making a supreme effort, she stood up without the aid of her staff and raised her arms.

"Boy!" she shouted. "Have you gone mad?"

Ulises jumped on her and plunged the knife into her naked breast. The grandmother moaned, fell on him, and tried to strangle him with her powerful bear arms.

"Son of a bitch," she growled. "I discovered too late that you have the face of a traitor angel."

She was unable to say anything more because Ulises managed to free the knife and stab her a second time in the side. The grandmother let out a hidden moan and hugged her attacker with more strength. Ulises gave her a third stab, without pity, and a spurt of blood, released by high pressure, sprinkled his face: it was oily blood, shiny and green, just like mint honey.

Eréndira appeared at the entrance with the plate in her hand and watched the struggle with criminal impassivity.

Huge, monolithic, roaring with pain and rage, the grandmother grasped Ulises' body. Her arms, her legs, even her hairless skull were green with blood. Her enormous bellows-breathing, upset by the first rattles of death, filled the whole area. Ulises managed to free his arm with the weapon once more, opened a cut in her belly, and an explosion of blood soaked him in green from head to toe. The grandmother tried to reach the open air which she needed in order to live now and fell face down. Ulises got away from the lifeless arms and without pausing a moment gave the vast fallen body a final thrust.

Eréndira then put the plate on a table and leaned over her grandmother, scrutinizing her without touching her. When she was convinced that she was dead her face suddenly acquired all the maturity of an older person which her twenty years of misfortune had not given her. With quick and precise movements she grabbed the gold vest and left the tent.

Ulises remained sitting by the corpse, exhausted by the fight, and the more he tried to clean his face the more it was daubed with that green and living matter that seemed to be flowing from his fingers. Only when he saw Eréndira go out with the gold vest did he become aware of his state.

He shouted to her but got no answer. He dragged himself to the entrance to the tent and he saw Eréndira starting to run along the shore away from the city. Then he made a last effort to chase her, calling her with painful shouts that were no longer those of a lover but of a son, yet he was overcome by the terrible drain of having killed a woman without anybody's help. The grandmother's Indians caught up to him lying face down on the beach, weeping from solitude and fear.

Eréndira had not heard him. She was running into the wind, swifter than a deer, and no voice of this world could stop her. Without turning her head she ran past the saltpeter pits, the talcum craters, the torpor of the shacks, until the natural science of the sea ended and the desert began, but she still kept on running with the gold vest beyond the arid winds and the never-ending sunsets and she was never heard of again nor was the slightest trace of her misfortune ever found.

Miss Florence's Trunk

by Ana Lydia Vega

translated by Andrew Hurley

Slavery per se is not a sin. It is a social condition ordained from the beginning of time for the wisest purposes, benevolent and disciplinary, by Divine Wisdom.

—Samuel F. B. Morse, *Letters and Journals,* published by his son E. L. Morse in 1914.

Folks here pity my loneliness, but I continue to exist.

—Susan Walker Morse, letter to Mary Peters Overman, Arroyo, Puerto Rico, February 28, 1848.

I

ON THE MORNING OF DECEMBER 8 1885, MISS FLORENCE JANE (OF the honest English Janes) went to her door, took up the *New York Times* that had arrived just moments before, and carried it into her small parlor. Idly she stood and scanned the news, but then, with a searing cry of pain, she flung the newspaper from her, as though it were a white-hot coal. Yet still, from the burgundy-velvet sofa where the journal lay, there continued to burn into her eyes (more accustomed to the softer lights and shadows of the novel) the fiery letters of a headline:

MYSTERIOUS DISAPPEARANCE AT SEA

Though laconic, the words were devastating, for the person who had disappeared, the person whose name the article revealed, had once been Miss Florence's dear benefactress, friend, and employer. It took Miss Florence several minutes to feel strong enough once again to trust her legs, and to go from the room in search of the smelling salts and lemon-balm water.

That night, in spite of the linden tea she sipped in extraordinary amounts, sleep would not come. The fragile, graceful figure of the woman who had once been her benefactress roamed, in a long white wispy robe, the somber hallways of her memory. Toward daybreak, exhausted from her long prayers for the repose of that soul which haunted her nightlong vigil, Miss Florence at last fled the warm refuge of her sheets.

Almost without realizing what she was about, she found herself kneeling on the floor, her back bent low and her head at a precarious angle. A quick glance sufficed to confirm that indeed the thing she looked to find was still beneath the bed, dark, somber and solid. No matter how hard she tried, though, she could not remember what drawer, chest, or nook it was to which she had entrusted the small key to the old lock, the one fragile protector of the trunk's inviolate privacy. Very much to her regret—and even more to that of the sleeping neighbors on the floor below—she determined to force the catch, her accomplice an old rusty hammer.

The smell of things locked away—moth balls and lavender sachets—made her draw her head back, and for a time she fought the compelling urge to sneeze. With a linen handkerchief held to her blushing nose, at last she nerved herself to disturb, for the first time in almost twenty years, the hermetic peace of those *souvenirs,* neatly organized by dates and places.

It did not take her long to find, in the sturdy black box with its lining of red taffeta, the volume whose cover of leather-grained cardboard bore a line of large gold letters:

JOURNAL: PUERTO RICO 1856–59

The yellowed pages clung to each other; they resisted the fingers that clumsily tried to turn them. Miss Florence's eyes nervously skipped about the pages, and as they alighted upon random words here and there, hushed sensations were awakened in her breast. There were moments when some ravelled piece of the past would play the tyrant to her attention, and upon that scrap her eyes would linger as though deciphering the enigmatic handwriting of a foreign manuscript.

La Enriqueta

I am here at last, after a horrendous—nay, hellish—voyage. Many times I thought the sea would receive the contents of my mutinous stomach. The captain that brought us from Saint Thomas must have made a pact with the devil to have tamed such waves. Mrs. Lind's letter and my British passport (much respected in these latitudes) saved me the discomforts of the formalities of Customs. A negro coachman in white livery—a curious colonial custom, not without a certain charm—was awaiting me, as I had been told he would be, in front of Mr. Lind's warehouse.

The hacienda lies some three miles from the harbor. We drove to the end of the main street of the village of Arroyo, and then we took a dusty, bumpy road that ran in absolute assurance to the gates of the estate picturesquely named La Enriqueta.

If the dry monotony of my journey had made me many times long for the English countryside, not so the splendid grounds of this palatial country place. I have used the word "hacienda," but I use it as those who live here use it, to refer not so much to a desert-like ranch such as those in the regions of Mexico and the southwestern territories of the United States (as I understand them to be), but rather to a sort of plantation, a veritable small city more like an English manor house and its many out-buildings than anything else of which I have experience. All is luxury and ostentation, though set in the country. There are artistically designed gardens in which a profusion of exotic flowers bloom. Before the grand mansion of wood and masonry, with wide porches all around it, a fra-grant fountain sprays rainbows of water over the finely sculpted heads of nymphs and dolphins. Parrots, monkeys, and even serpents are kept in spacious bamboo cages suspended by ropes and vines from the trees, many of which bear exotic fruit that I know not the names of. Towards the western and eastern boundaries of the immediate grounds, two arti-ficial pools, ringed with Greek and Roman statues and sailed upon by proud black swans, multiply the blinding glare of the tireless sun.

Mrs. Lind, who welcomed me with the greatest cordiality imagin-able, urged me to call her simply Miss Susan, as all the servants, she said, do. I could not hide the astonishment caused in me by that volun-tary abandonment of wedded title and name. Still, in order not to mar that first impression which is so important to the career of any gov-erness, I kept to myself as best I could my reservations.

Miss Susan's husband is away, travelling, as it appears he pretty often is. His simultaneous responsibilities as man of business and owner of a large hacienda almost constantly require his presence on the neighboring islands and in the nearby towns.

The young Charles—who but fleetingly showed himself—has the carriage and the aspect of any young European gentleman. His skin shows no sign whatever of that underlying yellowish sort of tint which so blemishes the appearance of white persons born in this part of the world. Miss Susan told me that they had just returned from the house of her father—the famous Mr. Samuel F. B. Morse—in Poughkeepsie, where they had spent the greatest part of the summer. One must, she added with a hint of sadness, retire to Locust Grove (as Mr. Morse calls his first fixed abode) in order to repair the harm done the lungs and the blood by the rigors of the tropics.

Before we sat down at table, which bore an impressive display of delicate porcelain and silverplate engraved with the ornate family *L*, Miss Susan took me into the kitchen, where I was introduced to the servants one by one. One of them, Bella, a negress of indeterminate age with sweetly canine eyes, was especially recommended to me. "She has been with me since the day I married," the lady of the house told me, embracing her with a certain unwonted—though sincere—affection.

If the meal had one fault, it was its abundance. Too spicy for my sober taste, the native dishes indisposed my stomach a bit, and so I was very glad indeed when Miss Susan asked Bella to go with me to my room. In this small room, then, on the second floor of the main house, its enormous window opening onto a spectacular cloud-filled sunset, I now sit, and perched as I am, I find that I too am mistress of this empire of sugar cane stretching as far as the eye can see toward the dark-blue Caribbean.

Master Charlie

My charge seems quite a temperamental child. His favorite victim is poor Bella, who shows him more affection than his own mother does. The boy has learned Spanish like a prodigy, but his accent, in no way befitting a member of his class, betrays the African origins of his school. It is in Spanish that he replies, impudently, when I try to catch his attention for some lesson.

I am not the first—though I hope to be the last—to have accepted the challenge of the domestication of this spoiled little wild beast of the Linds. The unfortunates who preceded me (and there have been, according to information that I believe to be trustworthy, no less than six) lasted but a few months, each one, before being replaced. I was warned by good Mrs. Travers of all this when she asked if she might recommend me for the post.

The boy detests history and arithmetic. Only drawing and singing can keep him at the desk, or even inside the room, on a sunny day. With more craft than patience, I have, however, been able to interest him in reading, thanks to two magnificent volumes of Sir Walter Scott that I found in the house. From the most violent antipathy toward literature, he has swung like a weathercock, and now exhibits the most effusive love for it. What would Mrs. Dayton say if she should see me turn from the solid virtues of the classics to the easy success of the moderns? It was, nonetheless, under her own teaching that I learned to value more the ends than the means. And as for my relations with this rebellious angel, I know not what will be worse: suffering his eternal contempt, broken by intermittent outbursts of childish perversity, or awakening his interest, with the uninterrupted questioning that is sure to ensue from that.

Early this afternoon we went on a little walk to Punta Guilarte. The excursion, out and back, took us a bit more than an hour. I used this time outdoors with Charles to test his knowledge of natural history. To my delighted surprise, my charge, very much of his own accord, and almost with pride, ticked off the names (in Spanish, almost always) of many plants and animals that we passed, names that I myself, of course, did not know. I will have to look out for some trustworthy source with the proper translations.

The sea was so still that one might have thought it a lake. I removed my shoes to test the temperature of the water, which shone almost white in the afternoon sun. As my feet sank into the moist sand, a warm sense of well-being ran up my legs, which had before been accustomed to the cruel cold of European waters. So absorbed was I in those comparisons that I almost forgot to oversee my charge. I got quite a start, even if only momentary, when I realized that the boy had disappeared, and without a word to me. But then I saw him leap, as agilely as a little rabbit, from a dense stand of sea-grapes. I could not help a cry of alarm at the sight of his totally naked body. I quickly turned my back so as not to be exposed more to that very primitive naturalness with which he reacted to my distaste. And then, informing me that he had his father's permission to bathe as God had brought him into the world, he ran (without bothering to request my own permission) happily off into the waves.

As Charlie's impetuous quickness had caught me off guard, I patiently waited for him to finish his impromptu swim. I did avoid, however, looking into his eyes, so as not to awaken in him, at such an early age, sentiments of a dubious nature. I supposed that he had acquired this and who knew how many other questionable habits in his contact with the African children who have always been his playmates. Small wonder Miss Susan has forbidden him to frequent the negro quarters.

On the way back to the house, a remark from Charlie satisfied my curiosity as to a matter that I would never have had the temerity to broach. He revealed to me very playfully that unlike Mr. Lind, who is, to all indications, quite given to nude bathing, Charlie's mother generally swam in a petticoat, out of fear of the stings of the men-of-war.

Miss Susan: Obverse and Reverse

Is one to think that it is the long absence of her husband that has sunk my mistress into these depths of melancholy and idleness? While

Charlie demands my attention almost twelve hours in the day, my mistress wanders like a discreet ghost about the house, the prey of an endless tedium. The heat and humidity of the afternoons confine her, as though she had been dramatically stripped of every ounce of *force vitale,* to the hypnotic web of the hammock. Almost nothing can persuade her to go out of the house without company, yet she has confided to me that most of her friends bore her. Her thin face grows every day sharper and more lean, and her waist can be encircled with the fingers of one hand. Bella's attentions are futile, her mistress's lassitude without salvation. Only the sea-baths, along the beaches that mark the southern boundary of the property, soothe her flesh, which is mercilessly devoured by the legions of mosquitoes that breed in the swampy regions of this coastal plain.

Suddenly, though, I discover that she is capable of enthusiasm. The news of the imminent arrival of Mrs. Molly Overman, a visit confirmed only days ago, seems to have had the power to transform her. Suddenly, the house is magically possessed; the grounds are a hive of feverish activity. Miss Susan directs the operations as though we were to be visited by royalty. Now if she is wearied, it is in bringing to the complicated preparations every nuance of elegance, and it is weariness that seems to vivify her. She has had the guest room redone as though for a princess: Louis XV gilt, Queen Anne chairs, damask bedcoverings and pillows. She has spent hours preparing the menu for the welcome dinner, which will be an impressive and delicious *mélange* of American and native dishes. She has had coconuts, mangoes, and passion-fruits brought directly from the trees for elaborate desserts and drinks. An immense bouquet of tropical flowers, whose names—bird of paradise, *flamboyán,* bougainvillea, shower-of-gold—make my sober head spin, will greet the triumphant entry of the New York guest into the house. Mrs. Molly is not just Miss Susan's niece, she is her best friend.

My Society Debut

Miss Susan and Mrs. Molly are like two girls, with that disconcerting combination of brashness and innocence so characteristic of certain American young ladies. At night I can hear (not without a certain twinge of discomfort) their gales of laughter. At table, it is Mrs. Molly who monopolizes the conversation with her racy stories. Smiling nostalgically, Miss Susan vicariously lives the sweet frivolity of the city life that her Antillean exile has so pitilessly robbed her of.

Yesterday, at the urging of the two ladies, I found myself accompanying them for tea *chez* Mrs. O'Hara, the wife of the British vice-consul. The grand wooden house of the O'Haras, located on Isabel Segunda Street, where many of the well-to-do families of the small town live, has a sober sort of elegance about it. As we approached it, I found it odd that the sight of the Union Jack snapping in the ocean breeze brought me neither pride for my origins nor longing for my old home. The years I have lived away from England have somehow blurred my pleasant memories of Oxfordshire, and I find that I recall only my father's long illness, his slow decay, and, upon the finality of his death, a deep sense of no longer belonging.

Mrs. O., as her friends and family call her, is a stout woman with wavy red hair, a most pleasant hostess eminently skilled at conversation—though to my taste she is a bit over-curious. In a flood of banal questions, there softly floated forth the inevitable inquiry as to my state of matrimony. "I am a free woman," I answered somewhat shortly, "and for the moment have no pressing reason for not continuing to be so."

When I turned my head to put an end to this interview, I found myself looking into the merry eyes of Miss Susan and Mrs. Molly, who could not altogether hide their surprise at my sharpness but who were mischievous enough to enjoy it. As the maid served tea and cakes, Mrs. O. returned to the subject, offering to present me to the "few acceptable unmarried men in the region" at the next *soirée*. At that, the providential arrival of two ladies (who turned out to be the vice-consul's sisters) prevented my compatriot's indiscretion from making me forget my manners.

I was relieved when we rose to take our leave, I must admit. The visit, which I had found interminable, made clear to me the reasons for my mistress's reluctance to frequent the salons of the foreign *crème de la societé*. Other people's lives are the only thing on the menu: the *plat de resistance*.

Enter Mr. Lind

The heat of this time of year (which is paradoxically called "winter" here) is worse than stifling. The oppressiveness of the weather sometimes makes me wish for a hard rain, a storm, a veritable hurricane to come and lash the countryside around. Fortunately, Charlie spends his afternoons swimming or splashing about in the creek with Miss Susan and Mrs. Molly (whom he adores), and that allows me to take refuge in the only cool place I have been able to find: the rear veranda. The roles have been unexpectedly reversed: Miss Susan bustles about while I languish in the hammock.

Tonight during dinner we heard a horse gallop up into the front garden of the hacienda. My mistress rushed euphorically out to the veranda as Bella scurried to set another place at the table. Charlie surprised me by remaining calmly in his chair, a miracle I attributed to his obvious fascination with the effervescent beauty of his cousin. Mrs. Molly went on eating imperturbably. For some reason, a growing nervousness evidenced itself in my hands, and I had to put down my fork in order not to betray the agitation caused in me by the sudden and unexpected arrival of the owner and master of La Enriqueta.

Miss Susan and her husband were a good while coming into the dining room. By a curious effect of the mirrors of the house, however, we could see their silhouettes as they embraced in the semi-darkness of the passage. Mr. Lind's arms passionately encircled his wife. I turned to the boy in order to distract his attention with some silly question, but as I turned back, I saw with some confusion that Mrs. Molly's eyes were brazenly fixed on the scene, the contemplation of which, I should have thought, even the most elementary sense of modesty would have prevented.

In spite of his penetrating green eyes, Edward Lind is not what the world generally calls a handsome man. His nose is too long and his lips too heavy to raise him to the plane of aesthetic harmony, not to mention the fact that when I first laid eyes on him he had not trimmed his beard or shaved for several days. He does, however, possess qualities capable of impressing certain women. His forthright manliness, his playful smile, and his slight foreign accent combine to give him a *je ne sais quoi* that a woman like Miss Susan must surely have found difficult to resist. Descended from a family that has lived for many years in St. Thomas, and of excellent Danish lineage, his conversation is varied and he has a sharp sense of humor, two qualities not a little surprising to find in a man accustomed principally to the society of animals and Africans.

After eating and drinking very well, not to say in abundance, he sent Charlie, who had remained pretty cool to the effusive greetings of his father, off to his room. Neither the pleas nor the heated protests nor, finally, the tears of his son could alter Mr. Lind's firm resolve. Neither of the ladies intervened, much less this woman who is but an employee of the family. The tantrum lasted but a moment, however. One word to the boy from my master (his voice, it is true, raised a bit) was all it took to send the child running from the room.

His good humor recovered, Mr. Lind asked Mrs. Molly to sit at the piano and he delighted us with sailors' ditties (if I can call delight that gay confusion that the frankly *risqué* nature of the numbers aroused in us females). As the laughter and the applause died, I could not help observing that Mr. Lind looked at me fixedly, and that Miss Susan never took her eyes off his face.

It must have been almost ten o'clock (an hour at which I could not but wonder at the untiring energy of a man just returned from a long journey) when Mr. Lind was struck by a sudden idea—he would give his guest a ride on his new horse. He has just bought a lovely *paso fino,* as the breed is known, a small horse with a canter that is, they say, as smooth as a rocking chair's.

"You come, too," he said to me with a boyish smile and sparkling eyes. "There's always room for more than one lady on my horse." I could not even raise my eyes for the confusion caused in me by the suggestive nature of his invitation, which I could only attribute to excess of drink. I courteously declined his offer, and, with my mistress's leave, I withdrew to my room as soon as I could. The shrieks of the new Amazon and the hilarious instructions of the experienced horseman have somewhat prevented my concentrating fully on these notes.

A LETTER

The Christmas season here, in spite of the all-embracing papism of the country, is, more than religious celebration, a pagan festival. We have already been treated to several *músicas,* as the tropical sort of carolling is called here in which neighbors journey to each other's houses to perform. La Enriqueta's rum is served abundantly to the carollers, and is accompanied by a great variety of fried delicacies generically known as *frituras.* Miss Susan seems to enjoy these impromptu parties very little. As she stands next the door to the veranda, her expression is one of impenetrable distance, while her husband mingles cordially with the creole visitors and even asks the ladies to dance.

Mr. Lind's sister and brother-in-law have replaced Mrs. Molly in the guest room. The aristocratic bearing of the Salomons, who have come from Ponce with servants and all, is not much to the liking of my incorrigible charge, who has begun to call them, to Miss Susan's delighted shock, "the Royal Couple." Even the dog they have brought along (a majestic collie whose rich coat makes him a pitiable victim of the heat of the tropics) perfectly suits their air of refinement.

Just three days ago it was that in the midst of great happiness I was delivered an urgent missive sent from St. Thomas. The bearer of the letter was Mr. Lind himself, whose horse had rushed like a black streak of lightning across the front of the house while I was having my five o'clock tea on the veranda. Seconds later he ran up the steps, three at a time, and put the letter in my hands.

"Miss Jane—your last name sounds more like a Christian name," he said, not yet releasing the envelope and looking very fixedly at me with that unsettling calmness that he has, as though he were expecting some happy phrase from me in order to open a long-postponed conversation. I could only produce a weak smile, however, as I lowered my eyes (as usual), now under the pretext of deciphering the illegible name of the sender.

With a rapidity almost feline, Mr. Lind took a step forward, coming so near me that I could very clearly hear, in the afternoon's silence, his labored breaths, redolent of rum and tobacco. Instinctively I took a step back. He stepped once again forward, and it was as though we were in a partnerless dance.

"Shyness is bad company," he softly murmured after a pause that seemed to me an eternity. It was utterly impossible for my paralyzed lips to speak a word. I know not what would have happened had not at that very moment Charlie's lithe figure appeared in the doorway. Mr. Lind took his eyes from mine and, turning to his son with somewhat exaggerated joviality, challenged him to a race to the other end of the veranda.

With a gesture of indifference the boy rejected his father's challenge; instead, he walked toward me, a look of questioning on his young face. It was only then that I realized I was holding the letter.

Once I reached my room, I broke the seal. Mr. Wolf, the Anglican pastor at Christiansted, had sent me the details of the rapid and painless (thank God!) death of my angelic protectress Mrs. Travers. The delay in the Spanish post had put off my grief for two long weeks.

Sitting at my dressing table, my forehead resting against the silvery cool mirror, I cried, tearlessly, for the perfection of my solitude in the world.

An Homage

This morning as I entered the library a little before eight, I found on my desk a drawing, very beautifully done. It showed me (the resemblance amazing in its detail) walking under the stars in the garden of La Enriqueta with my hair down and dressed in what I must say was very flimsy clothing—a fine lace petticoat and nothing else. At the bottom, there was a verse from Browning.

At first I could only smile at the somewhat over-idealized image of a nocturnal nymph that Master Charlie had drawn of me. Long later reflection, however, caused me to reconsider that smile. Clearly (and in spite of the tantrums that he sometimes still inflicts on us) my student is growing day by day farther from that childhood I continue to envisage him inhabiting, and entering the irreversible road to puberty. The equatorial heat, I understand, favors and accelerates that process. At thirteen years and two or three months, his angular, gangling body betrays the developing maturity that his childishly high and mighty airs sometimes deny. What silent transformations must be secretly at work in that mind so recently tender! White girls of his own age are conspicuous by their absence from these parts, and that is no doubt the explanation for this unhealthy attraction to adult women. Beginning today, and in spite of my natural affections, I shall have to keep a greater distance between us.

THE TABLEAU

The arrival of a new physician, come to take over old Dr. Tracy's practice, was the occasion for a reception that the Linds attended today. Though more than a bit reluctant to involve myself in social activities that hold so little interest for me, I was obliged to accompany them if I was not to risk committing an "offense to the British community," as my mistress was kind enough to tell me, quite ceremoniously.

In a dress from Miss Susan's vast collection, and selected and fitted by herself, I felt more inadequate than ever. Charlie, the insolent little imp, confirmed my fears; he made merciless fun of the high hemline of my dress, out from which peeked not only the toe but the entire top of my black lace-up shoes. He laughed so hard that Bella had to scold him, though that did not prevent him from making faces at me from behind her ample skirts.

As we were about to leave, with the buggy waiting in the drive in front of the house, I was witness to a most deplorable scene. Mr. Lind, who had been hearing with good patience the boy's insistent pleas to be included in the party, suddenly grew angry at Charlie's refusal to stay at home, and grabbing up the buggy-whip that stood beside the front door, he lashed out at the boy in rage. I could not speak, so great was my horror at the exaggerated violence of his reaction. The fury in the man's eyes made Miss Susan cry out and Bella take a step back, both women utterly terrified. The boy tried in vain to fend off the attack with his forearm. Impulsively, I stepped forward and before the father could bring the lash down again on his son's reddened skin, I seized the child and drew him to me and walked him, without a word, to his room.

Upon my return, the Linds were seated in the buggy. The driver helped me up, and I took my seat in silence beside Miss Susan, who discreetly squeezed my hand. Mr. Lind, his face turned away from us, spoke not a word during the trip, or even deigned to look at us.

In the entrance hall of the O'Hara residence, the butler awaited us, and this sight made my master exclaim, in an attempt to leaven the atmosphere: "There are two things the British never forget when they pack their bags for the colonies—their tea and their butlers!" I suppressed the smile that came to me, trying at all costs to keep my expression impassive, however falsely so.

The physician, it turns out, is a Frenchman some thirty years of age who has already been living for a short time in Arroyo. His name is Fouchard, and his English is very correct, though marked by the inevitable guttural r of the French. He seemed to me not only courteous and handsome enough but also somewhat shy, and of more than average intelligence.

As we talked, a young creole man with an extraordinarily long nose and an amazingly square chin came up to us and was at once introduced to me. His name is Alvaro Beauchamp, the son of a French father and Spanish mother, and his cordiality is quite disarming. In a few moments his sister Ernestina joined us, a young woman as affable as he. Almost at once, without a word from me, she began to tell me details of "our Dr. Fouchard." Her brother and the doctor had been introduced to one another in Paris, where they both studied medicine, by a mutual friend, a young man from Cabo Rojo (a town here in Puerto Rico) studying in France also. This young man Fouchard had known since his school days in Toulouse. Fouchard's interest in tropical diseases had brought him as far as the island of Guadeloupe (a French island, *naturellement*), and from there he had come on, at Beauchamp's urging, to Puerto Rico. The sparkle in Ernestina's eyes and the frank enthusiasm of her voice when she spoke of her brother's friend made me think at once that the presence of that friend on the island could mean but one thing.

As we sipped our drinks and enjoyed the hostess's good *hor d'oeuvres,* the conversation turned to the far-off events in Saint-Domingue (now Haiti) and the not-so-far-off French Antilles. The planters and men of business in the group could not hide the uneasiness they felt at the possibility of an African uprising, though it was a threat which the men of business preferred to make light of. With the greatest tact, Fouchard avoided being drawn into the discussion, an attitude I thought very prudent in one so recently arrived.

"God save Queen Victoria and deliver us from political and natural catastrophes," the vice-consul said, raising his glass in a toast. The guests most feelingly seconded him.

Mr. O'Hara's sisters had set up a stage for a *tableau,* and to carry it off enlisted the aid of their guests. I shrank into my armchair, hoping no one would conceive the misguided idea of including me in the cast. My fears, unfortunately, were not unfounded.

The protagonist of the plot, a predictable and (if I may confide my opinion frankly to my own notes) puerile one, was a very wealthy widower who publicly advertised for the "sincere and disinterested" love of a woman. Given such a premise, the candidates for the gentleman's wife were, predictably, not few. With his son's assistance, the gentleman managed to eliminate the female pretenders one by one as they revealed their venal flaws. As the discouraged gentleman (played by poor Dr. Tracy) is about to give up the search, he addresses the distinguished ladies present, among which—he has been told—is the Pure and Incorruptible Ideal Wife. In the starring role of the son, Mr. Reed (captain of one of Mr. Lind's ships) thereupon proposes that the young unmarried women of the company (six, including myself) pass one by one across the "stage" in order that we may be interviewed and appraised by the widower, with the kind collaboration of the other gentlemen as spectators and jury.

I was tempted to stand and, under any poor excuse that might occur to me, leave the room before my turn came. But my cowardice was greater than my sensitivity to ridicule, and so, in unspeakable misery, I awaited the fatal moment. To my misfortune, I was the last candidate to pass across the stage, after Miss Buckmar, Miss Balestière, Ernestina Beauchamp and Mrs. O.'s extroverted sisters-in-law, Lorna and Diana, had had their own opportunities to exhibit their many stunning talents.

With trembling hands and lips, I yielded myself up to the torture of the public eye. Dr. Fouchard, who looked even more uncomfortable than I, gave me a little wink of support, for which I showed my thanks with a sickly smile.

"Perhaps it should be our new *petit docteur* who interrogates Miss Jane," the ever-inopportune Mrs. O. quickly shrieked. I could have murdered her without a second thought had the moment allowed it. But to my profound dismay, before the shy Fouchard could react to our hostess's suggestion, we were addressed by the deep voice of Mr. Lind, which echoed above the gay chatter of the room:

"Let us declare winner by acclamation a candidate who does not have to speak to justify her victory."

A surge of boiling blood rushed to my head, and I thought for a moment my legs would fail me. General applause brought this vexatious episode to a close and enabled me to seek asylum once again in my deep armchair. As I received the effusive congratulations of Fouchard, I felt on the back of my neck the heat of a glance which I had not the courage to return.

THE MUSE

Taking advantage of his father's absence, and in open defiance of his mother's orders, Charlie went off today to see Carolina, the negress who suckled him until he was three years of age, and who is, it seems, in very delicate health. Fearful of the consequences, Bella came to tell me of Charlie's escape. I refused to intervene in the affair. My failure to act, however, was interpreted as tacit consent, and may earn me my patrons' censure. The risk of becoming the accomplice of a boy so given to disobedience should not be underestimated.

I devoted the free time given me by Charlie's escape to classifying the books in the library; they had been shelved by their only reader, Miss Susan, solely as her whim dictated. There is an impressive collection of French and British literature. Almost all the covers bear the initials SWM that Miss Susan has not wished to abandon. Some are gifts from Mr. Morse and have long dedications, signed, in every case, "Your most affectionate father."

As I opened one of the books—a volume by Mary Wollstonecraft on the equality of the sexes—there fell onto the table a pencil sketch. It showed the slender silhouette of Miss Susan dressed in the Greek robes of one of the nine Muses. Miss Susan often boasts of having once posed for a similar portrait, now famous, painted by her father.

How absurd seemed to me then the life which fate has given my mistress! How justified her *mal de vivre,* her indifferent surrender to the tedium of her days! She has abandoned modernity, the stir of the city, the intellectual ferment of her upbringing in order to pass her time, like the mockingbird her husband gave her on her wedding-day, in the perpetual lethargy of a golden cage. How powerful must be the magnet that holds her within it, and that weakens more and more each day the futile beating of her wings!

Although I am greatly moved by the sacrifice implied by that renunciation, a more obscure sentiment runs parallel to my pity, for I too am a prisoner, and likewise by my own will, though the loss of my freedom obeys causes much less sublime.

An emotion almost like envy steals from time to time into my soul.

THE SEQUESTRATION

Today I was the victim of a strange practical joke played on me by Charlie. I did not find it amusing. The two of us were in the garden, sitting on my favorite bench in the shade, when, suddenly taking my hand in his, he said with great urgency in his voice, "Come, come with me, I have something interesting to show you." Curious, I followed him at once. He took me to a little brick outbuilding occupied at night by the watchman, and stepping aside to let me pass, he told me to look inside. I should not have been so guileless, but the desire to find out what it was that was so "interesting" overcame my common sense.

Suddenly, I realized that the door had closed behind me, and that I was confined in that tiny space by thick brick walls. The heat was suffocating; the small openings that served as windows barely admitted air.

Outside there was no sound but Charlie's uncontrollable laughter.

"How do you like your new room?" he asked mockingly, his faced contorted with malicious hilarity.

I tried to keep calm, though I was far from feeling so, and I coldly instructed him to let me out.

"I'm going on a journey," he replied, his tone still insolent, "and when I come back, I want you to have dinner ready for me."

With these insolent words, he left me to my fate for a period of time which rage and impotence made seem immeasurably long.

I know not how many minutes, hours, centuries later, I felt upon my burning forehead a breath of cool air and I saw that the door was opening, little by little, as though by magic. Charlie's tall figure appeared suddenly on the threshold. Ready to box his ears, scratch his eyes out, anything to avenge the humiliating affront to myself, I rushed at him. With a quick, sure gesture he stopped my upraised hands, pulling them behind his back and forcing me by pure brute force to embrace his waist.

In that position, as uncomfortable as it was shameful, he held me for some time. At last, in a very low voice which did nothing to conceal the emotion he was feeling, he said, "Forgive me, Miss Florence, I only wanted you to understand what life is to a prisoner."

His arms dropped to his side. His lips trembled and tears spilled from his eyes. Then, casting aside my own resentments, it was I who held him against my breast.

THE EVE OF A VACATION

They all left yesterday, very early in the morning. Mr. Lind, forever occupied upon his affairs, could not or would not go with them to the harbor. My mistress looked radiant; her wide smile showed how happy she was to be departing for the continent. The serious look my charge put on, however, as he bade me good-bye, gave me pause. Seized by a sudden attack of sadness, Bella refused to come out even onto the veranda.

As the coach pulled away, I went (attracted by the fragrance of good coffee) into the kitchen, where I found Bella crying beside the great cookstove. Drying her tears on her apron, she shoved a letter at me. In it, my mistress very brusquely notified me of the arrangements she had made for me to take "a very well-deserved" vacation in Ponce as the guest of the Salomons. The coachman had been informed and the date of my departure set. I was given exactly a day and a half to make my preparations.

Miss Susan's decision (taken without having so much as consulted me, and announced this way in writing) took me very much aback. On the one hand, I was of course tempted by the idea of leaving, even for a short time, the narrow universe of La Enriqueta. On the other, the prospect of falling into the satin clutches of the "Royal Couple," collie and all, was not particularly pleasing to me. But as to all appearances I had no choice, I put the best face on things I could.

The torrential rains of the last few days have flooded the low-lying parts of the hacienda, and work has been stopped. Mr. Lind paces, the victim of chronic ill humor and a headache which Bella says can only be cured by two shots of rum and some lettuce tea. I too have felt somewhat indisposed. There is no doubt that the tropical climate, changeable and unhealthful as it is, does not sit well with us.

I was in the kitchen in the evening, helping (more out of boredom than obligation) make some candy and other little things to take with me to my hosts in Ponce, when Joseph, the overseer and Mr. Lind's most trusted employee, called at the window. Bella put her head out and they spoke for a while in the *patois* of the English islands. I saw her cross herself three times before allowing the poor rain-soaked man into her kitchen. No sooner was he inside than the two of them attempted to put upon my shoulders the responsibility of informing the master of the escape of a party of seven slaves. When I vehemently refused, Bella crossed herself again, gave Joseph a look of anguish, and went off to the parlor.

Mr. Lind's outburst of fury could have been heard in the farthest negro quarters, even above the sound of the rain. And no matter how absurd it was to try to follow the fugitives' tracks in the implacable deluge that was falling, Joseph was commanded to send out two bands along the most probable routes: the coastal region outside Guayama called Jobos and the steep, rugged mountains of Arroyo. Mr. Lind himself went out to saddle his horse, and cursing his blinding headache, rode off at the head of one of the search parties.

My spirits fallen and my body in the grip of a sort of chill brought on by the rain, I retired early. I made a place in my luggage for the jars I was to take to Ponce, and I sat down to finish some socks for Mr. Salomon. The indisposition that I had felt coming on since the morning at last made me put aside my work and lie down on my bed. My forehead was hot and I felt terribly tired.

I must have fallen asleep, dressed just as I was, because suddenly I awoke with a start. The clock in the dining room was striking twelve. The rain continued, and when I went to close my window (which was wide open), a wet, clammy cold gripped my feet.

I went back to sleep, but I was very agitated; I woke often to find my face bathed in icy sweat. In that intermediate state between waking and sleeping, I could hardly distinguish the whistling of the wind from the far-off howling of the dogs and the hoofbeats of the horses. I know not how much time passed before the wooden floor creaked under the slow footsteps that stopped inches from my door. I held my breath, and did not exhale again until the steps went away and I could hear the discreet but unmistakable sound of a bolt shot softly through its eye.

Today I am worse, and Bella has written to cancel my journey.

FEVER

While I suffered under the strange ailment that kept me in my bed for almost a month, and which even as late as yesterday gave signs of not having fully beaten its retreat, it was only rubdowns, herbal teas, and the pious mutterings of Bella that brought relief to my fever-racked body. Concerned by the ill health of his employee, Mr. Lind had sent at once for Dr. Tracy, begging him to make haste, but Dr. Tracy, in spite of his long years of experience, declared himself not competent to deal with tropical illnesses. Dr. Fouchard was away on a journey. Science, then, had perforce to yield to the secrets of homeopathy as practiced here, for which the word is *curandería*—what some might call witch-doctoring, if the "doctoring" part be emphasized.

As the housekeeper's many occupations prevented her devoting more time to the care of her new ward, a new servant, just recently (and upon the master's express orders) come into service in the house, took her place at the head of my bed. Her name was Selenia, and she was a tall, well-built mulatto woman who wore her wiry, disorderly hair long and loose. She would sit silent and sullen at the window of my small room, directly in the salty breeze that toyed with the covers of my bed.

For some reason impenetrable to me, Bella had declared war on this young woman from the outset. Myself unable to lift a finger to beg for silence and a measure of tranquility, I was forced to witness her bitter quarrels with my peevish nurse, over any little thing. Selenia, though, would haughtily bring forth this exasperating and unvarying pronouncement:

"Mr. Lind di'n bring me inta his house for that!"

On more than one occasion Bella had to take herself out of the room, else she'd have boxed the young woman's ears, while Selenia would smile to herself smugly and chill my soul with the icy indifference of her eyes' gaze upon me. How could so much beauty and so little human kindness combine in one face? Could it be true, as Mr. Lind says, that this hybrid race in the islands has been born without soul?

I had never felt so utterly alone and abandoned to my fate as during the course of that bedeviling sickness. Selenia would seize the least occasion to slip away from my bedside, while I would spend the greatest part of my day floating between the delirium of the fever and the agitated dreams of unrestful sleep. The hallucinations that I suffered swung, with a kind of mad illogicalness, between the most diverse episodes from my past and scenes from my residence in these latitudes: a mocking Charlie come to show me his drawing-pads covered with scrawls and indecencies, my deceased father seated beside my pillow softly caressing my fevered brow.

One night, in the midst of the confusion wrought upon my mind by the dreadful state of my body, I had the clear impression that I heard the shrill, rising notes of mad laughter. I turned my burning eyes to where the familiar silhouette of my caretaker ought to have been. My room appeared to be empty; yet my ears were still mercilessly assailed by those annoying shrieks—now counterpointed by a deeper voice, whispering intermittently. Following the pale track of a ray of moonlight that shone in through the half-open window, my eyes moved down to the floor and scanned across the shadows at the foot of my bed. As pale and disembodied as a spirit apparition, there glowed in the darkness the naked legs of a woman and a man, tangled in an obscene embrace on the plaited rush of the carpet.

I sank, unresistingly, into the deep waters of unconsciousness. When

I came to my senses again, all was silent, and my body was shaking violently from head to toe.

CONVALESCENCE

In time the fever subsided, yet the terrible weakness which was its legacy remained. I had lost a great deal of weight, and all the strength my racked frame had once had. I could hardly move about, and the mere thought of raising myself from the bed brought on nausea and dizziness.

Selenia had found entertainment to fill her time. Taking advantage of my utter inability to form the slightest protest, the crafty slut wandered freely about my bedroom, opening and closing drawers and boxes, fingering the objects on my dressing-table, poking about in the pockets of my dresses and trying on my shoes—which fit her, it pains me to say, perfectly.

"Miss Susan has better taste," she dared mutter one morning as she reviewed the few dresses modestly hanging in my wardrobe.

I witnessed these brazen violations of my little world with total impassivity, not for any lack of firmness of character but simply for lack of energy to make known my displeasure.

The efficacy of the chicken broth sent up by wise Bella soon was demonstrated. Slowly (too slowly for my own likes) the color began returning to my pale cheeks, life began returning to my movements. With the help of two plump pillows I could now sit up in my bed and take refuge in the refreshing world of a Charlotte Brontë novel. And so for brief periods I would withdraw from the calculated insolence of my companion.

So accustomed had I grown to a solitude interrupted only by Bella's sporadic visits and underscored by Selenia's ever more frequent absences, that I was startled one day to hear a decided knocking at my door. To my start was added confusion when, giving the permission my invisible visitor sought, I beheld the imposing figure of Edward Lind standing upon the threshold of my room, with his wet shirt clinging to his chest and his pants splattered with mud. With no further greeting than his smile, he came to my bed and announced in a falsely solemn voice:

"Miss Florence Jane, I hereby declare you survivor of the yellow fever. You've the stuff of an African woman in you—I never thought you would turn out so strong."

His mocking compliment brought the blood to my face. My discomfort increased when I saw Mr. Lind's eyes travel down my body, exposed under its linen nightdress to the curiosity of his gaze.

I turned my eyes away in confusion. From outside, a light mist blew in sidewise through the window. Mr. Lind's grave voice once more claimed my attention, and I found myself falling suddenly into the bottomless well of his dark eyes:

"The devil takes personal interest in the climate of these islands, you know. If it doesn't rain, we dry up and shrivel away; if it does, we're drowned."

Not knowing how to reply, I smoothed my disordered hair with my hand. Anything I might say seemed to me banal, unnecessary. Mr. Lind leaned over and touched my arm softly with his hand, with no more pressure than the furtive brush of a cat's paw. And then, without losing even for one second that smile, he said as he turned away:

"Take good care of yourself, Miss Florence. We'll see if we can't teach you to ride a horse one of these days."

It was only then that I became aware of the presence of Selenia. She was standing in a corner beside the silk-covered wall, strangely tense and mute. Her gaze was fixed on the door, which now stood wide open.

A VISIT

Yesterday for the first time in many weeks I went down to the garden, feeling as though I had been born anew. I took the precaution of wrapping myself in a shawl, to forestall the danger of a relapse. All seemed different: the rain had enlivened the colors of the foliage, and the sky gleamed clean and bright. The air was cooler, too, no doubt because the shade trees are swollen with sap. Upon my marble bench I let time drift idly by; I was bathed in the coolness of the breeze and I floated in the sweetest lethargy.

Bella came to interrupt my reverie, informing me of the most welcome arrival of a visitor. Moments later, there appeared before my eyes the kind and friendly face of Dr. Fouchard, whose greeting to me was one of his ever-unexpected winks. The frequency of these winks made me conclude that the doctor suffered from some sort of nervous tic, the product of his terrible shyness in the presence of the opposite sex.

"My dear Miss Florence!" he said, his voice trembling, "how happy it makes me to see you so recovered!"

He then explained to me, in a wealth of unnecessary detail, the fact already communicated to me by Dr. Tracy: he had been unable to attend me personally during my illness and long convalescence because he had been called away suddenly to Guadeloupe, to attend a hearing concerning an inheritance he had come into. He insisted so much and so perfectly contritely upon his powerlessness to put off the journey that at last I could only laugh. My thoughtless gesture somehow relieved the tension of our meeting, and likewise eased the flow of our conversation, which then went on for some two hours or more. I hardly noted how the time had passed, absorbed as I was by the fascinating stories of his life that René (for thus it is that he insists I am to call him) so skillfully wove to entertain me.

When the time came to end our talk, René said, in a new seizure of shyness that made him stammer and stumble over his words:

"If I were not afraid of tiring you, I would suggest a walk."

I did not think it prudent to accept his invitation just then, and so I asked that it be put off till the next morning. René agreed at once. He would not hear of my leaving my bench to accompany him to the gate, and he retired as discreetly as he had come.

When nightfall forced me to seek shelter in the parlor, I learned from Bella that more than a week ago Mr. Lind left for Hamburg, where he has both family and business dealings. That night I dined alone in the dining room, oppressed by the silence that reigned now, unchallenged, in the house.

An Outing

The doctor drove me in his buggy along a road as narrow as it was beautiful, down to the banks of the Guamaní River where an immense open-air market offers all sorts of merchandise for the daily life of those who live in the country.

My companion seems to know the area as well as if he had lived here for many years. His recounting of the fire that devastated Guayama more than two decades ago and of the cholera epidemic that decimated the population of that town a short time before I came to Puerto Rico so totally claimed my attention that I lost all sense of time and place. Sitting on a reddish rock jutting up in the middle of the river, the current running strong beneath our feet, far from the feverish bargaining going on in the market area, we conversed animatedly as noon came on. Suddenly realizing the time, René motioned me to wait for him while he went off to buy bread, cheese, and fruit for a little picnic lunch.

"What brought you to this island, Florence? What, or who, have you traded away your winters for?" he asked, handing me an orange he had peeled as the French do, and with the sections of it temptingly spread open.

I took the proffered fruit and put an end to his questioning with a shrug of my shoulders. "I do not talk about my past; there is nothing there that is worth remembering."

René's smile disarmed me.

"Let's forget the past, then," he said softly. "I consider it a privilege that you would allow me to figure in your present."

CONFIDENCES

Our outings have become an agreeable routine, a pleasant habit that breaks the tedium. I fear, on the other hand, that for René they may have taken on unwonted importance. Giving signs of total confidence in my ability to keep a secret, he has confided to me that he suffers the affliction of an unrequited love. He has been very careful, however, not to reveal the name of his beloved, and I, of course, have not asked. Something tells me that it is not Ernestina Beauchamp, about whom he speaks rarely, and without much enthusiasm.

Today an incident occurred which showed me another, and until now hidden, side of him. For my solitary walks I had always obeyed Miss Susan's admonitions and never penetrated the hedge of vines and taken the path to the negro quarters—the *batey*, as Charlie calls the little earthen plaza around which the negroes' rude houses are built. I had always chosen the other path, which leads through a stand of extraordinarily tall and graceful palm trees down to the very edge of the ocean. This day, however, at a little past six o'clock in the evening, as dusk was coming on, we took, at René's urging, a shortcut back to the house, and the path led us directly through the area of the negroes' dwellings. Under the pretext of weariness, my companion chose to enter that inhospitable and foul-smelling place about whose true life I knew naught but the echoes of voices and of drums wafted to me on the wind on certain nights.

A strong smell of boiled codfish hung over all. In great iron kettles of steaming water, plantains and green bananas bobbed. A hunchbacked old woman with a red kerchief knotted about her head was slowly stirring the cornmeal concoction that they call *funche*, a dish which, sprinkled with sugar, accompanies many a meal, even in the house of the master.

René's words, previously soft and melodious as he revealed to me his deepest emotions, now were strangely hard. All tenderness had fled his eyes, which looked upon me fixedly, with no flicker of a wink.

"It's curious that they are not called by their true name—slaves. It is as though we insisted upon denying their real condition, as though if we can but avoid naming it we may allow ourselves to be blind to the true horror of their state . . . But what are they if not slaves? They work in the fields from sun to sun; they live like beasts, one atop another, locked into these wretched hovels; they suffer punishments to their flesh that would shame the barbarians; they come, they go, they breathe to a rhythm set them by our mere wills . . . "

We had paused by the side of the road. The harsh expression on my companion's face disturbed me. I opened my mouth to say that I wished to go on toward the hacienda, but I closed it again upon seeing that René had turned on his heel and was attentively gazing into the green-black wall of sugar cane encircling the batey. As though in response to his gaze, a long cortège of ragged men and women, their bare feet, covered with mud, stumbling in the clumsiness of exhaustion, began to file slowly toward us. My heart beat violently in my breast. I raised my gaze to my companion's face, my eyes pleading for an answer to this spectacle.

"Look at them. Look well, Florence," he said, bringing his lips down to my ear, so close I could feel his breath. "These are the men and women who give the sweetness to our coffee."

My eyes clung fatally to those emaciated torsos, those scarred backs, those grim and hostile countenances that looked like faces issued from some dark cavern in the bowels of hell. Eager to erase the painful ugliness of that scene, which the failing light of evening invested with a spectral glow, I quickened my steps along the trail back to the house. René followed, but we spoke not a single word to each other until we were once again inside the magic circle of the gardens.

An odd being, this man capable of baring his heart while remaining shadowed in mystery. The more I try to persuade myself that my suspicions are irrational, the more tormented by uncertainty I am. Can Dr. Fouchard be one of those young idealists who preach the freeing of the black race? His obscure origins, his intriguing comings and goings, his impassioned denunciation of slavery—it all points toward that disturbing conclusion. And if my fears are unfounded, why place at risk our friendship with behavior that threatens not only my position but that of my protectors?

Tomorrow, when he comes for me, Bella will tell him that I am not in.

The Return

Miss Susan has come home again, loaded down with extravagant *bibelots* for her mahogany curio cabinets. There is a new set of china for the table, and two enormous agate vases from Italy. She has been kind enough to bring me two novels by George Sand. I am grateful, though the novels run directly counter to my usual literary taste. Taking the stairs two at a time, Charlie proclaimed to the world his happiness at seeing me again. In his eagerness to deliver my gifts to me, he accidentally tore one of the covers.

Trailing behind the son there appeared, much recovered from her previous thinness, the lady of the house. It was the first time she had deigned to enter my room; I presumed, therefore, that she had come to offer her sympathy for my illness of the summer past. I was not to be so honored, however. She sat for a long while telling me in great detail of her activities at Locust Grove and of her adventures in New York when she went with the Overmans to the theater or the opera.

"One gradually loses one's sensibility, seeing nothing but negroes and sugar cane," she sighed, lying back unthinkingly against my pillows.

With a total lack of reserve (which I found at once shocking and complimentary), she proceeded to disburden upon my ears her afflicted heart. As I am not one accustomed to being made privy to the intimate details of the lives of my superiors, I feared that my discomfort would be all too obvious to her, and I made an effort to conceal it.

Miss Susan revealed, with evident homesickness for the paternal estate, that she had never spent so much time before with Mr. Morse. The constant moving from house to house, the early widowhood, and the somewhat unstable personality of the genius who was her father—these things had conspired to deprive Miss Susan of the consolation of a paternal presence for many years. A real childhood, it could not be said she had, she continued with a slight stiffening of her lips, forced as she had been to take on (all unprotestingly) the mantle of substitute-mother for her two brothers. The ever-traveling father had not even been present when she and Edward, after the wedding in New Haven, had embarked for Puerto Rico. My mistress paused, barely able to contain her tears.

I remained silent, squeezing between my nervous hands a perspiration-soaked handkerchief which I did not think it prudent to offer her. Then, as suddenly as her words had begun to flow, Miss Susan said a hasty good-bye and abandoned my room. The boy, who had sat in silence through his mother's tale of tribulations, hesitated a moment beside the door, waiting for me to ask him to stay.

During the days that followed, my thoughts went many times over that troubling scene. I could not keep my mind from the image of the sad girl, grown up too quickly and now become, by a cruel twist of fate, an equally sad and solitary wife. Had Samuel Morse had his doubts before he had agreed to that sudden wedding of his daughter and the foreigner she had met but a year earlier at her uncle Charles Walker's house? Had he found unacceptable the idea that Miss Susan should go off to the ends of the earth to live, upon an island subject to earthquakes, hurricanes, and yet other trials? Had he been consoled by the knowledge that she would be the mistress of a prosperous estate of more than a thousand acres, with a windmill, a steam engine, and a hundred-sixty slaves?

I find myself, more often than I would like, reliving pieces of other person's lives—lives often more intense, more vivid, more real than these vapid chapters of my own.

THE INVITATION

It was Miss Susan who decided—without consulting me, as always—that I should attend. She was so intent upon telling me the news that she broke into our lessons, rendering naught my herculean efforts to hold Charlie's wayward attention to the lines of Milton assigned for that day.

"Can you guess who's coming? And coming next Sunday?!" she asked, her voice all animated delight. I immediately thought of Mr. Lind, who should be returning from Europe that same weekend. I let her, however, answer her own question, as had been her intention from the first. All right, she would tell me: the person who was coming was none other than Adelina Patti, the famed diva whose incomparable voice had seduced the entire Continent.

"In the company, of course," she added, her enthusiasm if anything greater, "of the great Moreau Gottschalk."

The little worldly culture I possessed prevented my sharing the intense pleasure which to all appearances my mistress was enjoying at the thought of receiving into her house the man I soon learned to be a famous piano virtuoso, the glory of the state of Louisiana. The information that made my pulse race was other—and contained in the speech she impulsively launched herself upon, no doubt so as not to give me time to prepare my own defensive broadside.

She began by scolding me for my "terrible shyness," which, she claimed, made me avoid parties and receptions "like the bubonic plague." She then proceeded to remind me, most untactfully, that "at one's age" it was never a bad idea to expose oneself to society and the possibility of making new friends. As she spoke, her voice grew more and more firm and her countenance more and more serious. She concluded her sermon with a statement which much resembled a command: she would hear no excuse for my not performing what she considered, without exaggeration, to be my sacred duty—if not out of obedience to the wishes of the family, then out of consideration for them.

I was doubly astonished. First of all, nothing in my mistress's previous behavior would have led me to suspect that she had such esteem for my humble self. In the second place, I was dumbstruck by this authoritarian outburst by a person who had, until that moment, shown me nothing but deference and consideration. When I could at last summon the strength to offer the excuse (a very weak one, as I recognized even as I spoke it) of the austerity of my wardrobe, my mistress produced another triumphant piece of news: she had already ordered me, from her own, quite well-known, seamstress in Guayama, "the perfect gown."

"I hope you won't be upset with me, dear Miss Florence," she said, reverting to her accustomed sweetness, "but in order not to disturb you, we have used Selenia's measurements, which we believe, as you will soon see, closely approximate your own."

The mere idea of wearing a dress sewn virtually upon the body of another woman, and more so when that woman was the hateful Selenia, was (to put the matter bluntly) repugnant to me. But I judged it inopportune of me to oppose Miss Susan's will just then, and essentially nil the possibility of changing her mind.

All these details disposed of, then, Miss Susan at once led me to her room, where I was given to admire, in all its splendor, the fine craftsmanship and impeccable cut of "the perfect gown." It goes without saying that the kind insistence of my protectress left me no alternative but to resign myself, and to slip the generous folds of that dream in white satin over my shoulders.

"It's made for you!" Miss Susan exclaimed, smiling with mischievous pride at the deed she'd done. "You look like a young bride!"

"The decolleté . . ." I began, trying to cover my exposed bosom with my hands.

Miss Susan laughed so spiritedly that she lost her balance and fell back onto the bed. In gales of laughter she buried her face in her pillow. Somehow, her hilarity vexed me more than the obligation to go to the reception.

The Toast

At six in the evening, the coaches and traps of the most prominent families of the entire coastal region around Guayama began turning into our drive. In the gardens, a group of the most select of our neighbors, among them more than a proportionate number of French and Englishmen and their families, awaited the arrival of the famous guests.

Shortly after seven, a servant came out onto the veranda and rang a little silver bell. All the guests began filing into the house, as though drawn inside by a power stronger than their own will. In the parlor, their hostess announced unexpected but happy news: the soprano and the pianist were awaiting us all in the dining room, where the event in their honor would begin. They had somehow outflanked all the gracious vigilance for their arrival and entered the house, secretly, through the back door.

From my place halfway down, I could keep my eye on what happened at both the head and the foot of the table. I could also see, thanks to the mirror at the other side of the room, the discreet and diligent attentions of the servants.

Seated between her father and a young Puerto Rican gentleman who hung on her every word and gesture, Patti looked like some pink-cheeked cherub. As to Gottschalk, I am not sure whether it was his voice or his remarkable height that impressed me more. But my gaze was drawn time and again not so much to our dazzling visitors as to that person who, by his rare presence among us, could be considered more a stranger than a member of our own circle.

Clean-shaven, smelling slightly of *eau de Cologne,* dressed in his formal suit and string tie, he was suddenly invested with a gentlemanly aspect that radically transformed the everyday roughness of his appearance. He sat at the table with perfect correctness, inclining his head from time to time to offer another portion to a guest or to reply politely to a question. At the other extreme of the table, flushed and a bit moist, Miss Susan could not be said to show the same composure.

The dinner, lavish in its assortment of wines and exquisite delicacies, was a long one. My immediate neighbors, who happened to be French, ignored me with that combination of indifference and arrogance that so often seems to characterize those from the other side of the Channel. Their affront, which could not be considered a serious one, had its advantages: it allowed me to observe without being observed.

More than once my eyes met those of my employer. I do not know whether from the effects of the wine or from my imagination, or from a secret alliance between the two, but I read in them the same curiosity that impelled my own. Made uneasy by the bold amusement of his gaze, I could not avoid the discomfiting reflex of putting a hand over my breast, which was much exposed by the graceful lines of my "perfect gown." My little trust in the confused perceptions of that moment prevent me from putting a very specific name to the enigmatic smile that my almost-involuntary movement caused the master of the house.

When the time came for dessert, our host called for the champagne, which flowed generously. He raised his glass and gave a long and brilliant toast to the glory of the celebrated *artistes* who were with us. Then he looked in turn directly into the eyes of every woman at the table, and pausing very deliberately (or at least, in my extreme nervousness, so I thought) at my own, he said, his voice suddenly silken:

"And a toast as well to the feminine beauty which, like the sea, surrounds us—and which, like the sea, is the cause of so much wealth and so many capsizings!"

My raised glass shivered a little in the air, and a few drops of wine spilled upon the tablecloth. Fortunately, the delighted applause that met our host's witty toast pretty much distracted the diners' attention. From that moment on, I tasted not a bite more, and my gaze (blurred not a little by the champagne) remained fixed on the mirror.

When we went into the music room for the concert by our guests of honor, Miss Susan showed me to a chair beside her own.

"Don't you find Dr. Fouchard's absence intolerable?" she whispered softly, not looking at me.

Exit Charlie

As I was finishing breakfast with my charge in the garden that same morning, I had been an involuntary witness of a deplorable scene. The angry voice of Miss Susan came to us through the thick hedge of jasmine in whose shade we were sitting.

"Why did you wait so long to tell me?" she remonstrated, and then, without waiting for a reply from that interlocutor whose identity I still knew not, she went on. "She will leave this minute! Tell her to get her filthy rags together and go to the field hands' quarters this instant!"

Suddenly, I was conscience-stricken at overhearing a conversation so clearly not intended for our ears. About to stand up and walk away and distract the boy's attention, I was interrupted in my plan by the gruff voice of Bella. With her usual good sense, she asked a question which, to judge by the silence it elicited, needed no answer:

"But Miss Susan, what will Mr. Lind say when he finds out?"

I did stand up then and with mock spontaneity ran off toward the pond, challenging my young ward to catch me if he could. And sure enough, Charlie, who never fails to take up the gauntlet of a dare, leapt up and was off like a little deer after me.

"I'll bet you don't know," he said when he caught me, his voice decidedly mischievous, and before he'd even recovered his breath again, "who they're talking about."

"I'm not certain I'm interested," I replied, feigning more indifference than I really felt, and adding for the moral edification of my indiscreet pupil, "Nor, for that matter, should you be."

The boy just laughed, shaking off the dart of my irony and taking my two hands in his own. Then, in a voice of extreme insolence, he said, "Sometimes, my dear Miss Florence, I have the impression that I am *your* tutor."

The heat I felt in my cheeks betrayed me. I quickly pulled my hands away and bent down to the water to touch a water-lily. My pupil leaned against the trunk of a royal palm, and his mocking voice (which was no longer the falsetto of before but rather a grave and disquieting baritone) came to me strong and clear across the morning's calm:

"You should know, even if you would rather *not* know, that Selenia's belly is swelling, and it's not from eating green mangoes."

At that moment there became abruptly transparent to me a fact which (for some reason I still cannot fathom) I was determined not to acknowledge: this skeptical and *blasé* young man had changed—he had ceased to be, for all time, my innocent little Charlie.

Hurricane

The mournful ululation of the wind upon the cliffs of Dover is pale beside the hellish howl of those gales that threatened to rip the roof from the house. The negroes had been closed up with the animals, under heavy lock and key, in the two strongest outbuildings. The owners of more fragile dwellings came to take refuge behind the solid walls of La Enriqueta, which was by far the most resistant structure in the entire area.

Even so, the house shivered from roof to foundation, and the concrete piles upon which it is constructed rocked. While Mr. Lind directed the neighbors in a constant opening and closing of doors and windows so as to channel, insofar as possible, the blasts of wind through the house, Miss Susan sobbed like a frightened girl in the arms of a proud brave Charlie. The din of shattering crystal exacerbated her desolation. With all the unconsciousness of youth, the boy was thrilled by what he considered this grand adventure.

In spite of the terror I myself was feeling, I distracted my nerves, which were keen to the point almost of temporary madness, by closely following the movements of Mr. Lind. With inexhaustible energy, he seemed to be everywhere, on every front, concerned with the slightest detail. In the midst of the gale, and against the desperate pleadings of his wife, he went up against the wrath of the elements and captured, with his own hands, an escaped horse. Wet to the bone but victorious, he returned to nail boards across the shattered windows of the second floor. Thanks to his able and courageous breasting of the storm, there was no major damage to the main house of the hacienda.

Huddled and cowering in a corner, feeling myself perfectly at the mercy of the elements (and knowing myself useless in the crisis), I watched him stride by me a thousand times. Though his eyes fell upon my body more than once, he spoke not a single word to me, nor did a single sign of recognition cross his features. Who is this contradictory, evasive creature, this unpredictable man at once attractive and repellant? However hard I try, I cannot assemble the jumbled pieces of his life into one true portrait of him. His distance can be glacial; his touch burns like fire. If I draw close, he retreats; if I avoid him, he seeks me out. Only in fugitive moments (as dreaded as desired, and now blurred in the sidelights of my memory) does his ardent flame take on more reality, does his violence clash with my fear.

Adieu

Mrs. O. and her sisters-in-law, come to the hacienda on virtually an official embassy, can talk of nothing else. The scandalous news of Dr. Fouchard's "flight" has spread like wildfire throughout the entire Guayama area. There is a great deal of speculation—though no foundation whatsoever, of course—as to the mysterious reasons that the doctor may have had for abandoning home and office in the middle of the night, without a word of goodbye for anyone, without a word of explanation for anyone, even his intimate friends the Beauchamps.

"*Cherchez la femme*, I say," pronounced Mrs. O. with a commiserating look at Lorna, the vice-consul's elder sister, whose open infatuation with the doctor had gone neither unobserved nor unremarked.

"No," I blurted out automatically, and without gauging the consequences my clumsy intervention might have. "René is not that kind of man."

When she realized that in my reflexive defense of the doctor I had called him by his Christian name and not his surname and title, Miss Susan looked over at me, clearly intrigued.

Mrs. O. wasted no time in following up on such a tempting clue.

"Oh?" she said mockingly, feigning a lack of interest she was far from feeling. "And what kind of man is he, then, Miss Florence, if you might be kind enough to enlighten us in that regard . . . ?"

I was silent a moment, while before my imagination's eye there paraded a train of unforgettable images and words which I would never have the courage or the right to reveal. My hesitation looked so suspicious, unfortunately, that I was obliged to cover my growing discomfort with a frivolous "Too timid for my own taste," which had the fortune to divert the conversation toward the "lack of boldness in the men of today" and the fateful consequences of that lack of spirit on the "state of matrimony of some ladies."

Having turned Mrs. O. into one of her favorite avenues of conversation, I lowered my gaze and took up the interrupted thread of my own thoughts. Out of the corner of my eye, I saw that Miss Susan followed my every reaction.

As I write these notes, a profound sadness overtakes me, so that I can hardly continue. I have been robbed of perhaps the only sincere friendship I have had in this country. If the causes of Dr. Fouchard's departure are really those that I suspect, it may be for the best—it may be preferable in the long run that our souls, so similar yet so different, have parted.

A BIRTHDAY

How quick time is, and how slow our perception of it! The fourteen years that Charlie observes today mark the beginning of the end. Little more than a year is left of my stay at La Enriqueta, and that year is justified only by the French lessons I give Charlie—the only subject that now seems to interest my restless pupil.

With great solemnity he has announced to me his plans to go off to Paris, where he says he will pursue his great passion—painting. I should be surprised if Mr. Lind allowed his only son to choose such an unpromising vocation. The father has little sympathy for art; his own talents, almost preternatural, are for business. In a very few years he has multiplied the acres of his property many times over, purchasing not only the cane fields of his sister Henrietta but also the adjacent lands of La Concordia. Moreover, the trade in Africans produces enough to offset the occasional loss in the fortunes of the sugar cane. It will no doubt take poor Charlie considerable work—and from what one sees, many tears—to persuade him. His father's iron will has now, more than ever, a concrete cause for being brought to bear: the future of the estate and of the business.

Miss Susan had asked that a very special meal be prepared for tonight's birthday celebration. When I came downstairs, dressed for dinner, to take my usual place at the table, the mother and son were impatiently awaiting Mr. Lind, who had been told of the dinner beforehand yet still had not come in. While Inés, the girl who has replaced Selenia, was serving the first course, the head of the household at last made his appearance.

His ill humor was evident. He did not even go upstairs to wash before dinner, but rather sat at the table and, sweaty and still panting from exertion as he was, he ordered his meal brought to him straightaway, as he informed us that he had to leave again at once. To Miss Susan's questions he replied grudgingly that there was a rumor of a rebellion in don Jacinto Cora's negro quarters, and that the landowners of the area were meeting to take measures against a possible uprising.

Charlie could hardly conceal his disappointment, though for obvious reasons he kept silent. Disregarding entirely the order and etiquette of the dinner, Mr. Lind attacked the main dish before our eyes: a fricasseed goat accompanied with rice and pigeon-peas. No sooner had he so precipitately supped, he passed the linen napkin across his beard and threw it (whether unconsciously or not, I cannot tell) to the floor and strode from the dining room without a further word.

We finished our dinner in silence, and with very little appetite. By the time Bella, in a heroic attempt to save the evening, placed in the center of the table the enormous coconut birthday cake that she had made herself in honor of her beloved Charlie, the party had turned into a wake—a strange wake without a corpse.

NEWS

Two letters arrived today. The first, brought by Mr. Lind, announced that Mr. Morse would soon be coming to Puerto Rico, and it has put Miss Susan into a state of absolute delight. The second has come into my hands through more secret means.

It was about four in the afternoon when, to seek a saving coolness, I started out onto the veranda for air. Just as I reached the door, Bella came into the room behind me with the unexpected announcement of a visitor. Moments later, Ernestina Beauchamp was shown in, looking much thinner than was her wont.

"I know you'll be surprised to see me, Miss Florence," she said weakly, and then without another word she put into my hands a sealed envelope, addressed to me. I hesitated a second before opening it. Suddenly I felt her hand, fragile and very cold, on mine.

"You must read it in private," she said, smiling sadly.

I offered her a chair, which she gratefully accepted. Her drawn and emaciated features revealed a most dolorous state of health, and this appearance was confirmed by her next words.

"I shall be only a short time longer in Puerto Rico. My brother has made arrangements for me at a sanatorium in the French Alps. I have come to say goodbye."

Her revelation surprised me less than the fact of her visit. Our meetings had been few, and our relationship somewhat superficial. The only thing we shared in common was our friendship with René Fouchard. I impatiently waited, letter in hand, for an explanation to justify her unusual action in coming to visit me this way. My wait was not long.

"He always spoke of you. He admired you."

I did not have to ask whom it was she referred to; her eyes, brimming with tears, told me. It was I, then, who put my hand upon hers, and that small gesture had the power to calm her. I sent for tea, and we made no further mention, during the rest of her brief visit, of the illness that afflicted her or of its cause. Her coachman was waiting for her in the drive; I accompanied her there, and stood on the veranda until the cloud of dust raised by the horses as she went had settled again.

I went to my room to break the seal on the letter. It was, of course, from René. The date—some months earlier—was an indictment of the Spanish mail service, or perhaps bespoke the reluctance of its more proximate messenger to deliver it. The sender apologized for our abrupt separation, and he attempted to explain his disappearance (an event as disconcerting as it was mysterious): "By the time you have consented to read this letter, I will be far from Arroyo, on my way to meet a destiny which I myself dare not predict. With a celerity that would not allow me the consolation of a goodbye, I had to leave—my continued presence on the Island, and the nature of the activities which, in the conscience of a fair and freethinking man, justified it, would sooner or later have compromised the welfare of my friends and contributed to the pleasure of my enemies."

His words throbbed with the force of the most authentic emotions, awakening in my own thoughts echoes, in spite of the unbridgable chasm that separated our two minds: "My dear friend—if I have any counsel for you, it is that you save yourself, that you flee that luxurious and pleasant prison in which you live, a prison built on the bones of so many of God's creatures. For if you do not, the brilliantly glittering lie of that rotten world will undermine your spirit and your will and turn them into the crushed and desiccated fibers of the sugar cane from which all the sweet life-juice has been squeezed."

The letter ended with a farewell which moved me greatly: "I send you, then, assurances of an affection blasted before it could bloom. I will never lose the hope of seeing you again."

The strident chords of a dizzying waltz resonate in my brain. Ernestina's desolation would drown my heart.

THE CHARLESTOWN PRODIGY

On the ship *Estelle,* of Long Island, and accompanied by his wife and the two children from his second marriage, the famous Mr. Morse has arrived from England, where he was vacationing. From the coast of Arroyo watchers might make out in the distance the American flag snapping in the wind atop the roof of the Lind mansion. The town doctor, a good-natured Irishman who turned red with pride upon shaking the inventor's hand, accompanied the family in the Ministry of Health launch to the place of disembarkation. There, a coach, crowned for the occasion with the imposing figure of an eagle admirably prepared by some remote taxidermist, awaited them, and in it a radiant Miss Susan, clapping her hands in delight, along with the slightly stand-offish Charlie and myself, filled with emotion.

The temperature was so oppressive that Mr. Morse could hardly believe it was December. He was fascinated, in spite of the suffocating heat, by the vision of those 1,400 acres of white-tasseled sugar cane swaying in the breeze that softly blew from the mountains down to the ocean. "A princely estate" were his precise astonished words as he contemplated the grandiose architecture of the house which for some months to come would be his home.

The Christmas festivities have taken on a special brilliance with the presence of the genius of Locust Grove. The inevitable Salomons have come from Ponce with a musical group—guitars and the smaller island *cuatro,* so named because of its four strings, plus the rhythm accompaniment of gourd-players—to initiate the visitors in the delights of the local folk traditions. The O'Haras, the Fantauzzis, the McCormicks, and the Aldecoas, among numerous other neighbors who wish to pay their respects to our international celebrity, frequent the house these days as never before.

To Miss Susan's grateful surprise, Mr. Lind has been the model husband and host. He has insisted on personally escorting his father-in-law about the estate, and about all the neighboring parts as well, taking him wherever he is invited. To reciprocate—or perhaps out of an inborn indisposition to leisure of any sort—Mr. Morse has promised to take upon himself the task of building a telegraph line between La Enriqueta and his son-in-law's warehouse on the docks.

Between overseeing all the many activities of the kitchen and attending to her step-mother and her half-siblings (who have fallen prey to an embarrassing infestation of head-lice), Miss Susan barely has time left over for a daughter's conversation with her father. And much less time, I suppose, to broach a subject as difficult as the little wrinkles that continue to furrow themselves into the terse skin of her happiness.

MELANCHOLY

The efforts of these three months have born fruit: the promised telegraph line is now complete and today Arroyo celebrated the occasion.

The authorities have spared no expense in impressing Mr. Morse. Baskets of flowers and fruits fill the veranda. A most *soigné* luncheon has mobilized the principal citizens of the town. The main orator was—as it must have been—the gentleman from Poughkeepsie, who, standing proudly between the flags of Spain and the United States, posed for a photograph to memorialize the day. I have all these details from none other than Charlie, who (thanks to the irresistible urging of his grandfather) accompanied the group through every minute. We women remained at home upon the hacienda assisting in the preparations for the domestic festivities.

In spite of the diversion that the presence of our famous guest means for Charlie, there is a melancholy, unseen by all but me, that has come over my pupil's spirit. I can guess its causes although I cannot be sure of them. Neither the comfort that surrounds him nor the granting of his every wish can fill that bottomless chasm that has opened in his heart. His loneliness, imperceptible to those who lack sensibility, is only comparable to that of this slave, who though not in chains finds her happiness dependent upon the caprices of a master who is forever absent.

THE ENCOUNTER

The departure of the Morses has left a terrible void in the house. Dispirited and aimless, Miss Susan drags herself about again. I would not be in the least surprised if she should fall ill, as she always does at this season. I miss Charlie's impish laughter. When I invite him to go with me on some outing, he makes absurd excuses.

My employer seems to have been swallowed up by the earth. No sooner had his distinguished father-in-law boarded the boat that would take him away than Mr. Lind disappeared into the cane fields as though desperate to regain a freedom that had been long withheld from him. Can the dimensions of this enormous house be too narrow for the adventuresome restlessness of his soul?

Today, determined to change my own habits and escape the tedium of this household, I went out on a walk by myself. Rising from the great cauldrons, the smell of molasses that permeates the atmosphere when the harvest of cane is ended followed me no matter how far I went. I took the road to Cuatro Calles, which I rarely take, so as to avoid the constant greetings in town. As I was walking back, late in the afternoon, I had a surprising and unpleasant encounter.

When I came to where the road to Guayama crosses Isabel Segunda Street, I recognized an unmistakable silhouette, tall, straight, and elegant in spite of the fact that upon its head there sat in perfect balance an enormous basket of fruit. It was Selenia, the woman cast out of our garden, and she had lost none of her beauty—or her arrogance. Slung from her back there was a baby, its skin lighter than her own, wriggling restlessly.

We came face to face, and inevitably we looked at one another. But neither of us showed the slightest sign of recognition. Seemingly oblivious to the most elementary principles of courtesy, the two of us walked on with the haughty indifference of two duchesses. The child turned its head to look after me. The open curiosity in its vivid green eyes brought me, almost in spite of myself, a smile.

What secret poison feeds dislike? What generous river brings the water of life to our affections? That wretched woman that fate set in my path has the power—though our lives have barely brushed against each other—to strangely disquiet me. What is this rude and obscure language that hunchbacked and wizened envy whispers into my ear now?

A CONFESSION

I could never have imagined that my pupil's moroseness owed less to his grandfather's absence than to the powerful influence of Cupid.

Yesterday he came to me with a confession. Her name is Carmelina, she is a creole, and she lives in town. Her father, a small businessman and a widower, keeps watch over her as he would a wife. She cannot so much as walk out upon her own balcony. It is truly remarkable that the two young people have even met.

Charlie's effusions, while those of one his age, are yet the product of a pretty indiscriminate taste. The girl (if one can call a person of twenty-one years still a girl) is far from his equal not only in age but also (and above all) in condition. Unless I err (and I will have to find a way to confirm this) I believe I have heard Mrs. O.—who knows everything and keeps back nothing—say that there are stories in Arroyo about the doubtful nature of the ties that bind her to her father.

Oh my poor innocent Charlie! Your blessed lack of experience may well yet be a curse!

A Wake

Last night Carolina, Charlie's old nurse, died of dropsy—or if Joseph is to be believed, from chewing tobacco. Stunned, the boy ran straight for Bella's comforting arms. Miss Susan did not dare try to stop him from running out to the negro quarters.

A group of men and women came later to ask permission to celebrate the event. Africans do not share our sense of mourning; death for them is a state akin to recaptured freedom, a final return to their homeland.

I was in the parlor giving the last touches to a violet shawl I was knitting for my mistress. It was almost eleven, and Mr. Lind had still not honored us with his presence. Through the open door, I heard Miss Susan's impatient voice; she was fearful of giving the negroes permission without first consulting with her husband. She therefore called for Joseph and sent him to look for Mr. Lind.

When she came back into the parlor, Miss Susan tried, with obvious effort, to smile at me. A profound uneasiness veiled her countenance. Strangely echoing her distress, I too sensed, as she did, that some misfortune loomed. And in fact that obscure intuition had made me postpone for upwards of an hour the moment of my retiring for the night. I had the feeling that Miss Susan was grateful to me for that, and that her laconic "Still up?" was less a question than a recognition.

I do not know how much time passed, but the wait seemed interminable. Miss Susan's restless silence paradoxically irritated me. As though the long-drawn-out wait for Mr. Lind were tacit consent, the drums now were beating in the batey.

Unable to control the trembling that had come over my hands, I put down my needles and got up with the false mission of bringing in the linden tea that Bella was preparing in the kitchen. More to hide my uneasiness than to make conversation, I shared with Bella my indignation that the men sent to find Mr. Lind had still not returned with any news of him.

"Oh, Miss Florence," the housekeeper exclaimed, her big eyes now almost starting from her head in fright, "somebody saw him at that woman's house, there in town. Who's going to dare go there and pull him out?"

Shaken by the compassion in her voice, and by its fatal certainty, I neither wished nor was able to ask more. By the time Bella went into the parlor bearing the silver tray with its two cups, I had bade good-night to Miss Susan and gone up to my room.

With the Margaret Fuller book I had taken from the library untouched on my night table (though the kerosene lamp glowed softly in the darkness), I spent the night unsleeping. The secret eruption of my fury kept me awake. I sat for hours thinking, remembering, going over the hopes and regrets held deep within my spirit. Little by little, reason began to comfort me, to make me understand the absurdity of dreams and illusions. I swore to myself then to advance the day of my departure, to escape forever from this accursed greenhouse existence in which, before they can bloom, hopes wither.

Very early in the morning, before sunrise, the sudden silence of the drums, the reddish glow in the sky, and the familiar sound of hoofbeats made me run like a madwoman to the window.

BLACK CLOUDS

As summer nears, I have thought it imprudent of me to keep my decision from Mr. and Mrs. Lind. I have completed the three years of my commitment to the education and moral upbringing of Charles Walker Lind, and nothing now holds me here. My pupil will depart soon for the United States, where (as his father expressly requires of him) he will study engineering. I too will take that northern route. And (should my mistress's generosity of spirit not extend to recommending me for some employment there, similar to my position here) I will place an announcement in a New York newspaper offering my services as tutor or lady's companion, and in the meantime take lodgings (with the savings I have been able to make) in a modest hotel.

I have told Charlie before anyone else. But his heart is the prisoner of new emotions which prevent his being stricken very much by the news. Perhaps I chose badly the moment to confide my plans to him. He had just vented his spleen at the "mute intransigence" of his father. He was sure, though he could not support his conviction with any proof, that Mr. Lind had discovered his infatuation with the famous Carmelina, and that that was the reason for his forced exile. In vain I assured him that the idea of sending him abroad was simply part of the normal expectations not simply of any father concerned about his son's future but in fact of every young man brought up in the narrow confines of the colonies.

What happened then has been a source of deep consternation for me. Not since those first turbulent months of my stay here have I seen Charlie so beside himself, so incapable of containing or even moderating the expression of his anger. Openly accusing me of having betrayed his confidence, he said such hurtful things to me that it was only my sense of decorum that allowed me to tolerate them. He threw in my face my supposed "prejudices," my "double standard," my position as a "paid spy." Rendered utterly speechless by the torrent of insults (which I knew myself far from deserving), I could only listen in silence. When the storm subsided at last, I picked up my books and papers with deliberate calm and left him alone with his conscience in the dimness of the library.

Miss Susan was less expressive but kinder. Not only did she assure me of her full protection and that of her friends in New York, but she promised me a letter of recommendation from Mr. Morse himself.

I had originally planned to sail in July on the same boat that Charlie sailed upon, but now, for obvious reasons, I have had to reconsider. I was greatly relieved when Miss Susan herself asked me to stay on until mid-August, when she once more expected a visit from Mrs. Molly Overman. The dull and lightless gaze that accompanied the kind words of my mistress told me that Miss Susan's desperation was even greater than my own.

LETHARGY

Charlie's last weeks in Puerto Rico have passed with maddening slowness. Relieved of the responsibility of his lessons, freed from the routine imposed by some fixed purpose, my days drag out like some long blank roll of parchment.

Mr. Lind is in Ponce, and is not expected back until Friday. Will it matter to him that I too am leaving, that I am leaving forever the protection of his house?

My ex-charge, now more the mutinous boy than ever, roams the gardens listlessly. Sometimes I see him walking pensively toward town. I know where he is going—to pay the bitter tribute of a love without future. Under the weak excuse of some vague indisposition, he hardly eats with us any more. It is as though he were already gone from us, while the ghost of his body has remained behind.

Most of my resentment has now dissipated—perhaps I should say my indignation. The romance between Charlie and Carmelina has reduced me to the sad role of a rival banished and without rights.

July is here, with its heat and mosquitoes. The preparations for Charlie's trip are going apace. His father has ordered a huge trunk for him, so that he can comfortably travel with all the wonderful clothes that his mother has had made for the young scion.

The Reconciliation

Attended by Dr. Tracy, the O'Haras, and other neighbors that in some cases affection and other cases courtesy made it necessary to invite, this evening the intimate farewell party took place.

"Master Charlie is already teaching us how much we shall miss him," remarked Dr. Tracy affectionately when at six o'clock the guest of honor had still not made his appearance. Perplexity was on every face but two: mine, for I knew the causes behind the effects, and that of his father, less confused than angry.

In an attempt to dispel her husband's obvious ill humor, Miss Susan had tea and cake brought in, a habit of the house since the arrival of this humble British subject. But the strategy did not have its hoped-for effect. Mr. Lind got up and took the stairs three at a time up to Charlie's room, where he burst in the door. Miss Susan sat utterly unmoving, her eyes fixed on me in clear but mute supplication.

I waited for Mr. Lind to find that his son was not in the house (a fact I had known from the first) and then before I could repent of my plan I intercepted him at the foot of the stairs. His green eyes interrogated my own with absolute coldness.

"I know where he is, let me go for him," was all I could manage to say, though I did have the temerity to brush his hand with mine. Miraculously, the tension fled his features.

"Go, then," he said with the softness that I had thought lost to me.

I went out into the garden without the slightest idea of where my steps ought to take me. What I wanted more than anything was to flee the oppressive air of that parlor. As I approached the gates, though, and was about to confront the decision as to which road to take, I came upon the overseer, returning at a gallop from the fields. When I asked where my pupil might be, he pointed down the Punta Guilarte road and said, "Down there."

Only the desperation of knowing how far away he was would have induced me to accept the bold invitation that came next. Impulsively, without thinking, I took the hand gallantly offered me and I mounted the horse in front of the overseer.

During that foolish race through the jungle of tall palm trees to the shore, I could feel my skirts flying and my hair come loose in the mad wind. And yet I felt I was safe. The veins on Joseph's arms swelled with the effort of holding me. My unruly fantasy made me close my eyes, change the horseman's name, the color of the skin of the hands that were tight about my waist.

The sun was low, and its sidelong rays tortured our eyes, but then suddenly the unmistakable figure of my dear Charlie appeared against the sky. He turned his head upon hearing the horse's gallop, and then came slowly toward us, though he did not return our greeting. Sliding carefully down, I asked Joseph to return to the house and send back two men with horses—a chore he could not have enjoyed doing but which he rushed off to perform.

A dense silence enveloped us after the sound of the horse's hooves had died away. We looked at each other, and the murmur of the waves drowned the beating of our anguished hearts. It was Charlie who with a single gesture cured all the hurt, all the pain of the wounds. My clumsy words were hushed by the close, warm embrace of his arms. We sat on a fallen treetrunk bleached by the waves and waited for the horses' return, remembering that day when, naked and innocent, he had shown himself to eyes that did not want to see.

FAREWELL

Today, very early in the morning, while the servants lashed the trunk to the roof of the coach, Bella took down my message: Miss Florence was indisposed. From my room I was the invisible witness of the impassive farewells of Charlie and the flowing tears of Miss Susan. The father, who had still not forgiven the terrible social affront committed by his son, showed his stubbornness by his absence.

Just as he was about to step into the carriage, the young voyager looked up toward my window. I waved my handkerchief softly. He blew me a kiss. And thus were separated Charles Walker Lind and his tutor: without promises and without tears.

The same route taken by my Charlie would lie before me in two weeks. Like a pain that sears my breast is the burning desire I feel to flee this little island forgotten by the world, and inhabited by none but birds of passage.

THE GRAND FINALE

With her habitual courtesy, Miss Susan offered me a wonderful dinner, and she set beside my plate an envelope swollen with money. Bella had made my favorite dish: roast turkey with minted rice stuffing. The master did us the supreme honor—all the more eloquent for its infrequency—of dining with us at the table.

After the delight of the superb dessert (*omelette norvégienne flambée*), Mr. Lind adroitly opened a bottle of his best champagne and raised his glass in an astounding toast—"To happiness."

"Does such a thing exist?" I asked, joking to hide a sudden access of anger.

Miss Susan smiled her approval and proposed another toast, this one less pretentious: "To serenity would be more like it, don't you think, Miss Florence?"

At that I raised my glass too, and inspired by some strange spirit of mockery (from my Celtic ancestors?), I drank "to chance, to ever-possible chance."

I refused to acknowledge the darts from his eyes nor to allow them to find their mark in the warm moistness of my own.

Tomorrow the boat will sail, and I will be taken forever from this bitter island. It is late, and my candle gutters. I have taken the latch off my door.

Miss Florence held the closed diary to her breast a moment before she put it carefully back into the small black box with its lining of red taffeta. Then she reached into the old trunk again and took from it a package of envelopes neatly tied together by pink ribbon. When she pulled one of the loose ends, the envelopes spilled onto the carpet like old playing-cards in a game without rules.

The French postage-stamps with the stern image of Napoleon III caught her eye at once. Opening one of the envelopes that had fallen a little apart from the rest, she recognized with a smile the long cursive strokes that invariably marked the handwriting of one of her own pupils.

The letter was not easy to read. Doubtlessly because of a scarcity of paper—or perhaps because of that incorrigible desire to mystify that he had always shown—the writer had covered both sides of the paper with horizontal and vertical lines superimposed upon each other.

Paris, May 24, 1866
10, rue du Roi-de-Rome

My dear Teacher,

You will surely wonder at having news of me after so long. Not a day, however, since we lost sight of you, now more than six years ago (almost a quarter of my life), has your memory ceased pursuing me. I will not say that I have deliberately thought of you every day of my tedious life. That would be to deceive you or, worse, flatter you—both of which your example always taught me to abhor. But I have frequently had the occasion to miss your witty British irony (which so often mortified me) and that constant disposition for indignation (which never failed to amuse me). Not to mention, of course, our infinite walks in quest of crabs and hibiscus flowers, or the inevitable five-o'clock tea in the garden of flesh-eating plants.

I take the liberty of recalling those sweet memories without even contemplating the possibility that you have cast all those years into oblivion. Is it true, Miss Florence? Can you have been so cruel, so strong? Have you erased from your mind those years of my innocence (and your own) in Puerto Rico?

Finding where to write you was more difficult than (if I do not misremember) obtaining your acquiescence to my childish afternoons when I wished to escape the school-room. No one knew anything about *la petite Anglaise,* save that she had arrived alive and well in New York and then had disappeared into thin air. No one, that is, except a good friend of the family (whose name I will not reveal) who had had the enviable fortune to come across you in the streets of Manhattan in the company of your current employer, one Mrs. Weston.

Why did you never write? What reasons did we give you (did *I* give you) to make you wish to uproot us in this way, so utterly, from your heart?

But I will not waste good time in recriminations, not when I have so much to tell you. (For you should know that you are even unto this moment my only, and exclusive, *confidante.* It is quite simple: I have never told anyone, nor ever will tell anyone else, my ridiculous "sorrows of young Werther.")

The last time we saw one another (I on the step of the carriage, you at the window of your dovecote), my sadness was my only baggage. Is one's first love the only one, or at least the most memorable? In that case, I am not certain who it was harder for me to abandon—the captive princess of Arroyo or the captivator of princes of La Enriqueta. Would that I possessed the gift of ubiquity, so that I might be witness at this instant to the color that has just come into your cheeks. I must content myself, unfortunately, with imagining it.

As to that dark and melancholic chapter of my life, only one piece of information is left me to tell you, the piece of information that paints this so-predictable fairy tale a dreadful red: the death of Carmelina a few months after my departure, a death by her own hands. Time passes, Miss Florence, though not so the tracks left upon us by the wounds that cut too deep.

It is not my intention to weary your nights with stories that will steal your sleep away. You are no doubt asking what a great engineering-fellow, who was graduated (and the passive tense of that verb is more than intentional) by force and against his natural inclinations, is doing wandering now about the streets of Paris. Well, I have returned to the calling that you yourself so wisely helped me discover—the vocation of art. I follow in the footsteps of my illustrious grandfather (who, as you well know, not only sent telegrams but also painted paintings) and more literally than you might think. At this very moment, for example, I am staying in the eleven-room apartment which Mr. Samuel F. B. Morse has just rented, a few steps from the Bois de Boulogne and not far—a bracing walk—from the Champs de Mars. Here my grandfather can enjoy, in the company of his wife, his children, and his parvenu relatives, the Grande Exposition Internationale, that material hymn to the technical and scientific glory of the Second Empire. Even Mrs. Goodrich, his sister-in-law, is here—with her entire southern clan—in order to spare themselves the "horrors of Reconstruction" after the Civil War that has left them virtually in the street. And where would we be without Mr. Prime, that excellent newspaperman in search of material for a biography (not mine, certainly).

As you will recall, I am not one for what might be called family reunions. I think, therefore, that I will be here on the rue du Roi-de-Rome for no longer than the time strictly needed to find a flat and a position as an apprentice in the *atelier* of some famous painter (M. Courbet, perhaps: I have ambitions). Mrs. Goodrich finds me a bit unsociable for her taste, and has said so to Mr. Morse, who (in defense of the family honor) unceasingly sings the praises of my venerable father. So you see, not even in France am I able to be anything but "Mr. Lind's son," that magical phrase which on the Island had the curious effect of simultaneously opening doors to me and shutting them.

But all is not as tragic as my telling of my tale might make one think, for my outlook has I'm sure been contaminated at least somewhat by the *esprit romantique* that infuses this nation. No, for there are amusing things as well, such as the vision of that wondrous patriarch Father Samuel (so republican in his convictions) dressed in the style of the French aristocracy, with a sword about his waist and all, climbing up on a chair with his wife Sarah in order to see, over the heads of the ten thousand citizens invited to the grand reception in the Hôtel de Ville, the Emperor in person.

I revel as you cannot imagine in the sheltering anonymity of this city's effervescent life, with all its multitudes and its overwhelming spaces. It makes me feel a kind of lightheadedness, almost a dizziness, like drinking too much champagne. In the narrow cobblestoned streets of this city where all is possible, I recover the faculty I thought lost—the faculty of trusting in the merits of my own decisions.

As I know you will judge harshly one who would dare close this epistle without one word about the elder Linds, I will send you *four* words, with my most cordial respects: *ça va, malgré tout.*

Is it too much vanity to hope for a reply? No matter—one can be arrogant with impunity at the age of twenty-three (precisely—my birthday is today).

Believe me, my dear Teacher, your most loving and grateful

—C.W.L

By one of those frequent caprices of fate, or of the postal service, Miss Florence's reply never reached her nostalgic former pupil. More than a year later, a second letter from France revealed at least part of the reason: the young man's address had changed.

Paris, September 16, 1867
39, rue de Douay

Ungrateful heart of ice—

Once again I dare offend you with a letter. I put aside the pride that has made me continue to await an impossible letter, and allow myself the hope that the most gratifying eventuality is in fact the true one—that you never received my first.

This one shall be much briefer. Speaking to an imaginary interlocutor is not the favorite pastime of a mind which, in spite of the overwhelming evidence against it, still aspires to the state of sanity. One simple anecdote will perhaps most efficiently serve to communicate to you how complex (and absurd) my current *état d'esprit* really is.

A French friend of mine took me a few days ago to the studio of an artist whose specialty is the fruits and vegetables of the tropics (in paint, I mean).

"I understand he is Puerto Rican, like you," my enthusiastic cicerone told me, and only my fear of offending him restrained me from laughing in his face. Puerto Rican? What does this new epithet mean, whose syllables never once assailed my ears in all the time I lived in Arroyo? Geographic proximity is surely not sufficient reason for bestowing adjectives of birth and antecedence so cavalierly, much less when one's parents have always behaved as though La Enriqueta were the displaced center of an eternally foreign universe. My upbringing, as you well know, only accentuated that distance. The summers in Poughkeepsie or Europe, or in the ancestral mansions of the Linds and Overmans in St. Thomas, served to remind me each and every year of my essential foreignness, my ancestry so little rooted in the land whose generous fruit nourished my family's wealth.

Yet, my dear friend, curiously, that word which I found so absurd had the power to shake me to the core. What has my life been but one long wanderlust without destination or compass? Where will it be that I, should that day come, plant my roots, however aerial they may be? When I stepped into that studio, the pineapples, the papayas and mameyes of the tropics, hanging in effigy and exile upon the walls, made me feel that I was once more close to the sea, feeling the cordial embrace of the sun as I lay upon the sand with you.

As for my artistic work, it saddens me to admit that my father's astute prophecy is very near coming true: "If you don't come back a second Delacroix, you'll have shamefully wasted your time and my money." After several unsuccessful attempts to be taken into a prestigious studio, I see that I cannot do without the letter of introduction that my famous grandfather so kindly handed me upon my arrival. I have discovered that in Paris, as in all cities, one must have a godfather if one is to be baptized.

One piece of encouraging news—which, in seeing the address above, you will have already noted: I live alone. I am renting a small room "under the roof," as the saying goes, with skylight and all, in a modest building just steps from Montmartre. Wouldn't you like to come back to

Europe? (Oh, forgive me, I know that England is another continent . . .)
You could walk with little Charlie along the mysterious Seine. This last
mad sentence will have shown you that I am still capable of daydreams
(at least).

Please, madam, receive the imperishable, though unrequited, affection of your ever-faithful

—C.W.L.

The day had long dawned upon the city, and the morning's gray light
was dripping thickly down the walls of the buildings, when the shutters
of the little room on Bleecker St. were drawn open and a window
raised. Inside, the stove cracked and ticked, and it gave off a smell of
gas that stung the nose. A freezing gust of air blew into the room. Miss
Florence Jane closed the window, yet she stood for a long while looking
down at the streets filled with dirty snow.

When she turned back, she saw the newspaper spreading its wings
like a black and white butterfly across the sofa and the open trunk,
which suddenly was as unsettling to her as a coffin without its corpse.
While the water whistled mockingly in the kettle and clouds of warm
steam filled the room, Miss Florence strode without the slightest hesitation to the wardrobe.

II

"It is the same sea, the same waves; their rhythm has not wavered or
abated in all this time. The smooth surface of the ocean does not
change like the fickle heart of men. And that blue drapery! How could I
have forgotten how intensely blue a sky can be which fears no winter?
The pelicans and sea gulls wheel and dive, heralding the land. It is difficult to believe that with that same grace they rip and devour their submarine prey—as mercilessly and relentlessly as, secret and terrible, the
very sharks."

With those words Miss Florence Jane began the diary of her return
to Puerto Rico. She followed the same route as on her first voyage,
twenty-seven years before. The cargo ship on which she had sailed
dropped anchor, as it had that other time, a prudent distance from the
dock. A little dinghy rowed her and the few other passengers to the
shore. There, an absent-minded customs officer, black-uniformed,
motioned that she could proceed.

Presenting herself at the hacienda without notice, her baggage slung over her shoulders as it were, seemed to her the most flagrant sort of breach of courtesy. Not even the respectable pretext of a visit to pay her condolences would justify such a violation of the rules of etiquette. With the aid of a small fistful of dollars, she persuaded the porter to take her bag—and her request for a room for the night—to a run-down-looking hotel on the main street, visible from the docks. The porter's hints as to the doubtful reputation of the place were in vain. To calm the man, Miss Florence finally had to assure him that she would not be staying there for any length of time at all.

As soon as I had taken a room at "El Marion"—whose reality only confirms the porter's apprehensions—I took off my hat in order to retouch my hair, which had been much blown by the wind. A mirror encroached upon from all sides by blotches gave back to me an image, in the stale shadow of the room, of a face much wearied by journeying. While I awaited the arrival of the coachman—who was taking his time, one might add—a whim made me change the sober gray dress that I had chosen for my voyage and put on one of pink silk whose cut favored me better. I then sat, nervously, upon the sway-backed cot which was to be my bed, if fortune smiled upon me, for but a single night.

The coachman's expression was one of perplexity when I asked him to take me to Mr. Edward Lind's residence. I repeated my request, attempting to Hispanicize my pronunciation of the name as best I could, but it was not until I mentioned the name of the hacienda that we could at last drive out toward Cuatro Calles—much more slowly than suited my impatience.

January was in its full tropical splendor. The white silk crown of the sugar cane swayed in the wind, and the deep green of the trees, thick with leaves, were a sign of benediction upon these lands of erstwhile drought. The warm wetness of the air, and the perspiration it provoked, bathed my face, and I was constantly obliged to mop my forehead and throat with a kerchief.

Up until that moment I had acted as though in a dream. I had been as though propelled by hidden clock-work springs, by irresistible winds blowing this way and that across the geography of my desires. Now, so near the truth, so near my destiny, I was assailed by the full violence of my consciousness of what was about to take place. What was I to gain from this absurd and unreasoning leap backward in time? Would I even be recognized by that person who for so many years had, alone, inhabited the shadows of my memory? Would I recognize him, who would have been tattooed, weathered, and scarred by life's storms? His features took on life once more, they sprang up again, lighted by sudden lightning-glare, and then once more faded, like a footprint in sand, under the cruel tide of my presentiments.

At last I saw the baronial gates, now gnawed by the salty air's erosion. Impelled by a need to step of my own power across that threshold of the paradise lost, I had the coachman stop the horses there. I felt it better to keep the secret and the surprise until the last. With more curiosity than good will, the man offered to wait for me. Handing him his money, I sent him off with an impatience I could not conceal.

Nature had made such incursions into the drive that my bootlaces tangled in the overgrown grass. Led by habit, I made my way, slipping and tugging, up the drive toward the house. The troublesome little burrs that I now again remember pulling from young Charlie's socks and pants-legs stuck to the silk of my dress, making a yellow fringe that mercilessly scratched my legs.

I rehearsed in my mind the impossible speeches of my return: the dutybound condolences, the hidden motive. What would be the new mask under which I faced anew his presence? Would time have tamed his old impetuosity? Would he, as he had of old, fall silent and withdraw his gaze? Fear whispered in my ear that a mere knock at his door would not suffice to undo the tight knots of unhappiness.

When I reached the turn in the drive and stood for a moment in the thick undergrowth that obscured what had once been the perfect design of the gardens, I suddenly caught sight of the spectral outline of the house. The mid-afternoon sun lit the scene, revealing to me the desolating vision that my incredulous eyes in vain attempted to discredit: Its roof sunken, its woodwork fallen and rotting, its regal staircase mutilated, its doors and windows hidden by enormous boards, the princely mansion of La Enriqueta stood, its death-throes long past, like a soulless body amid the green of the trees. What diabolic curse had spewed its poison over the glorious palace of my youth? What evil planet had now eclipsed the triumphant rainbow of my hopes?

Of what happened next I have but the vaguest memory. The blood rushed boiling to my brain; my knees buckled, my legs failed me. My breast, shaken by the commotion produced upon my senses by the spectacle of that ruin, struggled to breathe the suddenly rarefied air. A black curtain fell over my eyes, and I slipped, unresistingly, into the bottomless abyss of unconsciousness.

*   *   *

The first thing she felt as she regained consciousness was the warm touch of hands under her head. She tried futilely to rise, but she realized, with some alarm, that her body was as though hanging in the air. With the abrupt return to sensation, her blurred vision made out the distant lighthouse of a pair of green eyes looking with concern down upon her.

"What happened to you?" asked the voice that accompanied the eyes. Without waiting for the improbable reply of that pale woman borne in his anonymous arms, the green-eyed man deposited her very delicately in the grass.

At first, Miss Florence was frightened by that dark visage that leaned over her own bloodless one. If she did not get up, it was because her legs, still unsure, would not permit her. The open smile of the young mulatto, however, the rare color of those eyes observing her with a mixture of curiosity and compassion, little by little disarmed her mistrustfulness. At last she was able to murmur words of gratitude for his help, and even to make a weak attempt to open her purse, still hanging from her wrist, and offer him a few coins, which he would not accept.

As reply to the mute questioning reflected in the intense gaze of her rescuer, she asked with many gestures and few words about the whereabouts of the hacienda's owner. The man answered in Spanish, though his interlocutress could not decipher the meaning of his long explanation. After another such exasperating exchange, he courteously offered Miss Florence his arm.

Leaning upon that arm, she walked toward what had once been the batey of the negroes, now a clearing circled by little wooden cabins with thatched roofs. As she walked, she felt her strength gradually returning to her. In the earthern plaza that was the center of the rustic settlement, a group of children were noisily playing chase with pods of the locust tree.

The young man stopped before one of the cabins and signalled to her that she should wait outside. She leaned against a breadfruit tree and closed her eyes a moment. Almost immediately, her rescuer stuck his head out the door of the cabin and motioned for her to come inside. Timidly, Miss Florence approached the open door.

Her eyes had to accustom themselves to the dimness. The single window, open but a chink, allowed one thin ray of light to penetrate the room. It illuminated the white head of an old negro woman ceremoniously sitting in a rocking chair, rocking.

*   *   *

"What a sight for these sore eyes, miss! I thank heaven for letting me see you once more before I lose my sight forever!" The words, in the musical English of the islands, were immediately recognizable to me. Opening her arms, smiling an almost-toothless smile, she gave me the warmest reception I have ever received. The tears I had so far been able to contain ran freely now down my cheeks, mixing with Bella's own.

"Oh, Miss Florence, Miss Florence," were the only words her trembling old lips seemed capable of speaking. Moved and surprised, the young man who had brought me to Bella stared at us from the hammock.

When she recovered herself, Bella introduced me to Andrés, whom she insisted upon calling her grandson. This surprised me no end, as I knew that Bella had never had any children, and that when our lives diverged she had been a woman of some fifty years of age. Naturally I said nothing, accepting her statement as one accepts a mystery of the faith.

More restored now after the constant siege of emotions, I sipped the bitter coffee that Andrés, at his "grandmother's" bidding, served me, and I sat down on a low stool that the young man offered. I did not have to initiate the conversation (as I had rehearsed so often in my mind) with questions. Bella forestalled me by launching herself almost at once into a detailed accounting of the events that had so drastically transformed our respective lives. Andrés, smiling, listened attentively to the monologue, though his ignorance of English kept him from understanding much of it. His green eyes' insistence inexplicably disturbed me, and it required some effort on my part to avoid his glance.

"You know, Miss Florence, that we are free now?" Bella announced proudly. When I nodded, she went on without further interruption.

"Well, then . . . Mr. Morse, rest his soul, had died, when all of a sudden from over there, from Spain, came the news that we were free. No sooner had we heard, than Domingo and Juan Prim jumped on their horses and rode off down the coast yelling and carrying on to spread the word. You should have been at La Enriqueta that night! There were people from every hacienda in Arroyo, Patillas, and Guayama. The torch-lights lit up the place like it was high noon, and the drums beat till daybreak. Miss Susan and Master Charlie—the sweet boy had come back by this time—sat on the veranda and watched. He looked happy— he even pulled me out of the kitchen and made me go down to the batey, and he stood off and watched me, he waved at me to dance, and shake myself, and cast off all the shackles on my soul. Mr. Lind had gone to bed early. And the expression on his face . . . Things were not going well for him you know—money things. He had more debts than acres of land, and the government kept throwing monkey wrenches into any plan he invented to get a little ahead. They wouldn't even let him bring over an engineer from England so he could pipe water down from Ancones Creek so the cane fields could get some water. It was just too much for him, you see, to have to pay the folks that used to work for him for free."

My patience began to wear a bit thin, but fearing to show any too-forward (if not totally unjustified) interest in the family's private matters I kept my questions to myself and did not mention the name that trembled upon the threshold of my lips. Somehow Bella must have caught the silent plea in my eyes. Her next words seemed an attempt to satisfy my longings:

"You cannot imagine, Miss Florence, the things that a person heard in that house. They were like dogs and cats, the father and the son all day rowing and arguing, shouting at the top of their lungs at each other, right at the dinner table, over the crazy ideas that Mr. Lind said Master Charlie had brought back from France. Mr. Lind said he rued the day he'd ever wasted his money on such a trip as that. The child had always loved to paint—you know that better th'n anyone. But the master of the house wanted to put him behind the counter in the store, you might say. And Master Charlie more than thirty years old, while Mr. Lind was treating him like he was still a child. Until one day the poor thing could take no more . . ."

Bella paused, clearly affected by the vivid memories awakened in her by this emotional retelling of the past. But then with a deep sigh she went on with her distressing tale:

"Miss Susan had sent me to make up the room that used to be yours, the little one upstairs, remember? She didn't sleep with her husband anymore now. In fact, she kept so to her room that you almost never saw her anywhere else in the house anymore. It broke my heart to see her that way, so all alone, so shut up inside that room, inside herself. I even took her favorite parrot up to her so she could hear a human word now and then. Mr. Lind was never in the house, and when he did come home, the arguments with Master Charlie would drive him outside again in no time."

Andrés had closed his eyes, and his chest was rising and falling regularly; the hammock gently swayed. Bella smiled when she saw the direction my indiscreet gaze had taken.

"Young people aren't interested in these old folks' stories," she said. The words seemed to give new strength to her nostalgia, for she then continued.

"Well, then, Miss Florence—things were bad, and then all of a sudden they got worse. As though he hadn't made his father mad enough at him already, Charlie fell in love again. But don't misunderstand me— that wasn't the worst part of it. Mr. Lind did want to see the boy married, for it was his hope that his grandchildren would raise up that plantation again. But he didn't want him marrying the woman Master Charlie picked out, if you'll forgive me calling him Master Charlie still—it's that that's the way I always think of him, Miss Florence. Anyway, to keep himself occupied and to earn a little money now and again, Charlie would paint the portraits of the better families, you know, in the towns around, in Arroyo and Guayama especially. And that was how he came to meet Brunilda, which was the daughter that don Jacinto Cora had had by a servant girl. Brunilda was light-skinned, lighter-skinned than Selenia, if you remember her, Miss Florence. Her skin was as olive-colored as a gypsy, and she had big eyes the color of honey, and a nose that looked like somebody had whittled it down, it was so fine and narrow. The only thing that gave away her birth was her hair, which was just like mine, kinky, even though she wore it in a kind of a bun that favored her face wonderfully.

"When I say that Charlie fell in love, I'm not telling the half of it. The poor thing was like a puppy—he would send her flowers, he would take her candy, he would give her books to read, he would draw her . . . Every day on God's earth he would go out for a buggy-ride with her. The horse finally got to know the way—it never had to open its eyes after a while. And that girl's family, you can imagine, just delighted, delighted—why, they were the ones that would come out ahead in the match, of course.

"But I haven't mentioned the hurricane that was brewing in the *other* house. Mr. Lind did not approve of his son's intentions. Marrying a mulatto woman was not the same as sowing some wild oats with the negro girls. Oh, Miss Florence, like father, like son . . . But how could two men be so alike in their pleasures and so different in every other way?"

Instinctively I touched my forehead, a gesture that betrayed the discomfort brought me by such indiscreet words. Bella laid her rough hand over mine and went on, her smile full of wisdom:

"Master Charlie wouldn't budge. The more his father opposed the match, the more determined he was to marry the girl. In town it was all anybody could talk about—the vegetable-peddlers pushing their carts around town talked about it, and even the black sharecroppers made jokes about it, laughing over the way Mr. Morse would be spinning in his grave the day his dark-skinned great-grandson was born."

She sighed again, and her expression became grave. One would never have been able to predict that expression from the lightsome tone she had used to tell the story so far.

"Well," she said, crossing herself, "you know how the story ended. Let's not disturb the dead anymore than we have to."

These last words shook me from my previous reticence to speak, and I assured Bella of my total ignorance of the events to which she so mysteriously alluded. Her face underwent a transformation that made my blood freeze. A dry, cold knot gripped my throat.

"Then . . . you don't know?" she whispered, as though to convince herself of what was now a palpable reality. And in the face of the anguished silence that met her question, she broke into uncontrollable sobs, and cried out in pain, "Oh, Miss Florence! My God! . . . he's dead!"

At Bella's outburst and the cry that escaped my lips, Andrés sat up in the hammock. I could not move; I was seized with horror and astonishment, yet I would have postponed forever the moment of the bitter revelation. The tears refused to come. My dry eyes remained fixed on old Bella's face.

When I had gathered my little strength to mutter a few confused and incoherent words, I at last learned my poor ward's tragic ending. Five years had now passed since that fatal night, but Bella remembered the precise date and hour. It was exactly eight o'clock at night when the father and son, after bitter words of recrimination at the table, went off together into the darkness of the gardens. Perhaps they had wanted to spare the mother their angry shouting. Or perhaps, wishing to keep their differences between themselves, they had simply withdrawn out of earshot of the servants. Of what was said, no one was witness. How they offended one another, no one knows. All anyone ever knew was that without a backward glance, and as fast as the wind, Charlie fled his enchanted garden forever. Pale and wounded, he went to his room. His father dropped onto a marble bench, his head between his hands, and he did not lift his head again until he heard the shot. That was the beginning of his own death-in-life.

*   *   *

The day dawned gray and dreary. Haze floated heavily over the greenish sea around Arroyo and low black clouds smudged the far-off line of the horizon.

The town was still half asleep when Andrés gave a tug at the cord of the doorbell. He hadn't long to wait; the door opened almost instantly, and a small figure swathed in mourning emerged. The woman followed in the young man's quick steps with all the darting nearness of a shadow.

The town began to stretch. Some early fishing boats had already returned to the dock. A tramp sat up in his burlap bed to look with unconcealed curiosity upon that astonishing vision of a young mulatto man carrying a bunch of flowers followed by a phantasmagoric white woman dressed head to toe in black.

They made their way down San Fernando until they saw, from a curve in the street, the white wall upon whose dirty top there arose, like apparitions gauzed in mist, the enormous stone heads of two angels. The man and the woman stopped before the closed gates. The legend above them, encircled by a leafy crown that embraced a cross, proclaimed its hopeful yet mournful message:

> THIS, A GARDEN OF SILENCE AND CALM IS,
> WHICH NONE BUT THE SINNER NEED FEAR.
> BODIES ARE LAID IN THE EARTH HERE,
> WHILE THEIR SOULS TO NEW LIFE HAVE ARIS'N.

To Andrés' summons the gravedigger soon responded, slowly and laboriously dragging his bad leg. He leaned the shovel he had been carrying against the guardhouse wall and without so much as a good-morning told the waiting man and woman that this was no decent hour to be visiting the dead. Andrés lay the coin discreetly passed to him by his companion into the calloused hand of the growling Spaniard that tended the place, and without more ado the rusted chains parted.

While my guide asked for the exact place, I went on ahead, walking down between the two rows of stones and funerary monuments that formed the long main avenue. Suddenly I stopped and, led by blind intuition, traced my steps backward a few feet. The ill-humored gravedigger's directions were unnecessary. There, before me, but a few feet from the entrance to the graveyard, there rose a low house of red bricks, like an altar—my poor Charlie's last dwelling-place. The letters of his beloved name, cut into the sober marble gravestone, burned into the dry fibers of my eyes.

I knelt on the wet ground to murmur a prayer for the eternal rest of his afflicted soul. I lowered my eyes and called up the image of the mischievous child with round, rosy cheeks that he had once been. Sobs shook my body, and they somehow eased the pain in my breast, which had been wounded by a grief that I knew would never end. Confounded by the intensity of my tears, Andrés laid in silence, beside the tomb, the bunch of flowers so lovingly prepared by Bella for her dead babe.

I gave myself up to cruel reflections, which could only nourish my suffering. Again and again I remembered, though I had never lived, that terrible night that had cut off happiness forever. Had Charles Walker Lind sensed, two hours before dusk began falling, that that was to be his last sunset? When had there begun to germinate within him, like some black flower, the idea of death? Had he perhaps unknowingly sowed the design in his indifferent and mocking father's mind, so that in that distant and alien ground the burning seed would sprout? What was the angry fear, the cruel derision that crowned his daring? What fatal words dissolved the bonds? Who ripped, with a single slash, the placid canvas?

A sudden blinding flash of lightning cut the sky, and the thunder resounded in the desolate cemetery. The Spaniard crossed himself and limped off in search of shelter.

Andrés extended a hand, to help her to her feet. Before Miss Florence laid her trembling hand in his, however, she bent to leave a kiss upon the cold stone of the tomb. Needles of mist played their melancholy mazurka upon the wet marble.

It was true, horribly true—my own senses, oddly sharpened by suffering, had confirmed it. Now, no matter how hard I tried, I could never again deny it. My Charlie was—and I had to say the word—dead. His mortal body would never again tread the fertile earth. Only his memory, destined to suffer the slow fading of the emotions, would live with me.

Stricken with a grief that defies all attempts at description, I turned my back and covered my face. Long I stood like that. Thinking me disoriented, Andrés courteously showed me the path back to the entrance. I shook my head and asked him to leave me alone. He retired a little way, while I wandered down those paths flanked by imposing mausoleums. I do not know how long I walked, what miles I must have covered, how many hours passed, how many epitaphs with their futile cortege of surnames filed past my unseeing eyes. My black calico dress stuck wetly to my body, and a sharp wind mercilessly lifted the folds of my cape, cutting me to the bone. Almost as though in a trance I wandered, like another ghost in that precinct of the dead, breathing the fetid and poisonous air of the graveyard.

Exhausted at last from so much aimless wandering, I retraced my ever more lagging steps, leaving behind this place and returning, without happiness, to the world of the living. But a mute, deep voice drew me wordlessly once again to the scene of my previous weeping. If I had been able then to conquer the silent impulse, to break that macabre spell, my feet would not have returned to circumambulate the beloved remains of my rebellious angel and my wretched eyes would never have come to rest upon that stone which sealed forever my affliction—identical in cut and style, like a twinned bed, the red tomb of Edward Lind stood mutely confronting his son's, even after death.

The clouds opened then, emptying the rivers of the heavens. The dull scream from my very soul flooded my throat with fire.

Everyone wants to see the white lady, whose figure has floated like a virginal lay-sister through the cane fields. But Andrés has bolted the doors and windows of the cabin. Bella rocks in her rocking chair beside Miss Florence's cot, for Miss Florence is stricken with a fever that will not yield even to poultices and herbal teas. She speaks incomprehensible words to her dead loves. Tearful, downcast, the old servant blames herself for this, and day and night she sits with her rag, scented with eucalyptus, and wipes away the icy sweat that pearls the sick woman's brow.

How can one count the eternal nights of fever? Bella swears it was two nights, and that on the third I opened my eyes to ask what country I was in and if winter had never come. Her chicken broth and saintly patience saved me from the black pit my life had slipped away into since my pilgrimage to the cemetery.

Andrés would allow no one to talk to me of the past, yet the past was all I wanted to know. I had so many questions to ask, if I was to be able to go on living. As my strength grew, Bella gave in to me. Her cruel story filled the void of time with death.

"At first, Mrs. Lind refused to believe that Charlie was gone. She locked herself up all day, calling him and talking to the walls. At night, we'd see her walking through the gardens, looking for him behind the trees, crying and moaning like a soul in purgatory. Mr. Lind would send me out to get her, so she wouldn't get a mind to do somethin' crazy. Sometimes we'd be walking through the cane fields as the sun was coming up . . . And then when the sun was up, she would let me bring her back to her room . . ."

"No matter how hard anybody tried, Miss Susan didn't understand. All she wanted to do was tell us that waking nightmare that had tormented her since that night, tell us how it repeated itself over and over and over again . . . She kept seeing herself as a child in Locust Grove, sitting like a little lady at the long dining table there. She would be chatting as she served herself with the big copper ladle that her grandfather Jedediah had given her—pouring thick rivers of delicious-smelling sauce over a slice of glazed ham. So nobody would think she wanted to eat that whole sauce-boat of sauce herself, she would gracefully hold the sauce-boat up and then go to offer it to the rest of the guests. But when she would turn to her neighbor, her cold hands would drop it, and it would fall to the floor with a great crash. Horrified, she would look down to see the warm red lake spreading on the floor, bathing her bare feet, and as she looked up, apologizing, she would find nothing but two long rows of empty chairs.

"Little by little she got calmer, and then she would let me feed her. I would feed her with a spoon. In no more than a few months, she had dried up, she had got so old that it was almost hard to recognize her—a woman that had been so beautiful . . ."

"What about Mr. Lind?" I timorously whispered, both desiring and fearing the reply.

Bella paused, as though waiting for the right word to come to her. Her face hardened, and she took a deep breath before coldly pronouncing her next words.

"He never even wore mourning. Six months hadn't passed since Charlie's death, and he brought a black woman to live in the house."

Bella's voice now sounded distant. Though the tightness of my chest revealed how heavy upon me lay the anguish of this story, a curious sense of lightness possessed my brain, blunting a bit the knife-blade that probed the open wound of my emotions.

"She came in like a queen. She ruled the roost, all right, and she sat at the table and slept in Mr. Lind's bed. It was like Miss Susan had already died. I stayed there a while so as not to leave Miss Susan alone—the poor thing had nobody to take care of her. But one day I packed my things and went to town. I wasn't going to be no maid to a black woman. And the punishment was not long in coming, either, because the heavens are not deaf. Not long afterward, Mr. Lind fell sick, and his black mistress left him, and she took Miss Susan's jewelry and dresses with her. She went off to live the good life in Guayama . . ."

Hidden away on that dying hacienda, hounded night and day by debt, consumed by god only knows what inconfessable remorse, the father survived his son barely two years. It was Bella who had to see to the details of the funeral; no one else was left. She ordered the cedar coffin, mended the threadbare frockcoat he was buried in, notified the friends and neighbors, and made arrangements with the sacristan for the mass. It had been a quiet service: few mourners, no family, one or two of the official personages of the area. With no pomp or circumstance, his body had been lowered into the ground—and darkness had descended upon my soul.

From my cot I listened, eyes closed and my mind peopled with specters, to the melancholy story of Miss Susan's last days. The images of my fantasy mixed with those that Bella painted with the sure brush-strokes of her memories. Her emaciated face like that of a starving orphan, wearing the rent veil of a widow, Miss Susan rose from her own ashes.

Little by little she had given away everything: the damask bed-clothes, the Persian rugs, the mirrored silver tray. There was many a vis-itor who came through the gates of La Enriqueta, which were now always open, to leave loaded down with little treasures, from rock-crys-tal doorknobs pulled off the mahogany doors to linen pillowcases embroidered with the manorial L.

She would sit alone at her dining table. The dining room windows would be closed tight, to maintain that unchanging dusk. And Susan Walker Lind *née* Morse would play with invisible knives and forks upon cracked plates. From the other side of the table there would come, like the cawing of excited crows, indecent words and libertine laughter. Two voices clashed in feverish counterpoint: the deep, harsh tones of his and the strident falsetto of that other woman's. Miss Susan, thank god, could not see them. The screen painted with a scene of a woman sitting beside the ocean—painted one day by her now-dead son—fell, like a final curtain, between that inhuman *tête-à-tête* and her eyes now dry from so much weeping.

The image of that man who had so long dictated the rhythm and direction of my thoughts grew more dim to me with each word Bella spoke—like a shadow suddenly deprived of sun.

Slowly—all too slowly—my mind returned to what people call real-

ity. Bella's unwearying dedication once more returned strength to my
exhausted body. As soon as I could walk, Andrés took me down to the
ocean, where the salt air and the hypnotic rhythm of the waves might
restore to my spirit, at least in some measure, tranquility.

An inexplicable peace fell over all. Sitting beside me, my companion
did not move. He knew, without understanding why, that his silent
presence was balm to my wounded heart.

Suddenly Andrés raised his head and with curiosity followed the
erratic flight of a sea gull. The wondrous light of morning kindled the
startling beauty of his eyes, so astonishingly green against his dark skin.
An unexpected revelation, blindly intuited, and as blindly stifled, struck
me with the cunning speed of a bird of prey. Those green eyes, powerful, and so odd in one so dark—what indelible tattooing did they leave
upon my soul?

A wind from beyond the grave blew through the corridors of my
memory.

On January 30, 1886, Miss Florence Jane stood beside her luggage
on the dock in Arroyo, awaiting the dinghy that was to take her to the
boat. Leaning against a wall, the tall man with graying hair and mous-
tache never took his eyes off her. His indiscretion unsettled her so, that
she took a few deliberate steps, so as to put between herself and her
impertinent observer a more marked distance.

Unaffected by this, the man smiled a conciliatory smile (which was
not reciprocated) and quietly approached the traveler's bag, reading
there, stenciled upon it, its owner's name. Then, smiling again (and this
time with greater confidence), he spoke.

"Pardon me, Miss Florence . . . I had to be sure it was really you
before I dared say hello."

Though the face, transformed by years, was not the same, the voice
still had that youthful timbre of old. I instantly recognized, under the
disguise of age, that long nose, that small square chin.

"*Monsieur*," I replied, offering my hand. Alvaro Beauchamp (for that
was who the impertinent stranger was) promptly kissed it. "Fate never
ceases to surprise me."

He still had the instant charm and manly sweetness that had always
distinguished him. Having been recently widowed, he was on his way to
St. Thomas, where he was to take the steamer that would bear him
away to France. His two sons had returned to the land of their fore-

bears—one was now living in Toulouse, the other in Aix-en-Provence.

"And Ernestina, how is she?" I inquired, taking for granted that she was still in France and that M. Beauchamp intended to visit her there. He lowered his eyes, which suddenly clouded, and in a voice breaking with sorrow told me of the death, many years ago, of his unhappy sister. I murmured a few words of condolence, though I felt them terribly inadequate. Ernestina's name was barely an echo in my past, while for him it still embodied a beloved human presence.

The conversation seemed to flag, freighted as it was by the weight of the dead. The formulas of courtesy had deserted me, and I knew not how to go on, what to say. What possible interest could this profoundly grieving person have in the absurd story of my own journey to the depths of suffering? My lips wavered at the question that we both awaited, the name that neither of us could bring ourselves to speak. At last it was he who—knowingly or not—released me from my quandary.

"I have an appointment in Paris with a mutual friend of ours."

I could not pretend that the allusion went uncomprehended. After the loss of so many of our friends from those distant years, René Fouchard was the only remaining link that joined our lives. The conversation was coming to its end. The dinghy was approaching the shore and the passengers were moving toward the dock.

"Please give him my regards," I said, "and the assurance of my pleasant memory of those days."

The words tumbled out a bit clumsily as I violently signalled to a porter to help me with my bag.

M. Beauchamp kissed my hand again, and holding my gaze with almost fatherly tenderness, he whispered something.

"Place des Vosges, at the *Marais*. You can write him there."

The porter had already thrown my bag over his shoulder and was impatiently gesturing for me to follow him.

"14 Bleecker Street, New York," I replied, as I began to move away, and making the supreme effort to smile.

From the dinghy, I raised my hand in farewell. My cheeks burned under the stifling heat of the sun. The glare off the sea made my eyes water, and in a final act of mercy, the outlines of that island which I was now, truly forever, leaving, were softly blurred.

At two o'clock in the morning, the rearing and pitching of the waves has at last abated, and the sea is calm. Only a few hours remain before the boat, the *City of Santander*, reaches port in Havana. There, after unloading the mail sacks, it will remain at the dock only as long as necessary for the captain to be reassured as to the state of its engines. The few passengers it carries will then await the arrival of the ship that will take them to the United States.

On deck, up toward the bow, there is a woman, her gray hair in disarray, watching time pass. She trembles from head to foot, though the air is warm. She pulls the corners of her shawl around her and knots them upon her chest. She has not been able to sleep; she has been driven from her berth by an inconsolable wailing that comes from the sea and by a pale face, peering in the porthole window, that floats bodiless alongside the ship.

The moon illuminates the trail the ship leaves as it passes. In that trail I see the debris of my life. It was upon this very ship that, light with baggage but heavy with memories, my sad mistress set sail upon her own sea of exile, which soon became her bed of rest.

Perhaps just at the verge of a leap into the sea, fear made her waver, kept her, for one moment, from her desire. Perhaps she leaned gracefully over the rail, as though noting down a familiar name upon her dance card. Behold her there now, at last, the woman un-wed—with her crown of starfish, her scepter of seashells, her long mantle of seaweed, she is cleansed now of all foul betrayal, free now of her impossible love. She lies now at peace with herself. Her hardened features have felt the rest of softness; her withered skin has become smooth again. Once more she has become the pensive, beautiful Muse of the painting she once posed for, for her father.

Far away, in the distance, an identical moon shines over the darkness of the wild sugar cane. Its cruel rays wound the palace in ruins that no one now beholds with wonder. In the cracked mirrors of that solitude, in the desolate hallways of that nameless place, two wandering souls blindly seek each other through all eternity.

And what of me? Will I resist the dark temptation? Will I wear that widow's weed that has come so far to find me? Who will read these mute lips? Who will exhume my thwarted story of love and give it words?

III

It is a warm March day. Too warm to have the stove lighted. With the eager avidity of a starving animal, the flames devour the crumbs fed them by Miss Florence's hand. There is not much left: a foxed and faded drawing of a nymph in the moonlight, a napkin, stained with champagne, pressed between the pages of a book, and a yellow-striped rag that once tried to be the perfect dress.

Stripped of its erstwhile contents, the trunk now shows its naked lining. A thick cloud of smoke issues from the open window, up toward a sky traced by the first swallows of spring.

I Heard Her Sing

by G. Cabrera Infante

translated by Donald Gardner and Suzanne Jill Levine
in collaboration with the author

I knew La Estrella when she was only Estrella Rodríguez, a poor drunk incredibly fat Negro maid, long before she became famous and even longer before she died, when none of those who knew her well had the vaguest idea she was capable of killing herself but then of course nobody would have been sorry if she did.

I am a press photographer and my work at that time involved taking shots of singers and people of the *farándula*, which means not only show business but limelights and night life as well. So I spent all my time in cabarets, nightclubs, strip joints, bars, *barras, boîtes,* dives, saloons, *cantinas, cuevas, caves* or caves. And I spent my time off there too. My job took me right through the night and into dawn and often the whole morning. But sometimes, when I had nothing to do after work at three or four in the morning I would make my way to El Sierra or Las Vegas or El Nacional, the nightclub I mean not the hotel, to talk to a friend who's the emcee there or look at the chorus flesh or listen to the singers but also to poison my lungs with smoke and stale air and alcohol fumes and be blinded forever by the darkness. That's how I used to live and love that life and there was nobody or nothing that could change me because time passed so fast by my time that the days were only the waiting room of evening and evenings became as short as appointments and the years turned into a thin picture spread, and I went on my way, which means preferring nights to evenings, choosing night instead of day, living by night and squeezing my night, I mean my life, into a glass with ice or into a negative or into memory.

One of those nights I arrived at Las Vegas and I met up with all those people who like me had nobody who could change them and suddenly a voice came up to me from the darkness and said, *Fotógrafo,* pull up a seat please. Let me buy you a drink, and it was no longer just a voice but none other than Vítor Perla. Vítor has a magazine entirely devoted to half-naked girls or naked half-girls and captions like: A model with a future in sight—or rather two! Or: The persuasive arguments of Sonia Somethin, or: The Cuban BB says it's Brigitte who is her look-alike, and so on and so forth, so much so that I don't know where the hell they get their ideas from, they must have a shit factory in their heads to be able to talk like that about a girl or girls who only yesterday were or was probably just a *manejadora,* that is half maid and half baby-sitter, and now is half mermaid and half baby doll, or a part-time waitress who is now a full-time temptress, or who only yesterday worked in the garment center in Calle Muralla and who today is hustling her way to the top with all she's got. (Fuck, here I am, already talking like those people.) But for some mysterious reason (and if I were a gossip columnist I would spell it my$terious) Vítor had fallen into the deep, which was why it surprised me to find him in shallow waters and such spirits. I'm lying, of course. The first thing that surprised me was that he wasn't in the clink. So I told myself, He's loaded with shit but still manages to keep afloat: that's grace under morass, and I said it to him too but what I really said was, You keep afloat like good Spanish cork, and he burst out laughing. You're right, he said, but it's loaded cork! Confidentially, I must have a bit of lead somewhere inside—I'm keeling over. And so we began talking and he told me many things confidentially, he told me all his troubles, confidentially, and many other things, always confidentially, but I'm not going to repeat them because I'm a photographer not a press gossip, as I've said. Besides, Perla's problems are his own and if he solves them so much the better and if not it's curtains for Vítor. Anyway, I was fed up listening to his troubles and the way he twisted his face right and twitched his mouth left and as I had no wish to look at such ugly curly lips I changed the subject and we started talking about nicer things, namely women, and suddenly he said, Let me introduce you to Irena, and out of nowhere he produced the cutest little blonde, a doll who'd have looked like Marilyn Monroe if the Jívaros had abducted her and cut her down to size, not just shrinking her head but all the rest—and I mean *all* the rest, tits and all. So he hauled her by the arm like fishing her up from the sea of darkness and he said to me or rather to her, Irena, I want you to meet the best photographer in the world, only he didn't say the world but *el mundo,* meaning that I work for *El Mundo,* and the cutest little blonde, this incredible shrinking version of Marilyn Monroe smiled eagerly, turning up her lips and flashing her teeth like she was raising her skirt to show her thighs and her teeth gleaming in the darkness were the prettiest

thing I've ever seen: perfectly even, well-formed and sensual like a row
of thighs, and we started talking and every so often she would show off
her teeth without blushing and I liked them so much that after a while
I was meaning to ask her to let me touch her teeth or at least fondle her
gums, and we were sitting at the table talking when Vítor called the
waiter with this Cuban sucking sound we use to call waiters that is
exactly like an inverted kiss and the drinks came as if by themselves but
actually via an invisible waiter, his swarthy face and dirty hands lost in
the darkness, and we started drinking and talking some more and in
next to no time I'd very delicately as if I hadn't meant to place my foot
on top of hers and I swear I almost didn't notice it myself, her foot was
so tiny, but she smiled when I said sorry and I knew instantly that she
noticed it and in the next to no time I was holding her hand, which by
now she couldn't help noticing that I meant it but I lost one fucking
hour looking for it because her hand disappeared into my hand, playing
hide and seek in between my yellow fingers that are permanently
smeared with these hypo spots I pretend are nicotine stains, after
Charles Boyer, naturally, and now already after I had finally found her
hand I started caressing it without saying excuse me or anything
because I was calling her Irenita, the name was just her size, and in
next to no time we were kissing and all that, and when I happened to
look around, Vítor had already got up to leave, tactful as ever, very discreetly, and so there we were on our own for a long time alone touching
each other, feeling each other up, oblivious to everybody and everything, even to the show, which was over now anyway, to the orchestra
playing a dance rhythm, to the people who were dancing in and out of
the dark and getting tired of dancing, to the musicians packing up their
instruments across the dance hall and into the dark, going home, and
not noticing the fact that we were left alone there, very deep in the
darkness now, no longer in the misty shadows as Cuba Venegas sings
but in the deep darkness now, in darkness fifty, a hundred, a hundred
and fifty fathoms under the edge of light swimming in darkness, in the
lower depths, wet kissing, wet all over, wet in the dark and wet, forgotten, kissing and kissing and kissing all night long, oblivious to ourselves,
bodiless except for mouths and tongues and teeth reflected in a wet
mirror, two mouths and two tongues and four rows of teeth and gums
occasionally, lost in saliva of kisses, silent now, keeping silent silently
kissing, moist all over, dribbling, smelling of saliva, not noticing,
tongues skin-diving in mouths, our lips swollen, kissing humidly each
other, kissing, kissing before countdown and after blastoff, in orbit,

man, out of this world, lost. Suddenly we were leaving the cabaret. It was then that I saw her for the first time.

She was an enormous mulatto, fat-fat, with arms like thighs, with thighs like tree trunks propping up the water tank that was her body. I told Irenita, I asked Irenita, I said, who's the fat one? because the fat woman seemed to dominate the *chowcito*—and fuck! now I must explain what the *chowcito* is. (The *chowcito* was the group of people who got together to get lost in the bar and hang around the jukebox after the last show was out to do their own *descarga*, this Afro-Cuban jam session which they so completely and utterly lost themselves in that once they went down they simply never knew it was daylight some-where up there and that the rest of the world's already working or going to work right now, all the world except this world of people who plunged into the night and swam into any rock pool large enough to sustain night life, no matter if it's artificial, in this underwater of the frogmen of the night.) So there she was in the center of the *chowcito*, this enormous fat woman dressed in a very cheap dress made of caramel-colored cotton, dirty caramel confused fused with the fudge judged with her chocolate skin wearing an old pair of even cheaper san-dals, holding a glass in her hand, keeping time to the music, moving her fat hips, moving all her fat body in a monstrously beautiful way, not obscene but sexual and lovely as she swayed to the rhythm, crooning beautifully, scat-singing the song between her plump purple lips, wig-gling to the rhythm, shaking her glass in rhythm, rhythmically, beauti-fully, artistically now and the total effect was of a beauty so different, so horrible, so new, so unique and terrifying that I bitterly regretted I didn't have my camera along to catch alive this elephant who danced ballet, that hippopotamus toe-dancing, a building moved by music, and I said to Irenita, before asking what her name was, as I was on the point of asking what her name was, interrupting myself as I was asking what her name was, to say, She's the savage beauty of life, without Irenita hearing me, naturally, not that she would have understood if she had heard me, I said, I asked her, I said to her, to Irenita, Tell me, *tú*, who is it? And she said to me in a very nasty tone of voice, she said, She's the singing galapagos, the only turtle who sings boleros, and she laughed and Vítor slipped up beside me from the side of darkness just then to whisper in my ear, Careful, that's Moby Dick's kid sister, the Black Whale, and as I was getting high on being high I was able to grab Vítor by his sharkskin sleeve and tell him, You're a faggot, you're full of shit, you're a shitlicking bigot, you're a snot Gallego, a racist cunt and asshole: that's what you are, you hear me? *un culo,* and he said to me, calmly, I'll let it pass because you're my guest and you're drunk, that's all he said and then he plunged, like someone slipping behind curtains, into darkness. And I drew up closer and asked her who she was and she said to me, La Estrella, and I thought she meant the star so I said, No, no, I want to know your name, and she said, La Estrella, I am *La Estrella,* sonny boy, and she let go a deep baritone laugh or whatever you call the woman voice that corresponds to basso but sounds like baritone—cuntralto or something like that—and she smiled and said, My name is Estrella, Estrella Rodríguez if you want to know, Estrella Rodríguez Martínez Vidal y Ruiz, *para servirle,* your humble servant, she said and I said to myself, She's black, black, black utterly and finally eternally black and we began talking and I thought what a boring country this would be if Friar Bartolomé de las Casas had never lived and I said to him wherever he is, I bless you, padre, for having brought nigrahs from Africa as slaves to ease the slavery of the Injuns, who were dying off anyhow what with the mass suicides and the massacres, and I said to him, I repeated, I said, Bless you, padre, for having founded this country, and after making the sign of the cross with my right hand I grabbed La Estrella with my left hand and I said to her, I love you. La Estrella, I love *you!* and she laughed bucketloads and said to me, You're plastered, *por mi madre,* you're completely plastered! and I protested, saying to her, I said, No I'm not, I'm ferpectly so ber, and she interrupted me to say, You're drunk like an old cunt, she said and I said to her, But you're a lady and ladies don't say cunt, and she said to me, I'm not a lady, I'm an *artista* and youse drunk *coño* and I said to her, I said, You are La Estrella, and she said, And youse drunk, and I said to her, All right, drunk, as a bottle, I said to her, I said, I'm full of quote methylated spirits unquote but I'm not drunk, and I asked her, Are bottles drunk? and she said, *No, qué va!* and she laughed and I said, So please consider me a bottle, and she laughed again. But above everything, I said to her, consider me in love with you, La Estrella, I'm bottle-full of love for you. I like the Estrella better than I love the estrus, also called heat or rut, and she laughed again in bucketloads, lurching back and forward with laughter and finally slapping one of her infinite thighs with one of her never-ending hands so hard and loud the slap bounced back off the wall as if outside the cabaret and across the bay and in La Cabaña fortress they had just fired the nine-o'clock-sharp salvo like they do every evening at five past nine, and when the report or its echo ceased fire she asked me, she said to me, she said, You love me? and I said, Uh-huh but she went on, Kinkily? and I said, Kinkily, passionately, maddeningly, meaninglessly, foreverly but she cut me short, No, no, I meant, you love me with my kink, kinky hair and all, and she lifted a hand to her head meaning, grabbing more than meaning her fuzzy hair with her full-fat fingers, and I said to her, *Every* bit and piece of you— and suddenly she looked like the happiest whale in the whole world. It was then that I made my great, one and only, impossible proposition. I came closer to her to whisper in her ear and I said to her, I said, La Estrella, I want to make you a dishonorable proposal, that's what I said, la Estrella, let's do it, let's have a drink together, and she said to me, De- light-ed! she said, gulping down the one she had in her hand and already chachachaing to the counter and saying to the bartender, Hey, Beefpie, make it mind, and I asked her, What's mind and she answered, Not mind, baby, mind you I said mine, m-i-n-e, make it mine and mine is La Estrella's drink: no one can have what she has, not open to the public, see what I mean. Make it mine then, and she started laughing again in bucketfuls so that her enormous breasts began shaking like the fenders of a Mack truck when the engine revs up.

At that moment I felt my arm gripped by a little hand and there was Irenita. You gonna stay all night with La Gorda here? she asked, and as I didn't answer she asked me again, You gonna stay with Fatso, and I told her, *Sí*, nothing else, all I said was yes, and she didn't say anything but dug her nails into my hand and then Estrella started laughing in bucketloads, and putting on a very superior air, she was so sure of herself, and she took hold of my hand and said, Leave her alone, this little hot pussy can do better on a zinc roof, and to Irenita she said, Sit on your own stool, little girl, and stay where you belong if you don't mind, and everybody started laughing, including Irenita, who laughed because she couldn't do anything else, and showing the two gaps in her molars just behind her eyeteeth when she laughed, she exited into daylight.

The *chowcito* always put on a show after the other show had finished and now there was a rumba dancer dancing to the jukebox and as a waiter was passing she stopped and said, Poppy, turn up the lights and let's rock, and the waiter went off and pulled out the plug and had to pull it out again and then a third time, but as the music stopped every time he switched off the jukebox, the dancer remained in the air and made a couple of long delicate steps, her whole body trembling, and she stretched out a leg sepia one moment, then earth-brown, then chocolate, tobacco, sugar-colored, black, cinnamon now, now coffee, now white coffee, now honey, glittering with sweat, slick and taut through dancing, now in that moment letting her skirt ride up over her round polished sepia cinnamon tobacco coffee and honey-colored knee, over her long, broad, full, elastic, perfect thighs, and she tossed her head backward, forward, to one side, to the other, left and right, back again, always back, back till it struck her nape, her low-cut, gleaming Havana-colored shoulders, back and forward again, moving her hands, her arms, her shoulders, the skin on them incredibly erotic, incredibly sensual: always incredible, moving them around over her bosom, leaning forward, over her full hard breasts, obviously unstrapped and obviously erect, the nipples, obviously nutritious, her tits: the rumba dancer with absolutely nothing on underneath, Olivia, she was called, still is called in Brazil, unrivaled, with no strings attached, loose, free now, with the face of a terribly perverted little girl, yet innocent, inventing for the first time movement, the dance, the rumba at that moment in front of my eyes: all of my eyes and here I am without my fucking camera, and La Estrella behind me watching everything and saying, You dig it, you dig it, and she got up off her seat as though it was a throne and went toward the jukebox while the girl was still dancing, and went to the switch, saying, Enough's enough, and turned it off, almost tearing it out in a rage, and her mouth looked like it was frothing with obscenities, and she said, That's all, folks! Dancin's over. Now we'll have *real* music! And without any music, I mean without orchestra or accompaniment from radio record or tape, she started singing a new, unknown song, that welled up from her breasts, from her two enormous udders, from her barrel of a belly: from that monstrous body of hers, and I hardly thought at all of the story of the whale that sang in the opera, because what she was putting into the song was something other than false, saccharine, sentimental or feigned emotion and there was nothing syrupy or corny, no fake *feeling* or commercial sentimentality about it, it was genuine soul and her voice welled up, sweet, mellow, liquid, with a touch of oil now, a colloidal voice that flowed the whole length of her body like the plasma of her voice and all at once I was overwhelmed by it. It was a long time since anything had so moved me and I began laughing at the top of my voice, because I had just recognized the song, laughing at myself, till my sides ached with belly laughs because it was "Noche de Ronda" and I thought talking to Agustín, Lara, Agustín, you've never invented a thing, you've not ever invented a thing, you've never composed anything, for now this woman is inventing your song: when morning comes you can pick it up and copy it and put your name and copyright on it again: "Noche de Ronda" is being born tonight. *Esta noche redonda!*

La Estrella went on singing. She seemed inexhaustible. Once they asked her to sing "La Pachanga" and she stood there with one foot in front of the other, the successive rollers of her arms crossed over the tidal wave of her hips, beating time with her sandal on the floor, a sandal that was like a motorboat going under the ocean of rollers that were her leagues of legs, beating time, making the speedboat resound repeatedly against the ground, pushing her sweaty face forward, a face like the muzzle of a wild hog, a hairless boar, her mustaches dripping with sweat, pushing forward all the brute ugliness of her face, her eyes smaller now, more malignant, more mysterious under her eyebrows that didn't exist except as a couple of folds of fat like a visor on which were sketched in an even darker chocolate the lines of her eye makeup, the whole of her face pushed forward ahead of her infinite body, and she answered, La Estrella only sings boleros, she said, and she added, Sweet songs, with real feeling, from my heart to my mouth and from my lips to your ear, baby, just so you don't get me wrong, and she began singing "Nosotros," composing the untimely dead Pedrito Junco's melody all over again, turning his sniveling little *canción* into something real, into a pulsating song, full of genuine nostalgia. La Estrella went on singing, she sang till eight in the morning, without having any notion that it was eight until the waiters started to clear everything away and one of them, the cashier, said, Excuse me, family, and he really meant it, family, he didn't say the word for the sake of saying it, saying family and really meaning something quite different from family, but family was what he meant, really, and he said: *Familia,* we have to close. But a little earlier, just before this happened, a guitarist, a good guitarist, a skinny emaciated fellow, a simple and dignified mulatto, who never had any work because he was very modest and natural and goodhearted, but a great guitarist, who knew how to draw strange melodies out of any fashionable song no matter how cheap and commercial it was, who knew how to fish real emotion out of the bottom of his guitar, who could draw the guts out of any song, any melody, any rhythm between the strings, a fellow who had a wooden leg and wore a gardenia in his buttonhole, whom we always called affectionately, jokingly, Niño Nené after all the Niños who sang flamencos, Niño Sabicas or Niño de Utrera or Niño de Parma, so this one we called Niño Nené, which is like saying Baby Papoose, and he said, he asked, Let me accompany you in a bolero, Estrella, and La Estrella answered him getting on her high horse, lifting her hand to her breasts and giving her enormous boobs two or three blows, No, Niñito, no, she said, La Estrella always sings alone: she has more than enough music herself. It was then that she sang "Mala Noche," making her parody of Cuba Venegas which has since become famous, and we all died laughing and then she sang "Noche y Día" and it was after that that the cashier asked us *familia* to leave. And as the night had already come to an end, the *noche* already *día,* we did so.

La Estrella asked me to take her home. She told me to wait a minute while she went to look for something and what she did was to pick up a package and when we went outside to get into my car, which is one of those tiny English sports cars, she was hardly able to get herself in comfortably, putting all her three hundred pounds weight in a seat which was hardly able to take more than one of her thighs, and then she told me, leaving the package in between us, It's a pair of shoes they gave me, and I gave her a sharp look and saw that she was as poor as hell, and so we drove off. She lived with some married actors, or rather with an actor called Alex Bayer. Alex Bayer isn't his real name, but Alberto Pérez or Juan García or Something Similar, but he took the name of Alex Bayer, because Alex is a name that these people always use and the Bayer he took from the drug company who make pain-killers, and the thing is they don't call him that, Bayer I mean, these people, the people who hang out in the dive at the Radiocentro, for example, his friends don't call him Alex Bayer the way he pronounced it A-leks Báy-er when he was finishing a program, signing it off with the cast calling themselves out, but they called him as they still do call him, they called him Alex Aspirin, Alex Bufferin, Alex Anacin and any other pain-killer that happens to be fashionable, and as everybody knew he was a faggot, very often they called him Alex Evanol. Not that he hides it, being queer, just the opposite, for he lived quite openly with a doctor, in his house as though they'd been officially married and they went everywhere together, to every little place together, and it was in his house that La Estrella lived, she was his cook and sleep-in maid, and she cooked their little meals and made their little bed and got their little baths ready, little etceteras. Pathetic. So if she sang it was because she liked it, she sang for the pleasure of it, because she loved doing it, in Las Vegas and in the Bar Celeste or in the Café Nico or any of the other bars or clubs around La Rampa. And so it was that I was driving her in my car, feeling very much the showoff for the same reasons but the reverse that other people would have been embarrassed or awkward or simply uncomfortable to have that enormous Negress sitting beside them in the car, showing her off, showing myself off in the morning with everybody crowding around, people going to work, working, looking for work, walking, catching the bus, filling the roads, flooding the whole district: avenues, streets, back streets, alleyways, a constant buzzing of people between the buildings like hungry hummingbirds. I drove her right up to their house, where she worked, she La Estrella, who lived there as cook, as maid, as servant to this very special marriage. We arrived.

It was a quiet little street in El Vedado, where the rich people were still asleep, still dreaming and snoring, and I was taking my foot off the clutch, putting the car into neutral, watching the nervous needles as they returned to the point of dead rest, seeing the weary reflection of my face in the glass of the dials as if the morning had made it old, beaten by the night, when I felt her hand on my thigh: she put her 5 *chorizos* 5, five sausages, on my thigh, almost like five salamis garnishing a ham on my thigh, she put her hand on my thigh and I was amused that it covered the whole of my thigh and I thought, Beauty and the Beast, and thinking of beauty and the beast I smiled and it was then that she said to me, Come on up, I'm on my own, she said, Alex and his bedside doctor, she said to me and laughed that laugh of hers that seemed capable of raising the whole neighborhood from sleep or nightmares or from death itself, They aren't here, she said: They went away to the beach for the weekend, Let's go on up so we can be alone, she said to me. I saw nothing in this, no allusion to anything, nothing to nothing, but all the same I said to her, No, I've got to go, I said. I have to work, I've got to sleep, and she said nothing, all she said was, *Adiós,* and she got out of the car, or rather she began the operation of getting herself out of the car and half an hour later, as I was dozing off from a quick nap, I heard her say, from the sidewalk now, putting her other foot on the sidewalk (as she bent threateningly over the little car to pick up her package of shoes, one of the shoes fell out and they weren't woman's shoes, but an old pair of boy's shoes, and she picked them up again), she said to me, You see, I've got a son, not as an excuse, nor as an explanation, but simply as information, she said to me, He's *retardado,* you know, but I love him all the more, she said and then she left.

Ah Fellove they were playing your "Mango Mangüé" on the radio and the music and the speed and the night enveloped us as though they wanted to protect us or vacuum-pack us and she was riding beside me, singing, humming that rhythmic melody of yours I think and she wasn't she, I mean she wasn't La Estrella but Magalena or Irenita or Mirtila I think she was and in any case she wasn't she because I'm quite clear about the difference between a whale and a sardine or a gold fish and possibly it was Irenita because she really was a demoiselle kept in the fish tank of the night. Could her name be Gary Baldi? No, she looks damn selfish and in any case fishes' teeth can be seen sticking out of a little mouth not the great whale's maw of La Estrella which had room for a whole ocean of life, but: what the hell is one stripe more to a tiger? I picked this blond stripe up in Pigal when I was on my way to Las Vegas, late at night or early in the morning, and she was standing alone under the street light outside El Pigal and she shouted at me as I was slamming my brakes on, Stop your chariot, Ben Hurry, and I drew up to the curb and she said, Where you going pretty thing? and I said Las Vegas and she said couldn't I take her a little further, where I said and she said, South of the border, Where? and she said, Across Esquina de Texas, Texas she said not Texas corner and it was this that decided me to let her in, aside from the things I could see now that she was in the car and the street lights hit her enormous boobs bobbing up and down under her blouse, and I said, Is that for real, and she didn't answer, just opened her shirt, because what she was wearing was a man's shirt not a blouse and she unbuttoned it and she let her breasts, no: her tits, no: her udders hang loose: her enormous white round pointed boobs that were sometimes pink sometimes blue sometimes gray, and they began to look forever rosy under the lights of the streets we were passing and I didn't know whether to look to the side or the front and then I started worrying that someone would see us, that the police would stop us, because although it was twelve o'clock or two in the morning there were people everywhere in the street and I crossed Infanta doing sixty and at the seafood stand there were people eating shellfish and there are eyes like flashlights, eyesight tracking at the speed of light and sights more accurate than Marey's gun because I heard people shouting, Melons for the market! and I put my foot down on the accelerator and with my engine going at full throttle crossed Infanta and Carlos Tercero and suddenly the Esquina de Tejas disappeared behind Jesús del Monte and in Aguadulce I took the wrong turn and missed a number 10 bus by perhaps a couple of seconds and we arrived at El Sierra which was where this girl now very coolly buttoning up her shirt in front of the cabaret wanted to go and I say, O.K., Irenita and reach out a hand toward one of the melons which never made it to their market because they still had to be picked and be carried there, and she says to me, My name isn't Irenita, it's Raquelita, but don't call me Raquelita,

call me Manolito el Toro because that's what my friends call me and
that's what I am, a bull! and she removed my hand and got out, I'm
thinking of having myself rechristened. Legally I mean, she said and
started crossing the street toward the entrance of the cabaret where
there was this pinup of a beautiful chick waiting for her and they held
each other's hands and kissed on the mouth and began talking in whispers at the entrance under the neon sign which flashed on and off red
and black and I could see them and I couldn't and I could and I
couldn't and I could and I got fed up and up and out of the car and
crossed the street and joined them and I said, Manolito and she didn't
let me finish my sentence but said, And this one you see here is my gal
Joe, pointing to her friend who looked at me with a very solemn face,
but I said, Delighted to meet you Joe and she smiled and I went on,
Manolito, I said, I'll make it a round trip for the same price and she said
nothing doing and as I didn't want to go back into the Sierra because I
hadn't the slightest desire to meet up with that mulatto Eribó or with El
Beny the singer or with Cué who would begin with their music discus-
sions which belong in the library, all of them talking at once about
music as if it were the race question, arguing in unison that if two black
keys are worth one white, and about mixed bars and all that, then jumping from black keys to black magic and voodoo and *santería* and then
telling stories about ghosts not in haunted houses at midnight but in
front of a radio announcer's mike in the early morning or at midday in a
rehearsal and they talk of that piano in Radioprogreso which has played
by itself since Moisés Simons, the composer of "Peanut Vendor," died
and things like that which would keep me awake at night if I had to go
to bed alone. So I turned around and went back to my car but not
before I had said good-bye to Joe and Manolito, saying, naughty of me,
Good-bye *girls!* and off I went almost at a run.

    I went to Las Vegas and arrived at the coffee stand and met up with
Laserie and said to him, Hi, Rolando, how're things and he said, How're
you, *mulato* and so we began chatting and then I told him I was going
to take some pics of him here one of these nights when he was having a
cup of coffee, because Rolando really looks good, a real singer, a real
Cuban, a real regal *habanero* with his white drill suit, very neat and
dandy from the white tan shoes to the white straw hat, dressed as only
Negroes know how to dress, drinking his coffee very careful making
sure not to spill a drop and stain his spotless suit, with his body tilted
back and his mouth on the rim of the cup and the cup in one hand and
the other hand under it resting on the bar drinking the coffee sip by sip,

and I said good-bye to Rolando, See you soon, I said and he said, Whenever you feel up to it, *mulato,* and I'm just about to go into the club when you'll never guess whom I see in the door. None other than Alex Bayer who comes up to me and shakes my hand and says, I've been expecting you, in that very fine very educated very polished accent of his and I say, Who, me, and he says, Yes, you, and I say, Do you want me to take some shots of you and he says, No, I want to talk with you, and I say, Whenever you want, but isn't it a bit late now thinking he might or might not be trying to pick a fight, you never know with these people, like when José Mujica was in Havana he was walking along the Prado with an actress on each arm or a couple of singers or just two girls, and a fellow who was sitting on a bench shouted at them, Hi girls, and Mujica, very serious, very much the Mexican movie star, in pitch, as though he had been singing, went over to the bench and asked the fellow, 'Xcuse me, what did you say and he said, What you heard, miss, and Mujica, who was a really big man (or is, if he's still alive, though people tend to shrink as they get older) picked him up and held him over his head and threw him down on the street, not on the street but onto the grass borders between the Prado and the street, and went on his way as naturally and easily and unrivaled as though he were singing "Perfidia," Mexican accent and all, and I don't know if Alex was thinking what I was thinking or was thinking what Mujica was thinking or if he was thinking what he himself was thinking, all I know is that he laughed, he smiled and said, Let's go and I said, Let's sit at the bar and he shook his head, No, what I have to talk to you about it's better that I say it outside and I said, Better still, let's sit in my car then and he said, No, let's take a walk and I said, All right and we went off down along P Street and as we were walking he said, Night is made for walking in Havana, isn't it, and I nodded and then said, Yes, if it's cool, Yes, he said, if it's cool it's nice for walking. I do it very often, it's the best tonic there is for body and soul, and I felt like shitting on his soul thinking that all this faggot wanted to do was to walk around with me and pretend he was a philosopher. Peripathetic.

As we were walking along we saw the Cripple with the Gardenias coming out of the dark opposite, with his crutch and his tray of gardenias and his good evening said so politely and with such courtesy it seemed almost impossible he could be so sincere and crossing another street I heard the harsh, nasal and relentless voice of Juan Charrasqueado the Sing-Singing Charro singing the single verse of the lottery which he always sings and repeats a thousand times, Buy your number and buy your number and buy your number and buy your number and buy, meaning they should throw money into his sweaty sombrero as he forcibly passed it around, creating an atmosphere of mock obsession which is poignant because everyone knows he's incurably mad. I read the sign above the Restaurant Humboldt Club and thought of La Estrella who always ate there and I wondered what the illustrious baron who had discovered Cuba would say if he knew he is best remembered here as the name of a cheap restaurant, a dingy bar and a street famous for an infamous political massacre and also for a notorious brothel specializing in living pictures, featuring Superman! and Fernando's Hideaway and Bar San Juan and Club Tikoa and The Fox and the Crow and the Eden Rock where one night a black woman made the mistake of going down the flight of stairs to the door, in there to eat, and they threw her out with an excuse that was an exclusion and she began to shout LitelrocLitelrocLitelroc because Faubus was in the news and she started a great uproar down there, and La Gruta where all the eyes are phosphorescent because the creatures who inhabit this bar and club and bedroom are fish from the lower depths and Pigalle or Pigale or Pigal, it's called all these ways, and the Wakamba Self-Service and Marakas with its menu in English and its bilingual menu outside and its neon Chinese sign to confuse Confucius, and the Cibeles and the Colmao and the Hotel Flamingo and the Flamingo Club and on passing down N Street and 25th I saw under the lamppost outside in the street four old men playing dominoes in shirtsleeves and I smiled and even laughed and Alex asks me what I'm laughing about and I say, Oh nothing and he says I know he says. Do you? I asked and he says yes he says, At the poetry of this group portrait and I think, Fuck, an aesthete. But what I tell him is that he hasn't told me what he wanted to tell me and he says he doesn't know how to begin and I say that's very easy, begin at the beginning or at the end and he says, Easy for you because you're a journalist and I say, I'm not a journalist, I'm a photographer, Albeit a press photographer, he says and I say, Hélas yes I am and he says, Well, I'll begin in the middle and I say, Fine and he says, I take it you don't really know La Estrella and you go about telling lies about her and about us. Never mind that, I know what the truth is and I'm going to tell you, and I am not offended or anything and I see that he isn't offended or anything, so I say, Fine, shoot.

You are being *so* unfair! Alex said and I was about to protest when he said, No, let me speak and afterward you'll know that you really are being unfair, and I let him talk, I let him go on talking in that voice which was so rounded, so beautiful, so well-manicured, which pronounced all the *s*'s and all the *d*'s and in which all the *r*'s were *r*'s and I began to understand as he was talking just why he was so famous as an actor on the radio and why he got thousands of letters from women every week and I understood why he rejected their proposals and I also understood why he took such pleasure in making conversation, in telling stories, in talking: he was a Narcissus-cum-Echo who let his & her words fall into the pool of conversation and then listened to himself rapturously in the ripples of sound she made. Was it his voice that made him a faggot? Or the reverse? Or is it that in every actor there's an actress struggling to get out? Oh, well, asking questions is not my line.

What you are saying is not exactly true, he said. We, he said (and that *we* was all he conceded on his beautiful arrangement), we are not Estrella's masters, *La* Estrella as you call her. In actual fact we are more like Polyphemus's sheep. (A beauty, ain't it? But you'd have to hear him say it to get the full flavor.) She does what she likes in *our* house. She's not a servant or anything like that, but an uninvited guest: she arrived one day six months ago because we invited her one night when we heard her sing in the Bar Celeste: *I* invited her but just to have a drink with us. She overstayed, then she stayed over to sleep and she slept all day and when night fell she went away without saying a word. But the following morning she was knocking at the door. She went directly upstairs and lay down in the room we had given her the night before, my painting studio which, incidentally, I *traded* with her for the servant's room on the roof after *she* gave notice to *our* servant, who, poor soul, had been with us for years and years, taking advantage of the fact that we were away on holiday. Instead, she brought a cook into the house, a little Negro boy who obeyed her in everything and whom she went out with every night. Do you see what I mean? He used to carry her *neceser* for her, which at that time might be an old commando handbag or even a shopping bag with the label of El Encanto store still on. Then they would do the town at night and return in the wee hours of the morn. That was until we dismissed him. This happened, of course, much later. A week after that night she spent here as our guest she told us the story of her invalid son and taking advantage of the fact that we felt sorry for her—only for half a mo', let me tell you—she asked us if we could take her into our house, though as it was she could hardly ask us to allow her to stay, as she had already been staying with us a week. We *took* her in, as she called it, and after a few days she asked us if she could borrow a key. "So as not to disturb you," she told us. She gave it back the following day, it's true, but she didn't disturb us anymore, because she didn't knock on the door anymore. You know why? Because she had surreptitiously had another key made, her own of course.

I take it you were moved by the story of her idiot son, as we were. Well, I'm telling you, that's not true either: there is no son nor moron nor monster. It's her husband who has a daughter, a girl about twelve and perfectly normal. He had to send her to the country because she made life impossible for her. She is married, there's no doubt about it, to this man who owns a hotdog stand on the beach at Marianao. He's a poor man whom she blackmails and when she visits him in his shop it's to rob him of hot dogs, eggs, soft or hard-boiled, stuffed potatoes, the lot, which she eats in her room. I should mention by the way that she eats enough food for an army and that *we* have to buy all this food—and she's still hungry afterward. That's why she's so huge! She's as big as a hippo and like a hippo she's also amphibian. She takes a bath three times a day: when she arrives in the morning, in the afternoon when she wakes up to have her breakfast and in the evening before she goes out. To no avail, mind you, because you wouldn't *believe* how she sweats! She drips water as if she were in a permanent state of high fever. So she spends her life in the water: sweating and drinking water and taking baths. And she's always singing: she sings when she's getting ready to go out. She never stops singing! In the morning, when she comes in, we know she's arrived before she starts singing, because she holds onto the railings to climb the steps and you know what they're like, those marble steps and wrought-iron balusters of old Havana. So she climbs the stairs and as she climbs them she clings to the banister and the whole balustrade trembles and resounds right through the house and when the iron is loudly ringing against the marble she starts singing. We have had a thousand and one problems with the neighbors below, but nobody can say anything to her because she doesn't listen to reason. "They're jealous," she says, "real jealous. You'll see how they'll worship me when I'm famous." Because she has this obsession about being famous: and we too are obsessed with her becoming famous: we're crazy for her to become famous so she'll finally take her music or rather her voice—because she insists that you don't need musical backing to sing and that she carries her own accompanist inside her—her voice, then, someplace else.

When she's not singing she's snoring and when she's not snoring she floods the house with her perfume—Cologne 1800, can you imagine! although *I* shouldn't be talking *so* badly about my number-one backer— she sprays it all over, she showers herself with it and she's such a huge woman! Besides, she sprays herself with talcum like she sprays herself with perfume. That, plus the way she pours water all over herself and the way she eats, my dear, it's not human, believe you me, it's not human. Believe me! *Croyez-moi! Créeme!* (And this is one of the few Cubans who pronounce the second *e* of the verb *creer*.) Talcum for heaven's sake! Have you seen the folds of flesh, of fat on her neck? Then take a look next time and you'll see that in every crease there is a crust of talcum. To top it off—listen to this, I beg you—she's obsessed with the imperfections of her body and she spends the whole day pouring scents and perfumes and deodorants over herself and plucking out hairs from her eyebrows down to her feet. I swear I'm not exaggerating. One day we returned home unexpectedly and we found her walking up and down naked in her birthday suit all over the house and, alas, we got a very good view of her! Nothing but rollers of human flesh and not a *single* hair on her whole body. Believe me, this Estrella of yours is one of nature's true freaks! More than that, she's a cosmic case. Her one weakness, the only human thing about her, is her feet, not their shape, but because they hurt her, yes, she's flatfooted, and how she complains. It's the only thing she complains about. There are times when her feet really hurt. She just puts them palms up, legs perched high on any chair, and she lies on the floor complaining, complaining, complaining. Almost to the point when you begin to begin to feel sorry, almost pity for her, but that's when she gets up and starts shouting up and down the house, shouting at the poor neighbors, "But Ise gonna be famous! Ise gonna be famous! *Famous*, you fuckers!" You know who her enemies are aside from the invisible neighbors? (A) Old men, because she's only interested in young men and she falls in love with adolescent boys like a bitch in heat. (B) The impresarios who'll exploit her when she's famous. (C) People who will call her a nigger or allude to her black color behind her back. (D) *Dose* who'll make signs in front of her that she won't understand or who'll laugh without saying what they're laughing at or who'll use some private code or other which she'll have no means of deciphering. But the biggest unseen enemy is death. She's frightened to death that she'll die before she is, as she says, discovered. I know what you're going to say before you'll agree with me: that she's pathetic. Yes, she's pathetic, but, my dear, it's one thing being pathetic in a tragedy, and another being pathetic in a comedy. The latter is simply intolerable.

Have I forgotten anything? Oh, yes, to tell you that I prefer freedom to justice. You don't have to believe the truth. Go on being unfair to us. Love *La* Estrella. But, *please,* help her to be famous, see that she makes it big, rescue us from her. We will adore her like a saint, mystically. That is to say, in the ecstasy of her memory.

What do you want? I felt like Barnum and followed Alex Bayer's crooked schemes. It occurred to me that La Estrella had yet to be discovered, a verb invented for Eribó and all those Cuban Curies who spend their lives discovering the properties of radio, television and the silver screen. I told myself that the gold of her voice had to be separated from the muck in which Nature or Providence or whatever it was had enveloped her, that this diamond had to be extracted from the mountain of shit it had been buried in and what I did was to lay on a party, a *motivito* as Rine Leal would say, and it was to Rine that I went to make out as many invitations as possible. As for the rest, I would invite them myself. The rest included Eribó and Silvestre and Bustrófedon and Arsenio Cué and the Emcee who eats shit but I have to invite him because he's the compère at the Tropicana and Eribó would bring Piloto & Vera and Franemilio, who would enjoy the occasion more than anyone because he's a pianist who's very sensitive and besides he's blind, and Rine would bring Juan Blanco who's not a compère but a composer without a sense of humor (this music, not John White alias Johannes Witte or Giovanni Bianco: he's the composer of what Silvestre and Arsenio and Eribó, days when he's a reluctant mulatto, call *serious* music) and I even almost invited Alejo Carpentier and the only person we wouldn't have would be an impresario, because Vítor Perla wouldn't come on my account and Arsenio Cué would refuse even to speak to anyone in broadcasting and there the matter rested. But I could rely on publicity.

I gave the party or whatever it was in my house, in that single large room I had which Rine insisted on calling a studio and people began arriving early and others came who hadn't even been invited, like Gianni Boutade (or whatever his name is) who was French or Italian or from Monaco or all three of them at once and who was the king of *manteca* not because he was an importer of edible fats but because he was the biggest pusher of marijuana in the world and it was he who tried to apostle for Silvestre one night and he took Silvestre to hear La Estrella at Las Vegas some time later when she had become famous everywhere, and who really thought he was her impresario, and with him came

Marta Rayo and Ingrid Bergamo and Edith Cavello who I think were
the only women who came that evening because I was very careful that
neither Irenita or Magalena or Manolito el Toro née Gary Baldi or any
other creature from the black lagoon should turn up, whether they were
centauras (the *centaura* is half woman and half horse and is a mythical
beast from the Zoolympus of Havana-by-night and which I cannot or
won't describe now) or not or anyone like Lupa Féliz the well-known
composer of boleros, who is all horse, and Jesse Fernández came, a
Cuban photographer who worked for *Life en Español* and was doing a
story on Havana a city open day and night. The only person lacking was
La Estrella.

I loaded the cameras (my own) and told Jesse he could use any of
them and he chose a Hasselblad I had bought recently and said he
wanted to try it out that night and we started comparing the Rollei and
the Hassel and went on to talk about the Nikon as compared with the
Leica and then we got onto exposure times and Varigam paper which
was new in Cuba at that time and all those things photographers talk
about and which are the same as long and short skirts and the cut of
clothes for women and averages as ranking order for pelota fans and
sharps and flats plus pauses and demisemiquavers for Marta and Piloto
and Franemilio and Eribó and liver and mushrooms (that is, the nonedi-
ble ones: cirrhotic livers, athlete's foot) for Silvestre and Rine: themes
for the Boredom Variations, bullets of bullshit to kill time with, talking
about today what you can think about tomorrow and *Todo es posponer,* a
brilliant epigram Cué had stolen from somewhere or other. Rine meanwhile was pouring the drinks and passing the olives and hors d'oeuvres
around. And we were talking and talking and an owl flew past my balcony hooting and Edith Cavello hooted back *Solavaya!* which is an antidote for the bad luck hooting owls always bring when not hooted back
at. Then I remembered I had told La Estrella we were going to give the
party at eight so that she should turn up at least around half past nine. I
looked at my watch and it was ten past ten. I went to the kitchen and
said I was going out to buy some ice and Rine looked surprised because
he knew there was plenty of ice in the bathtub and I went down to
search all the seven seas of the night for this mermaid reincarnated as a
sea cow, for a Godzilla that sings when the water is running, for my Nat
King Kong.

I searched for her in the Bar Celeste, among the tables of people
eating, in Fernando's Hideaway like a blind man without his white cane
(because it would have been useless, because not even a white cane

could be seen in there), like a real blind man when I came out to the glare of the street on the corner of Humboldt and P, in the Café MiTío with its open terrace where all the drinks are fume-flavored, in the Las Vegas trying to avoid meeting Irenita or any of her species and in the Humboldt bar, and I went to Infanta and San Lazaro really fed up and didn't find her there either but when I returned, I passed the Celeste again and there she was at the back of the room absolutely drunk and alone and carrying on an animated conversation with the wall. She must have forgotten the whole thing because she was dressed as usual, wearing her habit of the Discalced Carmelites but when I appeared at her side she said, How's things Doll Face, come over and join the cause, and she smiled from ear to ear. I looked at her. She was being rude, of course, but she disarmed me by what she said next. I wasn't brave enough, she said, I didn't have the courage: you are too refined and well-bred and respectable for me. I'm just a poor nigger, she said, ordering another drink and gulping down the one she had, the glass a thimble in her hand. I made a sign to the waiter to forget it and sat down. She smiled at me again and began humming something I couldn't understand, but it wasn't a song. Come on, I said, let's go. No, no, she said, making it rhyme with yo-yo. Come on, I said, nobody's going to eat you. Me, she asked—it wasn't a question—eat me. Look, she said, raising her head, before any of you so much as touches one curl of my woolly-wig, I'll swallow you whole, she said, tugging hard on her hair dramatically or comically. Come on, I said, the whole of the western world's waiting for you at my house. Waiting for what, she said. Waiting for you to come and sing so they can hear you. Me, she asked, hear me, she asked, and they're in your house, they're in your house, right now, she asked, all I have to do then is to stay right here, because you live next door, don't you, and she began to get up, in the doorway and I'll start singing at the top of my voice and they'll hear me, she said, no, it won't work, and she fell back in her chair which didn't complain because it was no use to any chair, habituated and resigned as they are to being chairs. Yes, I said, it will work, but only if you come to my house because that's where it's all at, and I put on my confidential manner, there's an impresario there and all, and then she raised her head or rather she didn't raise her head, she tilted it on one side and raised one of the thin stripes she had painted over her eyes and looked at me and I swear by John Huston that this was how Movy Dick looked at Gregory Ahab. Had I succeeded in harpooning her?

I swear by my mother and by Daguerre that I thought of loading her

onto the freight elevator, but since that's the one the servants use and I
knew La Estrella didn't want to be hauled up like a piece of freight or
taken for a servant, the two of us took the little elevator facing us which
thought twice about going up with its strange cargo, and then ascended
the eight floors creaking painfully. We heard music from the corridor
and found the door open and the first thing La Estrella heard was the
sound of "Cienfuegos," that Montuno tune, and there was Eribó standing in the middle of a group of people endlessly explaining its *montuno*
or off-beat choruses and Cué with his cigarette-cumholder in his mouth
walking up and down, approving everything, and Franemilio standing
near the door with his hands behind his back, leaning against the wall
the way blind people do: knowing more by the tips of their fingers
where they are than other people do with their eyes and ears, and La
Estrella reacted badly on seeing him and shouted her vintage words
pickled in alcohol in my face, Shit, you motherfucker youse been conning me, and I didn't know what she meant and asked her why and she
said, Because Fran's here and I know he's come to play the piano and
Ise not singing with an accompanist, listen here, Ise not singing, and
Franemilio heard her and before I could think let alone say anything, he
said, Are you completely off your head? Me with a piano in the house!
he said in his soft voice. Come on, Estrella, come on in because here
it's you who brings the music, and she smiled and I called for attention
everybody and asked them to turn off the record player because La
Estrella was here and everybody applauded. See what I mean? I told
her, see what I mean? but she wasn't listening to me and was already
about to burst into song when Bustrófedon came out of the kitchen carrying a tray of drinks and Edith Cavello behind him with another and
La Estrella took a drink as she was passing and said to me, What's she
doing here? and Edith heard her and turned around and said, Listen
you, it's not me who shouldn't be here. I'm not a freak like you, and La
Estrella with the same movement she had made taking the glass threw
the drink in Franemilio's face because Edith Cavello for whom the
pitch was meant had ducked her head quickly but as she stepped aside
she stumbled and tried to cling onto Bustrófedon and grabbed his shirt
and he also tripped over, but since he has a great sense of balance and
Edith Cavello has a degree in gymnastics neither of them fell over and
Bustro made a gesture like a trapeze artiste who has just completed a
double somersault without a net and everybody except La Estrella,
Franemilio and I applauded. La Estrella because she was apologizing to
Franemilio and wiping his face with her skirt, which she had lifted

exposing her enormous purple thighs to the warm air of the evening and Franemilio because he couldn't see a thing and I because I was closing the door and asking everybody to turn it down to a dull roar please it was almost twelve and we didn't have permission for the party and the cops would be here any minute. They all shut up. Except La Estrella, who when she had finished apologizing to Franemilio turned to me and asked me, So where's the impresario? and Franemilio without giving me time to make anything up said, He didn't show, because Vítor didn't come and Cué is involved in some private feud with the television people. La Estrella gave me a real mean look, narrowing her eyes till they were as thin as her eyebrows, and said, So youse been conning me after all, and she didn't give me a chance to swear to her by all my fathers and old artificers as far back as Niepce that I didn't know nobody had come, I mean no impresario, and she said, Then you can go fuck yourself, I'm not singing, and she stomped off to the kitchen to pour herself a drink.

I think the feeling was mutual and La Estrella and my guests as well resolved to forget they lived on the same planet, because she stayed all the time in the kitchen eating and drinking and making a lot of noise and Bustrófedon back in the main room inventing tongue twisters and one of the ones I heard was the one of the *tres tristes tigres en un trigal* and the record player was playing "Santa Isabel de las Lajas," sung by Beny Moré, and Eribó was keeping time, beating on my dinner table and on one side of the record player and explaining to Ingrid Bergamo and Edith Cavello that rhythm was a natural thing, like breathing, he said, everybody has rhythm just like everybody in the world has sex and you know there are people who are impotent, men who are impotent, he said, same as there are women who are frigid and nobody denies the existence of sex because of this, he said, nobody can deny the existence of rhythm, what happens is that rhythm is a natural thing like sex, and there are people who are inhibited, he said—that was the word he used—who can't play an instrument or dance or sing in tune while there are other people who don't have this problem and can dance and sing and even play several percussion instruments at once, he said, and it's the same as with sex, impotence and frigidity are unknown among primitive people because they're not embarrassed by sex, nor are they embarrassed, he said, by rhythm and this is why in Africa they have as much sense of rhythm as of sex and, he said, I maintain, he said, that if you give a person a special drug which is not marijuana or anything like that, he said, a drug like mescalin, he said and he repeated the word so everybody should know he knew what he was talking about, or LYSERGIC ACID, and he was shouting now above the music, he will be able to play any percussion instrument, better or worse, the same as someone who is drunk can dance either better or worse. So long as he manages to stay on his feet, I thought and I told myself that that was a whole load of shit and I was thinking this word shit, it was at the exact moment I was thinking this word shit that La Estrella emerged from the kitchen and said, Shit, Beny Moré, you're singing shit, and she entered with *two* glasses in her hands, drinking left and right as she walked and she came to where I was standing and as everybody was listening to music, or talking or making conversation, and Rine was standing on the balcony getting miserable, playing those games of love that are called *el mate* in Havana, she sat down on the floor and leaned against the sofa and as she drank she rolled about on the floor and then she stretched herself out flat with the empty glass in her hand and lay down along one side of the couch which wasn't a modern one but one of those antique Cuban sofas, made of wicker and wood and woven straw or *pajilla* and she got right under it and stayed there sleeping and I could hear her snoring underneath me sounding like the sighs of a sperm whale and Bustrófedon who couldn't or didn't see La Estrella said to me, Nadar, *mon vieux,* are you blowing up one of your balloons? meaning (I knew him too well) that I was farting and I remembered Dali said once that farts are the body's way of sighing and I almost started laughing because it occurred to me that sighing is the soul's way of farting and snoring is the sighs and farts of dreaming. But La Estrella went on snoring without anything like this to bother her at all. Suddenly I realized that tonight's fiasco was mine and only mine, so I got up and went to the kitchen to pour a drink which I tossed down silently and I went silently to the door and left.

I don't remember how long I spent walking the streets nor where I was because I was everywhere at once and as I was returning home at two o'clock and was passing in front of the Fox and the Crow I saw a man and two girls come out and one of the girls was freckled and had big tits and the other was Magalena, and she greeted me and introduced me to her girl friend and boyfriend, a foreigner with dark glasses, who told me straight off that I looked like an interesting person and Magalena said, He's a photographer, and the fellow said with an exclamation that sounded like a belch, Agh, so you're a photographer, come along with us, and I wondered what he would have said if Magalena had told him I worked in a market: Agh, so you're a porter, a proletarian, how interesting, come with us and have a drink, and the fellow asked me what my name was and I said Moholy-Nagy and he said, Agh, Hungarian? And I said, Agh no, Vulgarian, and Magalena was dying of laughter, but I went along all the same and she walked in front with the woman, the wife she was of the man who was walking beside me, a Cuban Jew she was and he was Greek, a Greek Jew, who spoke with an accent which I didn't know where the fuck it came from, and I think he was explaining to me the metaphysics of photography, saying it was all a game of light and shadow, that it was so moving to see how the salts of silver (My God, the salts of silver: the man was a contemporary of Emile Zola!), that is to say the essence of money, could make men immortal, that it was one of the paltry (why not saltry) weapons that being had in its wars against nothingness, and I was thinking that I had the luck of the iris to be always meeting these well-stuffed metaphysicians, who ate the shit of transcendence as though it were manna from heaven, but we've just arrived at Pigal and are about to go in when Raquelita, sorry, Manolito el Toro runs into us and goes and kisses Magalena on the cheek and says, How're you, pal, and Magalena greets her like an old friend and this philosopher who's standing beside me says, She's very interesting, your lady friend, seeing her clasping my hand and saying, And how're you, you old Russian mulatto, and I tell the Greek by way of introduction and correction at the same time, My friend Señor el Toro, Manolito, a friend of mine, and the Greek says, That's even more interesting, meaning he had begun to know what I already knew, and as Manolito's leaving, I say, And how about you, Plato, so you like *efebos?* and he says, What's that you said? and I say, So you like young boys like Manolito, and he says, Young boys like her? I sure do! and we sit down to listen to Rolando Aguiló and his combo and soon the Greek is saying to me, Why don't you ask my wife for a dance? and I tell him I don't dance and he says, It's not possible, a Cuban who doesn't dance? and Magalena says, There's two of them because I can't dance either, and I tell her: A Cuban man and a Cuban woman, you mean, and Magalena starts humming "Fly Me to the Moon" which is what the band is playing but she stresses the word fly on every beat. Then she gets up, Excuse me, she says, emphasizing her s's which is the attractive mannerism of some mulatto women of Havana, and the Greek Jew's wife, this Helen who launched a thousand ships in the Dead Sea, asks her, Where are you off to? and Maga answers, Just the Ladies', and the other woman said, I'm going too, and the Greek, who's a modern Menelaus who couldn't care less about being betrayed by an odd Paris or two, gets up and when they've left he sits down again and looks at me and smiles. Then I understand. Fuck me, I tell myself, this is the island of Lesbos! And when they return from the "Ladies'," this combination of two tones of the same color, these two women whom Antonioni would call Le Amiche and Romero de Torres would paint with his broadest brush and Hemingway would describe just a little bit more subtly, when they sit down I say, 'Xcuse me but I'm leaving, because I've got to get up early, and Magalena says, *Ay*, but you're going much too soon! and I follow the thread of her song and say, Part of you I take with me, and she laughs and the Greek gets up and shakes my hand and says It's been a pleasure meeting you, and I say the pleasure's all mine, then I take the hand of this biblical high priestess for whom I would never be a Solomon or even a David and I say, *Encantado* and I'm off. Magalena catches up with me at the door and says, Are you really going? and I say, Why do you ask? and she says, I don't know, but you're going so early and so suddenly, and makes a gesture which would have been charming if she hadn't made it so often and I say, Don't bother, I'm quite all right: sadder but wiser, and she smiles and makes the same gesture again, *Adiós amor,* I say, and she says, *Ciao,* and goes back to her table.

I think of going back home and wonder if there would be anyone still there and when I'm passing the Hotel Saint John I can't resist the temptation not of the *tragamíqueles,* the coin-slot machines, the one-armed *bandidos* in the lobby which I would never put a dime in because I wouldn't ever get one out, but of the other Helen, of Elena Burke who sings in the bar, and I sit at the bar to hear her sing and stay on after she's finished because there's a jazz quintet from Miami, cool but good with a saxophonist who looks like the son of Van Heflin's father and Gerry Mulligan's mother and I settle down to listening to them play "Tonight at Noon" and to drinking and concentrating on nothing more than the sounds and I like sitting there at Elena's table and ordering her a drink and telling her how much I dislike unaccompanied singers and how much I like her, not just her voice but also her accompaniment, and when I think that it's Frank Domínguez who's at the piano I don't say a thing because this is an island of double and triple entendres told by a drunk idiot signifying everything, and I go on listening to "Straight No Chaser" which could very well be the title of how one should take life if it wasn't so obvious that that's how it is, and at that moment the manager of the hotel is having an argument with someone who just a

few moments ago was gambling and losing consistently and to top it off
the guy is drunk and pulls out a gun pointing it at the head of the manager who doesn't even wince and before he could say bouncer two enormous fellows appear and tackle the drunk and grab his gun and give
him two punches and flatten him against the wall and the manager
takes the bullets out and slides back the bolt and returns the empty gun
to the drunk who still doesn't know what's hit him and tells them to
frisk him and they shove him to the door and shove him out and he
must be some big shot as they haven't made mincemeat of him yet and
Elena and the people from the bar turn up (the music has stopped) and
she asks me what's happened and I'm just going to tell her I don't know
when the manager waves them back saying *Aquí no ha pasado nada* and
then with a flick of his hand orders the jazz-men back to their music,
something the quintet more asleep than awake do like a five-man
pianola.

I'm already on the point of leaving when there's another uproar in
the entrance and it's Colonel Ventura arriving, as he does every night, to
eat at the Sky Club and listen to poetess Minerva Eros, the alleged mistress of this assassin in uniform, she who bleats happily (for her and
myself) in the roof garden, and after greeting the manager Ventura goes
into the elevator followed by four gunmen, while another ten or twelve
remain scattered around the lobby, and as I'm sure I'm not dreaming
and add up all the disagreeable things that have happened to me
tonight and see that they were three in a row, I decide it's just the right
moment to try my luck at the crooked slot machines and I pull out of
my pocket, which feels more like a maze, a coin that doesn't have a
minotaur engraved on it because it's a genuine Cuban real not an
American nickel and I put it in and pull the handle, the single arm of
the Goddess of Fortune, and then put my other hand like an inverted
horn of plenty in the chute to catch the silver rush to come. The wheels
spin around and an orange comes up first, then a lemon and a little
later some strawberries. The machine makes foreboding rumbling, stops
finally and comes to rest in a silence that my presence renders eternal.

My door is locked. It must have been Rine who locked it, loyal as
ever. I open the door and I don't see the friendly chaos that supplanted
the alien order imposed by the cleaning woman just this morning, I
don't see it because I don't want to, because there are more important
things in life than disorder, because stretched out on the white covers
of my sofa-bed, yes sir, no longer a sofa but entirely a bed, on those
spotless Saturday sheets, I see the enormous, cetacean, chocolate-col-

ored stain, stretched out like a hideous blot, and it is of course, you've guessed it: Estrella Rodríguez, this star of the first magnitude who dwarfs the white heaven of my bed with her expanding black sun's appearance: La Estrella is sleeping, snoring, slobbering, sweating and making weird noises on my bed. I accept it all with the humble philosophy of the defeated and take off my coat and tie and shirt. I go to the refrigerator and take out a pint of cold milk, and pour myself a glass and the glass smells of rum not milk, though its contents probably taste of milk. I drink another glass. I put the half bottle back in the refrigerator and throw the glass into the sink, where it sinks in a sea of glasses. For the first time that night I feel how suffocatingly hot it is: it must have been like this all day. I take off my undershirt and trousers and remain there in my underpants which are short, and I take off my shoes and socks and feel the floor which is almost hot, but cooler than the city and the night. I go to the bathroom and wash my face and mouth and see there's a great pool of water under the shower, a mere memory of the ice it had once been, and I dip my feet in it and it's only moderately cool. I go back to the only room in this idiot pad that Rine Loyal calls a studio apartment and look for somewhere to sleep: the sofa, the one of wicker and wood, is very hard and the floor is soaking, dirty and littered with cigarette butts and if this was a film and not real life, this film in which people really die, I would go to the bath and there wouldn't be an inch of water in the bathtub, it would be a clean well-whitened place where I could sleep comfortably, the greatest enemy of promiscuity, and I would wrap myself in the blankets I don't have and sleep the sleep of the just and chaste, like an underdeveloped Rock Hudson (surely underdeveloped for lack of exposure) and the following morning La Estrella would be Doris Day singing without a band but with music by Bakaleinikoff, which has the extraordinary ability to remain invisible while sonorous. (Fuck Natalie Kalmus: I'm beginning to talk like Silvestre!) But when I return to reality it is dawn and this monster is in my bed and I'm exhausted and I do just what you, Orval Faubus, and anybody else in the world would do. I get into *my* bed. Onto an edge.

I dreamed I was an old man who'd gone out on a skiff into the Gulf Stream of the night and had gone 68 days now without catching any fish, not even a damselfish or a sardine. Silvestre had been with me for the first 66 days. After 67 days without a single fish Bustrófedon and Eribó and Arsenio Cué had told Silvestre that I was now definitely and finally *salao,* which is the worst form of salty. But on day number 69 (which is a lucky number in Havana-by-night: Bustrófedon says that it's because it's a *capicúa*, that's Cuban for a palindrome number, Arsenio Cué for a thing or two he knows about it and Rine for other reasons: it's the number of his house) on day or rather on night number 69 I was really at sea and all alone, when through the deep blue, violet, ultraviolet waters a phosphorescent fish came swimming. It was very large and bosomy and it looked like Cuba and then it became small and toothy and it was Irenita and then it got dark, blackish, pitch black and lissome and it was Magalena and when it bit my line and I caught it, it began to grow and grow and grow and it fought the line as it grew and it was as big as the boat now and it stayed there floating with strange sounds coming from its liver-lipped mouth, purring, groaning beside the boat, gaping, palpitating, making funny noises, noises more weird than funny like somebody choking as he swallows, and then the big fish was quite still, and then predatory fish began to arrive, sharks and barracudas and piranhas, all of them with faces I could recognize, in fact one of them looked very much like Gianni Boutade and another like the Emcee and it had a star on its mouth and yet another fish was Vítor Perla and I knew it was him because it had a throat like a tie made of blood and a pearl pinned on it, and I pulled the line quickly and fastened it to the side and, funny thing, I started talking to it, to the fish, Big fish, I said, fish that you are, fish, Nobel fish, I have lampooned you, harpooned I mean, it's true I caught you but I'm not going to let them eat you, and I began to haul it into the boat in a slow frenzy and I managed to get its tail into the boat and it was a radiant white now, the fish tail only, the rest of it being jet black, and suddenly I began to struggle with its soft, sticky, gelatin-flanks, gelatin because that side of it wasn't a fish but a jellyfish, an *aguamala,* but all the same I kept on pulling and suddenly I lost my balance and fell back into the boat, still pulling at its jelly side and the whole whale of a fish fell on top of me and the boat was too small for both of us and it, the fish not the boat, gave me no room to breathe and I was suffocating because its gills had landed on my face and over my mouth and nostrils and as this fish was all blubber it was spreading over me, smothering me as it sucked in my air, all the air, not only the air for breathing, the air outside but the already breathed air, the air *inside* as well, the air from my nostrils and from my mouth and from my lungs, and it left me with no air to breathe and I was suffocating badly, choking, asphyxiated. I was about to drown or choke when I woke up.

I stopped fighting the noble fish that was in my dream to begin

another struggle, kicking and wrestling with a villainous sperm whale in
real life which was lying on top of me and *kissing* me with its immense
lunglike lips, kissing me all over my face, kissing my eyes and nose and
mouth and who was now chewing my ear and biting my neck and sucking my breast and La Estrella kept sliding off my body and climbing
back onto it again making unbelievably weird noises, as if she were
singing and snoring at the same time and in between her groans she
was speaking to me, whispering, gasping in her rasping baritone *mi
amor* please kiss me *mi negro* please kill me *mi chino* come come come,
things which would have made me die laughing if I'd been able to
breathe and I pushed her with what strength I had left, using a half-
crushed leg as a fulcrum and making a springboard not of the bed but
of the wall (because I'd been driven back against the wall by that expan-
sion wave of fat, flattened, almost obliterated by that black universe
that was expanding in my direction at the speed of love), I managed to
give her a final big push and succeeded in putting her off balance and
out of bed, *my* bed. She fell on the floor and there she stayed puffing
and panting and sobbing but I leaped out of bed and switched on the
light and then I *saw* her. She was stark naked and her breasts were as
fat as her arms and twice as large as my head, and one of them fell over
on one side and touched the floor and the other jutted out over the central breaker of the three great rollers that separated her legs from what
would have been her neck if she had had one and the first roller above
her thighs was a sort of canopied extension of her mons veneris and I
could see how right Alex Bayer was when he said that "she depilated
herself completely" because there wasn't a single trace of hair, pubic or
otherwise, on her whole body and that couldn't have been natural, but
then nothing was natural about La Estrella. It was then that I began to
wonder whether she came from outer space.

If the dreams of reason beget monsters, what do the dreams of unrea-
son beget? I dreamed (because I had fallen asleep again: sleep can be as
stubborn as insomnia) that UFOs were invading the earth, not as Oscar
Hurtado threatened in ships that touched down noiselessly on the
rooftops or like Arsenio Cué's creatures quote hurld headlong flaming
from th'Ethereal Skie/ with hideous ruin and combustion down unquote
or as Silvestre feared infiltrating our lives in the form of microbes repro-
ducing silently, but with definitely Martian shapes, creatures with suck-
ers that could create total suction, as Rine would say, and adhere to
walls made of air and then descend or ascend invisible steps and with
majestic footfall could spread terror like an overflow of their black, bril-

liant, silent presences. In another dream or perhaps another form of the
same dream these alien beings were sound waves which mingled with us
and haunted us and enchanted us, like unseen sirens: from every corner
a music gushed out that made men stupid, a paralysing song ray which
nobody could resist and nobody could in fact do anything to fight this
invasion from outer space because nobody knew that music could be the
secret and final weapon, so nobody was going to stop his ears with wax
or even with his fingers and at the end of that dream I was the only man
on earth who could realize what was actually happening and I tried to lift
my hands to my ears and I couldn't because my hands were tied and
even my neck and shoulders were tied to the ground by some invisible
menders and it happened that I must have fallen off the bed because I
woke in a pool of sweat on the floor. I remembered then that I'd dragged
myself right across the floor to the opposite end of the room and had
gone to sleep right there near the door. Did I wake up with a motorman's
glove in my mouth? I can't tell but I can tell that I had a taste of bile on
my lips, and was terribly thirsty, and I didn't even drink so much as a cup
of coffee because I felt like vomiting, but I thought twice before getting
up. I wasn't at all keen to see La Estrella whether she was freak or foe,
sleeping in my bed, snoring with her mouth open and half-closed eyes,
rolling from side to side: nobody ever wants to meet the nightmare of the
night before when he wakes up. So I began to work out how I could get
to the bathroom to wash and return to look for my clothes and put them
on and go out into the street without disturbing her. When I'd done all
this in my mind I began to write a mental note to La Estrella to ask her
more or less when she got up to do me the favor of leaving without letting anyone see her, no that was no good: of leaving everything as she'd
found it, no that was no good either: of closing the door behind her: shit,
all this was childish and besides it was quite useless because La Estrella
might not know how to read, O.K. I'd write it in big bold caps with my
grease pencil but who told me she couldn't read? Racial segregation,
that's who, I said to myself as I was making up my mind to get up and
wake her up and talk to her openly. Of course I had to get dressed first. I
staggered to my feet and looked at the Castro convertible and she wasn't
there and I didn't have to look for her very far because I could see the
empty kitchen right in front of me and the bathroom door was open so I
could see the bath was empty as well: she wasn't here, she'd gone. I
looked at my watch which I had forgotten to take off last night and it
was two o'clock (in the afternoon?) and I thought she must have gotten
up early and left without making any noise. Very considerate of her. I

went to the bathroom and as I was sitting on the can, reading those instructions that come with every roll of Kodak film which had been left on the floor I don't know by whom, reading this conveniently simple division of life into Sunny, Cloudy, Shade, Beach or Snow (snow in Cuba, they must be joking!) and finally Clear Well-lighted Indoors, reading these instructions without understanding them, I heard the doorbell ringing and if I'd been able to jump up without foul consequences, I'd have done so because I was sure it was La Estrella's triumphal comeback, so I let the bell ring and ring and ring and I managed to silence my gut and my lungs and the rest of my body so I became the Silent Don. But a Cuban friend is more adhesive than a Scotch tape and someone shouted my name through the airshaft between the kitchen and bathroom, not a difficult operation for someone who knows the building, has the physique of a trapeze artiste, the chest of an opera singer, the persistence of memory and a stunt man's daring to risk his neck by sticking his head through the corridor window. It wasn't the voice of a Martian. I opened the door after performing some hygienic rituals and Silvestre burst through the doorway like a white tornado, livid, shouting excitedly that Bustro was sick, seriously ill. Who? I said, picking up the debris of my hair after the wind of his entry had scattered it over a radius of my face, and he said, Bustrófedon, I left him in his house early this morning because he was feeling sick, throwing up and all that and I laughed at him because I thought he was able to take his drink better than that but he told me to leave him alone and take him to his place and not disturb him but this morning when I went to look for him to go to the beach the maid told me there was nobody at home neither the señor nor the señora nor Bustrófedon because they'd taken him to the hospital so Silvestre told me all in one breath without a comma. And the maid called him Bustrófedon, just like that? A question that was my token gift of shit to this morning already brimming with drowsiness, hangover and diarrhea. No, you cunt, she didn't say Bustrófedon but of course it was Bustrófedon, who else. Did they tell you what was wrong with him? I said on my way to the kitchen to drink a glass of milk, that oasis well in the morning-after desert of us nomad drinkers. I didn't know, Silvestre said, I don't believe it's serious but I don't think he's at all well either. I don't like the sound of his symptoms, it could very well be aneurysm. A new *rhythm?* I asked in mock-disbelief. No, hell no! Cerebral *aneurysm,* an embolism of the brain arteries, I don't know, and I laughed at his words just before he said I don't know. What the fuck are you laughing at now? Silvestre said. You're on your way to becoming a famous diagnostician, *viejito*, I said. Why, he shouted and I could see he was getting angry, why did you say that? Forget it, I said. So you think I'm a hypochondriac too? he said and I said I didn't, I was merely laughing at his vocabulary but admiringly, dazzled by his instant diagnosis and stunned by his scientific knowledge. He smiled but didn't say anything and I narrowly missed hearing yet again his story of how he'd already started or was about to start studying medicine when he'd gone with a classmate of his to the faculty and straight into the dissection room and had seen the corpses and smelled the smell of formaldehyde and dead flesh and heard the ghastly sound of bones creaking when a professor cut them up with a saw, a *common* saw for chrissake! And so on and so forth. I offered him a grateful glass of milk and he said, No thank you I've already had breakfast and from the word breakfast he went on to what comes before breakfast—which is not the morning after but the night before.

What happened to you last night? he asked and I've never known anyone to ask more questions than Silvestre: Why should be his middle name. I went out, I said. For a walk. Where? Nowhere special I said. Are you sure? What do you mean, am I sure? Of cures I'm sure! At least nobody else was in my shoes, or were they? Ah! he said, making a guttural noise to show he understood what I meant, how interesting! I didn't want to ask him any questions and he took advantage of my disadvantage to ask me some more. So you don't know what happened last night? Here, I said, trying not to make it sound like a question. No, not here, he said, in the street. We were the last to leave, I believe. Yes, the last because Sebastián Morán left before you returned with La Estrella as he still had to do his show (I thought I heard a musical note of sarcasm in his voice) and then Gianni and Franemilio left and we stayed and by we I mean Eribó and Cué and Bustrófedon and me, talking, shouting rather above La Estrella's snores and Eribó and Cué and Piloto & Vera left together and Rine had gone earlier with Jesse and Juan Blanco, I think, I'm not sure, so Bustrófedon and I took Ingrid and Edith with us. I mean, what happened was that after closing up shop in your place Bustro and I picked up Ingrid and Edith as we planned to go to the Chori and on our way to La Playa Bustrófedon was in true form, you should have heard him, but we were already on the heavy side of the river when he began to feel ill and we had to go back and Edith finally told the driver to stop on the corner and she went to bed all by herself, Silvestre said.

In the room I come and go talking to my guardian angelo as I look for my socks which only last night came in pairs and have now all managed to become single specimens. When I got tired of searching for them through the universe of my studio I returned to my own private galaxy and went to the closet and pulled out a new pair and put them on while Silvestre went on talking, telling me his story, and I was working out what do with the rest of that Sunday. The thing is, he said, that I was making out with Ingrid (and now I should explain that Ingrid is Ingrid Bergamo but that's not her name, that's her nickname, we gave it to her because that's how she pronounces the name Ingrid Bergman: she's a *mulata adelantada,* as she herself puts it when she's in a good mood, meaning she can easily pass for white, and she dyes her hair ash blond and puts on lots of makeup and wears the tightest skirts of anyone in this island where the women don't wear dresses in any case but body gloves, and she's a very easy lay, which didn't do anything to diminish Silvestre's pleasure because no woman is easy on the eve of her bedding), so I picked her up and took her to the *posada* on 84th Street, he said, and after we were already inside the patio she started saying no, no and no, and I had to tell the driver to please drive on. But, he said, when we were back in El Vedado and the taxi had gone through the tunnel for the fourth or fifth time, we started kissing and all that and she let me take her to the *posada* on 11th and 24th Street and the same thing happened there except that the driver said he was a cab driver not a pimp and that I should pay him there and then so he could go away and then Ingrid started arguing with him for not taking her home and the guy was so cut up that I paid him quickly and he shot off. Of kosher, he said, Silvestre said, I took Ingrid with me and there in the intimate darkness she staged a big row and we went out onto the street again arguing with each other or rather she was doing all the arguing as I was trying to calm her down, as reasonable and cool as George Sanders in *All About Eve* (Silvestre always talks like that, in filmese: once he made a frame with his hands playing the photographer, and he said to me, Whoa! Budge an inch and you go out of frame! and another time I arrived at his house, which was dark, with the doors of the balcony closed because the evening sun hit them hard and I inadvertently opened the balcony and he said, You've just exploded twenty thousand full candles in my face! and the time he and Cué and I were talking about jazz and then Cué said something pedantic about its origins in New Orleans and Silvestre told him, Don't cut in with that flashback now, *viejito!* and other things I forget or can't remember now), and there we were walking and quarreling and crossing El Vedado from north to south, you know where we finally ended up? he asked but didn't wait

for my answer. We arrived at the *posada* on 31st Street and went in as
though there was nothing to it. I believe, he told me, I won the game by
default but this was only the first round and inside, once we were in the
room there was a wrestling match between a heroine from Griffith and
a Von Stroheim villain to get her to sit down, are you listening? just to
get her to sit down and not even on the bed but in a chair! After she'd
sat down she didn't want to let go of her handbag. Finally, he said, I got
her to calm down and sit quietly, almost relaxed and I go and take off
my jacket and she's up like a shot and runs to open the door to leave the
room and I zoom in on the door and see her hand in big close-up on the
bolt and I put my jacket back on and calm her down once more but in
calming her down she gets so nervous she makes a mistake and sits on
the bed and no sooner is she sitting than she leaps up as though it was
a fakir's bed of nails and I, playing the part of a man of the world, very
much a la Cary Grant, I manage to persuade her not to be frightened,
there's nothing to be afraid of, sitting on the bed is only sitting, and the
bed is just like any other bit of furniture, namely a chair, and like a
chair the bed could just as well be a seat and she's much quieter now,
so she gets up and leaves her handbag on the table and sits back on the
bed again. I don't know why, Silvestre told me, but I guessed I could
now take my jacket off, so I took it off and sat beside her and began to
caress and kiss her and having got this far I pushed her back, so she
would lie down, and she lies down only a second because up she pops
like on a spring again and I go on pushing her down and she goes on sitting up and I insist she lie down until something's got to give and this
time she lies down and stays down for good, very quiet and very much
the ingenue in a romantic-but-risqué scene, so I decide to take a
chance and begin telling her how hot it is and that it's a pity she's going
to fuck—pardon—to wreck her dress and how it's getting all rumpled
and how elegant it indeed is and she says, It's cute, isn't it? And with no
heralding effect whatsoever she tells me she's going to take it off so as
not to crease it, but that she won't take off anything more, that she will
definitely keep her slip on, and then she takes her dress off. She gets
back on the bed again and I've already taken my shoes off and I forget
the Hays code, I start working on her body in medium shot, and I plead
with her, I beg her, and I almost go down on my knees on the bed, asking her to take off her slip and I tell her I want to see her beautiful star-
let's body, that she needn't wear more than just panties and bra, that it's
only the same as a swimsuit except she's in bed not on the beach and I
succeed in convincing her with this argument, *viejito,* and she takes her

slip off though first she tells me that's all, she's not taking off anything more. But nothing. So then we start kissing and caressing and I tell her I'm going to get my pants rumpled unless I take them off so I take them off and I take my shirt off too and now I've got nothing on but my shorts and when I scramble back on the bed again she starts getting angry or pretends she's angry already and she won't let me caress her like before. But a minute later I'm touching her hand with a finger and then the finger climbs on top of her hand and then climbs up her arm not only one finger but two and then my hand climbs up the south face of her tit because it's there, and then I caress her body and we start feeling and fondling each other again and then I ask her, beginning in a whisper, almost in voice off, telling her, pleading with her to take off the rest of her clothes, or just her bra so I can see her marvelous breasts but she won't let me convince her and then just when I'm on the point of losing my cool, she says, O.K. and suddenly she's taken her bra off and what do you guess I'm seeing in the dim red light in the bedroom? That was the subject of another public debate: switching off the overhead light and switching on the bedside lamp. What I'm seeing is the eighth wonder of the world, the eighth and the ninth because there are *two* of them! And I start going crazy over them, and she starts going crazy and the whole atmosphere switches from suspense to euphoria like in a Hitchcock movie. The end of the sequence was, so as not to bore you with any more detail shots, that with the same or similar arguments that had become standard treatment by now I succeeded in persuading her to take off her pants, *but,* BUT, where old Hitch would have cut to insert and intercut of fireworks, I'll give it to you straight—I didn't get any further than that. Not even the Great Cary would have been able to persuade this poor man's Ingrid to do a love scene, torrid or horrid, and I came to the conclusion that rape is one of the labors of Hercules and that really there's no such thing as rape, because it can't be called a crime if the victim is conscious and only one person commits the act. No, that's quite impossible, dear De Sad.

I begin to laugh seismically but Silvestre interrupts me. Wait a moment, hang on a sec, as Ingrid says, that's not the end of the film. We spent the night, Silvestre tells me, or the bit of the night that was left on the best of terms and succored by her expert hands, satisfied more or less and in *Ecstasy,* a state of, I fell asleep and when I wake up it's already light and I look for my loved one and I see my costar has changed with the night, that sleep has transformed her and like poor Franz Kafka I call it a metamorphosis and even though it's not Gregor

Samsa whom I find beside me it sure is another woman: night and kisses and sleep have removed not only her lipstick but the whole of her makeup, the lot: the once perfect eyebrows, the large thick lovely black lashes, the phosphorescent and pale complexion that was so kissable the night before are no more, and, wait a moment, don't laugh please: you ain't heard nothing yet, so hold on, I'll be rocking the boat: there, by my side, between her and me like an abyss of falsyhood, there's a yellowish object, round more or less and silky in appearance but not in texture, and as I touch it I almost leap out of bed: it's hairy! I pick it up, he says, in my hands, very cautiously, and hold it up to the morning light to see it better and it is, a last tremolo of strings attached plus a clash of cymbals, yes, a wig: my leading lady becomes the American eagle because she is hairless or, he said, bald, bald, bald, bald! Well, not *completely* bald, which is even worse because she has a few bits of colorless fuzz here and there, quite disgusting I must say. So there I was, Ionesco Malgré Louis, Silvestre said, in bed with the bald soprano. I must have been thinking this so hard I said it out loud, because she began to stir and then woke up. In the immediately preceding shot I'd left the wig where it was, had lain down again and feigned sleep, and as she wakes up now the first thing she does is to put a hand to her head and in a frenzy she frisks around, she *leaps* around, looking for her hairpiece everywhere and she finds it and puts it on—but *upside down, chico,* upside down! Then she gets up, goes to the bathroom, closes the door and turns on the light and when she opens it again everything's in its place. She looks at me and then she does a double take because she was so worried about losing her hair she forgot I existed and it's only now she remembers she's in a *posada* and with me. She looks at me twice, Silvestre said, to make sure I'm sleeping, but she looks at me from a distance and there I am fast asleep with my eyes half opened, seeing everything: I'm a film camera. She picks up her handbag and her clothes and goes into the bathroom again. When she comes out she's another woman. Or rather she's the same woman you and I and everybody else know and who gave me such a hard time last night before she consented to let me be present at her unveiling, at her total striptease, *au dépouillement à la Allais.*

All this time I couldn't contain my laughter and Silvestre had to narrate his Odyssey above my guffaws and now the two of us laughed together. But then he signaled me to stop and said, But don't you laugh at Barnum, old Bailey, because we're both partners of Browning in *Freaks.* What do you mean, I say. Yes siree, you've been making love with the Negro nation's answer to Oliver Hardy. What do you mean, I repeat. Yes, yes. Listen, after I'd left the lie-detector chamber I took that delectable little blonde back to where she once belonged in an early taxi and after I'd seen her safely home I went off toward the sunrise and beyond, where my house is, and as I was passing here, it must have been about 5 o'clock A.M., there was La Estrella walking along the sidewalk up 23rd Street, looking real cross, and I don't mean her hair but her looks. So I called her and picked her up and took her home but along the way, my friend and lighting cameraman, she told me that a horrible thing happened to her on her way to stardom and she proceeded to tell me that she'd fallen asleep in your camera obscura and that you came back drunk and had tried to sodomize her, and she ended by swearing to me that she'd never never never put a foot inside your house again, and I'm telling you, she was really mad at you. So you see one freak equals another and a farce mirrors a fiasco or *fracaso*, failure's saddest form. Did she actually say that? I asked. No, not her but probably Carlos or Ernesto. Come on! Is that what she told you, is that what she said? Well, said Silvestre, she said you tried to bugger her, that's what she told me but I'm not keeping to the text. I'm giving you a fair film copy instead.

As I had no more laughter left in my body, I left Silvestre sitting on the bed or the sofa and went to brush my teeth. From the bathroom I asked him which hospital Bustrófedon was in and he told me he was in Antomarchi. I asked him if he was going to see him in the evening and he shook his head and said that at four o'clock he had a date with Ingrid the woman from Bergamo and he thought that today he shouldn't put off till tomorrow what he should have done yesterday. I smiled but without conviction now and Silvestre told me I shouldn't smile like that because it wasn't her body he was after but only that naked soul of hers and that I should also bear in mind her antecedents in film myth: Jean Harlow also wore a wig. Made by Max Factor of Hollywood.

Bustrófedon died yesterday, or is it today?

Is life a concentric chaos? I don't know, all I know is my life was a nocturnal chaos with a single center that was Las Vegas and in the center of the center there was a glass of rum and water or rum and ice or rum and soda and that's where I was from twelve o'clock on, and I turned up just as the first show was finishing and the emcee was thanking his charming and wonderful audience for coming and inviting them to stay for the third and last show of the night and the band was striking up its theme song with a lot of noise and nostalgia, like a circus brass band but changing from the umpa-pa to the two-four or six-eight beat of a *charanga* trying out a melody: the noise of a ragtime band coming on like a Kostelanetz string orchestra, something which depresses me even more than knowing I'm already talking like Cué and Eribó and all the other six million soloists of this island called Tuba and while I'm rubbing the glass in my hands and digressing that sober little man who sits inside me and speaks so low nobody but me can hear him tells me I'm losing my footing and as that genie of the bottle I am has just said very softly now *Cuba,* and Hey presto! there she was greeting me, popping out of nowhere to say, Hi there honey and at the same time giving me a kiss just there where the cheek meets the neck and I looked in the mirror, mirror on the wall (of bottles) and I saw Cuba, every inch of her, bigger and more beautiful and sexier than ever and she was smiling at me so I turned around and put my arm around her waist, And how're you Cuba baby, I said and I kissed her and she kissed me back and said, Be-au-ti-ful, and I didn't know if she was okaying the kisses she was testing with that sex sense she carries on the tip of her tongue or if she was extolling her soul, as Alex Bayer would say, because her body sure didn't need any padding. Or maybe she was simply glowing over the evening and our chance meeting.

I left the bar and we went over to a table but first she borrowed some change from me for the jukebox which was already playing none other than her "Sad Encounter" which is her theme song just as this music-killing band's is "The Music Goes Round 'n' Round," and we sat down. What are you doing here so early, I asked and she said, Didn't you know dear I'm singing now in the Mil Novecientos and I'm their star dear and I don't care what you say what matters is what they pay me and I'm sick and tired of the Sierra, and here I'm at the center of everything and I can get away to the San Yon or the Gruta or where I feel like between shows and that's what I'm doing now, capeesh? Sure I understand, you are the center of my chaos now Cuba I was thinking but I didn't say it though she knew what I meant because I was fondling her tits right there in the ultra-violet darkness where shirts and blouses turn into the shrouds of a pale ghost and faces turn a deep purple or can't be seen at all or else they look like wax it depends on their complexion or race or what drinks and where people slip away from one table to another and you see them crossing the dance floor deserted now and being first in one place and then another and doing the same thing in both, in other words making love, or *matarse* which means making death, a much better word because they were lethally exciting themselves to death and these gauche movements from one table to another changing company but not jobs made me think we were in a fish bowl, all of us, including me, though I thought, believed, allowed myself the luxury of thinking it was the others who were the fish in the bowl and suddenly we were all fish so I decided to drown myself, plunging into Cuba's cleavage, her melons coming out on their own from her blouse to surface to the open market, diving under her armpits left unshaved a la Silvana Mangano I think or a la Sofia Loren or some other star of the Italian screen, swimming, ducking under, totally immersed in her and suddenly I thought I was the Captain Cousteau of night waters.

And then I raised my face and saw an enormous fish, a galleon navigating underwater, a submarine of flesh that stopped short of colliding with my table and sending it sinking to the surface. Hey there baby said a voice deep and bass and shipwrecked as my own. It was La Estrella and I remembered when Vítor Perla, may he rest in peace, no, no, he's not dead but the doctor ordered him to go to bed early or he'd never get up again, I remembered that he knew what he was saying when he said that La Estrella was the Black Whale and I thought that one night she must have appeared to him just as she did to me now, and I said, High Estrella, and I don't know if it slipped out or if I just said it, the fact was she began lurching and swaying and she placed one of her hands like a black tablecloth on my table and recovered her balance again and said to me, as she always does, La, La La and for a moment I thought she was just warming up the tuba of her throat but she was correcting me so I said always willing to oblige, Yes *La* Estrella and she let out such a bellow of laughter it stopped the people in mid-table and I think it even froze the jukebox in mid-turntable and when she got tired of laughing she went off and I have to say that neither she nor Cuba had exchanged so much as a word because they weren't on speaking terms, I suppose because a singer who sings without music never speaks to someone whose singing is all music or more music backing that is than singing and with apologies to her friends who are also my friends Cuba reminds me of Olga Guillotine, who is the favorite singer of all those people who like artificial flowers and satin dresses and nylon-covered furniture: the fact is I like Cuba for other reasons than her voice anything but her voice definitely not her voice but for visual reasons, for the eye has reasons that the ear never knows, for reasons that not only can be seen but can be touched and smelled and tested, something that can't be done with a voice or perhaps only with one voice, with the voice of La Estrella, which is the voice that nature jokingly preserves in the excrescence of its pupa of flesh and fat and water. Am I still being unfair, Alex Bayer, alias Alexis Smith?

It was dancing time and I was falling all over the floor in rhythm and the voice I was holding in my arms was saying between giggling fits, You're pretty far gone, you know and I looked hard at her and saw it was Irmita and I wondered where Cuba had gone to but I didn't wonder how I came to be dancing with Irenita, I-re-ni-ta, Irenita that's her name, Irena if it really is her name and not an alias because I'm like Switzerland surrounded by allies and it was Irenita who said, You're going to fall over and it was the truth, I noticed it the moment I was telling myself, She must have come out from under the table, yes, that's where she comes from because she was always under the table where she fits very neatly but does she fit? She isn't as tiny as all that and I don't know why I had thought she was so tiny because she comes up to my shoulders and has a perfect body, perhaps her thighs or what you can see of her thighs are not so perfect as her teeth or what you, me I mean, can see of her teeth and I hope she's not going to invite us both to laugh together because I've no wish to see her thighs as far back as I've seen her teeth when she laughed and showed me her missing molar, but she had the cutest and best figure I've seen and the face of a swinger and her face was the mirror of her body missing molar excepted and I forgot about Cuba completely, totally, absolutely. But I couldn't forget La Estrella because she didn't let me. A great uproar exploded in the submerged cathedral, that is to say in the back room, and everybody was running toward it and we ran too. On the sofa near the entrance, next to the door, in the darkest corner of the room was an enormous black shadow shaking and roaring and falling on the floor and heaving it back onto the sofa and It was La Estrella, helplessly drunk and throwing a fit of crying and shouting and raving and as I went to see what was the matter with her I stumbled over one of her shoes lying on the floor and I fell on top of her and when she saw it was me she folded her Doric columns around me and held me tight and then she was giving me a missing molar with her crying, hugging me and saying, Ah *negro* it's hurting me, it's really hurting and I thought there was something in her body hurting and I asked her and she repeated it's hurting me, it really hurts and I asked her what it was that was hurting and she said, Ah *mulato* he's dead he's dead and she was crying and not saying who or what was dead and I managed to free myself and then she cried out,

My little son and finally she said, He's died! Ay how I miss him! and she fell to the floor and stayed here and looked as though she had died herself, or passed out but she was only asleep because she began snoring as loud as she'd been shouting and I slipped away from the group, come on all together now, which was still trying to lift her back onto the sofa and I groped my way toward the door and went out. I missed La Estrella as much as you miss a missing molar when it's still there and it hurts.

I walked the whole length of Infanta and when I got to 23rd I met up with this moveable coffee vendor who's always around and he offered me a cup and I said, No thanks I have to drive and it really was because I didn't want any coffee because I wanted to stay drunk and go around drunk and live drunk all my life which is the same as saying I wanted to drink myself to life. And as I didn't want just one coffee I took three and I got talking with the portable vendor and he told me that he worked nights from eleven to seven up and down La Rampa and I thought that's why we never run into each other because it's the same time I do my Rampa beat and I asked him how much he made and he told me 75 pesos a month no matter what he sold and that every day or rather night he sold between 100 and 150 cups of coffee and he told me, This, tapping his Goliath of a thermos with his David of a hand, makes about 300 pesos a month and I'm not the only vendor and it all goes to the boss. I don't know what I said to him about his missing molar of a boss because now I was drinking not coffee but a rum on the rocks not the beach rocks as you might imagine but bar rocks and I thought I would phone Magalena and when I got into the phone booth I remembered I didn't have her number but then I saw a whole telephone directory written over the walls and I selected a number because in any case I had already inserted a coin and I dialed it and waited while the phone rang and rang and rang and finally I heard a man's voice very weak and tired say Hello? and I said, Is that you, Hellen? and the man replied in his voice that wasn't a voice, No, señor and I asked him Who then, her sister? and he said, Hello hello and I said Ah so you're a double Hellen, and he said, almost screaming, What's the idea, waking people up at this time of the night! and I told him to go fuck his missing molar and hung up and picked up my fork and began cutting up my steak very carefully and I heard music behind me and there was a girl singing and lingering over the words and showing off her missing molar and it was this queen of musical suspense Natalia Gut (iérrez was her real name) singing a version of "Perfidia" that sounded like

"Porphyria," and I realized I was in Club 21 eating a T-bone steak and when I eat I sometimes have this habit of suddenly lifting my right hand so the sleeve of my shirt can disentangle itself from the sleeve and from the food and fall backward and when I lifted my arm a searchlight blinded me and I heard them saying a name which turned out to be my professional name and I stood up and people were applauding me, many people, an audience, but the light on my face went out and it hit a table several tables away and then someone said another name and I was eating the same steak but in a different place because I was in the Tropicana but not only do I not know how I got there whether on foot or in my car or whether they took me there and not only that but I no longer know if all this happened the same night and the emcee is continuing to present the guests as though the place was full of celebrities and fuck it! somewhere or other in the world there must be an original for this shitty parody, in Hollywood I bet, a word that gives me a missing molar, not only to pronounce but even to think of and I get up to go out and fall into the missing table between two tables and with the help of the captain of waiters I reach the patio and give him a military salute and say permission to go overboard sir, before going off, permission granted.

I return to the city and the cool night breeze makes me see the streets again and I reach La Rampa and continue along it and turn the corner into Infanta and park near Las Vegas, which is closed and there are two cops at the door and I ask them what's up and they tell me there's been trouble and ask me to keep moving pronto and I say I'm a reporter and they come on friendly and tell me they've arrested Lalo Vegas, the owner, because they've just discovered he's been pushing drugs, *Just?* C'mon, show me your missing molar I ask one of the cops and he laughs and tells me, Please *periodista* don't give us a hard time and I tell him there aren't any hard times telling him *No hay problema* just that and I go on my way past Infanta and Humboldt, on foot, and I come to a dark passage where there are some garbage cans and I can hear a song rising from the garbage cans and I walk around and around them to see which garbage can is singing so I can introduce her to her wonderful one-man audience and I go from one garbage can to another and then I realize that the honey-toned or honky-tonked words are rising from the ground, from among the scraps of food and filthy bits of paper and old papers which make a missing molar out of the words Sanit. Dept. written on these cans and I see that underneath the papers there's an iron grille on the sidewalk which must be the air vent of some joint down there under the street or in a basement or maybe it's the musical circle of hell, and I hear piano music and cymbals playing and a slow moist clinging bolero and then some applause and more music and another song and I stay there listening and feeling the music and the rhythm and the words climbing the legs of my pants and flowing into my body and when it stopped I realized that what was coming through this grille was the warm air pushed up by the air-conditioning of the Mil Novecientos and I turn the corner and go down the red staircase: the walls are painted red, the steps covered with red carpeting and the handrail striped red velvet and I shift toward the red to plunge down into the music and the noise of glasses and the smell of alcohol and the smoke and sweat and rainbow lights flooding the place and the people and I hear the famous finale of that bolero that goes *"Lights and liquor and lips/ Our night of love has ended/ Adiós adiós adiós"* which is one of Cuba Venegas' songs and I see her bowing all elegant and beautiful and dressed in sky blue from tits to toes and bowing again and displaying those great rounded half-uncovered breasts of hers that are like the lids of two marvelous stewing pots under which is bubbling the only food that makes men into gods, femmebrosia, and I'm happy to see her bowing and smiling and that her incredible body is swaying and that she's throwing back her breastaking head and above all that she's not singing anymore tonight because it's better, much much better to see Cuba than to hear her and it's better because anyone who sees Cuba falls in love with her but anyone who hears and listens to her can never love her again because her voice is her missing molar.

Now that it's raining, now that I have to look at the city lost in the smoke of the pouring rain, this city somewhere behind the vertical mist on the other side of my office window, yes, now that it's raining I remember La Estrella. Because the rain erases the city but it cannot erase memory and I remember La Estrella's hour of glory as I also remember when she fell from glory and where and how. I don't go to the nitecaves, as La Estrella called the nightclubs, any longer because the censorship has been lifted and they have moved me from the entertainment supplement to the front page and I spend my time taking pictures of political prisoners and bombs and Molotov cocktails and dead bodies the police leave lying where they fell to serve as an example, as though the dead were able to stop any other time than their own, and I'm again on night beat but it's downbeat.

I stopped seeing La Estrella I don't know for how long and I hadn't heard anything about her until the day I saw the copy about her opening at the Capri and I don't know to this day how her quantity of humanity had managed to make this great leap forward in quality. Someone told me an American impresario had heard her in Las Vegas or the Bar Celeste or at the corner of 0 and 23rd and had made a contract with her, I don't know, all I did know was her name was in the paper, my *own* newspaper, and I read it twice because I didn't believe it and when I was convinced it was true I felt really happy for her: so La Estrella has finally made it I said to myself and I was frightened like hell to see that her unshakable self-assurance had proved more prophetic than pathetic because I'm always alarmed by people who make a one-man crusade out of their destiny and who while denying luck and chance and even destiny have a feeling of certainty, a belief in themselves that's so deep it can't be anything but fate and now I saw her not only as a physical phenomenon but as a metaphysical monster: La Estrella played the Luther of Cuban music and she had always been dead right, as if she who couldn't read or write had in music her sacred scores.

I sneaked out of the city office that evening to go to the opening. Somebody told me she had been nervous during the rehearsals and although she was always on time at the beginning she missed out on one or two important rehearsals and they penalized her and almost took her off the program and if they didn't do it it was because of all the money they'd spent on her. This guy also told me she had refused to sing with a band, but what happened was that she'd paid no attention when they read her the contract which made it perfectly clear that she had to accept all the clauses of the company and there was a special clause in which they mentioned the use of transcriptions and arrangements, but she didn't know what the first word meant and it was quite clear she hadn't any notice of the second because underneath, next to the signatures of the managers of the hotel and the company, there was a gigantic X which was her signature in her own hand, and so she had to sing with a band. This is what Eribó told me. He's the bongo player at the Capri and he was going to play with her and he told me all this because he knew I was curious about La Estrella and he came to the office to explain things and patch up a fight we had because of something he did which almost killed this story and me with it. I was on my way from the Hilton to the Pigal and was just crossing N Street when I saw Eribó. He was standing under the pines near the car park facing the Retiro Médico skyscraper and talking to one of the Americans playing at the Saint John and I went up to them. He was the piano player and they weren't just chatting but arguing about something and when I greeted them I saw the American had a strange look on his face and Eribó took me aside and asked me if I spoke English, and I told him, Yes, a leetle, and he said, Listen, my friend here is in a tight spot, and he took me over to the American and in this weird state he formally introduced me and told the piano player in English that I would look after him and then he turned to me and said, You've got a car, haven't you? and I said sure and he said, Could you do me a favor and find a doctor, and I asked what for, and he said, This fellow needs a shot badly because he's in terrible pain and he can't sit down at the piano in the state he's in and he's on in half an hour, and I looked at the American and I could see from his face he really was in pain and I asked Eribó, What's the matter with him? and Eribó said, Nothing, he's just in pain, do me the favor will ya, look after him because he's a nice guy, and I got to go play because the first show is just about over, and then he turned to the American and explained what he'd said and turned to me and said, See you soon, and he left.

We went off in the car, me looking for a doctor not in the streets but in my mind, because to find a doctor during the day who's willing to give a junkie a shot of heroin is hard enough, let alone during the night, and every time we ran over a hole in the road or crossed a street the American gave a groan and once he screamed. I tried to get him to tell me what was wrong and he finally managed to get through, over, across to me that it was his anus. Your what? My asshole, man! and at first I thought he was just another pervert and then he told me it was only hemorrhoids and I told him I would take him to an outpatients' clinic, to an emergency clinic nearby, but he insisted all he needed was a shot to kill the pain and he'd be O.K. again and he was writhing on the seat and sobbing and as I'd seen *The Man with the Golden Arm* I hadn't the slightest doubt where it was hurting. Then I remembered that there was a doctor who lived in the Paseo building who was a friend of mine and I went and woke him up. He was scared because he thought it was someone wounded in a gunfight, a terrorist who'd been busted by his own petardo or drunk a Molotov cocktail or whatever or maybe someone who'd been hunted down by the S.I.M., but I told him I didn't get mixed up in things like that, I wasn't interested in politics and that the closest I'd been to a revolutionary was at a focal lens distance of 2.5 and he said all right, all right he'd have to go to his office and he gave me the address and said he'd follow us. I got to the office with the man fainting all over the place and as luck would have it a cop turned up just as I was trying to wake him so I could get him into the house and sit him down in the *portal* to wait for the doctor. The cop came up and asked me what was wrong and I told him he was a pianist and a friend of mine and that he was in pain. He asked me what was wrong and I said he had hemorrhoids and the cop repeated the word, Hemorrhoids? and I told him, Yes, piles, but he thought it was even weirder than I did and said, Are you sure he's not one of those guys, meaning was he dangerous, like a terrorist or something, and I said, Oh come on, he's a musician, and then this guy came round and I told the cop I was taking him inside and whispered to him he should try and make it by himself because this cop here was suspicious and the cop must have heard what I was saying, because he insisted on coming with us and I can still remember the iron gate creaking behind us as we entered the silent patio and the moon shining on the dwarf palm tree in the garden and the cold-looking iron garden chairs painted white and the strange group we made, the three of us, the American, the cop and myself sitting on the terrace in Vedado as the dawn was about to come up. Then the doctor arrived and when he turned on the light in the *portal* and saw the cop and us sitting there, the piano player in a half-swoon and me thoroughly frightened by now, he made the face Christ must have made when he felt Judas' lips on his own and saw the Roman sbirri over the apos(tate)tle's shoulder. We went in and the cop with us and the doctor got the piano player to lie down on a table and made me wait outside, but the cop insisted on staying and he must have inspected the anus with a vigilante's eye because he came out perfectly satisfied when the doctor called me and said, This fellow is very sick, and I saw that he was asleep and he said, I gave him an injection now, but he has a strangulating hemorrhoid and he'll have to be operated on at once and of course I was astonished then because I was lucky after all: I played the wrong number and it came up. I told the doctor who the piano player was and how I met him and he told me to go away, that he would take him to his clinic which wasn't far and he'd take care of everything and he walked me out and I thanked him and also the cop, who returned to his beat smiling.

At the Capri there were the same people as always, maybe a little more crowded than usual because it was Friday and an opening night, but I managed to find a good table. I was with Irenita who always likes to pay visits to fame even if she has to go by the way of hate to get there and we sat down and waited for the stellar moment when La Estrella would ascend to her musical heaven which was the stage and I kept myself busy looking around at the women in their satin dresses and the men who looked from their faces like they wore long underpants and the old women who would go crazy over a bunch of plastic flowers. There was a rolling of drums and then the emcee had the pleasure to introduce to the charming audience the discovery of the century, the greatest Cuban singer since Rita Montaner, the only singer in the world who could be compared with the greatest of the great in the world of international song like Ella Fitzgerald and Katyna Ranieri and Libertad Lamarque, which was like a salad for all seasons to be had with a soupçon of seltzer. Lights out and a searchlight tore a white hole in the purple backdrop and between the folds salami fingers were groping their way in and behind them there appeared a thigh in the shape of an arm and at the end of the arm La Estrella arrived with the black hand mike lost in her hand like a metal finger between those five nipples full of fat that are her actual fingers. Finally every inch of her sprawled on stage singing "Noche de Ronda" as she expanded forward in the general direction of a little round black table with a tiny black chair beside it, both shaking with more than stage fright as they waited for her freight to crash-land on them, and La Estrella spread out toward this sugges-tion of café chantant precariously balancing on her head a coiffure that Madame de Pompadour would have judged too much. She sat down and chair and table and La Estrella were within a thin inch of falling together to the ground and offstage, but she went on singing as though nothing had happened, steadying the tumbling table, silencing the creaking chair and drowning the loudsy band, all done with her voice, recovering from time to time her sound of yesteryear and filling the whole of that great hall with her incredible *voce e mezza* and for a minute I forgot her strange makeup, her face which was no longer ugly but simply grotesque up there, a purple mask with great scarlet-painted lips and the same defoliated eyebrows as before painted across in straight thin lines over the slitty eyes: all the ugliness the darkness of Las Vegas had always concealed. But a minute can only last a minute. If I stayed on until she had finished it was only out of solidarity and pity but all through the show I couldn't help thinking Alex Bayer would be doubly happy at this star-struck moment later known as the apotheosis of La Estrella.

When the show was over we went backstage to congratulate her and of course she didn't allow Irenita into her dressing room with its great silver star pasted on the door, the edges still sticky. I remember it well because I had time to study it in detail while I was waiting for La

Estrella: I was the last person she deigned to receive. I went in and the dressing room was full of flowers and fairies and two little mulatto acolytes who were combing her pompous pompadour and arranging her clothes. I greeted her and told her how much I had enjoyed her singing and how good she looked on stage and what a great singer she was, and then she offered me her hand, the left one, as though it was the Pope's hand, and I shook it limply and she answered with a sidewinding smile and didn't say a thing, but nothing, nothing, nothing, not a word: all she did was to smile her frozen lopsided smile and preen herself in the mirror on the wall and demand constant attention from her sycophants with a megalomania which like her voice, like her hands, like herself, was simply monstrous. I left the dressing room as best I could telling her I would come and see her again some other time when she wasn't so tired or nervous or busy, I can't remember which, and she smiled her lopsidewinding smile at me like a period or like a full stop.

Later I knew her Capri show had folded and that she moved to the Saint John, with only a guitar for backing, but the guitarist was not Niño Nené but somebody else. She had a genuine success there and she even cut a record (*I* know: I bought it and *listened* to it), and after that she went to San Juan, P.R., and to Caracas and to Mexico City and everywhere she went people were talking about her voice more than listening to it. She went to Mexico against the advice of her private doctor (no, *not* Alex Bayer's private doctor) who told her the altitude would kill her and she went in spite of his advice and in spite of everything she overstayed herself until one evening she ate a huge dinner and the next morning she had acute indigestion and called a doctor and the indigestion became a heart attack and she spent three days in an oversize oxygen tent and on the fourth day she got worse and on the fifth day she died. There ensued a legal battle between the Mexican impresarios and their Cuban colleagues about the cost of transport to take her back to Cuba for burial and they wanted to ship her as general freight and the air company said that a coffin wasn't general freight but came under special transport and then they wanted to put her in a frozen-goods container and have her sent the same way they fly lobsters to Miami and her faithful acolytes protested, outraged by this ultimate insult, but finally they had no other alternative than to leave her in Mexico to be buried there.

I don't know if all this is true or false but what is true is that she's dead and that soon nobody will remember her and that she was very much alive when I knew her and that now nothing remains of that fabulous freak, that enormous vitality, that unique human being but a skeleton like the hundreds, thousands, millions of true and false skeletons there are in Mexico, a country peopled by skeletons, once the worms have gorged themselves on the three hundred and fifty pounds of living flesh she bequeathed them. It is God's truth that she is gone with the wind which is the same as saying she's fucked and farted and that nothing remains of her but a lousy record with a shitty sleeve in obscenely bad taste on which the ugliest woman in the world appears in full sepia color: eyes slitting and mouth wide open between liver-colored lips and cradling a microphone in her hand very close to an avid muzzle, and although we who knew her know damn well this is not her, this is definitely not La Estrella, and the dead voice of that godawful record has nothing to do with her own live voice, this is all that remains of her and within six months or a year when all the dirty jokes about her photo finish and the micockphone she is about to blow in it are past and gone and forgotten, within two years at the most she will be completely forgotten herself—and this is the most terrible thing of all because the one thing I feel a mortal hatred for is oblivion.

But not even I can do anything, because you can't give a stop bath to life, so life must go on. Not so long ago, just before they transferred me to the front page, I went to Las Vegas on leave (yes, the nightclub has reopened and is continuing with its grand show of the evening and its chowcito and the same people go there every night and every dawn and on into the morning as before familia) and there were two girls singing there, new ones, two pretty little Negro girls singing and swinging without any backing. I instantly thought of La Estrella and her voice revolution in Cuban music and of her style which is a thing that lasts longer than a person and a voice and a revolution. La Estrella lives in these girls who call themselves Las Capellas in a homage that doesn't dare disclose its name, and they sing very well and in pluperfect pitch and what is more, they have a lot of success. I took them out, along with this critic friend of mine I don't know if you remember him, Rine Leal, to drive them home that same evening. On the way, right at the corner of Aguadulce, when I stopped at the red lights, we saw a boy playing the guitar and anybody who had eyes for music could see he was a kid from the sticks, a poor lonely kid who liked music and wanted to make it himself instead of having it canned or slaughtered on the premises. Rine made me park the car then and there and compelled us to go down under the May drizzle and into the bodegabar where the boy was, and I introduced him to Las Capellas though I didn't know him from anywhere and then told him the girls were crazy about music and that they sang but only in the shower because they hadn't yet dared to sing with accompaniment, and the kid with the guitar from the sticks was very humble and naïve and good-hearted and he said, Come on, let's try and don't be shy because I'll follow you and if you make a mistake I'll cover up for you and if you stray I'll go after you and bring you back to the bar, and he repeated, Come on, why don't you try for once, come on. So Las Capellas sang with him and he followed them as best he could and I think the two beautiful Negro singers had never sung better than at Aguadulce which once meant fresh water but not anymore, and Rineleal and I applauded and the owner of the place and the other people who were there applauded too, and then we went off running under the drizzle which had suddenly become a shower and the kid with the guitar followed us with his voice, shouting at Las Capellas, Don't be shy because you're very good and you'll go a long way if you want to, and we left Aguadulce running and got into my car and drove up to their house because Las Capellas are decentes but we stayed in the car waiting for the rain to stop or merely as a pretext for staying because after it had stopped raining we went on talking and laughing and so on and so forth until there was an intimate silence in the car and it was then we heard outside, quite distinctly, someone knocking on a door. Las Capellas thought it was their mother trying to attract their attention to order but they were surprised beyond belief because, as one of them said, their mother was very sensible and we heard the knocking again and we stood still and we heard it again and we got out of the car and the girls went into the house to find their mother sound asleep and nobody else lived with them and we could see the neighborhood was very quiet and orderly at that early or late hour. It was real spooky. Las Capellas began talking about dead people and the living dead and ghosts and Rine played some verbal games with the Bustrophantoms so I said I must split because I had to get to bed early, which was true, and we returned, Rine and I, to Havana and on my way back I thought of La Estrella but I didn't say anything not because it was uncanny but because it was unnecessary. Anyhow, when we got to the center of town which is La Rampa of course and we got out to have a coffee and so to bed, we met Irenita plus some nameless friend of hers who were just leaving Fernando's Hideaway and straight to bed so we invited them to go to Las Vegas where there wasn't a show or a chowcito or anything by now, only the jukebox and some very distant relatives so we only stayed there for about a half hour drinking and talking and laughing and listening to some unknown records till it was almost dawn, when we took them both to a hotel on the beach.

The Snow of the Admiral

by Alvaro Mutis

translated by Edith Grossman

For Ernesto Volkening
(ANTWERP, 1908—BOGOTÁ, 1983)

*In memory of, and in homage to,
his unshadowed friendship,
his unforgettable lesson*

N'accomplissant que ce qu'il doit,
Chaque pecheur peche pour soi:
Et le premier recueille, en les mailles qu'il serre,
Tout le fretin de sa misère;
Et celui-ci ramene a l'étourdie
le fond vaseux des maladies;
Et tel ouvre les nasses
Aux desespoirs qui le menacent;
Et celui-la recueille au long des bords,
Les épaves de son remords.

Emile Verhaeren, "Les Pecheurs"

I THOUGHT THAT THE WRITINGS, LETTERS, DOCUMENTS, TALES, AND
*memoirs of Maqroll the Gaviero (the Lookout) had all passed through my
hands, and that those who knew of my interest in the events of his life had
exhausted their search for written traces of his unfortunate wanderings,
but fate held in store a curious surprise just when it was least expected.*

*One of the secret pleasures afforded by walks through the Barrio Gótico
in Barcelona is visiting the secondhand bookstores (to my mind the best
stocked in the world), whose owners still preserve that subtle expertise,
rewarding intuition, and canny knowledge which are the virtues of the
authentic bookseller, a species well on its way to imminent extinction.
Recently, as I was walking down the Calle de Botillers, I was drawn to the
window of an old bookshop that tends to be closed most of the time but
offers truly exceptional works to the avid collector. That day it was open. I
walked in with the devotion of one entering the sanctuary of some forgotten rite. In attendance, behind an untidy heap of books and maps that he
was cataloguing in an exquisite, old-fashioned hand, was a young man
with the heavy black beard of a Levantine Jew, an ivory complexion, and
melancholy black eyes fixed in an expression of mild astonishment. He
gave me a thin smile and, like any good bookseller, allowed me to peruse
the shelves while he attempted to remain as unobtrusive as possible. As I
was putting to one side some volumes I intended to purchase, I unexpectedly came across a beautiful edition, bound in purple leather, of the book
by P. Raymond that I had been seeking for years and whose very title is
promising:* Enquête du Prévôt de Paris sur l'assassinat de Louis Duc
D'Orléans, *published by the Bibliothèque de l'Ecole de Chartres in 1865.
Many years of waiting had been rewarded by a stroke of luck I had long
since stopped hoping for. I took the copy without opening it and asked the
bearded young man for the price. He quoted the figure with that round,
definitive tone of finality which is also peculiar to his proud fraternity.*

Without hesitation I paid for it and my other selections, and I left to enjoy my acquisition alone, to savor it slowly, voluptuously, on a bench in the little square with the statue of Ramón Berenguer the Great. As I leafed through the pages, I noticed that inside the back cover a large pocket, originally intended for the maps and genealogical tables that accompanied Professor Raymond's exquisite text, contained instead a quantity of pink, yellow, and blue sheets that appeared to be commercial bills and accounting forms. When I inspected them more closely, I saw that they were covered by tiny, cramped writing, somewhat tremulous and feverish I thought, in an indelible violet pencil occasionally darkened by the author's saliva. The writing, on both sides of the page, carefully avoided the original printed material on what were, in fact, various kinds of commercial forms. A sentence suddenly caught my eye and made me forget the French historian's scrupulous research into the treacherous assassination of the brother of Charles VI of France by order of John the Fearless, Duke of Burgundy. At the bottom of the last page I read these words, penned in green ink by a somewhat steadier hand: "Written by Maqroll the Gaviero during his voyage up the Xurandó River. To be given to Flor Estévez, wherever she may be. Hotel de Flandre, Antwerpen." Since the book was underlined and annotated in the same violet pencil, it was not difficult to deduce that he had kept the papers in the pocket designed for more momentous academic purposes.

As the pigeons continued to sully the noble image of the conqueror of Mallorca, son-in-law to the Cid, I began to read the variegated pages where, in the form of a diary, Maqroll narrated his misadventures, memories, reflections, dreams, and fantasies as he traveled upriver, one man among the many who come down from the hill country to lose themselves in the half-light of the immeasurable jungle's vegetation. Many passages were written in a firmer hand, which led me to conclude that the vibration of the engine in the vessel carrying the Gaviero was responsible for the tremor I had at first attributed to the fevers which, in that climate, are as frequent as they are resistant to all treatment or cure.

As with so many other pages written by Maqroll in testimony to his contrary fate, this Diary is an indefinable mixture of genres, ranging from a straightforward narration of ordinary events to an enumeration of the hermetic precepts of what I assumed was his philosophy of life. Attempting to correct the manuscript would be both ingenuous and fatuous, and would contribute little to his original purpose: to record, day after day, his experiences on a voyage whose monotony and uselessness were, perhaps, alleviated by his work as chronicler.

On the other hand, it seemed a matter of elementary justice that the

Diary have as its title the name of the establishment where, for a long period of time, Maqroll enjoyed relative tranquillity along with the attentions of its owner, Flor Estévez, the woman who understood him best and shared the exaggerated scope of his dreams, the intricate tangle of his existence.

It has also occurred to me that readers might be interested in having access to information related, in one way or another, to the events and people Maqroll describes in the *Diary*. I have, therefore, appended several accounts that appeared in earlier publications but now occupy what I believe is their proper place.

THE GAVIERO'S DIARY

REPORTS HAD INDICATED THAT A GOOD PART OF THE RIVER WAS NAVIGABLE up to the foot of the cordillera. It isn't, of course. We're in a flat-keeled barge driven by a diesel motor that fights the current with asthmatic obstinacy. In the bow, under a canvas roof supported by an iron framework, hang four hammocks, two portside and two starboard. Other passengers, when there are any, stay in the center of the boat on palm leaves that protect them from the burning heat of the metal deck. Their footsteps resound over the empty hold with a bizarre, ghostly echo. We stop constantly to refloat the barge after it runs aground on the sandbars that form without warning and then disappear, following the whims of the current. Two of the four hammocks are used by those of us who boarded in Puerto España, and the other two are for the mechanic and the river pilot. The captain sleeps in the bow under a multicolored beach umbrella that he moves according to the position of the sun. He is always semi-inebriated, a condition that he skillfully maintains by a process of steady drinking, which keeps him in a state of mind where euphoria alternates with a drowsy stupor he never overcomes completely. His orders have no bearing on our progress, and they always leave me perplexed and irritated: "Courage! Watch out for the wind! Into the fray, away darkness! The water is ours! Burn the sounding line!" and on and on throughout the day and most of the night. The mechanic and the pilot pay no attention to this litany, yet somehow it keeps them awake and alert and gives them the skill they need to avoid the constant dangers of the Xurandó. The mechanic is an Indian whose silence would make you think he was mute if it weren't for an occasional conversation with the captain in a jumble of languages that is difficult to translate. Barefoot, bare-chested, he wears greasy jeans that he ties under his smooth, prominent belly; a protruding herniated navel expands and contracts as he struggles to keep the motor running. His relationship to the engine is a clear case of transubstantiation; they merge, they coexist in a single endeavor: the launch must move ahead. The pilot is one of those beings with inexhaustible mimetic abilities. His features, gestures, voice, and other personal traits have been carried to so perfect a degree of nonexistence that they can never stay in our memories. His eyes are very close-set, and I can remember him only by recalling the sinister Monsieur Rigaud-Blandois in *Little Dorrit*. Yet not even this unforgettable reference works for very long, and Dickens's character vanishes when I look at the pilot. A strange bird. My fellow passenger under the canvas is a calm blond giant who chews a few words in an almost incomprehensible Slavic accent, and constantly smokes the foul tobacco that the pilot sells to him at an exorbitant price. From what I can gather he and I are going to the same place: the factory that processes the lumber that will be shipped along this route, and whose transport I'll supposedly be in charge of. The word "factory" produces hilarity in the crew, which doesn't amuse me at all and leaves me prey to vague doubts. A Coleman lamp burns at night, and a parade of large insects smash into it, their colors and shapes so varied I occasionally have the impression that the order of their appearance has been arranged for some mysterious educational purpose. I read by the light of the glowing wicks until sleep overwhelms me like a fast-acting drug. The thoughtless frivolity of the Duke of Orléans occupies me for a moment before I drop into an irresistible stupor. The motor changes rhythm constantly, keeping us in perpetual uncertainty: at any moment it may stop forever. The current is becoming wilder, more capricious. It's all absurd, and I'll never understand why I set out on this enterprise. It's always the same at the start of a journey. Then comes a soothing indifference that makes everything all right. I can't wait for it to arrive.

What I feared has finally happened: the propeller hit roots on the riverbed and bent the axle. The vibration was alarming. We've had to pull up on a beach of slate-colored sand that gives off the sweetish, penetrating smell of rotting vegetation. Until I could convince the captain that the only way to straighten the axle was to heat it, several hours were spent in the suffocating heat in a struggle to perform the most dim-witted, thoughtless operations. A cloud of mosquitoes settled over us. Fortunately, we're all immune except the blond giant, who endured the attack with an angry, controlled look as if he didn't know the source of his persistent torment.

At nightfall a family of natives—a man, a woman, a boy of six, and a girl of four—appeared unexpectedly. All of them were completely naked. They stood watching the fire with the indifference of reptiles. Both the man and the woman are absolutely beautiful. He has broad shoulders, and the slow movements of his arms and legs emphasize his perfect proportions. The woman, as tall as the man, has large, firm breasts, and thighs that round into narrow, graceful hips. Their bodies are completely covered by a thin coat of fat that softens the angles of their joints. Their hair is cut in a helmet shape, and they dress and keep it in place with the juice of some plant that dyes it ebony black and makes it shine in the last rays of the setting sun. They ask a few questions in a language that nobody understands. Their teeth are filed to points, and their voices sound like the quiet coo of a drowsing bird. It was dark by the time we straightened the axle, but it can't be put back in place until morning. The Indians caught some fish along the shore and went to the far end of the beach to eat. The murmur of their childish voices lasted until dawn. I read until I fell asleep. The heat doesn't let up at night, and as I lie in my hammock, I think for a long while about the foolish indiscretions of the Duke of Orléans and about those character traits that will be repeated in other members of the "branch cadette," who come from different stock but have the same disposition to felony, gallant adventures, the dangerous pleasures of conspiracy, greed for money, and unrelieved disloyalty. One might think further about why such behavioral constants appear so relentlessly, almost up to our own time, in princes of such diverse backgrounds. The water slaps against the flat metal bottom of the boat with a monotonous gurgle that is, for some elusive reason, comforting.

MARCH 21

The family came on board the following dawn. While we struggled underwater to replace the axle, they stood on the palm leaves the whole day without moving or saying a word. The man and the woman have no hair anywhere on their bodies. Her sex swells like a freshly opened fruit, and his has a long foreskin that ends in a point. It resembles a horn or a spur, something totally foreign to the idea of sexuality, something without the slightest erotic significance. Occasionally they smile, which bares their filed teeth and eliminates any suggestion of cordiality or simple friendliness.

The pilot explains that it's common in these parts for Indians to travel the river in white men's boats. They usually offer no explanations, never say where they're going, and disappear one day as suddenly as they came. They're peaceful and never take anything that doesn't belong to them or share the food of the other passengers. They eat plants, raw fish, raw reptiles. Some come on board armed with arrows dipped in curare, the instantaneous poison whose preparation is a secret they've never revealed.

That night, while I was in a deep sleep, I was suddenly enveloped by a rank smell of decomposing mud and rutting snake that rose in a sweetish, unbearable stench. I opened my eyes. The Indian woman was staring at me, smiling with a provocativeness that was somehow carnivorous yet repulsively innocent. She put her hand on my sex, began to caress me, and lay down beside me. When I entered her, I felt myself sinking into a bland, unresisting wax that with immobile, vegetative passivity allowed me to move as I chose. The odor that had awakened me grew stronger as she drew closer; her soft body felt nothing like the touch of women. An uncontrollable nausea was rising inside me, and I finished quickly so I wouldn't have to withdraw and vomit before I reached a climax. She moved away in silence. In the meantime the Slav's hammock held two entwined bodies; the Indian was penetrating the Slav and screeching quietly like a bird in danger. Then it was the giant's turn, and the Indian continued to make his inhuman sound. I went to the bow and tried to wash away the putrid stench of rotting swamp that clung to my body. I vomited with relief. The stink still invades my nostrils without warning, and I'm afraid it will stay with me for a long time to come.

They stood there in the middle of the boat, their gaze lost in the treetops as they chewed a mash made of leaves that resemble laurel and the flesh of fish or lizards that they catch with uncommon skill. The Slav took the woman to his hammock last night, and this morning the man was sleeping on top of him in his arms. The captain separated them, not for the sake of decency but, as he explained, slurring his words, because the rest of the crew might follow his example and that would surely bring dangerous complications. The trip, he added, was a long one, and the jungle has an uncontrollable power over those not born there. It makes them irritable and tends to produce a delirium not free of risk. The Slav mumbled some explanation I couldn't understand and calmly returned to his hammock after drinking a cup of coffee brought to him by the pilot. I suspect they've met before. I don't trust the obedient docility of this giant—the shadow of a sad, weary madness can be seen occasionally in his eyes.

*   *   *

We've come to a wide opening in the jungle. After so many days we can finally see the sky and the clouds moving with benign slowness. The heat is more intense, but not as oppressive as that suffocating density under the green, shadowy dome of the great trees, where it becomes an implacable, persistent force that saps our strength. The noise of the engine dissipates into the air, and the boat slips along without our having to endure its desperate battle with the current. Something resembling happiness settles over me. It's easy to sense the relief in the others as well. But in the distance the dark wall of vegetation, waiting to swallow us up in a few hours, is beginning to take shape again.

I've used this peaceful interlude of sun and relative silence to examine the reasons that impelled me to undertake this journey. I first heard about the timber in The Snow of the Admiral, Flor Estévez's place in the cordillera. I lived with her for several months while I was recuperating from an ulcer on my leg caused by the bite of a poisonous fly from the mangrove swamps in the delta. Flor tended to me with distant but firm affection, and at night we made love, hampered by my disabled leg yet with a sense of redemption, of liberation from the old misfortunes that each of us carried like an oppressive burden. I believe I've written elsewhere about Flor's shop and the time I spent on the high plateau. A trucker with a load of cattle he'd purchased down on the plains stopped there and told us about wood that could be bought from a sawmill at the edge of the jungle, sailed down the Xurandó, and sold at a much higher price to the military posts under construction along the great river. When the ulcer dried, Flor gave me money and I went down to the jungle, although I had my doubts about the entire enterprise. The cold in the cordillera and the constant fog moving like a procession of penitents through dwarfed, shaggy vegetation, made me feel an urgent need to sink into the burning lowland weather. I'd received a contract to sail a freighter under Tunisian registry to Antwerp, where certain adjustments and modifications would convert it into a banana transport ship, but I mailed back the unsigned papers along with some clumsy excuses that must have intrigued the owners, who were old friends of mine, companions on other adventures and misadventures that deserve to be recorded someday.

When I boarded the barge I mentioned the sawmill, but nobody could tell me its exact location or even if it really existed. It's always the same: I embark on enterprises that are branded with the mark of uncertainty, cursed by deceit and cunning. And here I am, sailing upriver like a fool, knowing ahead of time how everything will end, going into the jungle where nothing waits for me. I am sickened and depressed by its monotony, its climate worthy of an iguana's cave. Far from the ocean, no women, speaking a language of mental defectives. And in the meantime Abdul Bashur—my dear comrade of so many nights on the shores of the Bosphorus, so many memorable attempts to make easy money in Valencia and Toulouse—waits for me and probably thinks I've died. I'm really intrigued: these disasters, these decisions that are wrong from the start, these dead ends that constitute the story of my life, are repeated over and over again. A passionate vocation for happiness, always betrayed and misdirected, ends in a need for total defeat; it is completely foreign to what, in my heart of hearts, I've always known could be mine if it weren't for this constant desire to fail. Who can understand it? We're about to reenter the green tunnel of the menacing, watchful jungle. The stink of wretchedness, of a miserable, indifferent grave, is already in my nostrils.

MARCH 27

This morning, when we stopped to unload some drums of insecticide at a settlement occupied by the military, the Indians went ashore. That's when I learned that my hammock neighbor is named Ivar. They stood on the bank chirping, "Ivar, Ivar," while he smiled as sweetly as a Protestant pastor. When night fell we were lying in our hammocks, the Coleman unlit to keep away the insects, and I asked him in German where he was from; he said Parnu, in Estonia. We talked until very late about our memories and experiences of places we both knew. As so often happens, language suddenly reveals a person entirely different from the one we had imagined. He strikes me as extremely cold, hard, cerebral—a man who feels absolute contempt for his fellow creatures, which he masks with formulas that he's the first to admit are false. Very dangerous. His comments on the erotic episode with the Indian couple amounted to an icy, cynical treatise by someone who has turned his back not only on modesty or social convention but on the most elementary, simple tenderness. He says he's going to the sawmill too. When I called it a factory, he began a confused explanation of what the installations actually contained, and this plunged me even further into despair and uncertainty. Who knows what's in store in that hollow at the foot of the cordillera? Ivar. Then, as I slept, I realized why the name was so familiar. Ivar was the cabin boy knifed to death on the *Morning Star* by a chief petty officer who insisted he'd stolen his watch when they went ashore to a brothel in Pointe-à-Pitre. Ivar, who could recite entire passages from Kleist and whose mother had made him a sweater that he wore proudly on cold nights. In my dream he welcomed me with his warm, innocent smile and tried to explain that he wasn't the other one, the one in the next hammock. I understood his concern immediately and assured him I knew that very well and there was no chance for confusion. I'm writing now at daybreak, when it's relatively cool. The long inquiry into the assassination of the Duke of Orléans is beginning to bore me. Only the most primitive, sordid desires can survive and grow in the irresistible flood of imbecility that washes over us in this climate.

But as I think of my recurrent failures, of how I keep giving destiny the slip in the same mindless way, I realize suddenly that another life has been flowing next to mine. Another life right beside me and I didn't know it. It's there, it goes on, it's composed of all the times I rejected a bend in the road or refused another way out, and the sum total of these moments has formed the blind current of another destiny that could have been mine, and in a sense still is mine, there on the opposite bank that I've never visited although it runs parallel to my ordinary life. Alien it may be, yet it carries all the dreams, illusions, plans, decisions, that are as much mine as this uneasiness I feel, that might have shaped the events of a history taking place now in the limbo of contingency. A history perhaps identical to the one I've lived, yet full of everything that didn't happen here but exists there, taking shape, flowing beside me like ghostly blood that calls my name yet knows nothing of me. The same insofar as I would have been the protagonist and colored it with my usual clumsy foundering, yet completely different in its events and characters. When the end comes, I think this other life, filled with the sorrow of something utterly lost and wasted, should pass before my eyes, and not my real life—its contents don't deserve the reconciliation of scrutiny, it isn't worth very much, I don't want it to be the sight that eases my final moment. Or my first? That's something to think about some other time. The enormous dark butterfly beating its woolly wings against the glass shade of the lamp is beginning to paralyze my attention, throwing me into an immediate, intolerable, disproportionate panic. I'm drenched in sweat as I wait for it to stop flying around the light and escape back to the night it belongs to. Ivar doesn't even notice

my temporary paralysis as he turns off the lamp and falls asleep, breathing deeply. I envy his indifference. Is there a crack in some hidden corner of his being where unknown terror lies in wait? I don't think so.
That's why he's dangerous.

APRIL 2

We're stranded again on sandbanks that formed in minutes while we
pulled ashore for repairs. Yesterday two soldiers came aboard who have
malaria and are heading for the frontier post to recuperate. They lie on
the palm leaves and shiver with fever, but they never let go of the rifles
that knock with monotonous regularity against the metal deck.

I know it's naive and useless, but I've established certain precepts,
one of my favorite exercises. It makes me feel better, makes me think
I'm bringing order to something inside me. Remnants of life at the
Jesuit academy, they do no good, lead nowhere, but they have that quality of benign magic I always turn to when I feel the foundations giving
way. Here they are:

Thinking about time, trying to find out if past and future are valid
and, in fact, exist, leads us into a labyrinth that is no less incomprehensible for being familiar.

Every day we're different, but we always forget that the same is true
for others as well. Perhaps this is what people call solitude. If not, it's
solemn imbecility.

When we lie to a woman, we revert to the helpless boy who has
nowhere to turn in his vulnerability. Women, like plants, like jungle
storms, like thundering waters, are nourished by the most obscure
designs of heaven. It's best to learn this early on. If we don't, devastating surprises await us.

A knife in the body of a sleeping man. The bare lips of a wound that
does not bleed. Vertigo, the death rattle, the final stillness. Like certain
truths that life fires at us—insoluble, unerring, erratic, indifferent life.

Some things must be paid for, others remain debts forever. That's
what we believe. The trap lies in the "must." We go on paying, we go on
owing, and often we don't even know it.

Hawks screaming above the precipices and circling as they hunt
their prey are the only image I can think of to evoke the men who
judge, legislate, govern. Damn them.

A caravan doesn't symbolize or represent anything. Our mistake is to
think it's going somewhere, leaving somewhere. The caravan exhausts

its meaning by merely moving from place to place. The animals in the caravan know this, but the camel drivers don't. It will always be this way.

Putting your finger in the wound. A human occupation, a debased act no animal would be capable of. The inanity of prophets and fortune-tellers. A gang of charlatans, yet so many seek them out and listen to them.

Everything we can say about death, everything we try to embroider around the subject is sterile, entirely fruitless labor. Wouldn't it be better just to be quiet and wait? Don't ask that of humans. They must have a profound need for doom; perhaps they belong exclusively to its kingdom.

A woman's body under the rush of a mountain waterfall, her brief cries of surprise and joy, the movement of her limbs in the rapid foam that carries red coffee berries, sugar cane pulp, insects struggling to escape the current: this is the exemplary happiness that surely never comes again.

In the ruins of the Krak of the Knights of Rhodes, standing on a cliff near Tripoli, a nameless tombstone bears this inscription: "This was not where." Not a day goes by that I don't think about those words. They're so clear, and at the same time they contain all the mystery it is our lot to endure.

Is it true we forget most of what has happened to us? Isn't it more likely that a portion of the past serves as a seed, an unnamed incentive for setting out again toward a destiny we had foolishly abandoned? A crude consolation. Yes, we do forget. And it's just as well.

It turns out that stringing together these hackneyed words of wisdom, these inane fake pearls born of idleness and the obligatory wait for the current to change its mood, has left me with even less of the energy I need to face the crushing hardship of this hellish climate. Once again I read the names and biographical sketches of those who attacked the Duke of Orléans on his gloomy corner of the Rue Vielle-du-Temple, and learn of their subsequent punishment at the hands of God or men, for both were involved.

APRIL 7

One of the soldiers died the day before yesterday. The sandbanks had just dissolved and the engine had started up, when one of the rifles suddenly stopped banging. The pilot called me to help him examine the body lying motionless in a puddle of sweat that was soaking through the palm leaves, its eyes staring at the thick jungle growth. His companion had taken the dead man's rifle and was looking at him, not saying a word. "He has to be buried right away," said the pilot in the tone of someone who knows what he's talking about. "No," answered the soldier, "I have to take him to the post. His things are there and the lieutenant has to make his report." The pilot said nothing, but it was clear that time would prove him right. Today, in fact, we pulled ashore to bury the body; it had swollen to monstrous size and gave off a stench that attracted a cloud of vultures. The king of the flock, a beautiful jet-black bird with an orange ruff and an opulent crown of pink feathers, had already settled on the framework supporting the canvas in the stern. A sky-blue membrane blinked down over his eyes as regularly as a camera shutter. We knew the others would never approach until he'd had his first peck at the corpse. When we dug the grave where the beach meets the jungle, he watched from his vantage point with a dignity not free of a certain disdain. And it must be noted that the beauty of the majestic creature lent the hurried funeral an air of heraldry and military arrogance in harmony with the silence that was barely broken by the slap of the current against the flat-bottomed boat.

We are traveling through a region of clearings so regularly spaced they seem man-made. The river is growing calmer, and the water's resistance to our progress is hardly noticeable. The surviving soldier is past the crisis and takes the white quinine pills with military resignation. Now he is in charge of both weapons and never lets them go. He chats with us under the captain's umbrella and tells us stories about the advance posts and how they get on with the soldiers across the border, about the bar fights on holidays that always end in several deaths on both sides, and how the dead are buried with military honors as if they had fallen in the line of duty. He has an uplander's cunning, and when he speaks he hisses the s and pronounces words with that peculiar rapidity which makes his sentences difficult to understand until we grow used to the rhythm of a language intended to conceal more than it communicates. When Ivar begins to ask details about the equipment and the number of conscripts stationed at the frontier post, the soldier half closes his eyes, gives a sly smile, and comes up with an answer that has nothing to do with the question. In any event he doesn't seem to like us very much, and I don't think he's forgiven us for burying his companion without his consent. But there's another, simpler reason. Like every person who has received military training, for him civilians are a kind of slow-witted obstacle that must be protected and tolerated; we're forever involved in shady deals and flagrantly stupid enterprises and we don't know how to command or obey, which is to say we cannot pass through this world without sowing disorder and unrest. Every one of his gestures tell us so. At bottom I feel envy, and although I'm constantly trying to undermine his unshakable system, I must recognize that it is what protects him from the silent ruination of the jungle, while the ominous signs of its effects on us become increasingly apparent.

The pilot prepares simple, monotonous food: rice cooked to a shapeless paste, beans with dried meat, fried plantains. Then a cup of something that passes for coffee but is really a watery slop of indefinable taste, with pieces of unrefined sugar that leave a worrisome sediment of insect wings, plant residues, and fragments of uncertain origin at the bottom of the cup. No one has alcohol except the captain, who always carries his canteen of aguardiente. He drinks with implacable regularity and never offers any to the other passengers. But it isn't the kind of liquor you'd want to taste, because judging by the captain's breath, it must be the worst bootleg cane liquor from some settlement in the interior, and its effects are all too obvious.

After supper, when the soldier finished his stories and the others had gone, I stayed in the bow hoping for a cool breeze. The captain sat with his legs hanging over the side and puffed on his pipe. Smoke is supposed to keep mosquitoes away, and in this case I wouldn't be surprised if it did, considering the filthy stuff he uses—its acrid smell bears no resemblance to tobacco. He was feeling communicative, which is rare for him, and he began to tell me the story of his life, as if the soldier's talkativeness had loosened his tongue by a process of osmosis that is very common when people are traveling. I couldn't help being interested in what I managed to understand of his disjointed monologue, spoken in a gravelly voice and filled with long, rambling circumlocutions that made no sense. Some episodes seemed familiar and might well have come from certain periods in my own life.

He was born in Vancouver. His father was a miner and later a fisherman. His mother was an Indian who ran away with his father. Her brothers chased them for weeks, and then one day his father arranged with a tavern owner he knew to make them drunk. When the brothers left, he was waiting for them on the outskirts of town, and that was where he killed them. The Indian girl approved of what her man had done, and they were married a few days later in a Catholic mission. The couple led an itinerant life. When he was born, they left him with the mission nuns. One day they never came back. When he was fifteen, the boy ran away and began to work as a cook's helper on the fishing boats. Later he signed on an oil tanker bound for Alaska. Then he sailed on the same ship to the Caribbean, and for a few years he made the run between Trinidad and the South American coastal cities, carrying airplane fuel. The ship's captain, a German with one leg who had been a submarine commander and had no family, took a liking to the boy and taught him the rudiments of navigation. From morning till night the German drank a mixture of champagne and light beer and ate sandwiches of black bread and herring, Roquefort cheese, salmon, or anchovy. One morning he was found dead, sprawled on the floor of his cabin and clutching the Iron Cross he kept under his pillow and showed off proudly during the high tides of his drunkenness. That was when the young man began a long pilgrimage through the ports of the Antilles that brought him to Paramaribo, where he set up housekeeping with a madam of mixed black, Dutch, and Hindu blood. Immensely fat and good-natured, she constantly smoked slender cigars made by the girls in the house. She loved gossip and managed her business with admirable skill. He developed a taste for rum with melted sugar and lemon, and ran three billiard tables located at the entrance to the establishment, more to distract the authorities than to entertain the clients. Several years passed; the couple got along and complemented each other in so exemplary a fashion that they became an institution, a topic of conversation throughout the islands. One day a Chinese girl came to work in the house. Her parents had sold her to the madam and used the money to establish themselves in Jamaica. They wrote two or three postcards and then were never heard from again. The new girl—tiny, silent, speaking no more than a few words of Curaçao pidgin—had not yet turned sixteen. She caught the sailor's eye, and he took her to his room a few times under the madam's tolerant, distracted gaze, but then he fell passionately in love with the girl and ran away with her, taking some of the madam's jewelry and the small amount of money kept in the billiard room cashbox. They wandered the Caribbean for a time and then sailed to Hamburg on a Swedish freighter, where he worked as a helper in the hold. In Hamburg they spent the little money they had saved, and she went to work in a Sankt-Pauli cabaret. Her number was a set of complicated erotic calisthenics performed with two other women on a small stage. The three of them spent many hours in an inexhaustible pantomime that excited the patrons but left them cold. They had robots' smiles on their faces and the unflagging elasticity of contortionists in their bodies. Then the Chinese girl did a routine with a huge Tartar suffering from giantism and a pallid clarinetist who made her musical commentary on the sketch assigned to the other two. One day the captain—that's what he was called by then—found himself implicated in a heroin-smuggling deal, and he had to leave Hamburg, and the girl, to avoid capture by the police.

Then the captain told an incomprehensible story that had something to do with Cádiz and the manufacture of signal flags that were altered almost imperceptibly to allow ships carrying illegal cargo to communicate with each other. I couldn't tell if the cargo was weapons, Levantine laborers, or raw uranium ore. Here too the story involved women. One of them talked, and the Civil Guard raided the shop where the altered flags were made. I didn't understand how the captain managed to escape in time, but he landed in Belém do Pará, where he traded in semiprecious stones and sailed upriver, engaging in all kinds of transactions. By this time he had fallen into hopeless alcoholism. He bought the barge at a military post where obsolete army equipment was sold at auction, and he sailed the intricate web of tributaries that crisscross the jungle in a dizzying labyrinth. Although he is enveloped in an alcoholic fog that dulls his faculties, for inexplicable reasons that escape all logic he has preserved both an infallible ability to orient himself and a power of command over his subordinates, who feel toward him a mixture of fear and unreserved trust that he exploits unscrupulously, and with cunning patience.

APRIL 10

The climate is gradually changing. We must be approaching the foothills of the cordillera. The current is stronger, and the riverbed is narrowing. In the mornings the birdsong sounds closer and more familiar, and the smell of vegetation is more noticeable. We're leaving behind the cottony jungle humidity that blunts the senses and distorts our perception of every sound, smell, or shape. The breeze at night is cooler and lighter. Its dying, sticky breath once kept us awake. At dawn I had a dream belonging to a very special group that come to me whenever I get close to the hotlands, with their coffee plantations, bananas, swollen murmuring rivers, interminable rains at night. The dreams announce happiness and release a peculiar energy, an anticipation of joy that is, of course, ephemeral and soon turns into the inevitable atmosphere of defeat I know so well. But that flash of lightning, gone almost at once, is enough for me to foresee better days, enough to sustain me in the chaotic landslide of schemes and wretched adventures that constitute my life. In the dream I take part in a historic moment, a crossroads in the destiny of nations, and at the critical moment I offer an opinion, a piece of advice that completely alters the course of events. My participation is so decisive, the solution I propose so brilliant and just, that it becomes the source of a confidence in my own powers that sweeps away shadows and guides me with such intensity toward the enjoyment of my own plenitude that the dream's restorative power lasts for several days.

I dreamed I had a meeting with Napoleon in a Flemish country house in Genappe or its environs, on the day after Waterloo. The Emperor, in the company of several stunned aides and civilians, is striding around a small room containing a few pieces of rickety furniture.

He greets me absentmindedly and continues his agitated pacing. "What do you plan to do, Sire?" I ask in the warm, firm tone of someone who has known him a long time. "I will surrender to the English. They are honorable soldiers. England has always been my enemy but they respect me, and they are the only ones who can guarantee my safety and the safety of my family." "That would be a grave error, Majesty," I respond with the same firmness. "The English are a perfidious people without honor, and their war on the seas has been filled with sly trickery and cynical piracy. They are islanders, which makes them suspicious, and they see the rest of the world as an enemy." Napoleon smiles and answers, "Have you forgotten, perhaps, that I am a Corsican?" I overcome the embarrassment I feel at my slip and continue arguing in favor of an escape to South America or the Caribbean islands. The others join in the discussion; the Emperor vacillates but finally accepts my suggestion. We travel to a port that resembles Stockholm, and set sail for South America in a steamer that is propelled by a large side wheel yet still carries sails to supplement its boilers. Napoleon remarks on the strangeness of such a peculiar ship, and I tell him that in South America they have been used for many years, that they are very fast and safe and the English will never be able to overtake us. "What is this vessel called?" Napoleon asks, his curiosity mixed with distrust. "*Marshal Sucre*, Sire," I reply. "Who was he? I have never heard that soldier's name before." I tell him the story of the Marshal of Ayacucho and the treacherous plot to assassinate him in the mountains of Berruecos. "And is that where you are taking me?" Napoleon rebukes me severely, looking at me with open distrust. He orders his officers to arrest me, and just as they are about to seize me, a change in the sound of the engines leaves them perplexed as they stare at the thick black smoke pouring out of the smokestack. I wake up. For a moment I still feel relief at being free, and satisfaction at giving timely advice to the Emperor and thereby sparing him the years of humiliation and misery on Saint Helena. Ivar looks at me in astonishment, and I realize I am laughing in a way that must seem inexplicable and disturbing. We've come to the first, almost imperceptible rapids. The motor's efforts have redoubled. That was the noise that woke me. The barge rocks and pitches as if it were shaking itself awake. A flock of parrots crosses the sky with a joyful gabble that fades in the distance like a promise of good fortune and unlimited opportunity.

The soldier announces that we'll soon reach the military post. I thought I caught a flash of uneasiness and disguised uncertainty on the faces of the pilot and the Estonian. Something is going on between these two; they're partners in some crooked deal, some dirty business. I took advantage of a moment when the captain was reasonably lucid and they were talking in low voices with the soldier, the three of them lying in the bow and pouring water on their faces to cool themselves, to ask if he knew what they were up to. He gave me a long look and would only say, "They'll end up six feet under one of these days. People already know more about them than they should. It's not the first time they've made this trip together. I could settle accounts with them now, but I'd just as soon let somebody else do it. They're a pair of fools. Nothing for you to worry about." Since a good part of my life has been wasted in dealing with fools just like them, it's not worry I feel but weariness as I watch the approach of one more episode in the old, tired story of the men who try to beat life, the smart ones who think they know it all and die with a look of surprise on their faces: at the final moment they always see the truth—they never really understood anything, never held anything in their hands. An old story, old and boring.

APRIL 12

At noon we heard the whine of a motor. A few minutes later a Junker seaplane, a model from the heroic days of aviation in the region, was circling the barge. I didn't think any were still in service—a six-seater with a fuselage made of corrugated metal. The motor tended to sputter, and when it did, the plane descended to water level in case the engine failed. A quarter of an hour later it flew out of sight, to the relief of the river pilot and Ivar, who had been tense and guarded the whole time it was flying around us. We ate the usual rations and were taking our siesta when the Junker suddenly landed on the water in front of us and approached the barge. An officer in a khaki shirt, wearing no cap or insignia, climbed down to the floats, pointed to a spot, and ordered us to pull ashore. His tone was authoritative and boded no good. We did as he ordered and were followed by the Junker, its engine at half speed. We moored, and two officers with pistols in their holsters climbed down from the plane and immediately jumped to the barge. Neither one had insignias, but their manner and tone of voice testified to their rank. The pilot of the Junker still wore his tattered flying gloves, and on his shirt he displayed the silver wings of the Air Force. He stayed at the controls while the two officers ordered us to bring our papers and stand under the canvas in the stern. The soldier went straight to his superiors, one of them took the dead man's rifle, and the officer who ordered us ashore began to question us, not even looking at our papers in his hand. It was clear he knew the captain and the mechanic. His only question to the captain was where he was going. The captain said to the sawmill, and then he took refuge under the umbrella after a drink from his canteen. The mechanic went back to his engine. The interrogation of the pilot and Ivar was much more detailed, and as their answers became vaguer and their fear more evident, the other officer and the soldier trotted to a position behind the suspects to prevent them from jumping into the water. When the first officer finished with them, he came over to me and asked my name and the purpose of my trip. I told him my name. The captain didn't allow me to continue and answered, "He's coming with me to the sawmill. He's a friend." The officer didn't take his eyes off me and seemed not to hear the captain's words. "Are you carrying weapons?" he asked with the dry voice of a man accustomed to command. "No," I answered quietly. "No sir, even if it takes a little more time," he added, tightening his lips. "Do you have any money?" "Yes . . . sir, a little." "How much?" "Two thousand pesos." He knew I wasn't telling the truth. He turned his back on me to give an order. "Put those two on the plane." The pilot and the Estonian made some effort to resist, but when they felt the rifle muzzles against their backs, they obeyed meekly. They were about to climb into the cabin, when the officer shouted, "Tie their hands behind their backs, assholes!" "There's no rope, Major," the other officer apologized. "With their belts, damn it!" While the soldier covered them with his rifle, the officer laid his weapon on the floor of the cabin and tied the prisoners with their own belts. The grotesque postures they assumed to keep their trousers from falling produced no reaction in anyone. They were put in the seaplane behind the pilot. The major stood looking at us and then turned to the captain and spoke to him in a neutral, less military tone. "I don't want any problems, Cap. You've always known how to handle yourself here and stay out of trouble—just keep on like that and we'll get along like we always have. And you"—he pointed his finger at me as if I were a recruit—"you do what you came to do and get out. We don't have anything against outsiders, but the fewer who come here the better. Watch your money. You can tell that fairy tale about two thousand pesos to your mother, but not to me. I don't care how much you have, but you ought to know that around here they'd kill you for ten centavos to buy some aguardiente. As for the sawmill, well, you'll find out for yourself. I want to see you going back down the Xurandó pretty damn quick, that's all." He turned without saying goodbye and climbed in beside the pilot, slamming the door with a clang of ill-fitting metal that echoed along both banks of the river. The Junker moved away and then climbed slowly, painfully, almost touching the treetops, until it disappeared in the distance.

The captain hadn't seemed to hear the major. He continued sitting in the hammock, not saying a word. Then he raised his head in my direction and said, "We're saved, friend, saved by the skin of our teeth. I'll tell you about it later. I had no idea he was back in command of the base. He knows about everybody around here. They transferred him to the General Staff, and I thought he wouldn't be back. That's why I took a chance with those two. I don't know why he didn't nab us too. He's arrested lots of people for less cause. I'll see if I can get another pilot at the post. I can't do that work anymore. You know where the supplies are. I don't eat much, so you'll have to make your own food. Don't worry about me. The mechanic can take care of himself too. He can't do the cooking anyway because he has to take care of the engine. He brings his own food and fixes it his own way down below. All right, let's go." The mechanic returned to the bow to take the pilot's place. He backed into the middle of the current and continued upriver. As night approaches, I realize that the tension is disappearing, the rarefied, malignant atmosphere the pilot and Ivar created with their exchanges of looks, their whispers, their unsettling, corrupt presence. The mechanic's blind loyalty to the captain, his silent devotion to the task of maintaining an engine that should have been junked and sold for scrap years ago, give him an air of ascetic heroism.

*   *   *

This contact with a world erased from memory by distance and the torpor in which the jungle buries us has, in a way, been encouraging despite the danger signs in the major's words and peremptory warnings. This very danger, in fact, returns me to the daily routine of the past, and the activation of my defenses, the alertness I need to face fairly predictable difficulties, are further incentives to shake off my apathy and climb out of the impersonal, paralyzing limbo I settled into with alarming willingness.

The vegetation is thinning out, becoming less dense. The sky is visible for a good part of the day. At night, close and familiar as they always are at the equator, the stars shine with a protective, watchful light that fills us with peace, with the certainty (fleeting, perhaps, but present in the restorative hours of night) that matters are following their course with the same fatal regularity that sustains us, time's human offspring, destiny's obedient children. I'm running out of the billing and customs forms I found in the hold, which the captain gave to me for writing this diary, my only escape from the tedium of the voyage. The indelible pencil is almost used up too. The captain claims I can get a new supply of paper and another pencil at the military base when we arrive there tomorrow. I can't imagine asking for so simple and openly personal a favor from the authoritarian major, whose voice still rings in my ears. Not the words but the metallic flat tone, as sharp as a gunshot, that leaves us defenseless, vulnerable, ready to obey blindly and in silence. I'm aware this is new for me, that I've never experienced anything like it, not at sea or in any of my various occupations and transformations on land. Now I understand how those incredible cavalry charges were accomplished. I wonder if what we call courage is simply unconditional surrender to the uncontrollable, neutral, overwhelming energy of an order issued in that tone of voice. More thought should be given to this.

Daybreak. We've arrived at the post. The Junker, tied to a small wooden dock, rocks with the current. This plane from another time, with its corrugated metal, painted black nose, radial motor, and half-rusted wings, is an anachronism, an aberrant ghost that I won't know where to place in my memory later on. The base consists of a structure

built parallel to the riverbed, with a zinc roof and metal mosquito netting on wooden stretchers. A small headquarters is in the center, and in
front of that a flag flies from a pole standing in the middle of a patch of
leveled ground that soldiers under disciplinary action spend the day
sweeping. The two wings of the building contain hammocks for the
troops and small cubicles for the officers, with a single hammock in
each. We were met by a sergeant who took us to headquarters. The
major greeted us as if he'd never seen us before. He wasn't polite, and
his military manner hasn't changed, but he maintains an indifference
and a distance that alleviate our fear of awakening his animosity and, at
the same time, indicate that his vigilance hasn't weakened but only
moved away slightly to include other areas of the post's daily routine.

They put us up at the far end of the wing on the right. The
mechanic preferred to return to the barge and sleep in his hammock
beside the engine. We ate outside with the soldiers at a long table
behind the building. Some river fish, and the chance to drink it down
with beer, made the meal seem like an unexpected banquet. After we
ate, the soldier who had traveled with us came over to say hello. We lit
the cigars he offered us and smoked, more to keep the mosquitoes away
than for the pleasure of tasting the tobacco, which was very strong. We
asked about the prisoners taken away in the Junker. He didn't answer
but looked up at the sky and then lowered his eyes to the ground with
an eloquence that made further explanation unnecessary. There was a
brief silence, and then in a voice that attempted to be natural he said,
"Executions are noisy and you have to fill out a lot of forms, but this
way they fall into the jungle where the ground is so marshy they dig
their own graves on impact. Nobody asks questions and that's the end
of it. There's a lot to do around here." The captain pulled on his cigar
and looked toward the jungle, fingering his canteen like a man making
sure he still has his charm against all misfortune. This summary
method of eliminating undesirables was no news to him. As for me, I
must confess that after the first chill down my spine I put the entire
business out of my mind. As I think about it now, I realize that when
life caves in on us, the first feeling to be blunted is pity. Human solidarity, so highly touted, has never meant anything concrete to me. We call
on it in moments of panic when we tend to think about the help others
can give us, not what we can offer them. Our traveling companion said
good night, and for a while we contemplated the starry sky and the full
moon, so disturbingly close we preferred to be in the room and rest in
our hammocks. I'd asked our friend if he could get me some paper and

a new pencil. In a little while he brought them and said, with a smile I couldn't decipher, "They're from the major. He wants me to say he hopes you use them to write what you ought to and not what you want to." It was clear he was repeating the message with an impersonal fidelity that made it even more sibylline. The stillness of the night and the absence of the noise of the motor, which I've grown used to, have kept me awake for some time. I'm writing in an effort to fall asleep. I don't know when we're leaving. The sooner the better. This isn't for me. Of all the places in the world I've been, and there are so many I've lost count, this is undoubtedly the only one where I've found everything hostile, alien, filled with a danger I don't know how to handle. I swear I'll never go through this again. I damn well didn't need it.

APRIL 15

This morning, as we were getting ready to leave, the Junker returned. It had left at dawn carrying the major and the pilot. The mechanic began to warm up the diesel engine, and the captain, with the new river pilot provided by the base, was loading provisions in the hold. A soldier called to me from shore. The major wanted to talk to me. The captain looked at me with suspicion and some fear. At that moment he was clearly thinking more about himself than about me. When I walked into headquarters, the major came out of his office. He made a gesture with his hand as if he wanted to take my arm for a stroll around the clearing. I followed him. His dark, regular features, adorned with a black mustache that he cared for meticulously but without vanity, wore an expression both ironic and protective, not quite cordial but inspiring a certain confidence.

"So you're determined to go all the way to the sawmills?" he asked as he lit a cigarette.

"Sawmills? I only heard about one."

"No, there are several," he answered, observing the barge with a distracted gaze.

"Well, I don't think that changes matters much. The important thing is to arrange to purchase the wood and then get it down-river," I said, while a familiar uneasiness came up through my stomach: it tells me when I'm beginning to stumble over the obstacles set up by reality if I've made the mistake of attempting to adjust it to the measure of my desires.

We finished our walk around the clearing. The major smoked with morose pleasure, as if this were the last cigarette of his life. Then he stopped, looked straight at me again, and said, "You'll manage one way or

the other. It's none of my business. But I want to warn you about something: You're not a man who can spend much time here. You're from
another place, another climate, another race. There's no mystery to the
jungle, regardless of what some people think. That's its greatest danger.
It's just what you've seen, no more, no less. Just what you see now.
Simple, direct, uniform, malevolent. Intelligence is blunted here and
time is confused, laws are forgotten, joy is unknown, and sadness has no
place." He paused and exhaled a mouthful of smoke as he spoke. "I
know you've heard about the prisoners. They each had enough history to
fill many pages of an indictment that will never be filed. The Estonian
sold Indians on the other side. The ones he couldn't sell he poisoned
and dumped in the river. He sold weapons to the coca and poppy grow-
ers and then told us the location of their plantations and camps. He
killed without reason, without anger. Just for the sake of killing. The
pilot was no better, but he was smarter, and it wasn't until a few months
ago that we could finally prove he took part in a massacre of Indians
arranged to allow someone else to sell the lands they had received from
the government. Well, there's no point in telling you any more about
those two. Crime is boring too, and has few variations. What I wanted to
say is this: If I send them under escort to the nearest court, it takes ten
days. I endanger six soldiers, who run the risk of getting caught in a
bribery scheme that can cost them their lives, or of being murdered by
the criminals' accomplices in the settlements. Six soldiers are very valuable to me. Indispensable, in fact. They can mean the difference
between life and death. Besides, the judges . . . Well, you can imagine. I
don't have to spell it out for you. I'm telling you this not to excuse myself
but to give you an idea of the way things are here." Another pause. "I see
you've become the captain's friend, haven't you?" I nodded. "He's a good
man as long as he has enough to drink. When he doesn't get his booze,
he becomes another person. Be careful that doesn't happen. He loses his
mind and is capable of the worst brutalities. Later he doesn't remember
a thing. I've also noticed that you don't like barracks life or people in uniform. You're not entirely wrong. I understand perfectly. But somebody
has to do certain jobs, and that's why there are soldiers. I've taken officer
training courses up north. I was in France for two years on a joint military mission. It's the same everywhere. I think I know what kind of life
you've led, and you may have had run-ins with my colleagues at one time
or another. When we're not on duty, we're more bearable. Our work
trained us to be . . . what you see." We were standing in front of the
dock. "Well, I won't keep you any longer. Be careful. The pilot you're tak-

ing with you is a reliable man. Drop him off here on the way back. Don't trust anybody, and don't expect much from the Army; we're busy with other things. We can't worry about foreign dreamers. You understand what I'm saying." He offered his hand, and I realized it was the first time we'd shaken hands. We walked to the end of the dock. As I climbed onto the barge, he patted my shoulder and said in a low voice, "Keep an eye on the aguardiente. Don't let it run out." He waved goodbye to the captain and walked toward his office with a slow, elastic step, his body erect and a little stiff. We moved to the middle of the river and began to ride against the current and away from the camp, which was starting to blend into the edge of the jungle. An occasional flash of sunlight on the Junker's fuselage, like an ominous warning, showed us its location.

APRIL 17

The new pilot is named Ignacio. His face is covered with pale wrinkles that make him look like a new-made mummy. When he talks he spits saliva through the few teeth left in his mouth, and he talks incessantly, more to himself than to anyone else. He respects the captain, whom he's known for a long time, and consequently he has a kind of friendship with the mechanic, to which he brings his conversation while the mechanic contributes his docile nature and inexhaustible talent for relating the life around him to the unpredictable behavior of the engine. Its sudden alterations threaten definitive, imminent collapse.

I was wrong to think that from now on the landscape and climate would become more and more like the hotlands. In the afternoon we entered the jungle again, the shadow created by the canopy of treetops and vines that crisscross from one bank to the other. The motor echoes like sounds in a cathedral. The incessant noise of birds, monkeys, insects. I don't know how I'll ever get to sleep. "The sawmills, the sawmills," I repeat in my mind to the rhythm of the water slapping against the prow. This was fated to happen to me. To me and nobody else. Some things I'll never learn. Their accumulated presence in one's life amounts to what fools call destiny. Cold comfort.

Today, during my siesta, I dreamed about places. Places where I've spent long, empty hours, and yet they're filled with some secret significance. They're the source of a message that is attempting to reveal something to me. The mere fact that I've dreamed about them is in itself a prophecy, but I can't decipher its meaning. Maybe if I list the places I'll discover what they're trying to tell me:

A waiting room in the station of a small city in the Bourbonnais. The train is due after midnight. The gas stove gives off too little heat, along with a swampy odor that clings to one's clothes and lingers on the damp-stained walls. Three faded posters proclaim the marvels of Nice, the charms of the Breton coast, the delights of winter sports in Chamonix. They only add to the sadness of the surroundings. The room is empty. The small alcove for the tobacco stand, which also sells coffee and crois-sants protected from flies by a glass cover on which suspicious traces of grease mix with the dust that floats through the air, is closed off with wire grating. I sit on a bench that is so hard I can't find a comfortable spot to fall asleep. I shift position from time to time and look at the tobacco stand, and at the covers of some crumpled magazines in a dis-play case that is also behind the wire grating. Someone is moving inside. I know this is impossible because the stand is up against a corner where there are no doors. And yet it's increasingly clear that someone is locked inside. The figure signals to me, and I can make out a smile on the blurred face but can't tell if it's a man or a woman. I walk to the stand, my legs numbed by cold and the uncomfortable position I've been in for so many hours. Someone inside is murmuring unintelligible words. I put my face up to the grating and hear a whispered "Further away, maybe." I put my fingers inside the wire, I try to move the grate, and just then someone walks into the waiting room. I turn around and see the guard in his regulation cap. He has one arm, and the sleeve of his tunic is pinned to his chest. He looks at me with suspicion, offers no greeting, and walks to the stove to warm himself, clearly intending to demonstrate that he's there to prevent any infringement of station rules. I go back to my seat in a state of unspeakable agitation: my heart is pounding, my mouth is dry, and I'm certain I've ignored a decisive message that will not be repeated.

In a swamp where clouds of mosquitoes approach and suddenly move away in dizzying spirals, I see the wreck of a large passenger seaplane. A Latecoére 32. The cabin is almost intact. I go in and sit down on a wicker seat with a little folding table in front of it. The interior has been invaded by plants that cover the walls and ceiling. High-colored, almost luminous yellow flowers resembling guaiacum blossoms hang down gracefully. Everything of any value was stripped away long ago. The atmosphere inside is serene and warm, an invitation to stay and rest for a while. A large bird—its breast an iridescent copper color, an orange marking on its beak—flies in through one of the windows, where the glass has been missing for years. It lands on the back of a seat three places in front of me and looks at me with small, copper-flecked eyes. Suddenly it begins to sing in an ascending trill that comes to an abrupt halt, as if my presence won't allow it to finish the phrase begun with so much verve. It flies along the ceiling of the Laté looking for a way out, and when it finally goes, leaving the echo of its song in the plant-filled interior, I feel as if I'd fallen under the evil spells reserved for those who visit forbidden places. Something has struck the helm in the most secret part of my soul, and I couldn't have done anything to prevent it; it didn't even know I was there.

A battlefield. The action ended the day before. Looters in turbans are stripping the corpses. The humid heat weakens one's limbs, like fever with no delirium. Among the fallen are bodies in red tunics. The insignias have disappeared by now. I approach a corpse wearing wide, pistachio-colored silk trousers and a short jacket embroidered in gold and silver. These have not been stolen because the body is run through by a lance that goes deep into the ground and pins down the clothing. He is a high-ranking officer with a young face and a slender, sleek body. I know by his turban that he is a Mahratta. The looters have disappeared. A horseman in a red tunic approaches from the distance. He stops his horse in front of me and demands, "What do you want here?" "I'm looking for the body of Marshal Turenne," I respond. He looks at me in surprise. I know this is the wrong battle, the wrong century, the wrong combatants, but I can't correct my mistake. The man gets off his horse and explains with greater courtesy, "This is the battlefield of Assaye in lands that once belonged to Peshwah. If you wish to speak with Sir Arthur Wellesley, I can take you to him right now." I don't know what to answer. I stand there like a blind man trying to orient himself in a crowd. The horseman shrugs his shoulders. "I can do nothing for you." And he rides back the way he came. It begins to grow dark. I ask myself where Turenne's corpse can be, and at that moment I know it's all a mistake and there's nothing I can do. A smell of spices, of patchouli, of bandages that haven't been changed for days, of sun beating down on dead men, of recently oiled saber blades. I awake to the depressing certainty that I've taken the wrong road and will never find the orderliness, made to the measure of my longing, that was finally waiting for me.

I'm in a hospital. Around my bed is a curtain that screens it from the other beds in the room. I'm not sick and don't know why I've been brought here. I move the curtain to one side and see another curtain around another bed. A woman's arm moves it aside, and there is Flor Estévez, dressed in the kind of skimpy gown worn by patients who've had surgery. She smiles as she looks at me, while her breasts, thighs, and partially hidden sex are exposed with a candor not typical of her in real life. As always, her hair is as wild as the mane of a mythological beast. I go to her bed. We begin to caress with the feverish haste of those who know they don't have much time because someone is arriving shortly. As I'm about to enter her, the curtain is pulled back abruptly. Altar boys hold it open while a priest insists on giving me communion. I struggle to close the curtain. The priest keeps the host in a chalice, and an altar boy passes him a small silver box containing the holy oil. The priest attempts to give me the last rites. I look at Flor Estévez again, but she averts her eyes in shame, as if she had arranged it all for some purpose that escapes me. Flor dips her fingers in the oil and tries to rub my member while she sings a song whose sadness leaves me helpless, and I experience the awful deception of the inevitable outcome. All eroticism has vanished. I try to scream, as desperate as a drowning man. I wake to the sound of my own voice fading to a grotesque howl.

I'm engrossed in thinking about the message hidden in these visions. Night has fallen and the boat moves slowly. The pilot and the captain argue with a faint irritation that feels intimate and inoffensive. The captain is at the critical point of his drunkenness and resumes his senseless orders: "Find the wind, you stubborn old fool, find it or we're lost, damn it!" "Okay, Cap, okay, don't hassle me. If we're not moving, it's because we can't." The pilot responds with the patience of someone talking to a child. "Ignacio, you navigate like a snake with its head cut off—there's a reason they weren't using you anymore at the base. Steady on the rudder, damn it, it's not a soup spoon!" And so on for a good part of the night. It's obvious they really enjoy this. It's how they communicate. They're old friends, so old that everything's already been said. My siesta lasted too long and I won't fall asleep until daybreak. I read and write in turn. John the Fearless had no valid excuse. When he condemned the brother of the king of France to death, he condemned his own race to inevitable extinction. What a shame. Perhaps a kingdom of Burgundy would have been the appropriate response to the inexorable series of disasters that rained down on Europe.

APRIL 18

As always, the possible keys to the visitations I experienced during yesterday's siesta have begun to reveal themselves today. They are my old demons, the stale phantoms that in different clothes, in another language, in a new twist of landscape, come to remind me of the constant threads that weave my destiny: living in a time completely alien to my interests and tastes, intimacy with the gradual dying that is each day's essential task, and the universe of eroticism always implicit for me in that task, my constant turning to the past in a search for the place and time when my life would have made sense, and a peculiar habit of always consulting the natural world and its presences, transformations, pitfalls, and secret voices, on which I still rely for the solution to my dilemmas and the final judgment on my actions, apparently so gratuitous but always obedient to their call.

Merely meditating on all of this has left me with a tranquil acceptance of the present that had seemed so confused and inimical to my affairs. Through an understandable error in perspective, I had been examining the present without taking into account those familiar elements revealed by yesterday's dreams. They were there, but I couldn't see them. I'm so accustomed to the prophetic quality of my dreams that although I haven't deciphered the message yet, I can already feel its beneficial, calming effect. I still don't understand Flor Estévez's actions: her initiative, her invitation to bed are so foreign to how she usually handles such situations. In fact, despite her savage appearance, her well-fleshed legs, her wild, disordered hair, her dark, rather moist skin, just slightly resistant to pressure as if it were made of invisible velvet, her full, sibyl's breasts partially exposed throughout the day—despite all these signs, Flor is a total stranger to flirtatious play and the sly erotic encounter. She erupts seriously, categorically, almost sadly, with the silent desperation of one who acts under the domination of an unleashed power, and she loves and takes her pleasure as wordlessly as a vestal. Perhaps Flor's provocative behavior in my dream is the result of my abstinence on this trip: the episode with the Indian was more disturbing then gratifying. It's more likely that it follows the classical confusion in dreams of traits and gestures belonging to different people. We can never be certain about the identity of the beings in our dreams. We never see just one person but a totality, an instantaneous, condensed parade of people rather than a single, definitive presence.

Flor Estévez. No one has been so close to me, no one has been so necessary to me, no one has cared for me with that secret tact buried in her wild, scowling aloofness so given to silence, to monosyllables, to simple grunts that neither affirm nor deny. When I talked to her about the lumber, her only comment was: "I didn't know you made money with wood. Houses, fences, boxes, shelves, whatever, but money? It's a fairy tale. Don't believe it." She went to the place where she hides her savings and gave me everything she had, without another word, without even looking at me. Flor Estévez, loyal and harsh in her anger, bold and sudden in her caresses. Absorbed, watching the fog roll in between the tall cámbulo trees, singing lowland songs, songs about fruit—joyful, innocent songs touched with a sharp nostalgia that remains forever in memory along with the tune and the transparent candor of their words. And here I am sailing up this river with a half-Comanche gringo drunk, a mute Indian in love with his diesel engine, and a ninety-year-old who looks as if he'd been born from the swelling bark of one of these gigantic trees with no name, no purpose. There is no cure for my reckless wandering, forever misguided and destructive, forever alien to my true vocation.

APRIL 20

We've entered another savanna, with small groves of trees and extensive marshes created by the floodwater. Flocks of herons cross the sky in regular formations that remind me of squadrons of reconnaissance planes. They circle the barge, land on the riverbank with impeccable elegance, and move in slow, prudent strides as they search for food. When a fish is caught, it struggles for a moment in the long bill, the heron shakes its head, and the victim disappears as if by magic. The sun goes down in a straight line over the featureless expanse of water gleaming through rushes and vines. From time to time, as if to remind us of its imminent return, a small taste of jungle appears, a dense cluster of trees where you can hear the chatter of monkeys, the screech of parakeets and other birds, the regular, drowsy singing of giant crickets. The solitude of the place makes us feel defenseless, and despite the lethal stench that is always present to warn us of its devastating proximity, we don't really know what causes the feeling here and not in the jungle itself. I lie in the hammock and watch the scenery with apathetic indifference. The only variation I can detect is a gradual change in the light as the afternoon advances. The current offers almost no resistance to the boat's progress. The motor acquires an accelerated knocking rhythm, which is very suspicious given the engine's advanced age and demented unpredictability. All of this barely registers on the almost depersonalized surface of my mind. As always after one of my prophetic dreams, I've fallen into a state of marginal indifference bordering on muffled panic. I view this as an inevitable assault against my being, against the forces that sustain me, against the uncertain, vain hope, but hope after all, that someday things will be better and everything will start to work out. I've grown so accustomed to these brief periods of dangerous neutrality that

I know I shouldn't examine them too carefully. That would merely pro-
long them. As with an accidental overdose of medicine, the effects will
disappear only when the body absorbs the foreign substance that is poisoning it. The captain comes over to tell me that at nightfall we'll stop at
a settlement for fuel and provisions. Remembering the major's recommendation, I ask about the condition of his canteen. He realizes I've
been warned and answers with some annoyance: "Don't worry, my
friend, I'll buy enough to last us the rest of the trip." He moves away,
exhaling pipe smoke in the irritated manner of someone trying to defend
an area of his inner life that has been trampled by strangers.

MAY 25

When we went ashore at the settlement, I never imagined I'd remain
there for weeks, hovering between life and death, or that the entire
aspect of the trip would change drastically into an exhausting struggle
against total despair and attacks of something akin to madness.

The settlement is composed of six houses around a pasture trying to
be a square. Two gigantic, incredibly leafy trees offer shade to the
wretched inhabitants who gather there in the afternoon to sit on rough
primitive benches hacked from tree trunks, smoking and commenting
on the vague, always disquieting rumors that reach them from the capital. The only building with a zinc roof and brick walls is a school that
also serves as a church when the missionaries come. It has one classroom, a small room for the teacher, and sanitary facilities that have
fallen into disuse and are covered with mold and filled with indeterminate trash. The teacher was kidnapped by Indians over a year ago, and
nothing more was heard about her until someone brought the news that
she was living with a tribal chief and had no intention of returning. The
military base keeps a meager complement of soldiers here, who sleep in
hammocks hung in what was once the classroom. They spend the days
cleaning their weapons and repeating a tedious litany of the minor mis-
eries that nourish barracks life.

The captain provisioned his canteen, and we began carrying drums
of diesel fuel to fill the storage tanks on the barge. The humidity, the
unbearable heat, and too few hands made the work exhausting. Nobody
wanted to help. The captain was drunker than ever, the pilot is so old
he can hardly move, and the mechanic and I had to do it by ourselves
under the indifferent gaze of the villagers, who are weakened by malaria
and have the glassy, empty eyes of people who long ago lost all hope of

escaping this place. On the afternoon of the first day I felt nauseated and had a dreadful headache, which I attributed to my having inhaled vapors from the fuel that we had to pour out with maddening slowness. The next day we continued the work. Rest and sleep seemed to have eased my symptoms somewhat, but at midday I began to feel an unbearable ache in all my joints, and shooting pains at the base of my skull immobilized me for minutes at a time. I went over to the captain to ask if he had any idea what was wrong with me. He looked at me for a time, and I could see by the expression on his face that it was serious. He took my arm, walked me to one of the hammocks in the school, helped me lie down, and had me drink a large glass of water with a few drops of a bitter, sticky, amber-colored liquid. He said something to the soldiers in a low voice. It evidently had to do with my condition. They looked at me as if I were about to undergo a terrifying trial they were all familiar with. In a little while the captain returned with my hammock from the barge. He hung it at the far end of the room, away from the soldiers' hammocks, and almost carried me there, holding me under the arms. I realized I had lost all feeling in my feet and didn't know if I was dragging them or trying to walk. It began to grow dark. With the slight drop in temperature and an almost imperceptible breeze blowing off the river, I began trembling violently in a shiver that seemed to have no end. A soldier gave me a hot drink whose taste I couldn't recognize, and then I fell into a profound stupor that was close to unconsciousness.

I lost all sense of the passage of time. Day and night merged in dizzying confusion. Occasionally one or the other would stop for an eternity I made no attempt to fathom. The faces that looked at me were totally alien, bathed in an iridescent light that made them seem like creatures from an unknown world. I had ghastly nightmares about the corners of the ceiling and the seams where the sheets of zinc were joined. I kept trying to fit one corner into another by modifying the structure of the beams or realigning the rivets that joined the sheets so they wouldn't show the slightest variation or irregularity. I brought to these endlessly repeated tasks all the strength of will born of fever and maniacal obsession. It was as if my mind had suddenly become stuck in an elementary process of learning the space around me, a process that in ordinary life is unconscious but now had become the only purpose, the ultimate, necessary, and inevitable reason, for my existence. In other words, I was nothing else but that process, and that process was my only reason for living. As my obsessions persisted and became more frequent and at the same time more fundamental, I began to slip irreversibly into madness, an inert, mineral dementia in which I, or rather what I had once been, was breaking down at an uncontrollable rate. As I try to describe what I suffered then, I realize that words can't convey all the meaning I want to give them. How can I explain, for example, the icy panic I felt as I observed this monstrous simplification of my faculties and the immeasurable length of time I endured this torment? It's impossible to describe. Simply because in a certain sense it is alien and entirely contrary to what we usually think of as human consciousness: we don't become another being, we turn into another thing, a dense mineral composed of infinitely multiplying interior edges whose inspection and documentation constitute the very reason for our survival in time.

The first intelligible words I heard were: "The worst is over. It's a miracle he's alive." A khaki shirt with no markings of any kind, a swarthy face with regular features and a straight, dark mustache—someone was speaking from a distance that was incomprehensible, since he was just a few centimeters from my face, staring at me. I learned later that the major had come in the Junker. From the medical kit he always carried with him he had taken a medicine that they injected every twelve hours, and this apparently saved my life. They told me too that in my delirium I sometimes mentioned the name of Flor Estévez, and at other times I insisted on the need to go upriver and take San Juan fort, which was under siege by Captain Horatio Nelson just a few kilometers from Lake Nicaragua. It also seems I spoke in other languages that no one could identify, although the captain told me later that when he heard me shouting "*Godverdomme!*" he was certain I was out of danger.

I'm still weak, my limbs respond with irritating slowness, I eat without appetite, and nothing can quench my thirst. It's not a thirst for water but for some drink with an intense vegetable bitterness and a white aroma like mint. It doesn't exist, I know, but my specific, clearly identifiable longing for it does, and one day I intend to find the potion I dream about constantly. I write with enormous difficulty, yet at the same time, as I record these memories of my illness I free myself from the madness that came with it and did me the most harm. My improvement is steady and rapid, and at times I think it all happened to someone else, someone who was nothing but the madness and disappeared when it did. I know it's not easy to explain, but I'm afraid that if I try too persistently, I'm in danger of falling into one of those obsessive exercises—my terror of them is boundless.

This afternoon the mechanic came over and started talking to me in a rapid mix of Portuguese, Spanish, and some jungle dialect I couldn't identify. For the first time, and on his own initiative, he began a conversation with someone on the barge other than the captain, with whom he communicates in bare monosyllables. His face, with Indian features that one must scrutinize carefully to avoid a serious misreading of each expression, revealed an uneasiness that went beyond mere curiosity. He began by asking if I knew what disease I'd had. I told him I didn't. Then, as if astounded by an inexcusable ignorance that he considered extremely dangerous, he said, "You had ditch fever. It attacks whites who sleep with our women. It's fatal." I said I was under the impression that I was cured, and with somewhat cryptic skepticism he answered, "Don't be so sure. Sometimes it comes back." Something in his words made me think he was moved by tribal jealousy, the dark struggle against the foreigner, to make me suffer the kind of doubt that was fit punishment for my transgression against the unwritten laws of the jungle. In retaliation for his malice I asked what the whites who had habitual relations with Indian women did to avoid the terrible fever. "They always finish outside, señor. It's no secret." He reproached me with the same arrogance, as if he were talking with someone who wasn't worth too many details. "You have to wash afterwards with honey water and put a leaf of jimsonweed between your legs, even if it burns, even if it leaves a blister." He finished enlightening me as he turned away and went back to his engine with the air of a man who has been distracted from very important work by some unimportant piece of foolishness. At midnight I was reading when the captain came to ask how I was feeling. I told him what the mechanic had said, and he reassured me with a smile. "If you pay attention to everything they say, my friend, you'll go crazy. Just forget it. You're better now. What more do you want?" The smell of cheap aguardiente hung over the foot of the hammock as he walked to the bow, shouting his usual lunatic orders: "Half steam and look alive! Don't burn out my magnetos with your damned tapir grease, assholes!" His voice faded into the limitless night until it reached the stars, so close they had a delicious palliative effect.

MAY 27

The captain has stopped drinking. I noticed it just this morning when he joined us for our daily breakfast of coffee and fried plantain. After his coffee he always takes a long drink of aguardiente. He didn't today, and he wasn't carrying his canteen. I saw a look of surprise on the mechanic's face, usually so impassive and remote. Since I know the captain put in a generous supply at the settlement, I don't think the reason is that he's run out of liquor. I've been observing him all day, and I can detect no other change except that he's also stopped giving those astonishing orders that had become for me a kind of invocation necessary to the boat's progress and the voyage in general. He didn't use the canteen all day. At night he came to lie down in one of the empty hammocks, and after a few preliminary remarks about the weather and the possibility of really torrential rapids ahead, launched into a long monologue about certain episodes in his life. "You can't imagine," he began, "what it meant for me to leave the Chinese girl in that Hamburg cabaret. I never had much luck with women. Perhaps the image I have of my mother is so different from the way white women are that my dealings with them have always been conditioned by my relationship to her. My mother was violent, silent, and blindly devoted to the ancestral beliefs and daily rituals of her tribe. She always thought whites were a necessary, unavoidable incarnation of evil. I think she loved my father very much but probably never showed it. My parents used to come to the mission occasionally. They would stay a few weeks and then leave again. During those visits my mother treated me with a gratuitous, almost animal cruelty. She belonged to the Kwakiutl people. I never learned a word of her language. I must have been marked for life, because until I met the Chinese girl, women always left me. There's something in me that they feel as rejection. I could have spent the rest of my life with the madam in Guiana. Our affair was based more on mutual interest than on sentiment. She was so good-natured and easygoing, there was never any reason to quarrel with her. In bed she displayed an unhurried, absentminded sensuality. Afterwards she would always burst into childish, almost innocent laughter. Everything changed when I met the girl. She penetrated a corner of my soul that had been kept sealed and even I didn't know was there. With her gestures, the scent of her skin, her sudden, intense glances that soon filled me with overwhelming tenderness, with her dependence that was a kind of unthinking, absolute acceptance, she could rescue me instantly from my confusions and obsessions, my discouragement and failure, or my simple daily routine, and leave me inside a radiant circle made of throbbing energy and powerful certainty, like the effects of an unknown drug that produces unconditional happiness. I can't think about all of this without asking myself how I could have left her for such trivial reasons, the kind of unimportant situation I had once faced very skillfully and settled almost effortlessly without ever being caught. Sometimes I wonder in desolate rage if I met her when it was too late, when I could no longer deal with so much life-giving joy, when the response that might have prolonged my happiness had already died. You understand what I'm saying. Some things come too soon and others come too late, but we only find out when there's nothing to be done, when we've already bet against ourselves. I think I know you well enough to suppose that the same kind of thing has happened to you and you know what I'm talking about. From the moment I left Hamburg, nothing has mattered. Something in me died forever. Alcohol and a passing acquaintance with danger have been the only things that gave me the strength to start again each morning. But I didn't know they could wear out too. Alcohol only provides a temporary reason for living, and danger disappears whenever we get close to it. It exists as long as we have it inside ourselves. When it leaves us, when we touch bottom and truly know we have nothing to lose and never did, danger becomes a problem for other people to deal with. Do you know why the major came back? That's why. I haven't talked to him about it, but we know each other well enough. While you were delirious in the classroom, we understood each other again. When I asked him why he had come back, all he would say was: "It's the same there as here, Cap, it's just faster here. You know that." And he's right. The jungle just speeds up the process. In and of itself it offers nothing unexpected, or exotic, or surprising. That's just the foolishness of people who live as if life lasted forever. There's nothing here, there'll never be anything here. One day it will disappear without a trace and fill up with roads, factories, people dedicated to working like mules for the empty thing they call progress. Well, it doesn't matter, I've never played that game. I don't even know why I mentioned it. What I wanted to tell you is not to worry. I didn't leave aguardiente, it left me. We'll keep going upriver. Like before. As long as we can. After that we'll see." He put his hand on my shoulder and stared at the current. He moved his hand away immediately. He didn't sleep but lay quiet and calm, with the serenity of the defeated. I write and then read, waiting for sleep. It always comes with the light breeze at daybreak. I'm certain the captain's words conceal a message, a secret sign that brings me a curious peace although it also tells me that the dice have been rolling for some time. The best thing is to let everything happen as it must. That's right. It's not a question of resignation. Far from it. It's something else, something to do with the distance that separates us from everything and everybody. One day we'll know.

*   *   *

In a curious way everything is becoming settled and calm. The dismal unknowns that loomed at the start of the trip have been clearing away, and now the outlook is simple and straightforward. The Indians left the barge and were forgotten. Ivar and his pal dug their own graves in the flooded earth of the jungle. The major has taken charge of us in a way that isn't explicit or even hinted at, but every day it becomes more evident. The captain stopped drinking and has entered a stage of peaceable dreaming, gentle nostalgia, harmless withdrawal. Day by day Ignacio seems to grow older and more like the protective jungle spirits. The mechanic has coaxed feats worthy of a cabalist from the motor. Along with the feeling that I've been saved by the skin of my teeth, convalescence affords me the tranquil security and invulnerable well-being of the chosen. I'm not oblivious to how precarious such guarantees can be, but as long as I submit wholeheartedly to their power, things file past in an orderly way and stay where they belong instead of attacking in an all-out assault on my identity. And this is why I can view even my relations with the Indian woman, and (if it's true) the fatal consequences I managed to escape, as trials I had to undergo in order to conquer the forces of this devouring, insatiable, vegetal universe which, I can see now, is simply one more place a man must visit to complete his passage through the world and avoid the torment of dying in the knowledge that he has dwelled in a limbo and turned his back on the splendid spectacle of life.

By the afternoon light, and even after I had to light the Coleman lamp, I continued reading Raymond's book on the assassination of the Duke of Orléans. There's a good deal to say about the matter. This isn't the time, and I'm not in the mood for that sort of speculation. But still, there's a curious lack of objectivity in the report on the crime submitted by the provost of Paris, and a concomitant lack of ill will on the part of the author who publishes and comments on it. The reasons for a political crime are always so complex, and the hidden, disguised motives mixed in with them so complicated, that recounting the facts in detail or recording what the people involved thought about it is not enough to form conclusions that are anywhere near definitive. The twisted soul of the Duke of Burgundy hides chasms and labyrinths infinitely more tortuous than anything the good provost can detect or Raymond attempt to elucidate. But what most attracts my attention, in this case and in all the others that have cost the lives of men who occupy an exceptional place in the chronicles, is the utter uselessness of the crime, the absolute lack of effect on the course of the shapeless, sightless magma that flows without definite purpose or reason and is called history. Only our incurable human vanity, the extraordinary narcissism of our claim to a place in the irresistible current that carries us, allows us to think that the assassination of a public figure can change a destiny that has been eternally charted in the infinite universe. But now it's my turn; I think I've exaggerated the true significance of the death of the Duke of Orléans. It's enough to trace the sordid envy and spite behind his assassination. Perhaps that's why the more I read the book, the less the issue interests me, and the more I assimilate it to the daily human spectacle wherever it may occur. In any one of the miserable hamlets we've passed, there's a John the Fearless, a Louis de Orléans, and a dark street corner like the one on the Rue Vielle-du-Temple, waiting for Orléans and his appointment with death. There's a monotony in crime, and it's not advisable to have too much to do with it in books or in life. Not even in their evildoing can humans surprise or intrigue each other. That's why the forest, the desert, the sea, do us good. I've always known it. Nothing new. I close the book, and a swarm of fireflies dances over the water, accompanies the boat for a while, and is lost finally in the distant swamps where the moon shines brightly and then hides behind the clouds. A cool breeze, the advance guard of an approaching squall, is carrying me gently toward sleep.

JUNE 2

This morning we passed a flat-bottomed barge very similar to ours. It was stranded in the middle of the river on sandbanks piled high with tree trunks and branches carried there by the current. It was heading downriver and had run aground during the night, when the pilot fell asleep. He's accompanied by a mechanic who watched, with resignation and indifference, as the pilot attempted to free the barge with a pole. While the captain tried to help by pushing against the side of their boat with our barge, I talked to the mechanic, who continued his skeptical observation of our efforts. I asked him about the sawmills. He told me they do, in fact, exist and are a week's travel away if we don't run into problems with the rapids upstream. He seemed intrigued by my interest in them. I told him I planned to buy lumber there and sell it in the ports along the river. He looked at me with a combination of bewilderment and irritation, and just as he began to explain something about the trees, the noise of our motor, accelerating and finally freeing the grounded barge, drowned out what he was saying. I shouted, asking him to repeat what he had said, but he shrugged his shoulders indolently and climbed down to start the motor while the rapid current was still pushing them forward. They disappeared around a bend in the river.

We continued upriver. I tried to learn more from the captain about what the other mechanic had begun to tell me. "Don't pay any attention," he commented. "There's a lot of stupid talk. You go and take a look and find out for yourself. I don't know much about it. The sawmills are real; I've seen them a few times and I've carried people who were working there. But they only speak their own language, and I haven't been interested in finding out what they do or what kind of business it is. They're Finns, I think, but they can understand a little German. But I'll say it again—don't pay attention to rumors or gossip. People here are very fond of making up stories. It's what keeps them alive in the settlements and army posts. They embroider and exaggerate and change them, and that's how they survive the boredom. Don't worry. You've gotten this far. Find out for yourself and then see what happens." I've been thinking about what the captain said, and I realize I've almost lost interest in the lumber. I wouldn't care if we turned back right now. I won't, through pure inertia. As if it were just a matter of making this trip, seeing the jungle and sharing the experience with the people I've met here, going back with new images, voices, lives, smells, deliriums, to add to all the other phantoms that walk with me, with no other purpose than to unravel the monotonous, tangled skein of time.

JUNE 4

The look of the current is changing radically. The bottom must be rough and rocky. The sandbanks have disappeared. The river is narrower and the first foothills are beginning to rise along the banks, exposing a reddish soil that sometimes resembles dried blood and then fades to a pinkish color. On these cliffs the tree roots are bared like recently polished bones, while their tops flower in an alternating rhythm of light violet and intense orange that almost seems intentional. The heat is increasing, but it no longer carries the suffocating, dense humidity that strips away all desire to move. Now a dry, burning heat envelops us and transmits intact the light that beats down on each object and endows it with absolute, inevitable presence. Everything is silent and seems to be waiting for some devastating revelation. The clattering engine is a blot on the rapt stillness all around us. The captain comes to warn me: "We'll be at the rapids in a little while. They're called Angel Pass. I don't know where the name comes from. Maybe it's because when you come downriver, this calm is waiting for you like a consolation and a promise that the danger is over. But when you travel upriver, the calm is deceptive, and that can be fatal for novices. This is where I always recite the prayer for travelers in mortal danger. I wrote it myself. Here. Read it. Even if you don't believe in it, at least it helps to take your mind off your fear." He handed me a paper in a plastic cover so smeared with the grease, mud, and grime that had accumulated with the passage of time and the touch of countless hands, that it was almost impossible to read the text, written on both sides of the paper in a haughty, angular, and defiantly clear feminine hand. I'll transcribe the captain's prayer as I wait for us to reach the rapids:

> High calling of my protectors, those who have gone before
> me, my constant guides and mentors,
>
> come now in this moment of danger, extend your sword,
> with firmness uphold the law of your purpose,
>
> revoke the disorder of birds and creatures of evil omen,
> wash clean the hall of innocents
>
> where the vomit of the rejected congeals like a sign of mis-
> fortune, where the garments of the supplicant
>
> are a blemish that deflects our compass, makes our calcu-
> lations uncertain, our forecasts mistaken.
>
> I invoke your presence at this hour and deplore with all
> my heart the manacles of my equivocations:
>
> my pact with man-eating leopards in the mangers,
>
> my weakness and tolerance for serpents that shed their
> skin at the mere shout of lost hunters,
>
> my communion with bodies that have passed from hand to
> hand like a staff to ford a stream, and on whose skin
> the saliva of the humble is crystallized,

*my ability to contrive the lie of power and cleverness that
    moves my brothers away from upright steadiness in
    their purposes,*

*my carelessness in proclaiming your power in customs
    offices and guardrooms, in pavilions of sorrow and on
    pleasure boats, in guard towers along the border and in
    the corridors of the powerful.*

*Wipe away in a single stroke all this misfortune and
    infamy, save me,*

*certain of my obedience to your bitter laws, your abusive
    haughtiness, your distant occupations, your desolate
    arguments.*

*I give myself completely to the domination of your unob-
    jectionable mercy, and with all humility I prostrate
    myself at your feet*

*to remind you that I am a traveler in mortal danger, that
    my ghost is worth nothing, that those who perish far
    from home are like trash swept into a corner of the
    market,*

*that I am your servant and am helpless, and that these
    words contain the unalloyed metal of one who has paid
    the tribute*

*owed to you now and forever throughout pale eternity.
    Amen.*

My doubts concerning the efficacy of so barbaric a litany were certainly reasonable, but I didn't dare express them to the captain, who
had handed me the text with evident devotion and faith in its preven-
tive, protective powers. I went to the bow where he was observing the
whirlpools that were beginning to shake the boat, I handed him the
paper, and he put it in a back pocket where he also keeps all the equipment for cleaning his pipe.

*   *   *

JUNE 7

We passed through the rapids without mishap, but in many ways it was a revealing test of what, until yesterday, had been my image of danger and the real presence of death. When I say "real," I mean it wasn't the phantom we call up in our imagination and concretize with elements taken from memories of the deaths we've witnessed under a variety of circumstances. No. This was a matter of perceiving, with all the fullness of our mind and senses, the immediate, unassailable proximity of our own death, the irrevocable cessation of our existence. There, within reach, beyond defiance. A good test, a long lesson. Come too late, like all the lessons that affect us in a direct, profound way.

On the day the captain gave me his extraordinary prayer, the mechanic decided we had to stop to overhaul the motor. When you're going against the current in the rapids, an engine failure means certain death. We pulled ashore, and he disassembled, cleaned, and tested every part of the machine. It was fascinating to see the patient knowledge that an Indian from the most isolated regions of the jungle uses to identify with a mechanism invented and perfected in countries whose advanced civilization rests almost exclusively on technology. His hands are so skillful they seem guided by some tutelary spirit of machinery, one that is completely alien to this Indian with his flat Mongolian face and his skin as hairless as a snake's. He could not rest until he had meticulously tested each stage in the motor's operation. Then, with a slight movement of his head, he let the captain know it was ready to carry us upstream through Angel Pass. Night had fallen, and we decided to stay where we were until dawn. Beginning the ascent is not something one does in the dark. We set out the next day at first light. Contrary to what I supposed, the rapids were not created by rocks on the surface blocking the river's movement and making it more violent. It all takes place down below, where the riverbed is full of hollows, uneven surfaces, caves, eddies, faults, while at the same time the angle of descent grows steeper and the water, with constant changes in direction and intensity, pours down in a deafening whirlpool of crushing force.

"Don't lie in the hammock. Stay on your feet and hold tight to the bars under the canvas. Don't look at the current, and try to think about something else." Those were the captain's instructions. He stayed in the bow the whole time, clutching a precarious bridge and standing beside the pilot, who handled the rudder with abrupt movements in his effort to avoid the crash of water and foam that would loom suddenly like the back of some unimaginable beast. The engine was constantly out of water, the propeller whirling in air with runaway, uncontrolled speed. As we entered the ravine that the current had been gouging for centuries, the light turned gray and we were wrapped in a veil of foam and mist that rose from the turbulent whirl of water as it smashed against the polished rock surface of the channel walls. Night seemed to fall for hours. The barge pitched and shuddered as if it were made of balsa wood. Its metal structure echoed with a muffled rumble of distant thunder. The rivets that held the metal plates together vibrated and jumped, shaking the entire frame with the instability that precedes disaster. Hours passed, and we couldn't tell if we were moving forward. It was as if we had settled forever into the implacable roar of the water, expecting at any moment to be sucked down by the whirlpool. An indescribable exhaustion began to paralyze my arms, and my legs felt as if they were made of something soft and numb. When I thought I couldn't bear any more, I heard the captain shouting in my direction. He gestured toward the sky with his head, and a crooked, enigmatic smile appeared on his face. I looked up and saw the light growing brighter. Some rays of sun broke through the cloud of foam and mist and made it shine with the colors of the rainbow. The howl of the torrent and the rumble in the hull began to diminish. The barge was moving forward, its rhythmic rocking controlled now by strong, regular turns of the propeller. When the pitching grew even gentler, the captain squatted on the deck and signaled to me to lie down in the hammock. His striped umbrella had disappeared. When I tried to move, my whole body ached as if I'd been beaten. I managed to stagger to the hammock and lie down, a feeling of relief spreading through me like a balm accepted gratefully by every joint and muscle, every centimeter of skin that had been numbed and whipped by water. As I celebrated the joy of being alive, I was overcome by a slight drunkenness, a peaceful drowsiness. The river was widening again, and flocks of herons flew out of the rushes to settle on treetops heavy with flowers. Once again the dry, unchanging, motionless heat reminded me that there had been other afternoons like the one now drawing to a close in benevolent, unbounded calm.

I fell into a deep sleep that lasted until the pilot brought me a cup of hot coffee and some fried plantain in a chipped pewter plate. "You got to eat something, boss. If you don't get your strength back, hunger wins out and you dream about the dead." His voice had a fatherly tone that left me awash in childish, gratuitous nostalgia. I thanked him and

gulped the coffee in one swallow. As I ate the slices of plantain, I felt
the gradual return of my old loyalties to life, to the world that holds
endless surprises, to the three or four beings whose voices reach me
despite time and my incurable wanderlust.

JUNE 8

The landscape is beginning to change. At first the signs are sporadic
and not always very clear. Even if the temperature stays the same, the
oven heat, as unmoving as a stubborn animal that refuses to budge, is
sometimes rippled by light, cool breezes. These exotic gusts from
another climate remind me of the veins in marble, alien in color, tone,
and texture to the mass. The swamps are disappearing and in their
place is a dense, dwarfed growth that gives off a mixture of smells like
the odor of pollen kept in a container. Something like honey with a very
pronounced vegetal accent. The riverbed is narrowing and deepening,
the banks are taking on a muddy consistency that feels like clay, and the
fresh, transparent water has a faint iron color. The changes are affecting
everyone's state of mind. There's a relief from tension, a desire to talk, a
gleam in our eyes, as if we knew that something long awaited was about
to happen. In the last light of afternoon a lead-blue line appears on the
horizon and becomes easily confused with storm clouds massing at a
distance impossible to determine. The captain comes over and points at
the spot I'm watching with so much interest. He makes a wavy motion
with his hand, sketching the outline of a cordillera, and without saying
a word he nods his head and smiles with a touch of sadness that makes
me uneasy again. "The sawmills?" I ask, as if I would like to avoid the
answer. He nods again, raises his eyebrows, and puckers his lips in a
gesture that means something like, "There's nothing I can do, but you
can count on all my sympathy."

I sit on the edge of the prow, my legs dangling over the water that
splashes me with a coolness I would have enjoyed more on other occa-
sions. I ponder the factories and what they conceal, sensing an unpleasant surprise that nobody has wanted to talk about in any detail. I think
of Flor Estévez, of her money about to be risked in an adventure heavy
with omens, of my habitual obtuse willingness to take on enterprises
like these, and I realize that I lost all interest long ago. Thinking about
it produces revulsion mixed with the paralyzing guilt of a man who
knows his work is about to begin, while he is only looking for a way out
of the commitment that is poisoning every moment of his life. A state of

mind that's all too familiar. I'm well aware of the openings I use to escape the troubling discomfort of being in the wrong, and that keep me from enjoying what life offers every day in dubious compensation for my remaining stubbornly at her side.

JUNE 10

A strange dialogue with the captain. Enigma flows beneath the words. That's why writing them down is not enough. His tone of voice, his gestures, his way of losing himself in long silences, helped to turn our conversation into one of those times when it isn't the words that communicate what we want to say. Instead they become obstacles, distractions that hide the true reason for talking. His voice from the hammock facing mine startled me. I thought he was asleep.

"Well, it's coming to an end, Gaviero. This adventure's almost over."

"Yes, it looks as if we're almost to the sawmills. I could see the cordillera clearly today," I replied, knowing there was more to his observation.

"I don't believe you're very interested in the sawmills anymore. I think the decisive thing this trip had in store for us has already happened. Don't you?"

"Yes, I do. Something like that," I said, giving him the chance to finish his idea.

"Look, if you think about it, you'll see that from our meeting the Indians to Angel Pass, everything has been linked, everything fits together perfectly. These things always happen in sequence and with a definite purpose. What's important is knowing how to interpret it."

"In my case you're probably right, Cap. But what about you?"

"Lots of things have happened to me along these rivers, along the great river. The same or almost the same as on this trip. But what intrigues me this time is the order in which they occurred."

"I don't understand, Cap. Naturally there's been one order for me and another for you. You didn't take the Indian to bed, you didn't get sick at the post, you didn't think you'd die at Angel Pass."

"When I meet someone who's lived your kind of life, who's undergone the trials that made you the man you are now, then being a witness and companion is as important as experiencing those things myself—perhaps even more important. The days I spent at the base sitting beside your hammock and watching your life slip away were a more decisive trial for me than for you."

"Is that why you stopped boozing?" My rather brutal question was an effort to make him be specific.

"Yes, that, and what it forced me to think about. As if I'd suddenly discovered I was playing the wrong game. It's bad enough to live part of your life in a role meant for somebody else, and even worse to find out when you no longer have the strength to make up for the past or get back what you've lost. Do you understand?"

"Yes, I think so. It's happened to me, too, lots of times, but only for short periods, and I've managed to recover and land on my feet." I was trying to change the direction our talk was taking and at the same time let him know I'd gotten the message.

"You're immortal, Gaviero. It doesn't matter that you'll die one day like the rest of us. That doesn't change anything. You're immortal for as long as you live. I think I've been dead a long time. My life is made as if scraps left over after cutting a dress had been patched together any which way. When I realized that, I stopped drinking. I can't go on fooling myself. When I saw you come back to life in that classroom and defeat the plague, I saw into myself very clearly. I saw my mistake and when it had begun."

"When you left Hamburg?" I asked, testing the ground.

"It doesn't matter. You know? It doesn't matter. It might have been when I ran away with her. When I left the Antilles. I don't know. It's not very important. It doesn't matter." I could hear the uneasiness in his voice, an irritation directed more at himself than at me, as if he hadn't expected to go this far when he began the conversation.

"Yes," I agreed, "you're right. It doesn't matter. When you come to this kind of conclusion, the beginning doesn't matter. It doesn't explain much."

A long silence made me think he'd fallen asleep. His voice startled me again.

"Can you guess who knows this as well as we do?" he asked in what might have been a joking tone.

"No. Who?"

"The major, man, the major. That's why he came back to the base. I've never seen him show so much interest in someone who was sick. Don't forget, he's seen his share of dying soldiers. He's not a man who's easily moved. You've seen him. I don't have to tell you. Well, the fact is he spent hours with me keeping watch over your delirium, following the battle you waged in that hammock, like an animal who's just been captured."

"Yes, I suspected something of the sort because of how he treated me when we said goodbye, and the things he said. He couldn't understand why I'd been saved, and that intrigued him."

"You're wrong. He understood as well as I do. He could see the immortality in you, and that baffled him so much it changed his character completely. The first chink I've ever found in him. I thought he was invulnerable."

"I'd like to see him again," I said, thinking out loud.

"You will. Don't worry. He's still intrigued too. When you meet again, you'll remember what I've told you." Now his voice was quiet, velvety, distant.

I understood that our talk was over. I was awake for a long time, turning over the hidden meaning that flowed out of the captain's words and dug deep inside me, working forgotten areas of my mind and setting warning lights everywhere. As if someone were cupping my soul.

JUNE 12

Ahead of us the cordillera looms on the horizon with overwhelming precision. I realize I'd forgotten how mountains make me feel, what they mean to me as a protective place, an endless source of challenges that strengthen me, sharpen my senses, awaken my need to defy fate and try to test its limits. At the sight of the mountain range misted over by the blue-tinged air, I feel a silent confession rise up from the depths of my soul and fill me with joy. Only I know how much it explains and lends meaning to every hour of my life: "It's where I come from. When I leave it, I begin to die." Maybe that's what the captain means when he talks about my immortality. Yes, that's it—now I understand completely. Flor Estévez and her untamable dark hair, her rough, kind words, her body in disarray, her songs to soothe hooligans and babies whose helpless innocence only she can understand, with the wisdom of a childless woman who shakes life by the shoulders until she forces it to hand over what she demands.

The cordillera. Everything had to happen to bring me to this experience of the jungle so that now, with the marks of the trials I had to undergo in my passage through its soft, decomposing hell still fresh on my body, I could discover that my true home is up there in the deep ravines where giant ferns sway; in the abandoned mine shafts and the damp, dense growth of the coffee plantings covered in the astonished snow of their flowers or the red fiesta of their berries; in the groves of plantain trees, with their unspeakably soft trunks and the tender green of their reverent leaves so welcoming, so smooth; in the rivers crashing down against the great sun-warmed boulders, the delight of reptiles that use them for their lovemaking and their silent gatherings; in the dizzying flocks of parrots that fly through the air, as noisy as a departing army, to settle in the tops of the tall cámbulo trees. That's where I come from, and I know it now with all the fullness of someone who has finally found the place for his business on earth. I'll leave it again, I don't know how often, but I'll never return to the places I'm leaving now. And when I'm away from the cordillera, its absence will pain me with a new pain, with the burning desire to go back and wander the paths that smell of woodland and yaraguá grass, of soil that's just been rained on, of sugar mills grinding.

Night has fallen and I'm lying in the hammock. The cool breeze comes like a promise and a confirmation, carrying an occasional scent of fruits that had been erased from my memory. I approach sleep as if I were going to relive my youth, just for the brief space of a night now, but having rescued it intact, unscathed by my own clumsy dealings with nothingness.

JUNE 13

Today I finished the book about the assassination of Louis de Orléans by order of John the Fearless, Duke of Burgundy. I keep it among my few belongings because I intend to reread certain details. It's clear there was a lengthy provocation on the part of the victim, who was supported by Isabel of Bavaria, his sister-in-law and most certainly his lover. The provost's modesty and the author's prudery don't permit them to elucidate a matter that seems of capital importance to me. The struggle between Armagnacs and Burgundians, especially its origin and the real reasons behind it, could be studied from very surprising angles. But this is something for the future. The archives of Antwerp and Liège must contain revealing documents that I'll have to investigate someday. I propose to do just that if I can still be of service to my dear friend Abdul Bashur and his associates. Abdul, what an extraordinary man he is: the warm, unconditional friend prepared to lose everything to help you, and the implacably astute businessman engaged in labyrinthine vendettas to which he's capable of devoting most of his time and fortune. We met in a café in Port Said. He was at a nearby table, trying to sell a collection of opals to a Jew from Tetuán who could not understand what Abdul was saying, or would not in the hope he would run out of arguments and sell the gems at a lower price. Abdul looked at me and, with the intuition of a Levantine who knows what language to speak with a stranger, asked me in Flemish for help in the transaction and offered me a percentage of the profits. I moved to his table and spoke in Spanish with the Jew. Abdul told me his terms in Flemish and I laid them out in Spanish. The deal was closed to Abdul's complete satisfaction. We stayed behind while the Jew walked away, fingering the stones and muttering oblique curses against all the seed of my ancestors. Abdul and I soon became good friends. He told me he was in the shipbuilding business with his cousins but that they were having a streak of bad luck. He was putting money together to go back to Antwerp and get the business on its feet. We wandered the Mediterranean until, in Marseilles, we managed to place an extremely compromising shipment that nobody else wanted to take a risk on. Our profits allowed Abdul to reorganize his company, and I sank my share in the lunatic venture of the Cocora mines, where I lost everything, and nearly lost my life. I've already written that story.

Later Abdul Bashur wrote to offer me a freighter under Tunisian registry, but I decided to try my luck with these sawmills that I now find promise little or nothing. As I recall all these events and projects from the past, I feel overcome by an indescribable fatigue, a torpor and loss of will, as if I'd spent ten years of my life here in these places of damnation and ruin.

JUNE 16

The day before yesterday at dawn I was awakened by a shadow obscuring the first ray of sun that usually shines in my eyes, and to which I've grown accustomed because it forces me to turn in my hammock without waking up completely and enjoy for another hour the particularly refreshing sleep that makes up for my restlessness at night. Something was hanging from the framework under the canvas and blocking the light. I awoke with a start: the body of the captain swung gently from the horizontal bar. His back was to me and his head rested on the heavy cable he'd used to hang himself. I called Miguel, and the mechanic came immediately and helped me take down the body. The purplish face had a wild-eyed, grotesque expression that made it unrecognizable. I realized only then that one of the captain's consistent traits, even in his most drunken states, was a kind of ordered dignity in his features that made one think of an actor who had once played the great tragic roles of Greek or Elizabethan theater. We searched his clothing for a note but found nothing. The mechanic's face was more closed and inexpressive than ever. The pilot came over to watch us and shook his head with an old man's resigned understanding. We pulled ashore when we found a place where we could bury the body. We wrapped it in the hammock that he used most often. The earth had the consistency of clay, and its reddish color grew more intense the deeper we dug the grave. The job took several hours. When we finished we were dripping with sweat and our limbs were aching. We lowered the body and covered it with earth. The pilot had made a cross of two guaiacum branches that he cut as soon as we landed and carved with fond patience while we worked the spades. With his knife he'd cut the words "The Kap" in painstaking letters on the horizontal branch. For a time we stood in silence around the grave. I thought about saying something but realized it would disturb our meditation. Each of us was recalling, in his own way and with his own collection of memories, the shipmate who finally found rest after living what he had called the life that wasn't his. We walked back to the barge, and I knew I was leaving behind a friend exemplary in his comradely discretion and firm, unflawed affection.

When the barge pulled out, I went to ask the mechanic about the rest of the trip. "Don't worry," he said in his barbaric but intelligible mix of languages, "we're going to the sawmills. I been the owner for two years. When Cap bought the barge at the base on the big river I put in this motor I been taking care of a long time just waiting for a chance like that. Later I bought it off him, but I never wanted him to leave. Where could he go and who would take him he drank so much? Those orders he shouted I think they made him feel he was still the owner and captain. He was a good man, he suffered a lot, who could understand him better than me? He called me Miguel. My real name's Xendú, but he didn't like it. He respected you a lot—sometimes he said he was sorry he didn't know you before. He said you could've done great things together." Miguel went back to his motor, and I leaned against one of the mooring posts and watched the current. It occurred to me again that we don't know anything about death, that all the things we say and invent and whisper about it are miserable fantasies that have nothing to do with the categorical, necessary, ineluctable fact whose secret, if it really has one, we take with us when we die. It was obvious the captain had decided to kill himself many days ago. When he gave up drinking, it was a sign that something had stopped inside him, something that had kept him alive and had broken down forever. Our conversation the other night comes back to me now with irrefutable clarity. He was telling me what he'd resolved to do. He wasn't the kind to suddenly say outright: "I'm going to kill myself." He had the defeated man's sense of decency. I didn't want to decipher the message, or more accurately, I chose to hide it in that corner of the soul where we keep irrevocable facts, the ones that no longer depend on us for their fateful realization. I think he must have been grateful for my attitude. What he said was to be remembered after his death and perpetuated along with his memory: he knew it would always be with me. He took his life so discreetly! He waited until I was sleeping soundly. It must have been just before dawn. He was obliged to use one of the crossbars. Any other method would have attracted our attention. That decency is in tune with the rest of his character and makes me feel he's even closer to an idea I have of men who know how to move through the world, through the corrupt, mindless mob. The more I think about him the more I see that I learned practically everything about his life, his way of being, his failures and his insistent hopes. It's as if I'd met his parents: his mother, the untamed Indian loyal to her man, and his father, lost in a dream of gold and unattainable happiness. I can see the fat madam at the Paramaribo brothel and hear her jovial laugh and the sound of her sensual, flat-footed walk. And the Chinese girl. The one I know best. There's a good deal to say about her and why he abandoned her in the great Sankt-Pauli sewer. It was a way to begin his death, to build it inside himself with one irremediable step, one incurable mutilation. I can't sleep. I've spent the night turning in the hammock, remembering, thinking, reconstructing a recent past in which I was taught lessons that will mark me for the rest of my life. Perhaps my own death is beginning now. I don't dare think about this too much. I want everything to fall back into place on its own. For now, the important thing is to get back to the uplands and take refuge in the blunt, wholesome safety of Flor Estévez. She would have understood Cap so well. But who knows, she has a sharp nose for losers and they're usually not to her liking. How complicated it all is. How many wrong turnings in a labyrinth where we do everything we can to avoid the exit, how many surprises and then the tedium of learning they weren't surprises at all, that everything that happens to us has the same face, exactly the same origin. I won't sleep tonight. I'll go have coffee with Miguel. I know where these tortured musings on the irremediable can lead. There's a dryness inside us we shouldn't get too close to. It's better not to know how much of our soul it occupies.

JUNE 18

I'm now writing on stationery with an official letterhead, which the captain kept in a box along with customs forms and other papers relating to the barge. I realize it's an effort for me to continue this diary. It's difficult to establish how, but in some way a good part of what I've been writing was connected to him. Not that I ever thought he would read it. Nothing further from my mind. But it's as if his presence, his figure, his past, the way he survived at the very edge of life, all served as a reference point, a guide—say it once and for all—an inspiration, despite all the inanity the word has acquired in the mouths of fools. Since what I now record on these pages deals exclusively with me, with what I see and the things that occur around me, it suffers from emptiness, a lack of weight that makes me feel like just another traveler searching for new experiences and unexpected emotions—the sort of thing, in other words, that I reject most deeply, almost physiologically. But on the other hand, it's clear that all I have to do is recall his phrases and gestures, his lunatic orders, to feel the impulse again to go on scribbling. Last night, in fact, I had a revealing dream so rich in detail and substance, and so coherent, that out of it will surely come the subterranean energy to continue the diary.

I was with Abdul Bashur on a pier in Antwerp—he always calls it Antwerpen, in Flemish—and we were on our way to visit the freighter whose command he was going to entrust to me. We stopped in front of the ship: it looked like new, recently painted and all its catwalks and pipes shining and neat. We walked up the gangway. A woman was scrubbing the wooden deck with unsettling energy and dedication. The rounded forms of her body were emphasized each time she bent over to scrape at a stain that resisted the brush. I recognized her immediately: it was Flor Estévez. She stood up smiling and greeted us with her usual brusque cordiality. Something she said to Abdul indicated they already knew each other. Then she turned to me and said, "We're almost finished. When this boat leaves port, it'll be the envy of the world. There's coffee and somebody waiting for you in the cabin." Her blouse was open. Her dark, full breasts were almost completely exposed. With some sorrow I left her on deck and followed Bashur to the cabin. When we walked in, there was the captain at a desk covered with disordered piles of papers and maps. He held his pipe in one hand and greeted us with the brisk, vigorous handshake of a gymnast. "Well," he said as he scratched his chin with the hand that held the pipe, "here I am again. What happened on the barge was only a rehearsal. It didn't pan out. We've worked very hard here, and whether we sell it or decide to operate it ourselves, buying the boat was a brilliant move. The lady thinks we should keep it. I told her we'd see what you two thought. And really,

Gaviero, she's been waiting for you very impatiently. She brought the things you left in the uplands and wasn't sure if anything was missing." I said we'd already spoken with her. "Let's go then," he said. "I want you to see everything." We went out. It began to grow dark very quickly. The captain walked ahead to show us the way. Each time he turned around, I could tell that his face was changing, that a sad, forsaken look was settling more and more firmly on his features. When he reached the machine room, I saw he was limping slightly. Then I was sure it wasn't him anymore, that we were following someone else, and in fact, when he stopped to show us the boiler, we saw a defeated, slow-witted old man mumbling some incoherent explanation totally unrelated to whatever he was pointing at with his trembling, grimy hand. Abdul was no longer with me. An icy wind blew through the hatchways and rocked the ship, whose impressive solidity had vanished. The old man moved toward a stairway that went down to the depths of the hold. I stood looking at a ramshackle collection of instruments, rods, and valves that hadn't been used in a very long time. I thought of Flor Estévez. Where was she? I couldn't imagine her connected with the sordid ruin that surrounded me. I ran toward the deck, longing to see her, tripped on a step that gave way under me, and fell into emptiness.

I woke drenched in sweat, my mouth filled with the bitter taste of rotten fruit. The current is stronger and rougher. A mountain breeze comes like an announcement that we've entered a region completely different from the ones we've passed through so far. The pilot, with his eyes on the cordillera, is cooking an insipid-smelling mixture of beans and yuca that reminds me of the jungle and its climate of exhaustion and mud.

JUNE 19

Today I had a conversation with the pilot that helped to clarify, at least partially, the enigma of the sawmills. In the morning he brought me coffee and the inescapable fried plantain. He stayed there, waiting for me to finish my breakfast, obviously wanting to tell me something.

"Well, we're almost there, aren't we?" I observed, giving him the chance to say what he had on his mind but didn't dare say because of that distance where old people hide to avoid being hurt or ignored.

"Yes, señor, just a few more days. You never been up there, right?" There was a touch of curiosity in the question.

"Never. But tell me, what's really in those factories?"

"Some men came from Finland to install the machines. That's three sawmills, set up a few kilometers apart. The soldiers guard them, but the engineers left. Some years ago now."

"And what timber did they plan to cut? I don't see enough trees around here to supply three installations like the ones you're telling me about."

"I think there's good timber at the foot of the cordillera. I heard about it one time or another. But it seems they can't get it to the mills."

"Why not?"

"I don't know, señor. Really. I couldn't say." He was hiding something. I saw a shadow of fear cross his face. His words weren't spontaneous and easy anymore. He'd lost his desire to talk, and as far as he was concerned, he'd already said enough.

"But who does know? Maybe the soldiers can give me some information when we get there. What do you think?" I didn't expect to get much more out of him.

"No, señor, not the soldiers. They don't like people asking questions, and I don't think they know much more than we do." He began to move away, picking up the empty cup and plate.

"And suppose I talk to the major?" I had touched a delicate nerve. The old man stood still and didn't dare look at me. "I'll talk to him if I have to. I'm sure he'll tell me what I want to know. What do you think?"

He walked slowly toward the stern, muttering and staring into the distance.

"Maybe he'll tell you something. Us folks around here, he never tells us nothing and he don't like us to stick our noses in. Talk to him if you want. It's up to you. I think he respects you." As he mumbled these words, he shrugged his shoulders with the resignation, especially pronounced in him, of old men faced with inevitability and the foolishness of others. I remembered his behavior when we cut down the captain's body, and then at the burial. He didn't want to participate in the destructive games of men. He had lived so long he must have found the sum total of human folly not only intolerable but completely alien.

There were no great surprises in what the pilot told me. I've put two and two together, and I've been convinced for some time that the trucker in the uplands and the people I talked to when I came to the jungle described an enterprise that is nothing but an illusion composed of scraps of rumors: vague miracles of wealth within reach, the kind of lucky break that never really happens to anyone. And I'm the ideal person to fall for it, no doubt about it. I've spent my whole life setting out on this kind of adventure and finding the same disillusionment in the end. Although I console myself eventually with the thought that the reward was in the adventure itself and there's no reason to search for anything but the satisfaction of trying every one of the world's roads, they all start looking suspiciously alike. And yet they're worth traveling if only to stave off tedium and our own death, the one that really belongs to us and hopes we can recognize her and take her as our own.

JUNE 21

Growing discouragement and lack of interest, not only with the factories but with the trip itself and all its events, difficulties, revelations. The landscape seems to match my state of mind: the vegetation, almost dwarfed and intensely green, has a smell of concentrated pollen that seems to stick to the skin; the light filters through a thin mist that confuses one's sense of distance and the size of objects. A steady drizzle has been falling all night, soaking through the canvas and running down my body in lukewarm drops of something that seems more like sap than rainwater. Miguel the mechanic talks constantly about his problems with the motor. I've never heard him complain before, not even when we had to face the rapids. Clearly he misses the jungle, and this country affects his mood and weakens his connection to the engine, as if he were suddenly defenseless and the motor were challenging him like a stranger, an enemy. The pilot continues to stare at the cordillera. From time to time he shakes his head like a man trying to banish a disturbing idea.

Not the best frame of mind for continuing these entries. I know myself fairly well, and if I keep sliding into this chasm, I can end up with nothing to hold on to. In the solitude of this country, with only these two ruins of the jungle's devastation for companions, there's a risk of not finding the slightest reason for staying alive. The drizzle came with the afternoon light: The mist evaporated and at times the air was as transparent as if the world had just been made. The pilot signaled from the bow to show me, straight ahead, there at the foot of the craggy mass of mountain, a metallic reflection shining in the last rays of the sun with a golden hue that reminds me of the domes of small Orthodox churches on the Dalmatian coast. "There they are. That's it. Tomorrow night we'll be there if all goes well." His slow, uninflected voice sounded as if it came from a ventriloquist's dummy. I found myself wanting the trip to go on indefinitely, wanting to put off the moment when I would have to face the troublesome reality of those huge structures whose brilliance is fading as darkness approaches, bringing with it the noise of crickets and flocks of parrots searching the foothills for shelter for the night. I've started to write a letter to Flor Estévez with no other purpose than to feel her near me and listening to the lunatic story of this voyage. I'm confident I'll give it to her one day. For now, the relief I feel in writing the letter is surely a way to escape this slide toward the nothingness that is overwhelming me and, sadly, is more familiar than even I imagine when I recall it as something gone without leaving a trace.

"Flor, my lady: If the pathways of God are mysterious, the ones I take here on earth are no less incomprehensible. Here I am, a few hours away from the famous factories, the ones the driver carrying the Llano livestock told us about, and I still don't know much more about them than what he said on that night of confidences and rum in The Snow of the Admiral, which is, by the way, where I would like to be now, not here. In fact, I have good reason to believe it will all come to nothing, at least according to the rather vague pieces of information I've been receiving as I sail up the Xurandó, a river with more whims, bad habits, and contrary moods than the ones you display when the upland closes in on itself and it rains all day and all night and even the blankets feel wet. The other night I dreamed about you, nothing I can tell you now because I'd have to fill you in on the other people in the dream whom you don't know, and that would cover many pages. I'm writing a diary, whenever I can and on whatever paper I can find, and I record every-thing, from my dreams to our mishaps, from the character and appear-ance of my traveling companions to the changes in landscape as we move upriver. But getting back to the dream, I should tell you that in it, or rather by means of it, I've come to realize your growing importance to me, how your body and not always docile spirit preside over my life and its misfortunes and the ruin where it takes shelter when I've grown sick of wandering and miscalculation. By now this should come as no sur-prise. I know your talents as a seer and hermetic oracle. And so I won't even take the time to tell you in detail how, in this hammock, I need to feel your turbulent body, need to hear you howl in love as if a whirlpool were swallowing you up. Such things should not be written, not only because it does no good but because, in memory, they suffer from a cer-tain rigidity and undergo such startling changes that it isn't worth expressing them in words. I don't know how things will go here. What I do know is that the cordillera is there in front of me, its aromas and whispers are reaching me. All I do is think of the place—it's clear to me

at last—that is my real home on earth. Your money is still safe and I suspect it will come back to you intact, which is what I truly want. I've
thought of telling you something about the jungle and the people who
live here, but I think you'll find out more about them in my diary if I can
get it and its author safely back to you. I've seen death twice, each time
with a different face and chanting her spells so close to me I didn't think
I'd return. Strange, but this hasn't changed me at all. It only taught me
that the lady has always watched over me and kept track of my wanderings. The captain (I hope we'll soon be talking about him at length) told
me that even though I'm obviously going to die one day, for as long as I
live I'm immortal. Well, that doesn't sound right. Of course, he said it
better, but that's basically the idea. The most striking thing is that I had
the same idea, but about you, because I think that inside The Snow of
the Admiral you've been weaving, building, raising the landscape around
you. I've often been convinced that you summon the fog and drive it
away, that you weave the giant lichen hanging from the cámbulo trees
and direct the course of the waterfalls that appear to burst from the
heart of the rocks and tumble over ferns and mosses of the most startling
colors, intense copper to the tender green that seems to shine with its
own light. We've talked so little despite the time we've been together
that perhaps these things come as a surprise, but they were what really
made me decide to stay with you on the pretext of healing my leg.
Speaking of which, it's still numb in places although I can use it to walk.
I'm not very good at writing to someone like you whom I carry deep
inside me and who wields so much power over the most secret corners
and convolutions of the Gaviero, who, if he had met you sooner, would
not have roamed so far or seen so much of a world that brought him so
little profit and even less wisdom. A man learns more with a woman like
you than by taking to the road and dealing with people who leave only
the sad wake of their disorder, the miserable limits of their ambition
measured against the ludicrous extent of their greed. The reason for
these lines has been just to talk with you a while to calm my fears and
feed my hope. I'll stop now and say goodbye until we meet again in The
Snow of the Admiral and drink coffee in the front passageway, watching
the fog come in and listening to the trucks drive up the mountain with
their motors straining, identifying the drivers by the way they shift gears.
This isn't all I wanted to tell you. I haven't even begun. Which doesn't
matter, of course. With you it isn't necessary to say things because you
already know them, you've always known them. Many kisses and all the
longing of one who misses you very much."

*   *   *

Today at dusk we reached the first sawmill. What we saw as right in front of us wasn't as close as we thought. The Xurandó makes a series of wide curves here that alternately move the brilliant aluminum and glass structure away and then bring it back again, turning it into a mirage—an impression that is heightened by how unexpected such architecture is in this place and climate. We moored at a small floating dock secured by yellow cables and impeccably maintained gangways made of light-colored wood. It reminded me of the Baltic. We came ashore and approached the building, which is surrounded by a barbed-wire fence over two meters high, with metal posts painted navy blue and placed every ten meters. We waited for some time by the sentry box at the entrance, and finally a soldier came out of the main building, arranging his clothing as if he'd been sleeping. He told us that the rest of the staff had gone hunting and would return tomorrow at dawn. Moved by an unexpected curiosity, I asked him what they hunted out there, and he stood looking at me with that astonished expression so characteristic of an ordinary soldier when he doesn't know how to hide something from civilians and finally decides to lie—a thing he would certainly never do with his superiors. "I don't know. I've never gone. Possum, I think, or something like that," he answered as he turned and walked toward the building. We went back to the barge to eat supper, get some sleep, and try again the next day. And again, in the fading afternoon light, the enormous metal structure was surrounded by a golden halo that made it look unreal, as if it were hanging in midair. It consists of a gigantic hangar, similar to the ones used for zeppelins, flanked by a small structure that apparently serves as a warehouse, and a row of three barracks, each containing four rooms, for the men who guard the site.

The hangar is built on an aluminum framework, with large, wide windows at the sides and front, and a dome on which a series of broad, tinted-glass canopies help keep out the sun. I remember seeing similar structures not only along Lake Constance and the shores of the North Sea and the Baltic, but also in ports in Louisiana and British Columbia where they load lumber cut into planks and ready to be shipped all over the world. The outlandish presence of a building like this on the banks of the Xurandó, at the edge of the jungle, is made even more startling by how meticulously it is maintained. Every centimeter of metal and glass gleams as if they'd just finished building it a few hours ago. A sudden loud noise indicated that a turbine had been switched on. The entire complex was illuminated by what appeared to be neon lighting, but much more subdued and diffuse. The light didn't reach the surrounding area, which explained why we hadn't seen it from a distance. The impression of unreality, of an unbearable nightmarish presence in the equatorial night, at first kept me awake and then visited my intermittent dreams, and each time, I found myself drenched in sweat, my heart racing. I knew I'd never have the chance to meet anyone who lived in this inconceivable building. A vague uneasiness has been taking hold of me, and now I'm trying to write in the diary so I won't look at the floating Gothic marvel of aluminum and glass lit by that morguish light and lulled by the gentle hum of its electrical plant. Now I understand the reservations and evasions of the captain, the major, the others, when I kept wanting to know what the sawmills really were. There was no point. The truth is impossible to communicate. "You'll see." That was what they all said in the end, refusing to go into detail. They were right. Once again Maqroll makes port at another of his extraordinary, unprofitable insights. It's hopeless. It will never change.

JUNE 24

This morning I went back to the sentry box. A guard listened to my request to speak with someone and closed the window without answering. I saw him talking on the phone. He opened the window again and said, "No visitors allowed at these installations. Good morning." He was about to close the window and I hurriedly asked, "The engineer? I don't want to talk to any of the guards, just to him. About lumber sales. Even if it's just by phone, I'd like to tell the engineer my reason for coming here." He looked at me for a moment with neutral, expressionless eyes as if he had heard my words through a distant loudspeaker. In a voice that was just as flat, almost energyless, he said, "There hasn't been an engineer here for a long time. Just soldiers and two sergeant majors. We have instructions not to talk to anybody. There's no point asking again." The telephone gave a frenetic ring. He closed the window, picked up the phone, listened intently, and finally nodded; he'd received an order. He opened the window a crack and said, "You have to remove the barge before noon tomorrow and stop asking to see somebody. And don't come back to the sentry box. I can't talk to you anymore." He slammed the glass shut and began to look over some papers on the desk. I felt immersed in another world, as if I'd sunk down to the depths of an uncharted, hostile ocean.

I went back to the barge and talked to the pilot. "I was afraid of this," he said. "I never tried to talk to them or go up to the gate. Those soldiers aren't from any base around here. They're relieved every so often. They come from the edge of the cordillera and they go back the same way, cutting across the mountain. Now you tell me what to do. Tomorrow noon we have to get out of here. I don't think it's a good idea to be stubborn." I suggested visiting the other factories further upriver. "No point in trying. They're all the same. Besides, we're running out of diesel. We'll have to go back at half speed and use the current. If we don't find fuel in one of the settlements, let's hope we have enough to get back to base." I lay down in the hammock and stopped talking. I was filled with a vague frustration, a silent irritation with myself and all the delays, negligence, and thoughtlessness that had brought me to this point and could have been avoided so easily if my character were different. We'll go back downriver. Crushed by irresistible despair I lay there trying to swallow the rage that swelled against everything and everybody. Knowing my anger was futile only increased it. At night, when I felt calmer and more resigned, I lit the lamp and wrote. The operating room light that floods the building, its aluminum and glass skeleton, the hum of the turbine, are becoming so intolerable that I've decided to leave tomorrow and get away from their devastating presence.

JUNE 25

We left this morning at dawn. As we cast off and let the current carry us to the middle of the river, the subdued howl of a siren could be heard coming from the building. In the distance another answered, and then another even further away. The factories were telling each other that the intruders had gone. The arrogant threat, the unspoken menace in those signals left us silent and debilitated for a good part of the day. We moved at a speed that at first pleased and surprised me. Then I suddenly thought of Angel Pass. A shudder went down my spine. Maybe it was easier going downriver. But I felt I wouldn't have the heart to face the crashing water again, its deafening noise and whirlpools, the overwhelming power of its unbridled energy. Late in the afternoon we came to a vast stillwater that turned the Xurandó into a lake, its shores lost in the distance no matter which way we turned. I was falling into a sleep that I hoped would revive me and help me forget the hostile world of the sawmills. A distant hum grew louder. I was torn between drowsiness and curiosity, and as sleep began to gain around, I heard a voice calling,

"Gaviero! Maqroll! Gaviero!" I woke up. The Junker from the base was slipping through the water alongside us. The major stood on the floats, his hand extended for a line that the pilot threw to him. He caught it on the second try and brought the plane close to the prow. "We're going ashore!" he ordered as he made a gesture of welcome with his free hand. He looked thinner, and his mustache wasn't as straight and neat as it had been. We moored the barge and secured the Junker to the prow. The major jumped on deck, as agile as a cat. We shook hands and went to sit on the hammocks. With no preliminaries and no questions about the trip, he came right to the point. "A patrol found Cap's grave. I went there last week. Some animal had tried to get to him. I had them dig deeper and we filled the top half with stones. In the jungle you can't just bury the dead. The animals get them in a few days. So you're on your way back? I can imagine what it was like. There was no point trying to warn you. Nobody believes you when you try to explain. Each man has to experience it for himself. What will you do now?" "I don't know," I answered, "I don't have many plans. I want to go back to the cordillera as soon as I can, but I don't know if there's a road on this side. But I wouldn't like to leave and still not know what's going on with those people in the factories. They say the machines are intact. I'm never coming back. Why don't you tell me?" He looked at his hands as he brushed away the leaves and mud left by the line. "All right, Gaviero," he began with a faint smile, "I'll tell you. In the first place, there's no mystery. The installations revert to the government in three years. Someone very high up is interested in them. He must be pretty influential because he could arrange for the Marines to guard and maintain them. And it's true, they are intact, but they were never put in operation because of an armed uprising in the timer area." He pointed to the mountain range. "Who's behind it? Not too hard to guess. On the reversion date, when the mills are turned over to the government, it's very possible the guerrillas will disappear as if by magic. Do you understand? It's very simple. There's always somebody smarter, isn't there?" Again that tone, that mixture of mockery and protectiveness, assurance and world-weariness. Before I could ask the question, he said, "Why didn't I tell you? We're big boys now, aren't we. I let you know as much as I could. Now that you're leaving and will certainly never come back, I can tell you everything. It's good you left when they told you to. Those people don't fool around. They say things only once. Then they open fire." I expressed my gratitude for his having given me as much warning as prudence would allow, and apologized for my obstinacy in pushing ahead. "Don't worry about it," he said. "It's not the first time. The business is very tempting—nothing harebrained about it. Except for what I told you: There's always somebody smarter. Always. It's just as well you're taking it philosophically. It's the only way. Well, now I have a proposition to make: If you want to go to the uplands, maybe I can help. Tomorrow, if you like, we'll fly to El Sordo Lagoon. It's in the middle of the cordillera. There's a village on shore where trucks leave for the uplands. Settle up with Miguel. I'll come at dawn tomorrow, and we can be there in an hour. What do you think?" "I don't know how to thank you," I answered, moved by his interest. "I really don't have the strength to go back to the jungle or face the rapids again. I'll pay Miguel and expect you tomorrow. Thanks again. I hope this doesn't put you out too much." "I told you the first time we met—you're not the man for this country. No, it's no trouble. The commander commands. The important thing is to know how far you can go, and I learned that when I was a second lieutenant. It's the only thing you have to know when you put on the braid. All right then, see you tomorrow. I'm leaving now because there's barely time to get back to base." He shook my hand, whistled to the pilot on the barge, and jumped onto the plane. He said something to the pilot beside him and looked at me with a smile more roguish than cordial.

This will be my last night here. I must admit to indescribable relief, as if I had drunk a potion that instantly restored all my strength and returned me to the world, the order of things that are mine. I talked to Miguel. He didn't mind settling now. I paid him and gave the pilot a good tip. I'm trying to sleep, but a wild excitement is churning inside me and keeping me awake. It's as if a great stone had been lifted from me, as if I'd been relieved of an overwhelming, painful, crushing task.

JUNE 29

The major came in the Junker at about seven in the morning. I picked up my gear and said goodbye to Miguel and Ignacio, who smiled the way old men do at the foolish stubbornness of others who repeat the mistakes they themselves have already made and forgotten. Miguel gave me his hand but there was no handshake. It was like holding a warm, damp fish. In his eyes I could see a distant, faint glimmer that revealed all the cordiality he was capable of feeling. At that instant I knew I was leaving the jungle. The mechanic not only is its perfect expression but is made of its very substance. He is an amorphous extension of that disastrous, faceless world. I climbed into the Junker, sat down behind the pilot and the major, and adjusted my seat belt. We moved in the water for a moment and then took off to the soothing vibration of the fuselage. I fell into a kind of trance until the major touched my knee and pointed to the lagoon down below. We landed gently in the water and taxied to a pier where a sergeant and three soldiers were waiting for us. The major climbed down with me. I said goodbye to the pilot, and then I realized he wasn't the one I had met before. He had one eye and a whitish scar on his forehead. The major left me with the sergeant and told him to find me a place to stay in the village until I located a truck going to the uplands. He gave me his hand and, with rather forced seriousness, cut off my attempts to thank him. "Please, from now on, think over your business ventures more carefully and don't take this kind of risk again. It's not worth it. I know what I'm talking about. You do too. Goodbye, and good luck." He climbed into the cabin and slammed the door, making the fuselage resonate with a familiar sound. The plane moved away, leaving a wake of foam that began to dissipate as the Junker disappeared into the low clouds of the cordillera.

Something has ended. Something is beginning. I saw the jungle. I had nothing to do with it, and I'm not taking anything away. Perhaps only these pages will bear dim witness to an episode that says little about my shrewdness and that I hope I'll forget very soon. In less than a week I'll be in The Snow of the Admiral, telling Flor Estévez things that surely will have little to do with what really happened. I can taste the aroma of bitter coffee on my palate.

Yesterday some Marines came to the village. They're part of the detachment that was relieved at the sawmills. They say the barge was wrecked at Angel Pass and the bodies of Miguel and the pilot haven't been found. The current must have carried them far downriver and washed them up on some beach in the jungle. The barge, stripped and battered, ran aground on a sandbar. Nobody came to claim it.

Inside the binder that held the pages of Maqroll's Diary was a loose sheet, written in green ink, with a hotel letterhead and no date. When I read it, I realized it was related to the diary, and for that reason it seems appropriate to transcribe it here. It may be of interest to those who have followed the Gaviero's story.

HOTEL DE FLANDRE ✱ *Quai des Tisserands No. 9 / Antwerp / Te. 3223*

. . . as we agreed. For three days we climbed a steep highway full of dangerous, carelessly engineered curves. At a certain point in the road I left the truck and rented a mule at the Cuchilla inn. For two days I wandered the uplands, looking for the highway that runs past The Snow of the Admiral. When I had lost all hope, I finally found it. I left the mule with the boy who had rented it to me and sat down in a gully to wait for a truck driving to the top. Two hours later an eight-ton Saurer came struggling up the grade like an asthmatic. The driver agreed to give me a ride. "I'm going all the way up," I explained, while he looked at me as if he were trying to remember who I was. We traveled all night. He woke me at dawn in a fog so thick it almost made driving impossible. "It must be around here. What're you looking for in this godforsaken place?" "A shop called The Snow of the Admiral," I answered as fear began to rise through my solar plexus." "Well," the driver said, "I'm going to stop for a while. You look around and see what you find. With this fog . . . " He lit a cigarette. I walked into a milky air so thick I could hardly see anything. The ditch beside the road helped to orient me, and in a little while I could make out the house. Letters were missing from the sign that hung by one corner from a rusty nail and blew in the wind. Everything was locked from the inside: doors, windows, shutters. Most of the glass was missing, and the building was on the verge of collapse. I went to the back door. Part of the balcony that used to extend out over a cliff had fallen in, and the thick wooden support beams, balancing on the edge of the ravine, were covered with moss and the droppings of parrots that rested there before flying on to the low country. It began to drizzle, and the fog cleared instantly.

I went back to the truck. "There's nothing left, señor. I knew the place but didn't know what it was called," the driver said with a compassion that wounded me deeply. "Ride with me, if you like. I'm going as far as La Osa coffee plantation. I think they know you there." I nodded in silence and climbed up beside him. The truck began the descent. A smell of burned asbestos indicated his constant working of the brakes. I thought about Flor Estévez. It would be very hard to get used to her absence. Something began hurting inside. It was the grinding of grief that would take a long time to heal.

The Road to Santiago

by Alejo Carpentier

translated by Frances Partridge

[The common Spanish name of the Milky Way is *el Camino de Santiago*: the high road of Saint James.]

I

Juan was walking along the bank of the River Scheldt with his own drum slung on his left hip, and another (won at cards) over his shoulder, when his attention was attracted by a ship which had just put in to shore and made fast to the bollards. The dusk, and the fine drizzle beating a gentle tattoo on that part of the drumhead which was unprotected by his hat-brim, made everything look a little hazy—hazier even than it looked already as a result of the brandy and beer provided by his friend the sutler, whose cart was spouting smoke from all its flues a little further downhill, close to the Lutheran church now being used as a stable. But such an atmosphere of sadness hung about this boat that it was as if the canal mist were pouring from inside her, like the breath of misfortune. Her sails were patched with pieces of old rusty-coloured canvas; her rigging was frayed, her yards mildewed, and streamers of dead seaweed were hanging from her un-careened sides. Here and there a seashell, like a star, a grey rose or a plaster coin, was embedded in this vegetation from far-off seas, now rotting and turning brown and dark green from contact with the icy cold of the water slumbering between sombre walls. The emaciated sailors looked like men sick of the scurvy, with their hollow cheeks, sunken eyes and toothless mouths. As they finished casting off from the long-boat that had brought them to the quay, their faces gave no sign of pleasure, even when they saw the lights of the taverns being lit. Both ship and men seemed to be sunk in the same remorse, as though the crew had called upon God blasphemously in a storm; and they were now winding up the ropes and hauling down the sails as reluctantly as if they had been condemned never to set foot on land. Then suddenly a hatchway opened, and it was as if the sun had lit up the Antwerp dusk. Small orange-trees, all ablaze with fruit and each planted in a half barrel, were being carried out of the darkness of the hold and set up in a scented avenue on the deck. The appearance of these trees decked in their brilliant globes transfigured the evening, and the mixed aroma of juice, pepper and cinnamon so amazed Juan that he took the drum from his shoulder, put it on the ground and sat astride it. It looked as though there were some foundation, then, for the rumours about the Duke's love affair, and his mistress's extravagant cravings for such presents as only an Alba could fetch her from the Spice Islands, or the Kingdoms of India or the city of Hormuz, to indulge her slightest whim. These small, heavily laden orange-trees must have been grown in the garden of some Christian Moor—no one else could perform such miracles with plants—before they braved storms and enemy ships, and came here to adorn a mirror-lined gallery in the palace of the woman who rouged her Flemish skin with the finest powdered coral from the Levant. For in the great days of voyages and discoveries, when a woman began to be demanding, the cosmetics that had been prized for centuries no longer satisfied her; she must have some new invention from Denmark, balms from Muscovy and essences extracted from rare flowers; if she wanted birds, they must be Indian parrots trained to use bad language; and as for dogs, no affectionate mongrel would do, she insisted on griffon-like lap-dogs, or creatures covered in long wool, that could be clipped to leave an outlandish tuft tied with coloured ribbon. So, naturally, whenever the soldiers got drunk on the Zamoran sutler's brandy, one of them was sure to get carried away and say that the reason the Duke had stayed so long at Antwerp, and that winter quarters were becoming spring quarters, was because he could not tear himself away from listening to a voice singing to the lute, as sweetly as the sirens sang long ago, according to the ancients. 'Siren?' exclaimed the girl who washed the dishes, a hard drinker who had trudged after the army all the way from Naples. 'Sirens? What you mean is that two tits are more of a draw than two carts!' Juan had not heard the rest, what with the commotion made by soldiers hurrying away from the sutler's cart without paying either for food or drink, for fear that one of the Duke's servants should come by and denounce this sally. But now, as he watched the orange-trees being carried on shore under the supervision of a newly arrived ensign, the girl's words came back to him, heavily underlined by this new evidence. Some covered carts belonging to the quarter-master's department were being loaded with the little trees. With his stomach hollowed by a sudden craving to eat stewed tripe or pick the meat off a calf's foot, Juan slung the drum he had won at cards over his shoulder again. Just then he noticed an enormous, swollen-looking rat, covered in pustules and with a naked tail, using a cable as a bridge to come ashore. With his free hand he caught up a stone and balanced it while he took aim. The rat had stopped still when it reached the quay like a stranger disembarking in an unknown town and wondering where the inns were. When it felt the pebble ricochet off its back before disappearing into the water of the canal, it started running towards the house of the preachers who had been burned at the stake, now a forage store. Without giving it another thought, Juan went back to the Zamoran sutler's cart. The soldiers of his company were baiting the dish-washer, by making up songs describing the girls of her village as tarnished virgins, cuckold-makers and bawds. But just then the carts loaded with orange-trees went by, and there was a sudden silence—broken only by a snort from the scullery-maid and the neighing of a stallion, which echoed through the nave of the Lutheran church like the laugh of Beelzebub himself.

2

At first it was thought that the trouble was only boils—nothing unusual in people coming from Italy. But when fevers that were certainly not tertian fevers appeared, and when five soldiers of the company were carried off vomiting blood, Juan began to feel afraid. He kept on exploring with his fingers the glands where the swelling from the French sickness usually began, expecting to find them like a chaplet of nuts. And although the surgeon was obviously reluctant to utter the name of a disease that had not been seen in Flanders for a long time, owing to the humidity of the air, his travels in the kingdom of Naples led him to conjecture that this was in fact the plague, and in a very severe form. He soon learned that all the sailors on the boat of the dwarf orange-trees were lying on their bunks, cursing the day they had ever breathed the air of Las Palmas, for the disease had been brought there by ransomed prisoners from Algiers, and was striking people down in the streets as if by lightning. And as if the fear of the scourge were not enough, that part of the town where the company was billeted was full of rats. Juan remembered that beast of ill-omen, the repulsive rat with the naked tail which his stone had missed by several inches; it must now be acting as a standard-bearer, or heretic priest, among the hordes running through courtyards, stealing into shops and polishing off all the cheeses on this bank of the river. His landlord, a fishmonger of Lutheran appearance, was in despair every morning to find his herrings half eaten, a skate minus its tail and a lamprey reduced to mere bones;

or worse still, one of the disgusting creatures lying drowned, belly upwards, in the eel-tank. Only a crab or a mussel could resist the ravenous greed of these festering purulent rats from God knows what Spice Island, who gnawed their way through the straps of armour and leather harness—and even profaned the Host before it had been consecrated by the company's chaplain. When a cold breeze blowing straight from the flooded pastures set the soldier shivering in his garret lodging under the tiles, he threw himself on his camp-bed groaning that his chest was on fire and his glands painful and swollen, and that he deserved death as a punishment for giving up teaching people to sing hymns to the glory of Our Lord, in order to become a regimental drummer—thus exchanging the art of the motet and the quadrivium for the music of the zambomba and the pig-gelder's whistle, such as the village youths played during the Corpus Christi festivities. But with a drum and two sticks one could go all over the world, from the kingdom of Naples to Flanders, beating out a march time beside the trumpet and the box-wood fife. And since Juan did not feel that he was a born priest or cantor, he had given up the probable honour of being allowed to join Maestro Ciruelo's class at Alcalá one day, and had followed the first recruiting officer who put three silver pieces of eight in his hand and promised him that a soldier's life would give him his fill of women, wine and cards. Now that he had seen the world, he understood the vanity of the desires that had cost his sainted mother so many tears. What good had it done him to sound the charge in the heat of three battles, and defy the thunder of the bombards, if he was doomed to die here in this garret—whose green window-panes were tinged with the gloomy light from the torches of the night patrol—listening to the muffled sound of drums beaten out of time by those beer-soaked Flemish? Juan had been groaning aloud that his chest was burning and his glands were swollen, in the hope that God would take pity on him, and refrain from sending him the disease in real earnest. But suddenly his body was seized by a horrible sensation of cold. Without taking his boots off, he got on to his bed, pulling a blanket over him, and a quilt on top of the blanket. But a blanket and a quilt were not nearly enough; he would have needed all the blankets of the whole company and all the quilts in Antwerp to give his ailing body that warmth that King David in his old age had hoped to find in the body of a young girl. Seeing him shivering so violently, the fishmonger, who had been summoned by his groans, shrank back in terror, and hurried down the rat-populated stairs crying out that the disease was in his house and the Catholics were being punished for their

simony and traffic in documents. Through a haze, Juan saw the face of
the surgeon who unfastened his belt and felt his groins, and then suddenly to the sound of a strange beating of drums—very rhythmical, yet
muffled—came the portentous arrival of the Duke of Alba.

He entered alone and unattended, dressed in black, with his ruff
very tight round his neck and his grizzled beard poking forwards, so
that he looked as if he had been decapitated, and his head was being
carried on a white marble platter. Juan made a tremendous effort to
get up from his bed and stand to attention as a soldier should, but his
visitor leapt over the quilt covering him, and sat down on the far side
on an esparto-grass stool with several earthenware flagons standing on
it. The flagons did not fall off or break, although a smell of hollands
spread through the room like the burning perfumes in a synagogue.
From outside came a confused discordant noise of trumpets, blown as
inharmoniously as if their notes were shivering in the same cold that
was making the sick man's teeth chatter. Without relaxing a frown that
might well have condemned Lutherans to be burned alive, the Duke
of Alba took three oranges which had been spoiling the fit of his dou-
blet and began playing with them like a juggler, throwing them from
hand to hand above his head with its Roman hair-cut, with surprising
agility. Juan wanted to compliment him on his unexpected skill in this
art, at the same time addressing him as Lion of Spain, Hercules of
Italy and Scourge of France, but no words came from his lips. Suddenly
the rain began violently drumming on the tiles of the roof. The window on to the street was blown open by a gust, extinguishing the
lamp. And Juan saw the Duke of Alba go out with the wind, his body
so elongated that it wound like a satin ribbon past the lintel, followed
by the oranges, which now had funnel-shaped hats and frogs' legs, and
were smiling with the wrinkles in their peel. Past the attic window,
from the courtyard to the street, a woman came floating astride the
handle of a lute; her breasts were hanging out of the low neck of her
dress, and her skirt was lifted to show her bare buttocks under the
wires of her farthingale. A gust which shook the whole house finally
carried off these horrifying figures, and, half fainting with terror, Juan
went to the window for air and saw that the sky was cloudless and
serene. For the first time since last summer, the Milky Way whitened
the firmament.

'The road to Santiago!' he groaned, falling on his knees before his
sword; its point was fixed in the floorboards, and its handle completed
the sign of the cross.

3

The pilgrim tramped the roads of France, grasping his staff in emaciated hands; he was wearing a cloak sanctified by beautiful shells sewn to the leather, and carried a gourd filled with pure stream water. His beard was growing longer under the drooping brim of his hat, and the frayed edge of his serge habit brushed against the worn sandals that had piously trod the streets of Paris, without ever crossing the threshold of a tavern, or deviating from the straight road to Santiago, except to admire from a distance the holy house of the monks of Cluny. Juan slept wherever he happened to be when night overtook him, and the kind inmates of several houses invited him in out of piety; but whenever he heard of a convent in the neighbourhood, he quickened his steps a little, so as to arrive at the hour of the angelus and ask shelter of the lay-brother who peered out of the wicket gate. He gave his scallop-shell to be kissed, and settled under the arches of the hospice, where hard stone benches provided all the comfort he could find for limbs weakened by illness and the first winter showers which had lashed his back all the way from Flanders to the Seine. Next day he was off at dawn, impatient to get at least as far as the Pass of Roncesvalles, for it seemed to him that his body would feel less broken once he was among his own countrymen. At Tours he was joined by the pilgrims from Germany, with whom he conversed by signs. At the hospital of St. Hilaire at Poitiers he met with twenty more pilgrims, and quite a large band of them set off towards the Landes together, leaving behind the fields of stubble wheat and making for the land of ripening vines. Here it was still summer, although the tasks of autumn were being done. The pine forests were denser, but the sun lingered on their topmost branches, and after picking a few grapes as they passed, their midday rests tended to grow longer among the aromatic plants and the cool shadows, and the pilgrims began to sing. The French sang of all the good things they had given up to fulfil their vows to Saint Jacques; the Germans rasped out some phrases in teutonic Latin, of which the most that could be understood was 'Herru Sanctiagu! Got Sanctiagu!' While the more musical Flemish intoned a hymn, which Juan ornamented with accompanying parts of his own invention: 'Soldier of Christ—with holy orisons—you shield us all—from misfortune!'

And so, walking slowly in a procession of more than eighty pilgrims, they arrived at Bayonne, in whose excellent hospital they could rid themselves of fleas, put new straps on their sandals, delouse each other in brotherly fashion, and get remedies for their eyes, many of them rheumy and inflamed from the dusty roads. The courtyards of the building swarmed with wretchedness in every form; men scratching their scabies, exhibiting their stumps and washing their sores in well-water. One was suffering from scrofula which even the touch of the King of France had been unable to cure, while another was sitting astride a bench to ease the discomfort of private parts so enormously swollen that they looked like the testicles of the giant Adamastor. Juan the Pilgrim was one of the few who asked for no remedies. The sweat that saturated his woollen garment as he walked through the vines in the sun had purged his body of its unhealthy humours. Afterwards, his lungs had delighted in the resinous aroma of the pines and the occasional waft of a breeze from the sea. And when he took his first bath in buckets of water drawn from the well that had been sanctified by the thirst of countless pilgrims, he felt so invigorated and joyful that he tossed off a jug of wine beside the river Adour, confident that there must be dispensation for a man who had just risked catching cold by wetting his head and arms for the first time for weeks. When he returned to the hospital his gourd was full of strong red wine instead of pure water, and he settled with his back against one of the pillars of the porch to drink in peace. In the sky, the Milky Way still indicated the road to Santiago. But Juan's spirits were lightened by the wine, and the starry heavens no longer looked to him as they had on the night when the plague brought him the dreadful warning that he was to be punished for his many sins. Just in time, he had made his vow to go and kiss the chain which had fettered the Great Apostle in prison in Jerusalem. But now that he was rested and washed, and had fewer lice, and more wine inside him, he began wondering whether his fever had been caused by the plague, and whether that diabolical vision was not merely the result of his fever. The groans of an old man lying beside him, with half his face eaten away by a tumour, reminded him that a vow is a vow, and burying his head in the cowl of his pilgrim's cloak, he rejoiced at the thought that he would arrive in bodily health, while others would drag their sores and scabs through the Puerta Francina, uncertain whether they would receive divine help. His restored health made him think with pleasure of the exuberant flesh of the Antwerp whores, who had delighted in the lean Spaniards, as hairy as goats, taken them on their ample laps before coming to business, and unfastened their cuirasses with arms as white as almond paste. The gourd hanging from the nails on Juan's staff now contained undiluted wine.

4

Entering burgos by the road from France, the pilgrim suddenly found himself in the bustle and hubbub of a fair. His desire to go straight to the cathedral was defeated by the steam of frying pancakes, and the smell of grilled meat, and tripe with parsley and pimento sauce, which delicacies he was generously invited to taste by a toothless old hag, from her booth by a gateway between two massive towers. After this, there was wine to be had much cheaper than in the taverns, from skins carried on donkeys. Then he was caught up in the swirling crowds gaping at the giant and the tight-rope walker, the broadsheet vendor and the man displaying highly coloured pictures illustrating the terrifying adventures of the woman who was made pregnant by the Devil and gave birth to a litter of piglets at Alhucemas. Further on a man was offering to pull out teeth painlessly, and giving the patient a crimson handkerchief to prevent his seeing the flow of blood, while his assistant beat on a bass drum with a mallet to drown the sound of his cries; at yet another stall a man was selling Bologna soap, ointment for chilblains, healing roots and dragon's blood. And there was the usual hullabaloo of frying doughnuts, flageolets playing out of tune, and an occasional dog dressed in coat and cap coming to beg alms for a poor cripple and walking on its hind legs like a man. Tired of being jostled, Juan the Pilgrim now stopped in front of some blind men sitting on a bench, who were just coming to the end of a song about the marvelous American Harpy—feared by both crocodile and lion—who lived in a foul-smelling den among broad mountain ranges and deserted forests:

> For an enormous sum
> A European bought her,
> With him she went to Europe;
> He landed her at Malta
> From there he went to Greece,
> Thence to Constantinople,
> The whole of Thrace exploring.
> 'Twas there she first refused
> The food they set before her,
> And in a few brief weeks
> She died raging and roaring.
>
> CHORUS: That was the end of the Harpy
> Monster most grim on earth,

> Oh that all such monsters
> Must surely die at birth!

Those who had been standing in the second row hurried away quickly to avoid having to give alms; they laughed at the blind men and left them venting their anger on the whole race of misers; but other blind men barred their way a little further on with a tableau of puppets representing the entry of the Moors into Cuenca disguised as sheep. Escaping from the American Harpy, Juan found himself transported to the land of Cockaigne, news of which was brought home after Pizarro had conquered the kingdom of Peru. This time the singers' voices were less cracked, and while one of them offered up prayers for barren women, the leader of the others, a very tall blind man wearing a black hat, touched his guitar with long finger-nails and sang the concluding verses of the romance:

> Every house has a garden
> Of gold and silver made
> And a marvellous abundance
> Of riches and good things.
> At the four corners
> Stand four tall cypresses,
> The first is full of partridges,
> The second of turkeys,
> Rabbits breed in the third
> And capons in the fourth.
> At the foot of each cypress
> Is a basin, encrusted
> With doubloons of eight reals
> Or doubloons of four.

And now, finishing his tune and assuming the solemnity of a recruiting sergeant, the blind man ended thus, in a voice loud enough to reach the four corners of the fair and with his guitar held up like a flag:

> Then, take heart, good sirs,
> Courage, poor gentlemen,
> Good news for the poor,
> And joy for those in trouble!
> For those who wish to go
> And see this new marvel,
> Ten ships will sail together
> From Seville this year!

Once again the audience began to steal away, while the singers hurled insults at them, and Juan found himself pushed to the end of an alley, where a cheap-jack, recently returned from the West Indies, was offering for sale with exaggerated gestures two alligators stuffed with straw, which he said came from Cuzco. He had a monkey on his shoulder and a parrot perched on his left hand. He blew into a large pink conch, and a black slave emerged from a crimson box like Lucifer in a miracle-play, proffering strings of pitted pearls, stones that would cure headaches, belts made of vicuña wool, tinsel earrings and other tawdry finery from Potosí. When he laughed, the negro showed teeth that had been curiously filed to a point, and his cheeks were scarred with knife slashes; then seizing a tambourine he began to dance in the wildest way imaginable, moving his waist as if he were broken in two, and making such outrageous gestures that even the old tripe-seller left her stew-pots to come and watch him. But just then it began to rain, and everyone ran to take shelter under the eaves—the puppet-master with his puppets under his cape, the blind men clutching their sticks, and the broadsheets of the woman who had given birth to piglets getting thoroughly soaked. Juan found himself in the parlour of an inn, where people were playing cards and drinking heavily. The negro dried the monkey with his handkerchief, while the parrot was preparing to take a nap, perched on the hoop of a barrel. The West Indian ordered wine, and began telling the pilgrim cock-and-bull stories. But although Juan had, like everyone else, been forewarned about West Indian romances, it occurred to him now that some wild stories had turned out to be true. That horrifying monster the American Harpy had in fact died at Constantinople, raging and roaring. The land of Cockaigne and its ponds encrusted with doubloons had actually been discovered by a fortunate captain called Longores de Sentlam y de Gorgas. Neither Peruvian gold nor silver from Potosí had been invented by West Indians. Nor had the golden shoes that Gonzalo Pizarro's horses had nailed to their hoofs. These things were well known to the paymaster of the King's fleet when the galleons came back to Seville loaded with treasure. His tongue loosened by wine, the West Indian now began describing some less celebrated marvels: a spring of such miraculous water that the crookedest and most crippled old men had only to bathe in it, and when they emerged their heads were covered in shining hair, their wrinkles were smoothed away, their health restored to them, their joints no longer swollen, and they were vigorous enough to make a whole army of Amazons pregnant. He spoke of amber from Florida, of the statues of giants seen by the other Pizarro at Puerto Viejo, and of the skulls found in the Indies with teeth as thick as three fingers, and only one ear—and that in the nape of the neck. There was also a sister city to Cockaigne, where everything was made of gold—even the barbers' basins, pots and pans, the rims of carriage wheels and oil-lamps. 'The inhabitants must have been alchemists!' exclaimed the astonished pilgrim. But the West Indian only asked for more wine and explained that the gold from the Indies had put a stop to the lucubrations of those who carried on the Great Work. Hermetic mercury, the divine elixir, moonwort, calamine and brass had all been abandoned by the followers of Morieno, Raimundo and Avicena, when they saw so many ships arriving laden with gold bars, gold vases and powder, precious stones, statues and jewellery. There is no object in being an alchemist in a country where there is as much of the best gold as would fill a room as high as an Estramaduran could reach.

It was night when the West Indian went off to his room, talking incoherently from all the wine he had drunk, while the negro, the monkey and the parrot went up to the loft over the stable. Nor was the pilgrim's head any clearer, and he swayed from side to side of his staff, and now and again described a circle round it, until at last he reached an alley in the suburbs, where a whore took him to bed with her until morning, in exchange for being allowed to kiss the holy shells that were already coming unsewn from his habit. A great many clouds drifted over the town that night, veiling the Milky Way.

5

Now he began to tell everyone who cared to listen that he was on his way home from a place he had never in fact been to. Saint James the Great and his prison chains and the axe that had decapitated him all lay behind him. So that he might still make use of convent hostels and enjoy their cabbage soup with slices of rye bread and other advantages, Juan was still wearing his pilgrim's dress and cloak and carrying his gourd— although it contained nothing but brandy. The road from France to Santiago lay far behind, abandoned in favour of another which passed through Ciudad Real and kept him for three days with his mouth to a leather bottle full of the most famous wine in the whole kingdom. As he went on his way he noticed a change in the inhabitants. They had little to say about what was happening in Flanders; their ears were pricked towards Seville, for news of an absent son, an uncle who had moved his forge to Cartagena, or someone who had lost his silver through not having registered it. There were villages whence whole families had departed: stone-cutters and their workmen, poor gentlemen with their horses and servants. And now drums were being beaten in every village square, to recruit men to go and conquer and colonise new provinces across the sea. All the taverns and inns were full of travellers. And so, having changed his scallop-shell for a compass, Juan arrived at the Casa de la Contratacion. He had completely forgotten that he had ever been a pilgrim, and looked more like an actor from some disbanded company, who had run short of money and rifled the box of costumes, finally appearing in the coat of the fool in the interlude, Biscayan breeches, Pilate's armour and the hat worn by Arcadio, the amorous shepherd of a comedy in the Italian style which had failed to please the public. Gradually, by collecting hose here, a cape there, exchanging his pilgrim's cloak for some shoes, and bargaining with the old-clothes man, Juan was fitted out in a style which no more suggested a pilgrim than it did a soldier in the Italian army. Nor had he any intention of responding to the recruiting sergeant's appeal, for the West Indian had told him that to travel in the fleet of a conqueror such as Cortes was not the best way to get rich. What paid best in the Indies at present was to have flair and a mind like a compass-needle, and be able to jump ahead of others; there was no need to pay attention to royal warrants, graduates' remonstrances and outcries from bishops. Over there, even the Inquisition had become easy-going, since very little could be done with all those negroes and Indians who were almost totally ignorant of religious matters. Besides it was common knowledge that if they started distributing sanbenitos most of them would fall to chaplains guilty of soliciting in the confessional, and since the excuse of having given way to sudden impulse is more valid in a hot country, the Holy Office in America had decided from the first to use its bonfires to heat up cups of chocolate, instead of bothering to establish the technical degrees of heresy—obstinate, negative, diminished, impenitent, perjured or enlightened. And besides, in a country where there were no Lutheran churches or synagogues, the Inquisition could afford to take a nap. Perhaps the negroes did sometimes beat their drums in front of wooden images smelling of the devil's cloven hoof. But that was their affair, and the monks shrugged their shoulders. They were more worried by heresies supported by pamphlets, writings and books. So, after bending their heads under the holy water sprinkler, the negroes and Indians often returned to their idolatry; but they were too badly needed in the mines and *repartimientos* for them to be treated, as the fourth apostle says, like withered vine-branches, to be gathered and thrown on the fire. The Spaniard from the West Indies had given Juan the benefit of his experience and recommended him to a Sevillian rope-maker, whose workshop was full of camp-beds and straw mattresses, where others like himself were awaiting permits to embark for New Spain with the fleet that was due to set sail from Sanlúcar in May with a crowd of lively adventurers. Juan's name had been entered in the books of the Casa de la Contratacion as Juan of Antwerp—for he must not forget that he was expected in Flanders once his vow was fulfilled—between those of a certain Jorge, the Bishop of Tarragona's negro slave, and an individual who denied rather too insistently that his father had returned to the old faith and his grandfather had been burned as a heretic. The next names on the page were those of a leather-dresser to the Empress, a Genoese merchant called Jacome de Castellón, several precentors, two firework-makers, the dean of Santa Maria del Darien with his page Francisquillo, a bone-setter skilled in mending broken limbs, priests, graduates, three newly converted Christians, and a woman called Lucia with a complexion like a stewed pear. As for complexions it would be better not to make distinctions concerning the colour of stewed pears or anything else, for in his wanderings through the labyrinthine Andalusian streets Juan was astonished by the marvellous varieties of human colour. Not only were there enfranchised negroes, dark as pitch or the skin of an aubergine, waiting for the day when they could leave with the fleet, but also dusky Cuban dancers of the *paracumbé,* Guinean women painted with kohl, and mulatresses from Zofalá. And during these last days before the embarkation a great many Indians were to be seen waiting to return to their native land among the followers of some prelate or captain who had come to do business at Court. The chief precentor of Guatemala, who was to sail with the fleet, had three servants to wait on him alone, each olive-skinned, with his brows bound with an embroidered fillet, and wearing a thick woollen blanket in all the colours of the rainbow thrown over his head like a cloak. All three wore crosses round their necks, but God alone knew what pagan ideas they exchanged in their gasping language, which sounded more like the whining of deaf-mutes than human speech. There were Indians from Hispaniola, natives of Yucatan in white trousers, and others, round-headed, with blubber lips and thick hair that looked as though it had been cut under a pudding basin, who came from the mainland; and sometimes Mass was attended by the eight Mexicans from the house of the Medina Sidonia family, who had played the flageolet—and very skilfully too—during the fiesta in honour of the meeting of Doña Maria and Prince Philip at Salamanca. There were eunuchs from Algiers and Moorish slaves with branded faces among this noisy, exotic crowd, brilliant with stuffs of many garish colours, beads and feathers, which brought a powerful aroma of adventure to Juan of Antwerp's nostrils. And then there was the brine in which the ships' stores were pickled, the caulker's tar, salted sardines from the white-wine shops, dicing going on all day and night and frenzied sarabands being danced in the brothels, where the sailors had introduced the custom of chewing a brownish plant that stained their saliva yellow and gave their beards a strong and lingering smell of liquorice, vinegar and spice.

And now Juan of Antwerp was on the high seas. They would not let him go to Mexico, because the Council wanted people to colonise regions impoverished by the raids of the French pirates, and to make good the shortage of labourers and the mortality among the Indians in the mines. Juan swore and stamped when he received this news. Then he reflected that it was God's punishment because he had not gone to Compostela. But the West Indian from the fair at Burgos had turned up most opportunely in the travellers' tavern, and told him that once he had crossed the ocean he could laugh at the Council's officials, and go wherever he liked, as all the more independent colonists did. So Juan recovered his good temper and beat his drum on the deck of the ship to announce that there would be a pig-race on the orlop before the animals succumbed to the cook's knife and were salted down. For want of other amusements, they tried to defeat the boredom of a dead calm and forget that the drinking-water in the barrels was already tainted, by racing pigs and calves until they dropped. Next there was a battle with syringes filled with sea water; a pole was tied to the neck of an infuriated dog, which broke more than one head with its gyrations; a blindfold man chased a cock tied between two planks and decapitated it with a single sabre-stroke; and when all this had become tedious and money had changed hands ten times over at games of quinola or rentoy, fevers broke out, people collapsed with sunstroke, someone left his teeth in a ship's biscuit already gnawed by mice, a dead man was thrown overboard, a jet-black negress gave birth to twins, some vomited, other scratched themselves, yet others voided their entrails; and when it seemed that the fleas, lice, filth and stench had got beyond endurance, a cry from the look-out announced one morning that at last he could see the headland by the port of San Cristobal at Havana. It was high time they arrived. Juan was already heartily sick of his thankless journey in search of a fortune, although some flying fish, seen a few days before, had seemed to him a portent announcing the proximity of American Harpies and the Land of Cockaigne. Delighted by the sight of a slender belfry rising above a collection of roofs and cabins which must surely be the town, he seized his drumsticks and beat out the rhythm of the march to which his company had entered Antwerp to take up winter quarters there, before making war against the heretics—those enemies of our holy faith.

6

But they found nothing but gossip there, nothing but scandal and scheming, letters going to and fro, mortal hatreds and boundless envy, all contained within eight stinking streets, deep in mud the whole year round, where a few black hairless pigs rootled happily in heaps of filth. Each time the New Spanish Fleet set sail for home, the ship's masters were entrusted with commissions, letters, lies and slanders, to be taken back to Spain and delivered to anyone who could best use them to harm someone else. What with the poisonous effect of the heat on tempers, the humidity rotting everything, the mosquitoes, and the jiggers laying their eggs under toenails, malevolence and greed for small benefits (for there were no large ones in that country) gnawed at men's souls like a canker. A man who could write did not use this advantage profitably, like the ancients, in composing a pastoral play or an entertainment for Corpus Christi, but in sending letters of complaint to the King, or long rigmaroles to the Council with a pen dipped in gall. While the Governor was trying to discredit the King's officers in an eight-page letter, the Bishop would be denouncing the Governor for living in concubinage; the Inspector accused the Bishop of usurping the money due to the Inquisitor without the consent of the Cardinal of Toledo; the Public Registrar accused the Treasurer of not paying the correct tithes, and the Treasurer (who was a friend of the Mayor's) accused the Registrar of dishonesty and swindling. And so a chain was formed, always ready to break at the weakest or most unexpected point. One man was denounced for having bought aphrodisiac herbs from a negro witch-doctor who had been whipped at Cartagena de Indias; the Town Crier was accused of committing the abominable sin; an *Encomendero* of moving the boundaries of State property; the Precentor of debauchery; the Chief Gunner of drunkenness, and the Beadle of pederasty. The town barber—whose squint was an offence in itself—forged the final link in the chain of infamy by declaring that Doña Violante, the wife of the last Governor, was an old harlot who had shameful relations with her own slaves. So that San Cristobal had become a hell, where men were dragging out the most wretched existence that could be found anywhere on this earth, among Indian servants stinking of rancid oil and negroes smelling like skunks. Ah! the Indies! the Indies! The only thing that cheered the spirits of Juan of Antwerp was the arrival of sailors from Mexico or Hispaniola. Then, for a few days, he would remember that he was a soldier, and perhaps he would steal a side of beef from the butchers, which several of them would cook in annatto sauce or powdered chillis from Veracruz; or else he would help break in the fishmonger's door and carry off baskets full of porgies and freshwater tortoises. During these months, for lack of more delicate fare, Juan developed a taste for such novelties as tomatoes, sweet potatoes and prickly pears. He filled his nostrils with tobacco, and on days when food was short—as it was more often than not—he dipped his manioc bread in cane syrup, afterwards burying his face in his bowl and licking it clean. And when the ships' crews came ashore, he danced with the enfranchised negresses who kept a wooden enclosure with bug-ridden mattresses, close to the careening-dock—they were ugly as sin, but women were scarce. The small sums he earned by beating his drum when a ship hove in sight, or by walking at the head of some procession, or trying to keep time with the mulatto women rattling their maracas at Christmas, he spent in the chop-house of a friend of the Governor's, close to the bakery, where casks of the worst possible red wine arrived now and again. No use asking here for wine from Ciudad Real, Ribadavia or Cazalla. The stuff he poured down his throat was rough to the tongue, bad, sour, and expensive into the bargain like everything else this island produced. Clothes rotted away, weapons rusted, mushrooms sprouted from documents, and when a carcass was thrown into the middle of the street, black bald-headed vultures would unwind its tripes like the ribbons on a maypole. Anyone falling into the water of the bay was devoured by an enormous fish, a sort of Jonah's whale, with its mouth somewhere between its neck and its stomach, known in the island as a shark. There were spiders as big as bucklers, snakes eight spans long, scorpions and countless other pests. In fact whenever the rough red wine rose to his head, Juan of Antwerp cursed that whoreson West Indian for persuading him to come to this miserable country, whose small supply of gold had vanished years ago into a few grasping hands. While the heat set his body on fire and his skin felt as though powdered with red-hot ash, he brooded over his misfortunes until his hypochondria became inflamed, and he grew as quarrelsome as his neighbours stewing in their own iniquity in the town; and one night, when the red wine had affected him particularly badly, he attacked Jacome de Castellón, the Genoese, for cheating at dice, struck at him with his knife and brought him down bathed in blood on top of a tripe-seller's stew-pots. Believing him dead, and alarmed by the cries of the negresses who came out of their rooms fastening their skirts, Juan seized a horse that he found tied up to a wooden fence and left the town at full gallop by the road from the docks, nor did he pause until he saw in the clear light of day the blue shapes of hills covered in palm-trees. Beyond them must lie the jungle, and there he would hide himself from the Governor's justice.

During several days Juan of Antwerp rode on, while his horse lost its shoes on the ever rougher ground. When he had left behind the last fields of sugar-cane, a range of mountains loomed up on his right, flanked by rounded spurs, like great dogs asleep under woollen blankets of forest. Following the banks of a stream which came leaping downhill between pools of arum lilies, bearing seeds and rotten fruit and little black-eyed fish that flickered against the current, the fugitive climbed till he reached a region of trees with purple flowers, some of whose forked trunks had been attacked by the tumour of a termite's nest, swarming with life. There were shrubs that seemed to be clothed in onion skins, and others weighed down by the nests of enormous rats. Juan left his horse tethered to the trunk of a silk-cotton tree, for he now had to clamber over great stones to reach the top of the ridge. He was soon descending the other side, where the jungle was less dense and the sea lay spread at his feet: a foamless sea, with waves that expired with a muffled impact in shadowy caves full of the thunder of rolling pebbles. At dusk he came to a beach covered in clams, where iridescent bladders were dying in the sun between sea-urchins, tawny apples and some large guamo shells that could be made to roar like bulls. Juan filled his lungs with the salty air; the fresh sea-breeze brought tears to his eyes, for it reminded him of the smell of Sanlúcar on the day of his departure, and also of his attic at Antwerp with the fishmonger's shop below—but just then a dog barked behind the coconut-palms, and turning round, the fugitive saw a bearded man aiming at him with an arquebus.

'I'm a Calvinist!' said the stranger defiantly.

'And I have killed a man,' replied Juan, trying to descend if possible to the level of someone who had confessed to the worst of all crimes. The bearded man let his bow-string go slack and studied him thoughtfully for a short while; then he shouted for a certain Golomon—a negro with slashed cheeks—who dropped from a tree almost on top of Juan and pressed his hat down over his face so violently that the crown split in two. Thus blindfolded by his hat, he was made to walk.

7

Six hundred Calvinists had been beheaded in Florida by the savagery of Menéndez de Avilés—so said the bearded man furiously, thumping the bible with his large fists, while Golomon sat a little way off, sharpening his machete on a stone. The Huguenot, a comrade of René de Landonnière, had miraculously escaped along with thirty men who later dispersed and went in search of Hispaniola. And mixing his exposition of the doctrine of predestination with blasphemies intended to be offensive to a Christian, he described the massacre, going into such details concerning cutting and thrusting with dented sabres that stuck half way through a man's neck and could only finish him off by sawing, and of axes falling on the spine with a sound like a butcher's cleaver, that Juan of Antwerp bowed his head with a grimace of disgust, implying that this seemed pretty severe punishment for praising God and Jesus Christ with fewer Latin phrases, especially in a country where the victims were in fact doing no harm to anyone. One man had had his left shoulder struck off along with his head, by a great blow with a two-handed sword.

'Another began to crawl on four legs after his neck had been severed and was spouting like a wine skin,' went on the bearded man furiously, wanting to get Juan to quarrel with him, so that he could order Golomon to strike off everything above his Adam's apple with his machete. But Juan of Antwerp made no sign. Although he had seen women buried alive and hundreds of Lutherans burned in Flanders, and had even helped bring wood for the fire and thrown Protestant women into the pit, everything appeared to him in a different light on an evening which might well be the last of his life, after he had endured so much misery in a country where a plough was a new invention, wheat unknown, the horse a prodigy, saddles unheard of, olives and grapes worth their weight in gold, and where the Holy Office in fact took little notice of the idolatry of the negroes (who did not call the Saints by their correct names) nor of the ladrinos (who still sang Indian songs) nor of the unscrupulous monks who carried off Indian women to their huts and indoctrinated them in such a manner that nine months later they returned the *Pater* from the Devil's mouth. It seemed to him right and proper that people should fight for theological doctrines concerning grace and incarnation, back there in the Old World. For the Duke of Alba to order someone like the bearded man to be burned, in a country where the heretics were trying to stir up whole provinces against King Philip, Champion of Catholicism and Demon of Noon, was merely an act of good statesmanship. But here he was among runaway slaves. He was on the run himself because he had committed a crime. He was a fugitive like the Calvinist, whose companion in flight was a new convert to Christianity—so new that he had forgotten his baptism and had had to fly from Havana after denouncing the Bishop for selling worthless plated monstrances in the cathedral as genuine, and demanding to be paid in good sound gold. So Juan had found a refuge from the Governor's justice with the Calvinist and the marrano, and he had also found the warmth of contact with other men. And women too. For when Golomon had led a party of slaves escaping from their sugar-cane plantation, the dogs had caught several of them who were afterwards put to death by their masters. But the women had meanwhile gone on ahead and reached the jungle. So Juan of Antwerp the drummer now had two negresses to wait on him, and gratify his lust whenever the urge seized him. The tall one, with ample breasts and her hair divided by eight partings, he called Doña Mandinga. The smaller one, whose buttocks jutted out like choirstalls and who had only a few hairs in that place where good Christians have a thick tuft, he named Doña Yolofa. As Doña Mandinga and Doña Yolofa spoke different languages, they did not quarrel when broaching fish through the gills to be roasted. And so the days passed in curing the flesh of wild boar or deer and storing heads of Indian corn. Time moved slowly; one day was just like the last in a land where the trees kept their leaves all through the year, and they measured the hours by the movement of shadows. When darkness fell, a profound sadness would overtake those living in the stockade. Each of them seemed to be remembering something, feeling nostalgia, regrets. Only the negresses sang, in the wood-smoke which hung over the calm sea like a mist smelling of the farmyard. Juan of Antwerp took off his hat, and with his face to the waves recited the Lord's Prayer and the *Credo,* his deep resonant voice testifying to his belief in the forgiveness of sins, the resurrection of the body and life everlasting. A little way off, the Calvinist was muttering a verse from the Genevan bible; while the marrano, with his back to the naked bodies of Doña Yolofa and Doña Mandinga, was reciting one of the Psalms of David in a voice that seemed full of suppressed tears: 'The Lord is merciful and gracious, slow to anger and plenteous in mercy' . . . The moon rose and the dogs of the stockade howled in chorus, sitting on the sand. The sea rolled its pebbles into the caves along the shore. And when, after prayers were over, the Jew accused the Calvinist of cheating at cards, all three men came to blows, hitting, falling, grappling with one another, calling for knives and sabres which no one brought them,

only to be reconciled afterwards and laugh as they shook the sand out
of their ears. As they had no money they played for shells.

8

But after countless months had gone by Juan languished and fell ill.
Doña Yolofa and Doña Mandinga fanned him with huge leaves and
drove away the tiny flies which rose from the mangrove-trees at that season; the Indians brought him delicious fish, caught by dazzling them
with torches in the caves on the shore. The drummer from Antwerp
spent long hours inhaling tobacco smoke from a pipe made out of a
bone, and thinking nostalgically of the days when he used to march into
towns beside the standard-bearer, the trumpet and the boxwood fife,
while as they advanced the green shutters with hearts cut in them
opened, and women leaned out over the flower-filled sills, seeming to
offer their rosy bosoms under the lace of their bodices—for the women
of Italy, Castile and Flanders were real women, very different from these
quarrelsome negresses, these wineskins with flesh too hard to pinch,
who had to serve as women here. How could a man who had been to
school at Alcalá talk to these pitch-black creatures about the thousands
of things he had seen and learned in his travels through the world? All
they understood was how to thump their barbarous drums and sing one
or two such senseless and monotonous songs that whenever they began
on this species of litany, shaking their tambourines and joining in a chorus to Golomon's full-throated solo, Juan the Student used to make off
into the jungle with the dogs, as a sign of his displeasure. For Juan really
had been a student—so he told the bearded man and the Jew—and had
learned the arts of the quadrivium as well as the musical notation for the
virginals, harp and vihuela, and the theory of modulation, variation and
medley-making, not to mention plain-chant and organ playing. And as
there was no spinet or vihuela on that coast, Juan used to demonstrate
by words and humming how well he could compose variations on a
pavane, or embellish the airs of *Conde Claro* or *Mirame como lloro* with
flourishes and grace-notes in the French or Italian style now fashionable
at Court. The fugitive's prestige had been so much increased by this display of his accomplishments that the others now took him for the son of
one of those poor squires who endured poverty with dignity, rather than
sell an ancestral home from the front door of which one could see, no
further off than that tree—and they all stared in that direction—the
façade of the Imperial University of San Ildefonso, the life of whose stu-
dents was described by the drummer in more inspired and circumstan-

tial detail every day. True, he had enlisted as a soldier, because he was in duty bound to serve the King, as all his ancestors had done ever since those remote times when they were involved in Charlemagne's campaigns. By thus glorifying his family tree, he relieved the tedium of eating so many clams and so much badly cooked turtle and meat smoked on the Calvinist's grills. His palate craved wine with almost painful urgency, and when his mind wandered off into imaginary chop-houses, he pictured enormous tables covered with partridges, capons, turkeys, calves' feet, cheeses full of huge holes, dishes of pickled fish, blanc-manges and honey from Alcarria. But Juan was not the only one to languish in the stockade, although the negroes and Indians enjoyed being far away from the rancher's mastiffs, and among women and bitches constantly giving birth. The Jew was dreaming of the Toledo Ghetto, where he had lived in peace for many years, and where one could enjoy weddings celebrated with much music, or listen to wise men reading their treatises aloud, without the house being drenched in tears and blood by the persecutions of the past. Closing his eyes, the marrano saw the narrow streets where makers of lanterns and knives had their workshops, near the confectioners with their puff pastry, rings of almond bread and crystallised citrons. Parents underwent purely formal conversion, and obediently taught their children some manual trade as well as making them study the Torah; so that if a boy did not want to be a balance-maker like his cousin Mossé, he could work in coral or paint playing-cards like Isaac Alfandari, or become a famous silver-smith like his other cousin Manahén, or master the art of healing wounds, like his relative Rabi Yudah. Jewesses would sing laments for money at Christian funerals, and from workrooms and shops there ceaselessly emerged the beautiful muffled music of beads being moved on an abacus. The Jew was dreaming of the Ghetto, and the bearded man of Paris, which he claimed as his native town, though in fact he was born in a suburb of Rouen, and had only spent a week under the walls of the Châtelet as cabin-boy on a logman's barge. But that week had been long enough for him to see the players acting comedies on a very beautiful bridge, and to brood over the vanity of the universe under the gallows at Montfaucon, and taste the wine in the taverns round the Madeleine and the Mule. He declared that there was nowhere to compare with Paris, and cursed this wretched country full of wild beasts; one was enticed here by tricksters, and suffered endless torments, in the hope of finding gold in a country where there was not even the glint of an ear of wheat to be seen. He went on to speak of fair-haired women, bubbling cider and a goose

sweating out its juices on a fire of vine-shoots, until at last the drummer's spleen was aroused, and he abused Golomon for idleness when
(after listening to all this) he began to talk confusedly about his own
ancestors and how they had been humiliated by the red-hot steel on
their flesh. They had all been important people, said the negro, and
although he could remember nothing more about his native land than a
very wide river full of turbulent rapids, and a few huts built of mud
mixed with dung, the negro described a world in which his father wore a
crown of feathers and drove in carriages drawn by white horses, just like
those in which the Medina Sidonias drove down the Alameda at Seville
during a fiesta. They all pursued their dreams gloomily, while around
them crabs set the dried coconuts rolling. They munched the small purple fruit of a sea-shore shrub, which tasted something like grapes and
brought the taste of wine back to mouths that were weary of manioc and
chicha. Their minds were full of things they had desired and imagined,
but never really possessed, when all of a sudden the rain began to fall in
torrents, bringing with it a plague of insects. Juan stamped and cried out
with rage when he saw the cloud of little black flies that surrounded
him, buzzing in his ears and steeping themselves in his blood when he
slapped his cheeks. And one morning he awoke shivering, with a face
like wax and a red-hot bar across his chest. Doña Yolofa and Doña
Mandinga went to the mountains in search of herbs that could be got
from a certain Lord of the Woods, who must have been yet another diabolic inmate of this lawless and barbarous country. There was nothing to
be done but swallow their brews; but while he slept the sick man had a
terrible dream: he suddenly saw in front of his hammock the Cathedral
of Compostela, its towers reaching to the sky. In his delirium it seemed
to him that the belfries rose to such a height that they were lost in the
clouds, far above the vultures floating on the wind with motionless
wings, like black crosses of ill omen floating in the waters of the firmament. Although it was mid-day, the Milky Way stretched so white and
clear above the Portico de la Gloria that the starry skies looked like the
angels' table-cloth. Juan watched himself—as he might have watched
another man from where he lay—approaching the holy basilica, alone,
strangely alone in that city of pilgrims, dressed in a cloak sewn with scallop-shells and resting his staff on the grey paving-stones. But the doors
were shut against him. He wanted to go inside, but he could not. He
called out and no one heard him. Juan the Pilgrim knelt and prayed,
groaned, scratched at the sacred wood, writhed on the ground like an
exorcised spirit, imploring to be let in. 'Saint James!' he sobbed. 'Saint

James!' Then he choked on some salt water and found himself on the sea
shore begging to be allowed to embark in a boat he saw moored there,
though no one else could see anything but a rotten tree-trunk. He wept
so bitterly that Golomon had to tie him with lianas into his hammock,
where he lay as if dead. And when he opened his eyes that evening there
was noise and excitement in the stockade. A ship in distress, dismantled
by storms in the Bermudas, had run aground on a reef opposite the shore.
The voices of sailors crying for help were carried to them on the wind.
Golomon and the man with a beard pushed the canoe into the water, while
the marrano fetched the oars.

9

At dawn the shape of the Teide was outlined against the sky like an
enormous mountain of blue haze. The man with a beard, who was pretending to be a Christian from Burgundy with the King's permit to go to
the Indies (he promised to show it when they arrived), knew that his
travels would very soon be at an end. Since the Grand Canary traded
with the English and Flemish, and several Calvinist or Lutheran captains unloaded their merchandise there, and were not asked whether
they believed in predestination, or fasted in Lent or wanted to buy
cheap seals for documents, he knew it would be easy to get lost in the
town, and later on find some way of escaping from the island and getting to France. He gave Juan a conspiratorial look, but did not speak of
what they both knew. Meanwhile, there was the delight of rediscovering
the taste of lentils and salmagundi, cheese and pickles, which they had
hankered after all too often back in the stockade. They had left Doña
Yolofa and Doña Mandinga behind, in tears of rage rather than grief;
when they discovered that they were the concubines of someone as
grand as a Squire, they began to behave to the other negresses as if they
were Castilian ladies. The sick man felt health returning to his body as
soon as he was on board the ship, which finally dropped anchor in
Sanlúcar, where a pilgrim's cloak and sandals were awaiting him—for a
vow was a vow, and misfortunes had rained down on him ever since he
failed to carry out his own. And now that he was really going to set foot
on land after long weeks at sea, he felt as happy as he remembered having been one afternoon after washing himself in the hospice at
Bayonne. It suddenly occurred to him that since he had been to the
West Indies he was now a West Indian. So when he landed he would be
Juan the West Indian. Then he heard a clamour among the sailors on
the poop and supposing that they were celebrating their arrival he ran

to look, followed by the man with a beard. But what was happening there was no laughing matter: the men were crowding round the new Christian and jostling him roughly. One of them tripped him up and threw him on the ground, and then taking him by the scruff of the neck forced him to kneel: 'The Lord's Prayer!' he shouted in his face. 'The Lord's Prayer and after that the *Ave Maria!*' And Juan realised that the sailors had been spying on the marrano for several days, and had heard from the cook that, on the pretext of working as scullion, he had stolen some flour to make himself some unleavened bread. And today being Saturday, they had noticed that he washed himself very early and put on clean clothes. 'The Lord's Prayer!' they were all shouting now, and kicking him at the same time. The marrano whined out wild entreaties, but no one listened, and when they beat him with a knotted rope, he began muttering something which was neither the Lord's Prayer nor the *Ave Maria,* but the Psalm of David that he used to recite in the stockade three times a day: 'The Lord is merciful and gracious, slow to anger and plentiful in mercy.' Before he had finished speaking, they all hurled themselves upon him and kicked him, while one of them ran to get some irons. And as soon as he was chained up and spitting out the teeth they had knocked out with a stick, they all turned on the bearded man, and pinned him against the gunwale, calling him a Lutheran pirate. But he stood up to them, and protested so resolutely, threatening to complain to the Council, that the coxswain wavered and finally called for calm. After some hesitation, he decided to hand the self-styled Burgundian over to the courts of Las Palmas, and let them decide whether he should be given leave to go on to the West Indies or not. With an ashen face, the man with a beard watched the irons being fastened round his ankles, while they led away the marrano amid insults, and threw bucketfuls of dirty water in his face. They had treated him so roughly that he left a trail of blood behind him. Juan saw them push him down the companion ladder and shut the hatch on his last despairing cry. He had just learned that the Grand Canary, once an island where both Moors and converts could live in peace, was now the chief observation post of a Champion of Catholicism, as personified in a redoubtable inquisitor who had set up the Green Cross of the Holy Office in Las Palmas and seized whole ship's crews as suspects. His dungeons were full of Dutch coxswains and Anglican captains waiting to be handed over to the secular arm. Squatting at the foot of the foremast, Golomon was trembling like a man with fever, terrified lest he should be asked why, when he prayed to Our Lord Jesus Christ in the hacienda of the master whose brand was plainly visible on his skin, he did not address the Redeemer by name, but worshipped him in his own language, after first hanging a great many strings of beads round his neck. Juan tried to quiet him, as one might a good dog, by patting him on the shoulder; but he could not tell him—for fear of being over-heard—that on important execution days the Inquisitors were much less likely to waste faggots on burning negroes, than on learned men who knew too much Arabic, sharp-eared theologians, Protestants and propagators of a heretical book much sought after in parts where Dutch ships put in, entitled *Praise of Folly* or *Praise of Madmen,* or something of the sort. And as it would soon be Trinity Sunday, a favorite day of autos-da-fé, Juan the West Indian already pictured the marrano dressed in a black sanbenito, and the bearded man in a yellow one embroidered with a red St. Andrew's cross on back and front. After receiving the blessing beneath the flag-staff, both of them would climb on to their donkeys amidst the shouts and gibes of people who had come a long way to enjoy these forty days of indulgence, and be driven towards the burning faggots with a great many other heretics, carrying aloft the por-traits of those who had escaped and must therefore be burned in effigy.

10

One market-day, Juan the West Indian stood at the end of a blind alley, loudly offering for sale two alligators stuffed with straw, which he claimed to have brought from Cuzco, though he had actually bought them from a pawnbroker in Toledo. He had a monkey on his shoulder and a parrot perched on his hand. He blew into a large pink conch, and Golomon emerged from a crimson box, like Lucifer in a miracle play, proffering strings of pitted pearls, stones that would cure headaches, belts made of vicuña wool, tinsel earrings and other tawdry finery from Potosí. When he laughed, the negro displayed teeth filed to a point and cheeks marked with three knife slashes according to the custom of his tribe; then, picking up a tambourine, he started dancing, swaying from the waist so energetically that even the old tripeseller left her stall by the arch of Santa Maria to come and watch him. Now that the sara-band, the guineo and the chaconne were all the rage in Burgos, he was applauded by a large crowd, who begged for another new dance from the New World. But just then it began to rain; everyone ran to take shelter under the eaves, and Juan the West Indian found himself in the parlour of an inn, with another pilgrim called Juan who had been wan-dering through the fair in his cloak sewn with shells. He had come from

Flanders to fulfil a vow made to St. James during a terrible epidemic of the plague. Juan the West Indian, who had landed at Sanlúcar, with the staff and gourd that symbolised a pilgrim's fulfilment of his vows, divested himself of his habit in Ciudad Real one day when Golomon, providing himself with a monkey and a parrot to help him sell trinkets at fairs, showed him that with any luck he could earn enough in two days by hawking novelties from the Indies to feast himself on wine and girls for a whole week. The negro was afire with eagerness to sample white bodies responsive to his vigorous virility; the West Indian, on the other hand, lost his head whenever a negress went by, with her rump as high as a choirstall. At present, Golomon was drying the monkey on his handkerchief, while the parrot was preparing to take a nap, perched on the hoop of a barrel. The West Indian ordered wine, and began telling cock-and bull stories to the pilgrim called Juan. He described a spring of such miraculous water that the crookedest and most crippled old men had only to bathe in it, and when they emerged their heads were covered in shining hair, their wrinkles smoothed away, their health restored to them, their joints no longer swollen, and they were vigorous enough to make a whole army of Amazons pregnant. He spoke of amber from Florida, of statues of giants seen by Francisco Pizarro in Puerto Viejo, and of skulls with teeth as thick as three fingers and only one ear, and that in the nape of the neck. But Juan the Pilgrim, fuddled by the wine he had drunk, told Juan the West Indian that people coming from the Indies always kept maundering on about marvels such as these, and in the end no one believed them. Nobody now had any faith in Springs of Eternal Youth, nor did the story of the American Harpy, sold on broadsheets by blind men, have any foundation in fact. The burning subject of the moment was the city of Manoa in the Kingdom of the Omeguas, where there was more gold to be had for the taking than the fleets had brought back from New Spain and Peru. The regions between enchanted Bogota and Potosí (an even greater miracle of nature) and the mouths of the Amazon were filled with marvels more wonderful than any that had yet been seen: islands of pearl, the country of Cockaigne, and the earthly paradise that the Great Admiral claimed to have seen—as everyone knew from his letter to King Ferdinand— with a mountain shaped like a woman's breast. A German was said to have died taking with him the secret of a kingdom where barbers' basins, cooking-pots, kettles, the rims of carriage-wheels, and lamps were made of precious metals. The drums were still being beaten to announce yet more voyages of discovery . . . But here Juan the West

Indian interrupted Juan the Pilgrim to say that such victories as those of Pizarro and his fleet were not the most profitable. What paid best in the Indies was to have flair and a mind like a compass-needle, and to be able to jump ahead of others; there was no need to pay attention to Royal warrants, remonstrances of graduates or outcries of bishops, in a country where the Inquisition itself had become easy-going, and cups of chocolate were more often heated on their fires than heretics' flesh. . . . The drums sounding here in Spain would not lead to riches. The drums that should be listened to were those sounding across the sea, because they told of new openings for men to make fabulous fortunes with less fighting than before, taking with them doctors wonderfully skilled in mending broken bones or healing the bites of wild beasts with the Indians' own herbs.

II

Next day, after giving the scallop-shells from his cape to the girl he had spent the night with, Juan the Pilgrim rejected the road to Santiago and set off towards Seville. Juan the West Indian followed behind, coughing and wheezing, for he had caught cold in the wind blowing off the sierras. When he lay shivering on his pallet bed in a wayside inn he thought longingly of the warmth contained within the coarse skins of Doña Yolofa and Doña Mandinga. He looked up at the cloudy sky and prayed for sun, but he was answered by a shower of rain falling on the grey and sulphur-coloured stones of the plateau, where the soaked sheep huddled together in the green grass round a waterhole, burying their hoofs in the clay. Golomon came behind, bare-footed, with the monkey and the parrot covered with his cloak, and his straw hat butting against a freezing wind. In Valladolid they were greeted by the stench of faggots burning to death the wife of the Emperor's counsellor, in whose house the Lutherans had met and held services. Here everything smelt of scorching flesh, burning sanbenitos, grilling of heretics. From Holland and from France came drifting the shrieks of prisoners, the weeping of women buried alive, the tumult of slaughter, the terrible cries of denunciation issuing from unborn children pierced by swords in their mother's wombs. Some said that better days would emerge from all this blood and tears; others cried that the Sixth Seal had been broken, and that the sun would turn as black as a cilice, and that the kings of the earth, princes, rich men and leaders, all those in power, all slaves and free men, would take to the caves and mountains. But beyond Ciudad Real, people seemed to be different. They hardly talked at all about what was happening in Flanders, and lived with their ears pricked towards Seville for news of absent sons, of an uncle who had moved his forge to Cartagena, and another who kept a good inn at Lima. There were some villages which had been deserted by whole families; stone-cutters with their workmen, poor gentlemen with their horses and servants. Juan the West Indian and Juan the Pilgrim hastened their steps when they saw the first orange grove between the purple of the aubergines and the copper of the pumpkins, banded by a field of water-melons. White-wine shops reappeared, and negresses with tawny skins the colour of a stewed pear and buttocks as high as choirstalls. Odours of brine, tar and resinous woods mingled with the noises of a port of embarkation. And when the two Juans arrived at the Casa de la Contratacion, along with the negro who was carrying their beads, they looked such a pair of rogues that the Virgin of Navigators frowned when she saw them kneeling in front of her altar.

'Let them pass, Holy Mother,' said St. James, son of Zebedee and Salome, thinking of the hundreds of new cities he owed to similar scoundrels. 'Let them go; they will keep their promise to me over there.'

And Beelzebub, ingenious as ever, disguised himself as a blind man dressed in rags with a great black hat on his horns, and when he saw that it had stopped raining in Burgos, he climbed on a bench in one of the alleys of the fair, and sang, while his long fingernails roamed over the strings of his vihuela:

> Then, take heart, good sirs,
> Courage, poor gentlemen,
> Good news for the poor
> And joy for those in trouble!
> For those who wish to go
> And see this new marvel,
> Ten ships will sail together
> From Seville this year!

The starry heavens above were white with galaxies.

The Pursuer

by Julio Cortázar

translated by Paul Blackburn

In memoriam Ch. P.

Be thou faithful unto death
Apocalypse 2:10

O make me a mask
Dylan Thomas

Dédée had called me in the afternoon saying that Johnny wasn't very well, and I'd gone to the hotel right away. Johnny and Dédée have been living in a hotel in the rue Lagrange for a few days now, they have a room on the fourth floor. All I have to do is see the door to the room to realize that Johnny's in worse shape than usual; the window opens onto an almost black courtyard, and at one in the afternoon you have to keep the light on if you want to read the newspaper or see someone else's face. It's not that cold out, but I found Johnny wrapped up in a blanket, and squeezed into a raunchy chair that's shedding yellowed hunks of old burlap all over the place. Dédée gotten older, and the red dress doesn't suit her at all: it's a dress for working under spotlights; in that hotel room it turns into a repulsive kind of coagulation.

"Faithful old buddy Bruno, regular as bad breath," Johnny said by way of hello, bringing his knees up until his chin was resting on them. Dédée reached me a chair and I pulled out a pack of Gauloises. I'd brought a bottle of rum too, had it in the overcoat pocket, but I didn't want to bring it out until I had some idea of how things were going. I think the lightbulb was the worst irritation, its eye pulled out and hanging suspended from a long cord dirtied by flies. After looking at it once or twice, and putting my hand up to shade my eyes, I asked Dédée if we couldn't put out the damned light and wouldn't the light from the window be okay. Johnny followed my words and gestures with a large, distracted attention, like a cat who is looking fixedly, but you know it's something else completely; that it is something else. Finally Dédée got up and turned off the light. Under what was left, some mishmosh of black and grey, we recognized one another better. Johnny had pulled one of his big hands out from under the blanket and I felt the limber warmth of his skin. Then Dédée said she'd make us some nescafé. I was happy to know that at least they had a tin of nescafé. I always know, whatever the score is, when somebody has a can of nescafé it's not fatal yet; they can still hold out.

"We haven't seen one another for a while," I said to Johnny. "It's been a month at least."

"You got nothin' to do but tell time," he answered. He was in a bad mood. "The first, the two, the three, the twenty-one. You, you put a number on everything. An' that's cool. You wanna know why she's sore? 'Cause I lost the horn. She's right, after all."

"Lost it, but how could you lose it?" I asked, realizing at the same moment that that was just what you couldn't ask Johnny.

"In the metro," Johnny said. "I shoved it under the seat so it'd be safe. It was great to ride that way, knowing I had it good and safe down there between my legs."

"He finally missed it when he was coming up the stairs in the hotel," Dédée said, her voice a little hoarse. "And I had to go running out like a nut to report it to the metro lost-and-found and to the police." By the silence that followed I figured out that it'd been a waste of time. But Johnny began to laugh like his old self, a deep laugh back of the lips and teeth.

"Some poor devil's probably trying to get some sound out of it," he said. "It was one of the worst horns I ever had; you know that Doc Rodriguez played it? Blew all the soul out of it. As an instrument, it wasn't awful, but Rodriguez could ruin a Stradivarius just by tuning it."

"And you can't get ahold of another?"

"That's what we're trying to find out," Dédée said. "It might be Rory Friend has one. The awful thing is that Johnny's contract . . ."

"The contract," Johnny mimicked. "What's this with the contract? I gotta play and that's it, and I haven't got a horn or any bread to buy one with, and the boys are in the same shape I am."

This last was not the truth, and the three of us knew it. Nobody would risk lending Johnny an instrument, because he lost it or ruined it right off. He lost Louis Rolling's sax in Bordeaux, the sax Dédée bought him when he had that contract for a tour in England he broke into three pieces, whacking it against a wall and trampling on it. Nobody knew how many instruments had already been lost, pawned, or smashed up. And on all of them he played like I imagine only a god can play an alto sax, given that they quit using lyres and flutes.

"When do you start, Johnny?"

"I dunno. Today, I think, huh De?"

"No, day after tomorrow."

"Everybody knows the dates except me," Johnny grumbled, covering himself up to the ears in his blanket. "I'd've sworn it was tonight, and this afternoon we had to go in to rehearse."

"It amounts to the same thing," Dédée said. "The thing is that you haven't got a horn."

"What do you mean, the same thing? It isn't the same thing. Day after tomorrow is the day after tomorrow, and tomorrow is much later than today. And today is later than right now, because here we are yakking with our old buddy Bruno, and I'd feel a lot better if I could forget about time and have something hot to drink."

"I'll boil some water, hold on for a little."

"I was not referring to boiling water," Johnny said. So I pulled out the bottle of rum, and it was as though we'd turned the light on; Johnny opened his mouth wide, astonished, and his teeth shone, until even Dédée had to smile at seeing him, so surprised and happy. Rum and nescafé isn't really terrible, and all three of us felt a lot better after the second swallow and a cigarette. Then I noticed that Johnny was withdrawing little by little and kept on referring to time, a subject which is a preoccupation of his ever since I've known him. I've seen very few men as occupied as he is with everything having to do with time. It's a mania of his, the worst of his manias, of which he has plenty. But he explains and develops it with a charm hard to resist. I remember a rehearsal before a recording session in Cincinnati, long before he came to Paris, in forty-nine or fifty. Johnny was in great shape in those days and I'd gone to the rehearsal just to talk to him and also to Miles Davis. Everybody wanted to play, they were happy, and well-dressed (this occurs to me maybe by contrast with how Johnny goes around now, dirty and messed up), they were playing for the pleasure of it, without the slightest impatience, and the sound technician was making happy signs from behind his glass window, like a satisfied baboon. And just at that moment when Johnny was like gone in his joy, suddenly he stopped playing and threw a punch at I don't know who and said, "I'm playing this tomorrow," and the boys stopped short, two or three of them went on for a few measures, like a train slowly coming to a halt, and Johnny was hitting himself in the forehead and repeating, "I already played this tomorrow, it's horrible, Miles, I already played this tomorrow," and they couldn't get him out of that, and everything was lousy from then on, Johnny was playing without any spirit and wanted to leave (to shoot up again, the sound technician said, mad as hell), and when I saw him go out, reeling and his face like ashes, I wondered how much longer that business could go on.

"I think I'll call Dr. Bernard," Dédée said, looking at Johnny out of the corner of her eye, he was taking his rum in small sips. "You've got a fever and you're not eating anything."

"Dr. Bernard is a sad-assed idiot," Johnny said, licking his glass. "He's going to give me aspirin and then he'll tell me how very much he digs jazz, for example Ray Noble. Got the idea, Bruno? If I had the horn I'd give him some music that'd send him back down the four flights with his ass bumping on every step."

"It won't do you any harm to take some aspirin in any case," I said, looking out of the corner of my eye at Dédée. "If you want, I'll telephone when I leave so Dédée won't have to go down. But look, this contract . . . If you have to start day after tomorrow, I think something can be done. Also I can try to get a sax from Rory Friend. And at worst . . . The whole thing is you have to take it easier, Johnny."

"Not today," Johnny said, looking at the rum bottle. "Tomorrow, when I have the horn. So don't you talk about that now. Bruno, every time I notice that time . . . I think the music always helps me understand this business a little better. Well, not understand, because the truth of the matter is, I don't understand anything. The only thing I do is notice that there is something. Like those dreams, I'm not sure, where you begin to figure that everything is going to smash up now, and you're a little afraid just to be ready for it; but at the same time nothing's certain, and maybe it'll flip over like a pancake and all of a sudden, there you are, sleeping with a beautiful chick and everything's cool."

Dédée's washing the cups and glasses in one corner of the room. I noticed they don't even have running water in the place; I see a stand with pink flowers, and a wash-basin which makes me think of an embalmed animal. And Johnny goes on talking with his mouth half stopped up by the bottle, and he looks stuffed too, with his knees up under his chin and his black smooth face which the rum and the fever are beginning to sweat up a little.

"I read some things about all that, Bruno. It's weird, and really awful complicated . . . I think the music helps, you know. Not to understand, because the truth is I don't understand anything." He knocks on his head with a closed fist. His head sounds like a coconut.

"Got nothing inside here, Bruno, what they call, nothing. It doesn't think and don't understand nothing. I've never missed it, tell you the truth. I begin to understand from the eyes down, and the lower it goes the better I understand. But that's not really understanding, oh, I'm with you there."

"You're going to get your fever up," Dédée muttered from the back of the place.

"Oh, shut up. It's true, Bruno. I never thought of nothing, only all at once I realize what I thought of, but that's not funny, right? How's it funny to realize that you've thought of something? Because it's all the same thing whether you think, or someone else. I am not I, me. I just use what I think, but always afterwards, and that's what I can't stand. Oh it's hard, it's so hard . . . Not even a slug left?"

I'd poured him the last drops of rum just as Dédée came back to turn on the light; you could hardly see in the place. Johnny's sweating, but keeps wrapped up in the blanket, and from time to time he starts shaking and the chair legs chatter on the floor.

"I remember when I was just a kid, almost as soon as I'd learned to play sax. There was always a helluva fight going on at home, and all they ever talked about was debts and mortgages. You know what a mortgage is? It must be something terrible, because the old lady blew her wig every time the old man mentioned mortgage, and they'd end up in a fistfight. I was thirteen then . . . but you already heard all that."

Damned right I'd heard it; and damned right I'd tried to write it well and truly in my biography of Johnny.

"Because of the way things were at home, time never stopped, dig? From one fistfight to the next, almost not stopping for meals. And to top it all off, religion, aw, you can't imagine. When the boss got me a sax, you'd have laughed yourself to death if you'd seen it, then I think I noticed the thing right off. Music got me out of time, but that's only a way of putting it. If you want to know what I think, really, I believe that music put me *into* time. But then you have to believe that this time had nothing to do with . . . well, with us, as they say."

For some time now I've recognized Johnny's hallucinations, all those that constitute his own life, I listen to him attentively, but without bothering too much about what he's saying. On the other hand, I was wondering where he'd made a connection in Paris. I'd have to ask Dédée, ignoring her possible complicity. Johnny isn't going to be able to stand this much longer. Heroin and poverty just don't get along very well together. I'm thinking of the music being lost, the dozens of sides Johnny would be able to cut, leaving that presence, that astonishing step forward where he had it over any other musician. "I'm playing that tomorrow" suddenly fills me with a very clear sense of it, because Johnny is always blowing tomorrow, and the rest of them are chasing his tail, in this today he just jumps over, effortlessly, with the first notes of his music.

I'm sensitive enough a jazz critic when it comes to understanding my limitations, and I realize that what I'm thinking is on a lower level than where poor Johnny is trying to move forward with his decapitated sentences, his sighs, his impatient angers and his tears. He gives a damn where I think everything ought to go easy, and he's never come on smug that his music is much farther out than his contemporaries are playing. It drags me to think that he's at the beginning of his sax-work, and I'm going along and have to stick it out to the end. He's the mouth and I'm the ear, so as not to say that he's the mouth and I'm the . . . Every critic, yeah, is the sad-assed end of something that starts as taste, like the pleasure of biting into something and chewing on it. And the mouth moves again, relishing it, Johnny's big tongue sucks back a little string of saliva from the lips. The hands make a little picture in the air.

"Bruno, maybe someday you'll write . . . Not for me, dig, what the hell does it matter to me. But it has to be beautiful, I feel it's gotta be beautiful. I was telling you how when I was a kid learning to play, I noticed that time changed. I told that to Jim once and he said that everybody in the world feels the same way and when he gets lost in it . . . He said that, when somebody gets lost in it . . . Hell no, I don't get lost when I'm playing. Only the place changes. It's like in an elevator, you're in an elevator talking with people, you don't feel anything strange, meanwhile you've passed the first floor, the tenth, the twenty-first, and the city's down there below you, and you're finishing the sentence you began when you stepped into it, and between the first words and the last ones, there're fifty-two floors. I realized that when I started to play I was stepping into an elevator, but the elevator was time, if I can put it that way. Now realize that I haven't forgotten the mortgage or the religion. Like it's the mortgage and the religion are a suit I'm not wearing at the moment; I know that the suit's in the closet, but at that moment you can't tell me that that suit exists. The suit exists when I put it on, and the mortgage and religion existed when I got finished playing and the old lady came in with her hair, dangling big hunks of hair all over me and complaining I'm busting her ears with that god-damned music."

Dédée had brought another cup of nescafé, but Johnny was looking with misery at his empty glass.

"This time business is complicated, it grabs me. I'm beginning to notice, little by little, that time is not like a bag that keeps filling up. What I mean is, even though the contents change, in the bag there's never more than a certain amount, and that's it. You see my suitcase,

Bruno? It holds two suits and two pairs of shoes. Now, imagine that you empty it, okay? And afterwards you're going to put back the two suits and the two pairs of shoes, and then you realize that only one suit and one pair of shoes fit in there. But that's not the best of it. The best is when you realize you can put a whole store full of suits and shoes in there, in that suitcase, hundreds and hundreds of suits, like I get into the music when I'm blowing sometimes. Music, and what I'm thinking about when I ride the metro."

"When you ride the metro."

"Oh yeah, that, now there's the thing," Johnny said, getting crafty. "The metro is a great invention, Bruno. Riding the metro you notice everything that might end up in the suitcase. Maybe I didn't lose the horn in the metro, maybe . . . "

He breaks into laughter, coughs, and Dédée looks at him uneasily. But he's making gestures, laughing and coughing at the same time, shivering away under the blanket like a chimpanzee. His eyes are running and he's drinking the tears, laughing the whole time.

"Don't confuse the two things," he says after a spell. "I lost it and that's it. But the metro was helpful, it made me notice the suitcase bit. Look, this bit of things being elastic is very weird, I feel it everyplace I go. It's all elastic, baby. Things that look solid have an elasticity . . . "

He's thinking, concentrating.

". . . a sort of delayed stretch," he concludes surprisingly. I make a gesture of admiring approval. Bravo, Johnny. The man who claims he's not capable of thinking. Wow. And now I'm really interested in what he's going to say, and he notices that and looks at me more cunning than ever.

"You think I'll be able to come by another horn so I can play day after tomorrow, Bruno?"

"Sure, but you'll have to take care of it."

"Sure, I'll have to take care of it."

"A month's contract," explains poor Dédée. "Two weeks in Rémy's club, two concerts and the record dates. We could clean up."

"A month's contract," Johnny imitates her with broad gestures. "Rémy's club, two concerts, and the record dates. Be-bata-bop bop bop, chrrr. What I got is a thirst, a thirst, a thirst. And I feel like smoking, like smoking. More'n anything else, I feel like a smoke."

I offer him my pack of Gauloises, though I know perfectly well that he's thinking of pot. It's already dark out, people are beginning to come and go in the hallway, conversations in Arabic, singing. Dédée's left, probably to buy something to eat for that night. I feel Johnny's hand on my knee.

"She's a good chick, you know? But I've had enough. It's some time now I'm not in love with her, and I can't stand her. She still excites me, she knows how to make love like . . . " he brought his forefinger and middle finger together, Italian-fashion. "But I gotta split, go back to New York. Everything else aside, I gotta get back to New York, Bruno."

"What for? There you were worse off than you are here. I'm not talking about work but about your own life. Here, it looks like you have more friends."

"Sure, there's you, and the marquesa, and the guys at the club . . . Did you ever make love with the marquesa, Bruno?"

"No."

"Well, it's something that . . . But I was talking about the metro, and I don't know, how did we change the subject? The metro is a great invention, Bruno. One day I began to feel something in the metro, then I forgot . . . Then it happened again, two or three days later. And finally I realized. It's easy to explain, you dig, but it's easy because it's not the right answer. The right answer simply can't be explained. You have to take the metro and wait until it happens to you, though it seems to me that that only would happen to me. It's a little like that, see. But honestly, you never made love with the marquesa? You have to ask her to get up on that gilt footstool that she has in the corner of her bedroom, next to that pretty lamp and then . . . Oh shit, she's back already."

Dédée comes in with a package and looks at Johnny.

"Your fever's higher. I telephoned the doctor already, he's going to come at ten. He says you should stay quiet."

"Okay, okay, but first I'm going to tell Bruno about the subway. The other day I noticed what was happening. I started to think about my old lady, then about Lan and the guys, an' whup, it was me walking through my old neighborhood again, and I saw the kids' faces, the ones from then. It wasn't thinking, it seems to me I told you a lot of times, I never think; I'm like standing on a corner watching what I think go by, but I'm not thinking what I see. You dig? Jim says that we're all the same, that in general (as they say) one doesn't think on his own. Let's say that's so, the thing is I'd took the metro at Saint-Michel, and right away I began to think about Lan and the guys, and to see the old neighborhood. I'd hardly sat down and I began to think about them. But at the same time I realized that I was in the metro, and I saw that in a minute or two we had got to Odéon, and that people were getting on and off. Then I went on thinking about Lan, and I saw my old lady when she was coming back from doing the shopping, and I began to see them all around, to be with them in a very beautiful way, I hadn't felt that way in a long time. Memories are always a drag, but this time I like thinking about the guys and seeing them. If I start telling you everything I saw you're not going to believe it because I would take a long time doing it. And that would be if I economized on details. For example, just to tell you one thing, I saw Lan in a green suit that she wore when she came to Club 33 where I was playing with Hamp. I was seeing the suit with some ribbons, a loop, a sort of trim down the side and a collar . . . Not at the same time, though, really, I was walking around Lan's suit and looking at it pretty slow. Then I looked at Lan's face and at the boys' faces, and then I remembered Mike who lived in the next room, and how Mike had told me a story about some wild horses in Colorado, once he worked on a ranch, and talked about the balls it took for cowboys to break wild horses. . . ."

"Johnny," Dédée said from her far corner.

"Now figure I've told you only a little piece of everything that I was thinking and seeing. How much'll that take, what I'm telling you, this little piece?"

"I don't know, let's say about two minutes."

"Let's say about two minutes," Johnny mimicked. "Two minutes and I've told you just a little bitty piece, no more. If I were to tell you everything I saw the boys doing, and how Hamp played *Save it, pretty mama,* and listened to every note, you dig, every note, and Hamp's not one of them who gets tired, if I told you I heard an endless harangue of my old lady's, she was saying something about cabbages, if I remember, she was asking pardon for my old man and for me, and was saying something about some heads of cabbage . . . Okay, if I told you all that in detail, that'd take more than two minutes, huh, Bruno?"

"If you really heard and saw all that, it'd take a good quarter-hour," I said, laughing to myself.

"It'd take a good quarter-hour, huh, Bruno. Then tell me how it can be that I feel suddenly the metro stop and I come away from my old lady and Lan and all that, and I see that we're at Saint-Germain-des-Prés, which is just a minute and a half from Odéon."

I never pay too much attention to the things Johnny says, but now, with his way of staring at me, I felt cold.

"Hardly a minute and a half in your time, in her time," Johnny said nastily. "And also the metro's time and my watch's, damn them both.

Then how could I have been thinking a quarter of an hour, huh, Bruno? How can you think a quarter of an hour in a minute and a half? That day I swear I hadn't smoked even a roach, not a crumb," he finished like a boy excusing himself. "And then it happened to me again, now it's beginning to happen to me everyplace. But," he added astutely, "I can only notice in the metro, because to ride the metro is like being put in a clock. The stations are minutes, dig, it's that time of yours, now's time; but I know there's another, and I've been thinking, thinking . . . "

He covers his face with his hands and shakes. I wish I'd gone already, and I don't know how to get out now without Johnny resenting it, he's terribly touchy with his friends. If he goes on this way he's going to make a mess of himself, at least with Dédée he's not going to talk about things like that.

"Bruno, if I could only live all the time like in those moments, or like when I'm playing and the time changes then too . . . Now you know what can happen in a minute and a half . . . Then a man, not just me but her and you and all the boys, they could live hundreds of years, if we could find the way we could live a thousand times faster than we're living because of the damned clocks, that mania for minutes and for the day after tomorrow . . . "

I smile the best I can, understanding fuzzily that he's right, but what he suspects and the hunch I have about what he suspects is going to be deleted as soon as I'm in the street and've gotten back into my everyday life. At that moment I'm sure that what Johnny's saying doesn't just come from his being half-crazy, that he's escaping from reality; I'm sure that, in the exchange, what he thinks leaves him with a kind of parody which he changes into a hope. Everything Johnny says to me at such moments (and it's been five years now Johnny's been saying things like this to me and to people) you can't just listen and promise yourself to think about it later. You hardly get down into the street, the memory of it barely exists and no Johnny repeating the words, everything turns into a pot-dream, a monotonous gesticulating (because there're others who say things like that, every minute you hear similar testimony) and after the wonder of it's gone you get an irritation, and for me at least it feels as though Johnny's been pulling my leg. But this always happens the next day, not when Johnny's talking to me about it, because then I feel that there's something that I'd like to admit at some point, a light that's looking to be lit, or better yet, as though it were necessary to break something, split it from top to bottom like a log, setting a wedge in and hammering it until the job's done. And Johnny hasn't got the strength to hammer anything in, and me, I don't know where the hammer is to tap in the wedge, which I can't imagine either.

So finally I left the place, but before I left one of those things that have to happen happened—if not that, then something else—and it was when I was saying goodbye to Dédée and had my back turned to Johnny that I felt something was happening, I saw it in Dédée's eyes and swung around quickly (because maybe I'm a little afraid of Johnny, this angel who's like my brother, this brother who's like my angel) and I saw Johnny had thrown off the blanket around him in one motion, and I saw him sitting in the easy-chair completely nude, his legs pulled up and the knees underneath his chin, shivering but laughing to himself, naked from top to bottom in that grimy chair.

"It's beginning to get warm," Johnny said. "Bruno, look what a pretty scar I got between my ribs."

"Cover yourself," Dédée ordered him, embarrassed and not knowing what to say. We know one another well enough and a naked man is a naked man, that's all, but anyway Dédée was scandalized and I didn't know how to not give the impression that what Johnny was doing had shocked me. And he knew it and laughed uproariously, mouth wide open, obscenely keeping his legs up so that his prick hung down over the edge of the chair like a monkey in the zoo, and the skin of his thighs had some weird blemishes which disgusted me completely. Then Dédée grabbed the blanket and wrapped it tightly around him, while Johnny was laughing and seemed very cheerful. I said goodbye hesitatingly, promised to come back the next day, and Dédée accompanied me to the landing, closing the door so Johnny couldn't hear what she was going to say to me.

"He's been like this since we got back from the Belgian tour. He'd played very well everyplace, and I was so happy."

"I wonder where he got the heroin from," I said, looking her right in the eye.

"Don't know. He'd been drinking wine and cognac almost constantly. He's been shooting up too, but less than there . . . "

There was Baltimore and New York, three months in Bellevue psychiatric, and a long stretch in Camarillo.

"Did Johnny play really well in Belgium, Dédée?"

"Yes, Bruno, better than ever, seems to me. The people went off their heads, and the guys in the band told me so, too, a number of times. Then all at once some weird things were happening, like always with Johnny, but luckily never in front of an audience. I thought . . . but you see now, he's worse than ever."

"Worse than in New York? You didn't know him those years."

Dédée's not stupid, but no woman likes you to talk about her man before she knew him, aside from the fact that now she has to put up with him and whatever "before" was is just words. I don't know how to say it to her, I don't even trust her fully, but finally I decide.

"I guess you're short of cash."

"We've got that contract beginning day after tomorrow," said Dédée.

"You think he's going to be able to record and do the gig with an audience too?"

"Oh, sure." Dédée seemed a bit surprised. "Johnny can play better than ever if Dr. Bernard can get rid of that flu. The problem is the horn."

"I'll take care of that. Here, take this, Dédée. Only . . . Maybe better Johnny doesn't know about it."

"Bruno . . . "

I made a motion with my hand and began to go down the stairway, I'd cut off the predictable words, the hopeless gratitude. Separated from her by four or five steps, made it easier for me to say it to her.

"He can't shoot up before the first concert, not for anything in the world. You can let him smoke a little, but no money for the other thing."

Dédée didn't answer at all, though I saw how her hands were twisting and twisting the bills as though she were trying to make them disappear. At least I was sure that Dédée wasn't on drugs. If she went along with it, it was only out of love or fear. If Johnny gets down on his knees, like I saw once in Chicago, and begs her with tears . . . But that's a chance, like everything else with Johnny, and for the moment they'd have enough money to eat, and for medicines. In the street I turned up the collar on my raincoat because it was beginning to drizzle, and took a breath so deep that my lungs hurt; Paris smelled clean, like fresh bread. Only then I noticed how Johnny's place had smelled, of Johnny's body sweating under the blanket. I went into a café for a shot of cognac and to wash my mouth out, maybe also the memory that insisted and insisted in Johnny's words, his stories, his way of seeing what I didn't see and, at bottom, didn't want to see. I began to think of the day after tomorrow and it was like tranquillity descending, like a bridge stretching beautifully from the zinc counter into the future.

When one is not too sure of anything, the best thing to do is to make obligations for oneself that'll act as pontoons. Two or three days later I thought that I had an obligation to find out if the marquesa was helping

Johnny Carter score for heroin, and I went to her studio down in Montparnasse. The marquesa is really a marquesa, she's got mountains of money from the marquis, though it's been some time they've been divorced because of dope and other, similar, reasons. Her friendship with Johnny dates from New York, probably from the year when Johnny got famous overnight simply because someone had given him the chance to get four or five guys together who dug his style, and Johnny could work comfortably for the first time, and what he blew left everyone in a state of shock. This is not the place to be a jazz critic, and anyone who's interested can read my book on Johnny and the new postwar style, but I can say that forty-eight—let's say until fifty—was like an explosion in music, but a cold, silent explosion, an explosion where everything remained in its place and there were no screams or debris flying, but the crust of habit splintered into a million pieces until its defenders (in the bands and among the public) made hipness a question of self-esteem over something which didn't feel to them as it had before. Because after Johnny's step with the alto sax you couldn't keep on listening to earlier musicians and think that they were the end; one must submit and apply that sort of disguised resignation which is called the historical sense, and say that any one of those musicians had been stupendous, and kept on being so, in his moment. Johnny had passed over jazz like a hand turning a page, that was it.

The marquesa had the ears of a greyhound for everything that might be music, she'd always admired Johnny and his friends in the group enormously. I imagine she must have "loaned" them no small amount of dollars in the Club 33 days, when the majority of critics were screaming bloody murder at Johnny's recordings, and were criticizing his jazz by worse-than-rotten criteria. Probably also, in that period, the marquesa began sleeping with Johnny from time to time, and shooting up with him. I saw them together often before recording sessions or during intermissions at concerts, and Johnny seemed enormously happy at the marquesa's side, even though Lan and the kids were waiting for him on another floor or at his house. But Johnny never had the vaguest idea of what it is to wait for anything, he couldn't even imagine that anyone was somewhere waiting for him. Even to his way of dropping Lan, which tells it like it really is with him. I saw the postcard that he sent from Rome after being gone for four months (after climbing onto a plane with two other musicians, Lan knowing nothing about it). The postcard showed Romulus and Remus, which had always been a big joke with Johnny (one of his numbers has that title), said: "Waking alone in a multitude of loves," which is part of a first line of a Dylan Thomas poem, Johnny was reading Dylan all the time then; Johnny's agents in the States agreed to deduct a part of their percentages and give it to Lan, who, for her part, understood quickly enough that it hadn't been such a bad piece of business to have gotten loose from Johnny. Somebody told me that the marquesa had given Lan money too, without Lan knowing where it had come from. Which didn't surprise me at all, because the marquesa was absurdly generous and understood the world, a little like those omelets she makes at her studio when the boys begin to arrive in droves, and which begins to take on the aspect of a kind of permanent omelet that you throw different things into and you go on cutting out hunks and offering them in place of what's really missing.

I found the marquesa with Marcel Gavoty and Art Boucaya, and they happened just at that moment to be talking about the sides Johnny had recorded the previous afternoon. They fell all over me as if I were the archangel himself arriving, the marquesa necked with me until it was beginning to get tedious, and the boys applauded the performance, bassist and baritone sax. I had to take refuge behind an easy-chair and stand them off as best I could, all because they'd learned that I'd pro-vided the magnificent sax with which Johnny had cut four or five of the best. The marquesa said immediately that Johnny was a dirty rat, and how they'd had a fight (she didn't say over what) and that the dirty rat knew very well that all he had to do was beg her pardon properly and there would have been a check immediately to buy a new horn. Naturally Johnny hadn't wanted to beg her pardon since his return to Paris—the fight appears to have taken place in London, two months back—and so nobody'd known that he lost his goddamned horn in the metro, etcetera. When the marquesa started yakking you wondered if Dizzy's style hadn't glued up her diction, it was such an interminable series of variations in the most unexpected registers, until the end when the marquesa slapped her thighs mightily, opened her mouth wide and began to laugh as if someone were tickling her to death. Then Art Boucaya took advantage of the break to give me details of the session the day before, which I'd missed on account of my wife having pneumonia.

"Tica can tell you," Art said, pointing to the marquesa who was still squirming about with laughter. "Bruno, you can't imagine what it was like until you hear the discs. If God was anywhere yesterday, I think it was in that damned recording studio where it was as hot as ten thou-sand devils, by the way. You remember *Willow Tree*, Marcel?"

"Sure, I remember," Marcel said. "The fuck's asking me if I remember. I'm tattooed from head to foot with *Willow Tree*."

Tica brought us highballs and we got ourselves comfortable to chat. Actually we talked very little about the recording session, because any musician knows you can't talk about things like that, but what little they did say restored my hope and I thought maybe my horn would bring Johnny some good luck. Anyway, there was no lack of anecdotes which stomped that hope a bit, for example, Johnny had taken his shoes off between one cutting and the next and walked around the studio barefoot. On the other hand, he'd made up with the marquesa and promised to come to her place to have a drink before the concert tonight.

"Do you know the girl Johnny has now?" Tica wanted to know. I gave the most succinct possible description of the French girl, but Marcel filled it in with all sorts of nuances and allusions which amused the marquesa very much. There was not the slightest reference to drugs, though I'm so up tight that it seemed to me I could smell pot in Tica's studio, besides which Tica laughed in a way I've noted in Johnny at times, and in Art, which gives the teahead away. I wondered how Johnny would have gotten heroin, though, if he'd had a fight with the marquesa; my confidence in Dédée hit the ground floor, if really I'd ever had any confidence in her. They're all the same, at bottom.

I was a little envious of the equality that brought them closer together, which turned them into accomplices so easily; from my puritanical world—I don't need to admit it, anyone who knows me knows that I'm horrified by vice—I see them as sick angels, irritating in their irresponsibility, but ultimately valuable to the community because of, say, Johnny's records, the marquesa's generosity. But I'm not telling it all and I want to force myself to say it out: I envy them, I envy Johnny, that Johnny on the other side, even though nobody knows exactly what that is, the other side. I envy everything except his anguish, something no one can fail to understand, but even in his pain he's got to have some kind of in to things that's denied me. I envy Johnny and at the same time I get sore as hell watching him destroy himself, misusing his gifts, and the stupid accumulation of nonsense the pressure of his life requires. I think that if Johnny could straighten out his life, not even sacrificing anything, not even heroin, if he could pilot that plane he's been flying blind for the last five years better, maybe he'd end up worse, maybe go crazy altogether, or die, but not without having played it to the depth, what he's looking for in those sad *a posteriori* monologues, in his retelling of great, fascinating experiences which, however, stop right there, in the middle of the road. And all this I back up with my own cowardice, and maybe basically I want Johnny to wind up all at once like a nova that explodes into a thousand pieces and turns astronomers into idiots for a whole week, and then one can go off to sleep and tomorrow is another day.

It felt as though Johnny had surmised everything I'd been thinking, because he gave me a big hello when he came in, and almost immediately came over and sat beside me, after kissing the marquesa and whirling her around in the air, and exchanging with Art and her a complicated onomatopoetic ritual which made everybody feel great.

"Bruno," Johnny said, settling down on the best sofa, "that's a beautiful piece of equipment, and they tell me I was dragging it up out of my balls yesterday. Tica was crying electric-light bulbs, and I don't think it was because she owed bread to her dressmaker, huh, Tica?"

I wanted to know more about the session, but Johnny was satisfied with this bit of braggadocio. Almost immediately he turned to Marcel and started coming on about that night's program and how well both of them looked in their brand-new grey suits in which they were going to appear at the theater. Johnny was really in great shape, and you could see he hadn't used a needle overmuch in days; he has to take exactly the right amount to put him in the mood to play. And just as I was thinking that, Johnny dropped his hand on my shoulder and leaned over:

"Dédée told me I was very rough with you the other afternoon."

"Aw, you don't even remember."

"Sure. I remember very well. You want my opinion, actually I was terrific. You ought to have been happy I put on that act with you; I don't do that with anybody, believe me. It just shows how much I appreciate you. We have to go someplace soon where we can talk over a pile of things. Here . . . " He stuck out his lower lip contemptuously, laughed, shrugged his shoulders, it looked like he was dancing on the couch. "Good old Bruno. Dédée told me I acted very bad, honestly."

"You had the flu. You better now?"

"It wasn't flu. The doc arrived and right away began telling me how he liked jazz enormously, and that one night I'd have to come to his house and listen to records. Dédée told me that you gave her money."

"So you could get through all right until you get paid. How do you feel about tonight?"

"Good, shit, I feel like playing, I'd play right now if I had the horn, but Dédée insisted she'd bring it to the theater herself. It's a great horn, yesterday it felt like I was making love when I was playing it. You should have seen Tica's face when I finished. Were you jealous, Tica?"

They began to laugh like hell again, and Johnny thought it an opportune moment to race across the studio with great leaps of happiness, and between him and Art they started dancing without the music, raising and lowering their eyebrows to set the beat. It's impossible to get impatient with either Johnny or Art; it'd be like getting annoyed with the wind for blowing your hair into a mess. Tica, Marcel and I, in low voices, traded our conceptions of what was going to happen that night. Marcel is certain that Johnny's going to repeat his terrific success of 1951, when he first came to Paris. After yesterday's job, he's sure everything is going to be A-okay. I'd like to feel as confident as he does, but anyway there's nothing I can do except sit in one of the front rows and listen to the concert. At least I have the assurance that Johnny isn't out of it like that night in Baltimore. When I mentioned this to Tica, she grabbed my hand like she was going to fall into the water. Art and Johnny had gone over to the piano, and Art was showing him a new tune, Johnny was moving his head and humming. Both of them in their new grey suits were elegant as hell, although Johnny's shape was spoiled a bit by the fat he'd been laying on these days.

We talked with Tica about that night in Baltimore, when Johnny had his first crisis. I looked Tica right in the eye as we were talking, because I wanted to be sure she understood what I was talking about, and that she shouldn't give in to him this time. If Johnny managed to drink too much cognac, or smoke some tea, or go off on shit, the concert would flop and everything fall on its ass. Paris isn't a casino in the provinces, and everybody has his eye on Johnny. And while I'm thinking that, I can't help having a bad taste in my mouth, anger, not against Johnny nor the things that happen to him; rather against the people who hang around him, myself, the marquesa and Marcel, for example. Basically we're a bunch of egotists; under the pretext of watching out for Johnny what we're doing is protecting our idea of him, getting ourselves ready for the pleasure Johnny's going to give us, to reflect the brilliance from the statue we've erected among us all and defend it till the last gasp. If Johnny zonked, it would be bad for my book (the translation into English or Italian was coming out any minute), and part of my concern for Johnny was put together from such things. Art and Marcel needed him to help them earn bread, and the marquesa, well, dig what the marquesa saw in Johnny besides his talent. All this has nothing to do with the other Johnny, and suddenly I realized that maybe that was what Johnny was trying to tell me when he yanked off the blanket and left himself as naked as a worm, Johnny with no horn, Johnny with no money and no clothes, Johnny obsessed by something that his intelligence was not equal to comprehending, but which floats slowly into his music, caresses his skin, perhaps is readying for an unpredictable leap which we will never understand.

And when one thinks things out that way, one really ends up with a bad taste in the mouth, and all the sincerity in the world won't equalize the sudden discovery that next to Johnny Carter one is a piss-poor piece of shit, that now he's come to have a drink of cognac and is looking at me from the sofa with an amused expression. Now it's time for us to go to the Pleyel Hall. That the music at least will save the rest of the night, and fulfill basically one of its worst missions, to lay down a good smokescreen in front of the mirror, to clear us off the map for a couple of hours.

As is natural, I'll write a review of tonight's concert tomorrow for *Jazz*. But now at intermission, with this shorthand scrawl on my knee, I don't feel exactly like talking like a critic, no comparative criticisms. I know very well that, for me, Johnny has ceased being a jazzman and that his musical genius is a façade, something that everyone can manage to understand eventually and admire, but which conceals something else, and that other thing is the only one I ought to care for, maybe because it's the only thing really important to Johnny himself.

It's easy to say it, while I'm still in Johnny's music. When you cool off . . . Why can't I do like him, why can't I beat my head against the wall? Pickily enough, I prefer the words to the reality that I'm trying to describe, I protect myself, shielded by considerations and conjectures that are nothing other than a stupid dialectic. I think I understand why prayer demands instinctively that one fall on one's knees. The change of position is a symbol of the change in the tone of voice, in what the voice is about to articulate, in the diction itself. When I reach the point of specifying the insight into that change, things which seemed to have been arbitrary a second before are filled with a feeling of depth, simplify themselves in an extraordinary manner and at the same time go still deeper. Neither Marcel nor Art noticed yesterday that Johnny was not crazy to take his shoes off at the recording session. At that moment, Johnny had to touch the floor with his own skin, to fasten himself to the earth so that his music was a reaffirmation, not a flight. Because I feel this also in Johnny, he never runs from anything, he doesn't shoot up to get out of it like most junkies, he doesn't blow horn to squat behind a ditch of music, he doesn't spend weeks in psychiatric clinics to feel protected from the pressures he can't put up with. Even his style, the most authentic thing he has, that style which deserves all the absurd names it's ever gotten, and doesn't need any of them, proves that Johnny's art is neither a substitute nor a finished thing. Johnny abandoned the language of *That Old Fashioned Love* more or less current ten years ago, because that violently erotic language was too passive for him. In his case he preferred desire rather than pleasure and it hung him up, because desire necessitated his advancing, experimenting, denying in advance the easy rushing around of traditional jazz. For that reason, I don't think Johnny was terribly fond of the blues, where masochism and nostalgia . . . But I've spoken of all that in my book, showing how the denial of immediate satisfaction led Johnny to elaborate a language which he and other musicians are carrying today to its ultimate possibilities. This jazz cuts across all easy eroticism, all Wagnerian romanticism, so to speak, to settle firmly into what seems to be a very loose level where the music stands in absolute liberty, as when painting got away from the representational, it stayed clear by not being more than painting. But then, being master of a music not designed to facilitate orgasms or nostalgia, of a music which I should like to call metaphysical, Johnny seems to use that to explore himself, to bite into the reality that escapes every day. I see here the ultimate paradox of his style, his aggressive vigor. Incapable of satisfying itself, useful as a continual spur, an infinite construction, the pleasure of which is not in its highest pinnacle but in the exploratory repetitions, in the use of faculties which leave the suddenly human behind without losing humanity. And when Johnny, like tonight, loses himself in the continuous creation of his music, I know best of all that he's not losing himself in anything, nothing escapes him. To go to a date you can't get away from, even though you change the place you're going to meet each time. And as far as what is left behind, can be left, Johnny doesn't know or puts it down supremely. The marquesa, for example, thinks that Johnny's afraid of poverty, without knowing that the only thing Johnny can be afraid of is maybe not finding the pork chop on the end of the fork when it happens he would like to eat it, or not finding a bed when he's sleepy, or a hundred dollars in his wallet when it seems he ought to be the owner of a hundred dollars. Johnny doesn't move in a world of abstractions like we do; the reason for his music, that incredible music I've listened to tonight, has nothing to do with abstractions. But only he can make the inventory of what he's taken in while he was blowing, and more likely, he's already onto something else, losing that already in a new conjecture or a new doubt. His conquests are like a dream, when he wakes up he forgets them, when the applause brings him back from his spin, that man who goes so far out, living his quarter of an hour in a minute and a half.

It would be like living connected to a lightning rod in the middle of a thunderstorm and expecting that nothing's going to happen. Four or five days later I ran into Art Boucaya at the Dupont in the Latin Quarter, and he had no opportunity to make his expression blank as he gave me the bad news. For the first second I felt a kind of satisfaction which I find no other way of qualifying except to call it spiteful, because I knew perfectly well that the calm could not last long; but then I thought of the consequences and my fondness for Johnny, thinking of them, made my stomach churn; then I downed two cognacs while Art was telling me what had happened. In short, it seems that Delaunay called a recording session to put out a new quintet under Johnny's name, with Art, Marcel Gavoty and a pair of very good sidemen from Paris on piano and drums. The thing was supposed to begin at three in the afternoon, and they were counting on having the whole day and part of the night for warmup and to cut a number of tunes. And what happened? It started when Johnny arrived at five, Delaunay was boiling already, then Johnny sat down on a chair and said he didn't feel very well and that the only reason he came was not to queer the day's work for the boys, but HE didn't feel up to playing.

"Between Marcel and me, we tried to convince him to lie down for a bit and rest, but he wouldn't do anything but talk about, I don't know, he'd found some fields with urns, and he gave us those goddamned urns for about a quarter of an hour. Finally, he started to haul out piles of leaves that he'd gathered in some park or another and had jammed into his pockets. The floor of the goddamned studio looked like a botanical garden, the studio personnel were tromping around looking as mean as dogs, and all this without laying anything down on the acetate; just imagine the engineer sitting in his booth for three hours smoking, and in Paris that's a helluva lot for an engineer.

"Finally Marcel convinced Johnny it'd be better to try something, the two of them started to play and we moved in after a bit, better that than sitting around getting tired of doing nothing. After a while I noticed that

Johnny was having a kind of contraction in his right arm, and when he began to blow it was terrible to watch, I'm not shitting you. His face all grey, you dig, and every once in a while a chill'd shake him; and I didn't catch that moment when it got him on the floor. After a few tries he lets loose with a yell, looks at each of us one by one, slowly, and asks us what the hell we're waiting for, begin *Amorous*. You know, that tune of Alamo's. Well, Delaunay signals the engineer, we all start out the best possible, and Johnny opens his legs, stands up as though he were going to sleep in a boat rocking away, and lets loose with a sound I swear I'd never heard before or since. That goes on for three minutes, then all of a sudden he lets go with a blast, could of split the fuckin' celestial harmonies, and he goes off into one corner leaving the rest of us blowing away in the middle of the take, which we finish up best we can.

"But now the worst part, when we get finished, the first thing Johnny says was that it was all awful, that it came out like a piece of shit, and that the recording was not worth a damn. Naturally, neither we nor Delaunay paid any attention because, in spite of the defects, Johnny's solo was worth any thousand of what you can hear today. Something all by itself, I can't explain it to you . . . You'll hear it, I guess. I don't imagine that either Delaunay or the technicians thought of wiping out the acetate. But Johnny insisted like a nut, he was gonna break the glass in the control booth if they didn't show him that the acetate had been wiped. Finally the engineer showed him something or other and convinced him, and then Johnny suggested we record *Streptomycin,* which came out much better, and at the same time much worse, I mean it's clean and full, but still it hasn't got that incredible thing Johnny blew on *Amorous*."

Breathing hard, Art had finished his beer and looked at me, very depressed. I asked him what Johnny had done after that, and he told me that after boring them all to tears with his stories about the leaves and the fields full of urns, he had refused to play any more and went stumbling out of the studio. Marcel had taken his horn away from him so that he couldn't lose it or stomp on it again, and between him and one of the French sidemen, they'd gotten him back to the hotel.

What else was there to do except to go see him immediately? But what the hell, I left it for the next day. And the next morning I found Johnny in the Police Notices in *Figaro,* because Johnny'd set fire to the hotel room during the night and had escaped running naked down the halls. Both he and Dédée had gotten out unhurt, but Johnny's in the hospital under observation. I showed the news report to my wife so as to cheer her up in her convalescence, and dashed off immediately to the hospital where my press pass got me exactly nowhere. The most I managed to find out was that Johnny was delirious and had enough junk in him to drive ten people out of their heads. Poor Dédée had not been able to resist him, or to convince him to not shoot up; all Johnny's women ended up his accomplices, and I'm sure as can be that the marquesa was the one who got the junk for him.

Finally I ended up by going immediately to Delaunay's place to ask if I could hear *Amorous* as soon as possible. To see if *Amorous* would turn out to be Johnny's last will and testament. In which case, my professional duty would be . . .

But not yet, no. Five days later Dédée's phoned me saying that Johnny is much better and that he wants to see me. I'd rather not reproach her, first of all because I imagine it'd be a waste of time, and secondly because poor Dédée's voice sounds as though it were coming out of a cracked teakettle. I promised to go immediately, and said that perhaps when Johnny was better, we could organize a tour through the provinces, a lot of cities. I hung up when Dédée started crying into the phone.

Johnny's sitting up in bed, in a semi-private with two other patients who are sleeping, luckily. Before I can say anything to him, he's grabbed my head with both paws and kissed me on the forehead and cheeks numerous times. He's terribly emaciated, although he tells me that he's got a good appetite and that they give him plenty to eat. For the moment the thing that worries him most is whether the boys are bad-mouthing him, if his crisis has hurt anyone, things like that. It's almost useless to answer him, he knows well enough that the concerts have been canceled and that that hurt Art and Marcel and the others; but he asks me like he expected that something good had happened meanwhile, anything that would put things together again. And at the same time he isn't playing me a trick, because back of everything else is his supreme indifference; Johnny doesn't give a good goddamn if everything goes to hell, and I know him too well to pay any attention to his coming on.

"What do you want me to tell you, Johnny? Things could have worked out better, except you have this talent for fucking up."

"Okay, I don't deny that," Johnny said tiredly. "And all because of the urns."

I remembered Art's account of it and stood there looking at him.

"Fields filled with urns, Bruno. Piles of invisible urns buried in an immense field. I was wandering around there and once in a while I'd stumble across something. You'd say that I'd dreamt it, huh? It was just like that, believe it: every once in a while I'd stumble across an urn, until I realized that the whole field was full of urns, that there were miles and miles of them, and there were a dead man's ashes inside every urn. Then I remember I got down on my knees and began to dig up the ground with my nails until one of the urns appeared. Then I remember thinking, 'This one's going to be empty because it's the one for me.' But no, it was filled with a grey dust like I knew all the others were I hadn't seen yet. Then ... then that was when we began to record *Amorous,* if I remember."

I glanced discreetly at the temperature chart. According to it, reasonably normal. A young intern showed up in the doorway, acknowledging me with a nod, and made a gesture indicating food to Johnny, an almost sporty gesture, a good kid, etc. But when Johnny didn't answer him, when the intern had left, not even entering the door, I saw Johnny's hands were clenched tight.

"They'll never understand," he said. "They're like a monkey with a feather duster, like the chicks in the Kansas City Conservatory who think they're playing Chopin, nothing less. Bruno, in Camarillo they put me in a room with another three people, and in the morning an intern came in all washed up and all rosy, he looked so good. He looked like the son of Tampax out of Kleenex, you believe it. A kind of specimen, an immense idiot that sat down on the edge of the bed and was going to cheer me up, I mean that was when I wanted to kill myself, and I hadn't thought of Lan or of anyone, I mean, forget it. And the worst was, the poor cat was offended because I wasn't paying attention to him. He seemed to think I should sit up in bed en-goddamn-chanted with his white skin and beautifully combed hair and his nails all trimmed, and that way I'd get better like the poor bastards who come to Lourdes and throw away the crutches and leave, really jumping . . .

"Bruno, this cat and all the cats at Camarillo were convinced. You know what I'm saying? What of? I swear I don't know, but they were convinced. Of what they were, I imagine, of what they were worth, of their having a diploma. No, it's not that. Some were modest and didn't think they were infallible. But even the most humble were sure. That made me jumpy, Bruno, *that they felt sure of themselves.* Sure of what, tell me what now, when a poor devil like me with more plagues than the devil under his skin had enough awareness to feel that everything was like a jelly, that everything was very shaky everywhere, you only had to concentrate a little, feel a little, be quiet for a little bit, to find the holes. In the door, in the bed: holes. In the hand, in the newspaper, in time, in the air: everything full of holes, everything spongy, like a colander straining itself . . . But they were American science, Bruno, dig? White coats were protecting them from the holes; didn't see anything, they accepted what had been seen by others, they imagined that they were living. And naturally they couldn't see the holes, and they were very sure of themselves, completely convinced of their prescriptions, their syringes, their goddamned psychoanalysis, their don't smoke and don't drink . . . Ah, the beautiful day when I was able to move my ass out of that place, get on the train, look out the window how everything was moving backward, I don't know, have you seen how the landscape breaks up when you see it moving away from you . . . "

We're smoking Gauloises. They've given Johnny permission to drink a little cognac and smoke eight or ten cigarettes a day. But you can see it's not *him,* just his body that's smoking, and he's somewhere else almost as if he'd refuse to climb out of the mine shaft. I'm wondering what he's seen, what he's felt these last few days. I don't want to get him excited, if he could speak for himself . . . We smoke silently, and occasionally he moves his arm and runs his fingers over my face as though he were identifying me. Then he plays with his wrist watch, he looks at it tenderly.

"What happens to them is that they get to think of themselves as wise," he said sharply. "They think it's wisdom because they've piled up a lot of books and eaten them. It makes me laugh, because really they're good kids and are really convinced that what they study and what they do are really very difficult and profound things. In the circus, Bruno, it's all the same, and between us it's the same. People figure that some things are the height of difficulty, and so they applaud trapeze artists, or me. I don't know what they're thinking about, do they imagine that you break yourself up to play well, or that the trapeze artist sprains tendons every time he takes a leap? The really difficult things are something else entirely, everything that people think they can do anytime. To look, for instance, or to understand a dog or a cat. Those are the difficult things, the big difficulties. Last night I happened to look in this little mirror, and I swear, it was so terribly difficult I almost threw myself out of bed. Imagine that you're looking at yourself; that alone is enough to freeze you up for half an hour. In reality, this guy's not me, the first second I felt very clearly that he wasn't me. I took it by surprise, obliquely, and I knew it wasn't me. I felt that, and when something like that's felt . . .

But it's like at Atlantic City, on top of one wave the second one falls on you, and then another . . . You've hardly felt and already another one comes, the words come . . . No, not words, but what's in the words, a kind of glue, that slime. And the slime comes and covers you and convinces you that that's you in the mirror. Sure, but not to realize it. But sure, I am, with my hair, this scar. And people don't realize that the only thing that they accept is the slime, and that's why they think it's easy to look in a mirror. Or cut a hunk of bread with a knife. Have you ever cut a hunk of bread with a knife?"

"I'm in the habit of it," I said, amused.

"And you've stayed all that calm. Not me, Bruno, I can't. One night I shot all of it so far that the knife almost knocked the eye out of a Japanese at the next table. That was in Los Angeles, and there was such a fantastic brawl . . . When I explained to them, they dumped me. And it seemed to me so simple to explain it all to them. At that time I knew Dr. Christie. A terrific guy, and you know how I am about doctors . . . "

One hand waves through the air, touching it on all sides, laying it down as though marking its time. He smiles. I have the feeling that he's alone, completely alone. I feel hollow beside him. If it had occurred to Johnny to pass his hand through me I would have cut like butter, like smoke. Maybe that's why once in a while he grazes my face with his fingers, cautiously.

"You have the loaf of bread there, on the tablecloth," Johnny says looking down into the air. "It's solid, no denying it, toasted a lovely color, smells beautiful. Something that's not me, something apart, outside me. But if I touch it, if I move my fingers and grasp it, then something changes, don't you think so? The bread is outside me, but I touch it with my fingers, I feel it, I feel that that's the world, but if I can touch it and feel it, then you can't really say it's something else, or do you think you can say it's something else?"

"Oh baby, for thousands of years now, whole armies of greybeards have been beating their heads to solve that problem."

"There's some day in the bread," murmured Johnny, covering his face. "And I dared to touch it, to cut it in two, to put some in my mouth. Nothing happened, I know; that's what's terrible. Do you realize it's terrible that nothing happened? You cut the bread, you stick the knife into it, and everything goes on as before. I don't understand, Bruno."

Johnny's face was beginning to upset me, his excitement. Every time, it was getting more difficult to get him to talk about jazz, about his memories, his plans, to drag him back to reality. (To reality: I barely get that written down and it disgusts me. Johnny's right, reality can't be this way, it's impossible to be a jazz critic if there's any reality, because then someone's pulling your leg. But at the same time, as for Johnny, you can't go on buying it out of his bag or we'll all end up crazy.)

Then he fell asleep, or at least he's closed his eyes and is pretending to be asleep. Again I realize how difficult it is to tell where Johnny *is* from what he's doing. If he's asleep, if he's pretending to sleep, if he thinks he's asleep. One is much further away from Johnny than from any other friend. No one can be more vulgar, more common, more strung out by the circumstances of a miserable life; apparently accessible on all sides. Apparently, he's no exception. Anyone can be like Johnny if he just resigns himself to being a poor devil, sick, hung up on drugs, and without will power—and full of poetry and talent. Apparently. I, who've gone through life admiring geniuses, the Picassos, the Einsteins, the whole blessed list anyone could make up in a minute (and Gandhi, and Chaplin, and Stravinsky), like everyone else, I tend to think that these exceptions walk in the clouds somewhere, and there's no point in being surprised at anything they do. They're different, there's no other trip to take. On the other hand, the difference with Johnny is secret, irritating by its mystery, because there's no explanation for it. Johnny's no genius, he didn't discover anything, he plays jazz like several thousand other black and white men, though he's better than any of them, and you have to recognize that that depends somewhat on public taste, on the styles, in short, the times. Panassié, for example, has decided that Johnny is outright bad, and although we believe that if anyone's outright bad it's Panassié, in any case there's an area open to controversy. All this goes to prove is that Johnny is not from some other world, but the moment I think that, then I wonder if precisely so there is not in Johnny something of another world (he'd be the first to deny it). Likely he'd laugh his ass off if you told him so. I know fairly well what he thinks, which of these things he lives. I say: which of these things he lives, because Johnny . . . But I'm not going that far, what I would like to explain to myself is the distance between Johnny and ourselves that has no easy answer, is not based in explainable differences. And it seems to me that he's the first to pay for the consequences of that, that it affects him as much as it does us. I really feel like saying straight off that Johnny is some kind of angel come among men, until some elementary honesty forces me to swallow the sentence, turn it around nicely and realize that maybe what is really happening is that

Johnny is a man among angels, one reality among the unrealities that are the rest of us. Maybe that's why Johnny touches my face with his fingers and makes me feel so unhappy, so transparent, so damned small, in spite of my good health, my house, my wife, my prestige. My prestige above all. Above all, my prestige.

But it turns out the same old way, I leave the hospital and hardly do I hit the street, check the time, remember what all I have to do, the omelet turns smoothly in the air and we're right side up again. Poor Johnny, he's so far out of it. (That's the way it is, the way it is. It's easier for me to believe that that's the way it really is, now I'm in the café and the visit to the hospital was two hours ago, with everything that I wrote up there forcing me, like a condemned prisoner, to be at least a little decent with my own self.)

Luckily, the business about the fire got fixed up okay, or it seemed reasonable to imagine that the marquesa did her best to see that the fire business would be fixed up okay. Dédée and Art Boucaya came looking for me at the paper, and the three of us went over to *Vix* to listen to the already famous—still secret—recording of *Amorous*. Dédée told me, not much caring to, in the taxi, how the marquesa had gotten Johnny out of the trouble over the fire, that anyway there was nothing worse than a scorched mattress and a terrible scare thrown into all the Algerians living in the hotel in the rue Lagrange. The fine (already paid), another hotel (already arranged for by Tica), and Johnny is convalescing in an enormous bed, very pretty, drinking milk out of a milkcan and reading *Paris Match* and *The New Yorker*, once in a while changing off to his famous (and scroungy) pocket notebook with Dylan Thomas poems and penciled notations all through it.

After all this news and a cognac in the corner café, we settled down in the audition room to listen to *Amorous* and *Streptomycin*. Art had asked them to put out the lights, and lay down on the floor to hear better. And then Johnny came in and his music moved over our faces, he came in there even though he was back in the hotel propped up in bed, and scuttled us with his music for a quarter of an hour. I understand why the idea that they were going to release *Amorous* infuriated him, anyone could hear its deficiencies, the breathing perfectly audible at the ends of the phrase, and especially the final savage drop, that short dull note which sounded to me like a heart being broken, a knife biting into the bread (and he was speaking about bread a few days back). But on the other hand, and it would escape Johnny, there was what seemed to us a terrible beauty, the anxiety looking for an outlet in an improvisation full of flights in all directions, of interrogation, of desperate gestures. Johnny can't understand (because what for him is a calamity, for us looks like a road, at least a road-sign, a direction) that *Amorous* is going to stand as one of jazz's great moments. The artist inside him is going to blow his stack every time he hears this mockery of his desire, of everything that he'd wanted to say while he was fighting, the saliva running out of his mouth along with the music, more than ever alone up against that he was pursuing, against what was trying to escape him while he was chasing it. That hard. Curious, it had been indispensable to listen to this, even though already everything was converging into this, this solo in *Amorous,* so that I realized that Johnny was no victim, not persecuted as everyone thought, as I'd even insisted upon in my biography of him (the English edition has just appeared and is bound to sell like Coca-Cola). I know now that's not the way it is, that Johnny pursues and is not pursued, that all the things happening in his life are the hunter's disasters, not the accidents of the harassed animal. No one can know what Johnny's after, but that's how it is, it's there, in *Amorous,* in the junk, in his absurd conversations on any subject, in his breakdowns, in the Dylan Thomas notebook, in the whole of the poor sonofabitch that Johnny is, which makes him larger than life, and changes him into a living weirdo, into a hunter with no arms and legs, into a rabbit running past a sleeping tiger's nose. And I find it absolutely necessary to say that, at bottom, *Amorous* made me want to go vomit, as if that might free me of him, of everything in him that was going up against me and against everybody, that shapeless black mass without feet or hands, that crazy chimp that puts his fingers on my face and looks at me tenderly.

Art and Dédée don't see (I think they don't want to see) more than the formal loveliness of *Amorous.* Dédée even like *Streptomycin* better, where Johnny improvises with his usual ease and freedom, which the audience understands perfectly well and which to me sounds more like Johnny's distracted, he just lets the music run itself out, that he's on the other side. When we got into the street, I asked Dédée what their plans were, and she said that as soon as Johnny was out of the hotel (for the moment the police had him under surveillance), a new record company wanted to have him record anything he wanted to and it'd pay him very well. Art backed her up, said Johnny was full of terrific ideas, and that he and Marcel Gavoty were going to do this new bit with Johnny, though after the past few weeks you could see that Art wasn't banking on it, and privately I knew that he'd been having conversations with his agent about going back to New York as soon as possible. Something I more than understood, poor guy.

"Tica's doing very well," Dédée said bitterly. "Of course, it's easy for her. She always arrives at the last minute and all she has to do is open her handbag and it's all fixed up. On the other hand, I . . . "

Art and I looked at one another. What in hell could we say? Women spend their whole lives circling around Johnny and people like Johnny. It's not weird, it's not necessary to be a woman to feel attracted to Johnny. What's hard is to circle about him and not lose your distance, like a good satellite, like a good critic. Art wasn't in Baltimore at that time, but I remember from the times I knew Johnny when he was living with Lan and the kids. To look at Lan really hurt. But after dealing with Johnny for a while, after accepting little by little his music's influence, his dragged-out terrors, his inconceivable explanations of things that had never happened, his sudden fits of tenderness, then one understood why Lan wore that face and how it was impossible that she live with Johnny and have any other face at all. Tica's something else, she gets out from under by being promiscuous, by living the dolce vita, and besides she's got the dollar bill by the short hairs, and that's a better scene than owning a machine gun, at least if you believe what Art Boucaya says when he gets pissed off at Tica or when he's got a hangover.

"Come as soon as you can," Dédée said. "He'd like to talk with you."

I would have liked to lecture the hell out of him about the first (the cause of the fire, in which he was most certainly involved), but it would have been almost as hopeless to try to convince Johnny that he should become a useful citizen. For the moment everything's going well (it makes me uneasy) and it's strange that whenever everything goes well for Johnny, I feel immensely content. I'm not so innocent as to think this is merely a friendly reaction. It's more like a truce, a breather. I don't need to look for explanations when I can feel it as clearly as the nose on my face. It makes me sore to be the only person who feels this, who is hung with it the whole time. It makes me sore that Art Boucaya, Tica or Dédée don't realize that every time Johnny gets hurt, goes to jail, wants to kill himself, sets a mattress on fire or runs naked down the corridors of a hotel, he's paying off something for them, he's killing himself for them. Without knowing it, and not like he was making great speeches from the gallows or writing books denouncing the evils of mankind or playing the piano with the air of someone washing away the sins of the world. Without knowing it, poor saxophonist, as ridiculous as that word is, however little a thing it is, just one among so many other poor saxophonists.

What's terrible is if I go on like that, I'm going to end up writing more about myself than about Johnny. I'm beginning to compare myself to a preacher and that doesn't give me too big a laugh, I'm telling you. By the time I got home I was thinking cynically enough to restore my confidence, that in my book on Johnny I mention the pathological side of his personality only in passing and very discreetly. It didn't seem necessary to explain to people that Johnny thinks he's walking through fields full of urns, or that pictures move when he looks at them; junk-dreams, finally, which stop with the cure. But one could say that Johnny leaves these phantoms with me in pawn, lays them on me like putting a number of handkerchiefs in a pocket until the time comes to take them back. And I think I'm the only one who can stand them, who lives with them and is scared shitless of them; and nobody knows this, not even Johnny. One can't admit things like that to Johnny, as one might confess them to a really great man, a master before whom we humiliate ourselves so as to obtain some advice in exchange. What is this world I have to cart around like a burden? What kind of preacher am I? There's not the slightest bit of greatness in Johnny, I've known that since I've known him, since I began to admire him. And for a while now this hasn't surprised me, although at the beginning the lack of greatness upset me, perhaps because it's one quality one is not likely to apply to the first comer, and especially to jazzmen. I don't know why (I don't *know* why) I believed at one time that Johnny had a kind of greatness which he contradicts day after day (or which we contradict, it's not the same thing really; because, let's be honest, there is in Johnny the phantom of another who could be, and this other Johnny is very great indeed; one's attention is drawn to the phantom by the lack of that quality which nevertheless he evokes and contains negatively).

I say this because the tries Johnny has made to change his life, from his unsuccessful suicide to using junk, are ones you finally expect from someone with as little greatness as he. I think I admire him all the more for that, because he really is the chimpanzee who wants to learn to read, a poor guy who looks at all the walls around him, can't convince himself, and starts all over again.

Ah, but what if one day the chimp does begin to read, what a crack in the dam, what a commotion, every man for himself, head for the hills, and I first of all. It's terrible to see a man lacking all greatness beat his head against the wall that way. He is the critic of us all with his bones cracking, he tears us to shreds with the opening notes of his music. (Martyrs, heroes, fine, right: one is certain with them. But Johnny!)

*   *   *

Sequences. I don't know how better to say it, it's like an idea of what abruptly brings about terrible or idiotic sequences in a man's life, without his knowing what law outside the categories labeled "law" decides that a certain telephone call is going to be followed immediately by the arrival of one's sister who lives in the Auvergne, or that the milk is going to be upset into the fire, or that from a balcony we're going to see a boy fall under an automobile. As on football teams or boards of directors, it appears that destiny always appoints a few substitutes when those named to the positions fall out as if by themselves. And so it's this morning, when I'm still happy knowing that things are going better and more cheerfully with Johnny Carter, there's an urgent telephone call for me at the paper, and it's Tica calling, and the news is that Bee, Johnny and Lan's youngest daughter, has just died in Chicago, and that naturally Johnny's off his head and it would be good of me to drop by and give his friends a hand.

I was back climbing the hotel stairs—and there have been a lot of them during my friendship with Johnny—to find Tica drinking tea, Dédée soaking a towel, and Art, Delaunay, and Pepe Ramírez talking in low voices about the latest news of Lester Young, Johnny very quiet on the bed, a towel on his forehead, and wearing a perfectly tranquil and almost disdainful air. I immediately put my sympathetic face back into my pocket, restricting myself to squeezing Johnny's hand very hard, lighting a cigarette, and waiting.

"Bruno, I hurt here," Johnny said after a while, touching his chest in the conventional location. "Bruno, she was like a small white stone in my hand. I'm nothing but a pale horse with granulated eyelids whose eyes'll run forever."

All of this said solemnly, almost recited off, and Tica looking at Art, and both of them making gestures of tender forbearance, taking advantage of the fact that Johnny has his face covered with the towel and can't see them. Personally, I dislike cheap sentimentality and its whole vocabulary, but everything that Johnny had just said, aside from the impression that I'd read it somewhere, felt to me like a mask that he'd put on to speak through, that empty, that useless. Dédée had come over with another towel to replace the one plastered on there, and in the interval I caught a glimpse of Johnny's face uncovered and I saw an ashy greyness, the mouth twisted, and the eyes shut so tight they made wrinkles on his forehead. As always with Johnny, things had happened in a way other than what one had expected, and Pepe Ramírez who doesn't know him very well is still flipped out and I think from the scandal, because after a time Johnny sat up in bed and started slowly, chewing every word, and then blew it out like a trumpet solo, insulting everyone connected with recording *Amorous*, without looking at anyone but nailing us all down like bugs in a box with just the incredible obscenity of his words, and so for two full minutes he continued cursing everyone on *Amorous*, starting with Art and Delaunay, passing over me (but I . . .) and ending with Dédée, Christ omnipotent and the whore who without exception gave birth to us all. And this was profoundly, this and the small white stone, the funeral oration for Bee, dead from pneumonia in Chicago.

Two empty weeks will pass; piles of work, journalism, magazine articles, visits here and there—a good résumé of a critic's life, a man who only lives on borrowed time, borrowed everything, on novelties for the news-hungry and decisions not of one's making. I'm talking about what happened one night Tica, Baby Lennox and I were together in the Café de Flore humming *Out of Nowhere* very contentedly and talking about a piano solo of Bud Powell's which sounded particularly good to all three of us, especially to Baby Lennox who, on top of being otherwise spectacular, had done herself up à la Saint-Germain-des-Prés, and you should have seen how great it looked on her. Baby will see Johnny show up with the rapturous admiration of her twenty years, and Johnny look at her without seeing her and continue wide of us and sit alone at another table, dead drunk or asleep. I'll feel Tica's hand on my knee.

"You see, he started shoving needles in his arm again last night. Or this afternoon. Damn that woman . . . "

I answered grudgingly that Dédée was as guilty as anyone else, starting with her, she'd turned on with Johnny dozens of times and would continue to do so whenever she goddamn well felt like it. I'd feel an overwhelming impulse to go out and be by myself, as always when it's impossible to get close to Johnny, to be with him and beside him. I'll watch him making designs on the table with his finger, sit staring at the waiter who's asking him what he would like to drink, and finally Johnny'll draw a sort of arrow in the air and hold it up with both hands as though it weighed a ton, and people at other tables would begin to be discreetly amused, which is the normal reaction in the Flore. Then Tica will say, "Shit," and go over to Johnny's table, and after placing an order with the waiter, she'll begin to talk into Johnny's ear. Not to mention that Baby will hasten to confide in me her dearest hopes, but then I'll tell her vaguely that she has to leave Johnny alone and that nice girls are supposed to be in bed early, and if possible with a jazz critic. Baby will laugh amiably, her hand stroking my hair, and then we'll sit quietly and watch the chick go by who wears the white-leaded cape up over her face and who has green eyeshadow and green lipstick even. Baby will say it really doesn't look so bad on her, and I'll ask her to sing me very quietly one of those blues that have already made her famous in London and Stockholm. And then we'll go back to *Out of Nowhere,* which is following us around tonight like a dog which would also be the chick in the cape and green eyes.

Two of the guys from Johnny's new quintet will also show up, and I'll take advantage of the moment to ask how the gig went tonight; that way I'll find out that Johnny was barely able to play anything, but that what he had been able to play was worth the collected ideas and works of a John Lewis, assuming that the last-named could manage any idea whatsoever, like one of the boys said, the only one he having always close at hand being to push in enough notes to plug the hole, which is not the same thing. Meanwhile I'll wonder how much of this is Johnny going to be able to put up with, not to mention the audience that believes in Johnny. The boys will not sit down and have a beer, Baby and I'll be sitting there alone again, and I'll end up by answering her questions and explain to Baby, who is really worthy of her nickname, why Johnny is so sick and washed up, why the guys in the quintet are getting more fed up every day, why one day the whole shebang is going to blow up, in one of those scenes that had already blown up San Francisco, Baltimore and New York half-a-dozen times.

Other musicians who work in the quarter'll come in, and some'll go to Johnny's table to say hello to him, but he'll look at them from far off like some idiot with wet mild eyes, his mouth unable to keep back the saliva glistening off his lips. It will be interesting to watch the double maneuvers of Tica and Baby, Tica having recourse to her domination of men to keep them away from Johnny, turning them off with a quick explanation and a smile, Baby whispering her admiration of Johnny in my ear and how good it would be to get him off to a sanitorium for a cure, and all because she's jealous and would like to sleep with Johnny tonight even, something impossible furthermore as anyone can see and which pleases me considerably. For ever since I've known her, I've been thinking of how nice it would be to caress, to run my hand over Baby's thighs, and I'll be a step away from suggesting that we leave and have a drink someplace quieter (she won't care to, and at bottom, neither will I, because that other table will hold us there, attached and unhappy) until suddenly, no notice of what's coming, we'll see Johnny get up slowly, looking at us, recognizing us, coming toward us—I should say towards me, Baby doesn't count—and reaching the table he'll bend over a little naturally as if he were about to take a fried potato off the plate, and we'll see him go to his knees just in front of me, with all natural-ness he'll get down on his knees in front of me and look me in the eye, and I'll see that he's crying and'll know without any say-so that Johnny is crying for little Bee.

My reaction is that human, I wanted to get Johnny up, keep him from making an ass of himself, and finally I make myself the ass, because there's absolutely nothing more ridiculous than a man trying to move another who is very well off where he is and comfortable and feels perfectly natural in that position, he likes it down there, so that the customers at the Flore, who never get upset over trifles, looked at me in a rather unfriendly fashion, none of them knowing, however, that the Negro on his knees there is Johnny Carter, they all look at me as if they were looking at someone climbing up on the altar to tug Christ down from his cross. Johnny was the first to reproach me, just weeping silently he raised his eyes and looked at me, and between that and the evident disapproval of the customers I was left with the sole option of sitting down again in front of Johnny, feeling worse than he did, wanting to be anywhere else in the world but in that chair face to face with Johnny on his knees.

The rest hadn't been so bad, though it's hard to tell how many centuries passed with no one moving, with the tears coursing down Johnny's face, with his eyes fixed on mine continuously, meanwhile I was trying to offer him a cigarette, to light one for myself, to make an understanding gesture toward Baby who, it seemed to me, was on the point of racing out or of breaking into tears herself. As usual, it was Tica who settled the problem, sitting herself down at our table in all her tranquility, drawing a chair over next to Johnny and putting a hand on his shoulder, not pushing it, until finally Johnny rose a little and changed from that horror into the conventional attitude of a friend sitting down with us, it was a matter only of raising his knees a few centimeters and allowing the honorable comfort of a chair to be edged between his buttocks and the floor (I almost said "and the cross," really this is getting contagious). People had gotten tired of looking at Johnny, he'd gotten tired of crying, and we of sitting around like dogs. I suddenly understood the loving attitude some painters have for chairs, any one of the chairs in the Flore suddenly seemed to me a miraculous

object, a flower, a perfume, the perfect instrument of order and upright-
ness for men in their city.

Johnny pulled out a handkerchief, made his apologies without
undue stress, and Tica had a large coffee brought and gave it to him to
drink. Baby was marvelous, all at once dropping her stupidity when it
came to Johnny, she began to hum *Mamie's Blues* without giving the
impression that she was doing it on purpose, and Johnny looked at her
and smiled, and it felt to me that Tica and I at the same time thought
that Bee's image was fading slowly at the back of Johnny's eyes, and that
once again Johnny was willing to return to us for a spell, keep us company until the next flight. As usual, the moment of feeling like a dog
had hardly passed, when my superiority to Johnny allowed me to be
indulgent, talking a little with everyone without getting into areas rather
too personal (it would have been horrible to see Johnny slip off the
chair back onto his . . .), and luckily Tica and Baby were both acting
like angels and the people at the Flore had been going and coming for
at least the length of an hour, being replaced, until the customers at
one in the morning didn't even realize that something had just happened, although really it hadn't been a big scene if you think of it
rightly. Baby was the first to leave (Baby is a chick full of application,
she'll be rehearsing with Fred Callender at nine in the morning for a
recording session in the afternoon) and Tica had downed her third
cognac and offered to take us home. When Johnny said no, he'd rather
stay and bat the breeze with me, Tica thought that was fine and left,
not without paying the rounds for us all, as befits a marquesa. And
Johnny and I ordered a glass of chartreuse apiece, among friends such
weaknesses are forgiven, and we began to walk down Saint-Germain-
des-Prés because Johnny had insisted that he could walk fine and I'm
not the kind of guy to let a friend drop under such circumstances.

We go down the rue de l'Abbaye as far as the place Furstenberg,
which reminds Johnny dangerously of a play-theater which his godfather seems to have given him when he was eight years old. I try to head
for the rue Jacob afraid that his memories will get him back onto Bee,
but you could say that Johnny had closed that chapter for what was left
of the night. He's walking along peacefully, not staggering (at other
times I've seen him stumble in the street, and not from being drunk;
something in his reflexes that doesn't function) and the night's heat and
the silence of the streets makes us both feel good. We're smoking
Gauloises, we drift down toward the river, and opposite one of those
galvanized iron coffins the booksellers use as stands along the quai de

Conti, some memory or another or maybe a student whistling reminds us of a Vivaldi theme, humming it, then the two of us begin to sing it with a great deal of feeling and enthusiasm, and Johnny says that if he had the horn there he'd spend the night playing Vivaldi, I find the suggestion exaggerated.

"Well, okay, I'd also play a little Bach and Charles Ives," Johnny says condescendingly. "I don't know why the French are not interested in Charles Ives. Do you know his songs? The one about the leopard, you have to know the one about the leopard. 'A leopard . . .'"

And in his weak tenor voice he goes on at great length about the leopard, needless to say, many of the phrases he's singing are not absolutely Ives, something Johnny's not very careful about while he's sure that what he's singing is something good. Finally we sit down on the rail opposite the rue Gît-le-Coeur and smoke another cigarette because the night is magnificent and shortly thereafter the taste of the cigarette is forcing us to think of having a beer at a café, just thinking of the taste of it is a pleasure for Johnny and me. I pay almost no attention when he mentions my book the first time, because right away he goes back to talking about Charles Ives and how numerous times he'd enjoyed working Ives's themes into his records, with nobody even noticing (not even Ives, I suppose), but after a bit I get to thinking about the business of the book and try to get him back onto the subject.

"Oh, I've read a few pages," Johnny says. "At Tica's they talk a lot about your book, but I didn't even understand the title. Art brought me the English edition yesterday and then I found out about some things. It's very good, your book."

I adopt the attitude natural in such a situation, an air of displeased modesty mixed with a certain amount of interest, as if his opinion were about to reveal to me—the author—the truth about my book.

"It's like in a mirror," Johnny says. "At first I thought that to read something that'd been written about you would be more or less like looking at yourself and not into a mirror. I admire writers very much, it's incredible the things they say. That whole section about the origins of bebop . . ."

"Well, all I did was transcribe literally what you told me in Baltimore," I say defensively, not knowing what I'm being defensive about.

"Sure, that's all, but in reality it's like in a mirror," Johnny persists stubbornly.

"What more do you want? Mirrors give faithful reflections."

"There're things missing, Bruno," Johnny says. "You're much better informed than I am, but it seems to me like something's missing."

"The things that you've forgotten to tell me," I answer, reasonably annoyed. This uncivilized monkey is capable of . . . (I would have to speak with Delaunay, it would be regrettable if an imprudent statement about a sane, forceful criticism that . . . *For example Lan's red dress*, Johnny is saying. And in any case take advantage of the enlightening details from this evening to put into a new edition; that wouldn't be bad. *It stank like an old washrag*, Johnny's saying, *and that's the only value on the record*. Yes, listen closely and proceed rapidly, because in other people's hands any possible contradiction might have terrible consequences. *And the urn in the middle, full of dust that's almost blue*, Johnny is saying, *and very close to the color of a compact my sister had once*. As long as he wasn't going into hallucinations, the worst that could happen would be that he might contradict the basic ideas, the aesthetic system so many people have praised . . . *And furthermore, cool doesn't mean, even by accident ever, what you've written*, Johnny is saying. Attention.)

"How is it not what I've written, Johnny? It's fine that things change, but not six months ago, you . . . "

"Six months ago," Johnny says, getting down from the rail and setting his elbows on it to rest his head between his hands. "Six months ago. Oh Bruno, what I could play now if I had the kids with me . . . And by the way: the way you wrote 'the sax, the sex,' very ingenious, very pretty, that, the word-play. *Six months ago. Six, sax, sex*. Positively lovely. Fuck you, Bruno."

I'm not going to start to say that his mental age does not permit him to understand that this innocent word-play conceals a system of ideas that's rather profound (it seemed perfectly precise to Leonard Feather when I explained it to him in New York) and that the paraeroticism of jazz evolved from the washboard days, etc. As usual, immediately I'm pleased to think that critics are much more necessary than I myself am disposed to recognize (privately, in this that I'm writing) because the creators, from the composer to Johnny, passing through the whole damned gradation, are incapable of extrapolating the dialectical consequences of their work, of postulating the fundamentals and the transcendency of what they're writing down or improvising. I should remember this in moments of depression when I feel dragged that I'm nothing more than a critic. *The name of the star is called Wormwood*, Johnny is saying, and suddenly I hear his other voice, the voice that comes when he's . . . how say this? how describe Johnny when he's beside himself, already out of it, already gone? Uneasy, I get down off the rail and look at him closely. And the name of the star is called Wormwood, nothing you can do for him.

"The name of the star is called Wormwood," says Johnny, using both hands to talk. "And their dead bodies shall lie in the streets of the great city. Six months ago."

Though no one see me, though no one knows I'm there, I shrug my shoulders at the stars (the star's name is Wormwood). We're back to the old song: "I'm playing this tomorrow." The name of the star is Wormwood and their bodies'll be left lying six months ago. In the streets of the great city. Out, very far out. And I've got blood in my eye just because he hasn't wanted to say any more to me about the book, and truly, I don't know what he thinks of the book, which thousands of fans are reading in two languages (three pretty soon, and a Spanish edition is being discussed, it seems that they play something besides tangos in Buenos Aires).

"It was a lovely dress," Johnny says. "You do not want to know how beautifully it fit on Lan, but it'll be easier to explain it to you over a whiskey, if you got the money. Dédée sent me out with hardly three hundred francs."

He laughs sarcastically, looking at the Seine. As if he hadn't the vaguest idea of how to get drink or dope when he wanted it. He begins to explain to me that really Dédée is very goodhearted (nothing about the book) and that she does it out of kindness, but luckily there's old buddy Bruno (who's written a book, but who needs it) and it'd be great to go to the Arab quarter and sit in a café, where they always leave you alone if they see that you belong a little to the star called Wormwood (I'm thinking this, and we're going in by the Saint-Séverin side and it's two in the morning, an hour at which my wife is very used to getting up and rehearsing everything she's going to give me at breakfast, along with the cup of coffee, light). So I'm walking with Johnny, so we drink a terrible cognac, very cheap, so we order double shots and feel very content. But nothing about the book, only the compact shaped like a swan, the star, bits and hunks of things, that flow on with hunks of sentences, hunks of looks, hunks of smiles, drops of saliva on the table and dried on the edge of the glass (Johnny's glass). Sure, there are moments when I wish he were already dead. I imagine there are plenty of people who would think the same if they were in my position. But how can we resign ourselves to the fact that Johnny would die carrying with him what he doesn't want to tell me tonight, that from death he'd continue hunting, would continue flipping out (I swear I don't know how to write all this) though his death would mean peace to me, prestige, the status incontrovertibly bestowed upon one by unbeatable theses and efficiently arranged funerals.

Every once in a while Johnny stops his constant drumming on the tabletop, looks over at me, makes an incomprehensible face and resumes his drumming. The café owner knows us from the days when we used to come there with an Arab guitarist. It's been some time now that Ben Aifa has wanted to go home and sleep, we're the last customers in the filthy place that smells of chili and greasy meat pies. Besides, I'm dropping from sleepiness, but the anger keeps me awake, a dull rage that isn't directed against Johnny, more like when you've made love all afternoon and feel like a shower so that the soap and water will scrub off everything that's beginning to turn rancid, beginning to show too clearly what, at the beginning . . . And Johnny beats a stubborn rhythm on the tabletop, and hums once in a while, almost without seeing me. It could very well happen that he's not going to make any more comments on the book. Things go on shifting from one side to another, tomorrow it'll be another woman, another brawl of some sort, a trip. The wisest thing to do would be to get the English edition away from him on the sly, speak to Dédée about that, ask it as a favor in exchange for so many I've done her. This uneasiness is absurd, it's almost a rage. I can't expect any enthusiasm on Johnny's part at all; as matter of fact, it had never occurred to me that he'd read the book. I know perfectly well that the book doesn't tell the truth about Johnny (it doesn't lie either), it just limits itself to Johnny's music. Out of discretion, out of charity, I've not wanted to show his incurable schizophrenia nakedly, the sordid, ultimate depths of his addiction, the promiscuity in that regrettable life. I set out to show the essential lines, emphasizing what really counts, Johnny's incomparable art. What more could anyone say? But maybe it's exactly there that he's expecting something of me, lying in ambush as usual, waiting for something, crouched ready for one of those ridiculous jumps in which all of us get hurt eventually. That's where he's waiting for me, maybe, to deny all the aesthetic bases on which I've built the ultimate structure of his music, the great theory of contemporary jazz which has resulted in such acclaim from everywhere it's appeared so far.

To be honest, what does his life matter to me? The only thing that bothers me is that if he continues to let himself go on living as he has been, a style I'm not capable of following (let's say I don't want to follow it), he'll end up by making lies out of the conclusions I've reached in my book. He might let it drop somewhere that my statements are wrong, that his music's something else.

"Hey, you said a bit back that there were things missing in the book."

(Attention now.)

"Things are missing, Bruno? Oh yeah, I said there were things missing. Look, it's not just Lan's red dress. There're . . . Will there really be urns, Bruno? I saw them again last night, an enormous field, but they weren't so buried this time. Some had inscriptions and pictures on them, you could see giants with helmets like in the movies, and monstrous cudgels in their hands. It's terrible to walk around between the urns and know there's no one else, that I'm the only one walking around in them and looking for . . . Don't get upset, Bruno, it's not important that you forgot to put all that in. But Bruno," and he lifts a finger that does not shake, "what you forgot to put in is me."

"Come on, Johnny."

"About me, Bruno, about me. And it's not your fault that you couldn't write what I myself can't blow. When you say there that my true biography is in my records, I know you think that's true and besides it sounds very pretty, but that's not how it is. And if I myself didn't know how to blow it like it should be, blow what I really am . . . you dig, they can't ask you for miracles, Bruno. It's hot inside here, let's go."

I follow him into the street, we wander a few feet off and a white cat comes out of an alley and meows at us; Johnny stays there a long time petting it. Well, that does it; I'll find a taxi in the place Saint-Michel, take him back to the hotel and go home myself. It hasn't been so awful after all; for a moment there I was afraid that Johnny had constructed a sort of antitheory to the book's and that he was trying it out on me before spilling it at full speed. Poor Johnny petting a white cat. Basically, the only thing he said was that no one can know anything about anyone, big deal. That's the basic assumption of any biography, then it takes off, what the hell. Let's go, Johnny, let's go home, it's late.

"Don't think that that's all it is," Johnny says, standing up suddenly as if he knew what I was thinking. "It's God, baby. Now that's where you missed out."

"Let's go, Johnny, let's go home, it's late."

"It's what you and people like my buddy Bruno call God. The tube of toothpaste in the morning, they call that God. The garbage can, they call that God. Afraid of kicking the bucket, they call that God. And you have the barefaced nerve to mess me up with that pigsty, you've written that my childhood, and my family, and I don't know what ancestral heritage of the Negro . . . shit. A mountain of rotten eggs and you in the middle of it crowing, very happy with your God. I don't want your God, he's never been mine."

"The only thing I said is that Negro music . . ."

"I don't want your God," Johnny says again. "Why've you made me accept him in your book? I don't know if there's a God, I play my music, I make my God, I don't need your inventions, leave those to Mahalia Jackson and the Pope, and right now you're going to take that part out of your book."

"If you insist," I say, to say something. "In the second edition."

"I'm as alone as that cat, much more alone because I know it and he doesn't. Damn, he's digging his nails into my hand. Bruno, jazz is not only music, I'm not only Johnny Carter."

"Exactly what I was trying to say when I wrote that sometimes you play like . . ."

"Like it's raining up my asshole," Johnny says, and it's the first time all night that I feel he's getting really sore. "A man can't say anything, right away you translate it into your filthy language. If I play and you see angels, that's not my fault. If the others open their fat yaps and say that I've reached perfection, it's not my fault. And that's the worst thing, the thing you really and truly left out of your book, Bruno, and that's that I'm not worth a damn, that what I play and what the people applaud me for is not worth a damn, really not worth a damn."

Truly a very rare modesty at this hour of the morning. This Johnny . . .

"How can I explain it to you?" Johnny yells, putting his hands on my shoulders, jerking me to the right and to the left. (Cut out the noise! they scream from a window). "It isn't a question of more music or less music, it's something else . . . for example, it's the difference between Bee being dead and being alive. What I'm playing is Bee dead, you dig, while what I want to, what I want to . . . And sometimes because of that I wreck the horn and people think that I'm up to my ears in booze. Really, of course, I'm always smashed when I do it, because, after all, a horn costs a lot of bread."

"Let's go this way. I'll get a taxi and drop you at the hotel."

"You're a mother of goodness, Bruno," Johnny sneers. "Old buddy Bruno writes everything down in his notebook that you say, except the important things. I never would have believed you could be so wrong until Art passed that book on to me. At the beginning I thought you were talking about someone else, about Ronnie or about Marcel, and then Johnny here and Johnny there, I mean it was about me and I wondered, but where am I?, and you dish it out about me in Baltimore, and at Birdland, and my style . . . Listen," he added almost coldly, "it isn't that I didn't realize that you'd written a book for the public. That's very fine, and everything you say about my way of playing and feeling jazz seems perfectly okay to me. Why are we going on talking about the book? A piece of garbage floating in the Seine, that piece of straw floating beside the dock, your book. And I'm that other straw, and you're that bottle going by bobbing over there. Bruno, I'm going to die without having found . . . without . . . "

I catch him under his arms and hold him up, I prop him against the railing above the pier. He's slipping into his usual delirium, he mutters parts of words, spits.

"Without having found," he repeats. "Without having found . . . "

"What is it you want to find, brother," I tell him. "You don't have to ask the impossible, what you have found is enough for . . . "

"For you, I know," Johnny says bitterly. "For Art, for Dédée, for Lan . . . You donno how . . . Sure, every once in a while the door opens a little bit . . . Look at the two straws, they've met, see they're dancing, one in front of the other . . . It's pretty, huh . . . It began to open out . . . Time . . . I told you, it seems to me that time business . . . Bruno, all my life in my music I looked for that door to open finally. Nothing, a crack . . . I remember in New York one night . . . A red dress. Yeah, red, and it fit her beautifully. Okay, one night we were with Miles and Hal . . . we were carrying it for about an hour I think, playing the same piece, all by ourselves, happy . . . Miles played something so lovely it almost pulled me out of my chair, then I let loose, I just closed my eyes and I flew. Bruno, I swear I was flying . . . And I was hearing it like from a place very far away, but inside me just the same, beside myself, someone was standing there . . . Not exactly someone . . . Look, the bottle, it's incredible how it bobs along . . . It wasn't anyone, just that you look for comparisons . . . It was the sureness, the meeting, like in some dreams, what do you think?, when everything's resolved, Lan and the chicks waiting for you with a turkey in the oven, you get in the car and never hit a red light, everything running as smooth as a billiard ball. And who I had beside me was like myself but not taking up any space, without being in New York at all, and especially without time, without afterwards . . . without there having to be an afterwards . . . for a while there wasn't anything but always . . . And I didn't know that it was a lie, that

that happened because I was lost in the music, and that I hardly finish playing, because after all I had to give Hal his chance to do his thing at the piano, at that same moment my head would fall out, I'd be plunged into myself . . . "

He's crying softly, he rubs his eyes with his filthy hands. Me, I don't know what to do, it's so late, the dampness coming up from the river, we're going to catch cold, both of us.

"It felt like I wanted to swim with no water," Johnny murmurs. "It felt like I wanted to have Lan's red dress but without Lan inside it. And Bee's dead, Bruno. And I think you're right, your book really is very good."

"Let's go, Johnny, I'm not getting offended at what you think's bad about the book."

"It's not that, your book is okay because . . . because it doesn't have urns, Bruno. It's like what Satchmo blows, that clean, that pure. Doesn't it seem to you that what Satch's playing is like a birthday party or a decent action? We . . . I tell you I felt like I wanted to swim without water. It seemed to me . . . no you have to be an idiot . . . it seemed to me that one day I was going to find something else. I wasn't satisfied, I thought that the good things, Lan's red dress, even Bee, were like rat traps, I don't know how to put it any other way . . . Traps so that you would conform, dig, so that you would say everything's all right, baby. Bruno, I think that Lan and jazz, yeah, even jazz, were like advertisements in a magazine, pretty things so that I would stay conformed like you stay because you've got Paris and your wife and your work . . . I got my sax . . . and my sex, like the good book say. Everything that's missing. Traps, baby . . . because it's impossible there's nothing else, it can't be we're that close to it, that much on the other side of the door . . . "

"The only thing that counts is to give whatever one has that's possible," I say, feeling incredibly stupid.

"And win the poll every year in *Down Beat*, right," Johnny agrees. "Sure, baby. Sure. Sure. Sure. Sure."

I'm moving little by little toward the square. With any luck there'll be a taxi on the corner.

"On top of everything, I don't buy your God," murmured Johnny. "Don't come on to me that way, I won't put up with it. If it's really him on the other side of the door, fuck it. There's no use getting past that door if it's him on the other side opening it. Kick the goddamn thing in, right? Break the mother down with your fist, come all over the door, piss all day long against the door. Right? That time in New York I think I opened the door with my music, until I had to stop and then the son-ofabitch closed it in my face only because I hadn't prayed to him ever, because I'm never going to pray to him, because I don't wanna know nothing about that goddamned uniformed doorman, that opener of doors in exchange for a goddamned tip, that . . . "

Poor Johnny, then he complains that you can't put these things in a book. Three o'clock in the morning, Jesus Christ.

Tica went back to New York, Johnny went back to New York (without Dédée, now happily settled at Louis Perron's, a very promising trombonist). Baby Lennox went back to New York. The season in Paris was very dull and I missed my friends. My book on Johnny was selling very well all over, and naturally Sammy Pretzal was already talking about the possibility of an adaptation for Hollywood; when you think of the relation of the franc-rate to the dollar, that's always an interesting proposition. My wife was still furious over my passage with Baby Lennox, nothing too serious overall finally, Baby is promiscuous in a reasonably marked manner and any intelligent woman would have to understand that things like that don't compromise the conjugal equilibrium, aside from which, Baby had already gone back to New York with Johnny, she'd decided that she'd enjoy returning on the same boat with Johnny. She'd already be shooting junk with Johnny, and lost like him, poor doll. And *Amorous* had just been released in Paris, just as the second edition of my book went to press and they were talking about translating it into German. I had thought a great deal about the changes possible in a second edition. To be honest within the limits permitted by the profession, I wondered whether it would not be necessary to show the personality of my subject in another light. I discussed it at different times with Delaunay and with Hodeir, they didn't really know what to advise me because they thought the book terrific and realized that the public liked it the way it was. It seemed I was being warned that they were both afraid of a literary infection, that I would end up by riddling the work with nuances which would have little or nothing to do with Johnny's music, at least as all of us understood it. It appeared to me that the opinion of people in authority (and my own personal decision, it would be dumb to negate that at this level of consideration) justified putting the second edition to bed as was. A close reading of the trade magazines from the States (four stories on Johnny, news of a new suicide attempt, this time with tincture of iodine, stomach pump and three weeks in the hospital, working in Baltimore again as though nothing had happened) calmed me sufficiently, aside from the anguish I felt at these ghastly backslidings. Johnny had not said one compromising word about the book. Example (in *Stomping Around*, a music magazine out of Chicago, Teddy Rogers' interview with Johnny): "Have you read what Bruno V—— in Paris wrote about you?" "Yes, it's very good." "Nothing to say about the book?" "Nothing, except that it's fine. Bruno's a great guy." It remained to be seen what Johnny might say if he were walking around drunk or high, but at least there were no rumors of the slightest contradiction from him. I decided not to touch the second edition, to go on putting Johnny forth as he was at bottom: a poor sonofabitch with barely mediocre intelligence, endowed like so many musicians, so many chess players and poets, with the gift of creating incredible things without the slightest consciousness (at most, the pride of a boxer who knows how strong he is) of the dimensions of his work. Everything convinced me to keep, no matter what, this portrait of Johnny; it wasn't worth it to create complications with an audience that was crazy about jazz but cared nothing for either musical or psychological analysis, nothing that wasn't instant satisfaction and clear-cut besides, hands clapping to keep the beat, faces gone beatific and relaxed, the music that was driving through the skin, seeping into the blood and breath, and then finish, to hell with profound motives.

First two telegrams came (one to Delauney, one to me, in the afternoon the newspapers came out with their idiotic comments); twenty days later I had a letter from Baby Lennox, who had not forgotten me. "They treated him wonderfully at Bellevue and I went to fetch him when he got out. We were living in Mike Russolo's apartment, he's gone on tour to Norway. Johnny was in very good shape, and even though he didn't want to play dates, he agreed to record with the boys at Club 28. You I can tell this, really he was pretty weak"—I can imagine what Baby meant by that after our affair in Paris—"and at night he scared me, the way he'd breathe and moan. The only thing that softens it for me," Baby summed it up beautifully, "is that he died happy and without knowing it was coming. He was watching TV and all of a sudden slumped to the floor. They told me it was instantaneous." From which one inferred that Baby had not been present, and the assumption was correct because later we found out that Johnny was living at Tica's place and that he'd been there with her for five days, depressed and preoccupied, talking about quitting jazz, going to live in Mexico and work in the fields (he'd handed that to everybody at some time or other in his life, it's almost boring), and that Tica was taking care of him and doing everything possible to keep him quiet, making him think of the future (this is what Tica said later, as if she or Johnny had ever had the slightest idea of the future). In the middle of a television program which Johnny was enjoying, he started to cough, all at once he slumped down all of a sudden, etc. I'm not all that sure that death was as instantaneous as Tica declared to the police (Johnny's death in her apartment had put her in an unusually tight spot she was trying to get out of, pot was always within reach, and probably a stash of heroin somewhere, poor Tica'd had several other bad scenes there, and the not completely convincing results of the autopsy. One can imagine completely what a doctor would find in Johnny's lungs and liver). "You wouldn't want to know how painful his death is to me, although I could tell you some other things," sweet Baby added gently, "but sometime when I feel better I'll write you or tell you (it looks like Rogers wants to get me contracts in Paris and Berlin) everything you need to know, you were Johnny's best friend." And after a page dedicated to insulting Tica, you'd believe she not only caused Johnny's death but was responsible for the attack on Pearl Harbor and the Black Plague, poor Baby ended up: "Before I forget, one day in Bellevue he asked after you a lot, he was mixed up and thought you were in New York and didn't want to come see him, he was talking all the time about fields full of things, and after he was calling for you, even cussing you out, poor baby. You know what a fever's like. Tica told Bob Carey that Johnny's last words were something like: 'Oh, make me a mask,' but you can imagine how at that moment . . . " I sure could imagine it. "He'd gotten very fat," Baby added at the end of her letter, "and panted out of breath when he walked." These were details you might expect from a person as scrupulous as Baby Lennox.

All this happened at the same time that the second edition of my book was published, but luckily I had time to incorporate an obituary note edited under full steam and inserted, along with a newsphoto of the funeral in which many famous jazzmen were identifiable. In that format the biography remained, so to speak, intact and finished. Perhaps it's not right that I say this, but naturally I was speaking from a merely aesthetic point of view. They're already talking of a new translation, into Swedish or Norwegian, I think. My wife is delighted at the news.

My Uncle, the Jaguar

by João Guimarães Rosa

translated by Giovanni Pontiero

HUM? . . . YEAH. OF COURSE, SIR. AHA, YOU WANT TO COME IN, COME in then . . . How did you know I live here? How did you find out? . . . Eh. No, sir, . . . Is that the only horse you've got? Ixe! The horse's lame and diseased. It's finished. Axi . . . Sure. Hum, hum. Did you see this little fire of mine from a distance? Yeah. Come on in then, you're welcome to stay.

Ha-ha. This isn't a house . . . I know. I wish it were. I'm not a farmer, just a tenant . . . not even a tenant. I'm—all over the place. I'm here, when I feel like it I move on. Yeah. I sleep here. Hum. Nhem? You were saying. No, sir . . . Are you coming or going? Bring your things inside. Erê! I'll help you to unsaddle the horse. Let me give you a hand to hobble the horse . . . Bring the saddle-bag inside, bring the sack and your blankets. Hum, hum! Of course you can. You've come to see me, to visit me: Good. Fine. Why don't you sit down, stretch out on the bunk? The bunk isn't mine. I've got a hammock. That's where I sleep. The bunk belongs to the black man. I'm going to squat down here. It's just as comfortable. I'll blow on the fire. Nhem? The hammock's mine. Yeah. No, sir. Hum . . . Now then, why don't you open the sack, sort your things out? Atié! You're a fat wolf . . . Atié . . . Is any of this for me? What's this got to do with me? I won't steal your things, I'm not a thief. A-hé, yes, sir, I would. I like it. You can pour it in the gourd. I love the stuff . . . Nice. Fine. A-hã! This rum of yours is great. I could drink it by the litre . . . Ah, munhã-munhã: I'm joking. I'm only joking, munhamunhando. I feel good. Apê! You're a fine man and so rich. No, sir. Sometimes. I enjoy it. Almost never. I know how to make rum: I make it with cashew nuts, wild berries and maize. But it's not much good. It don't give you this warm feeling. It's hard work. I haven't got any today. I've run out. You wouldn't like it. It's filthy rum, only fit for a poor man . . .

A-hã, the black man won't be coming back. The black man's dead.

How do I know? He died somewhere around here, died from some disease. Disease soon wore him down. That's the truth. I'm not lying . . . Hum . . . It'll take your friend some time to get here, he won't arrive until late tomorrow. Some more? Yes sir, I enjoy a drink. Apê! This is great rum. Is this the only big bottle you brought? Eh, eh. Is your mate driving here tomorrow? Is he? Have you got a fever? Your friend's sure to bring some medicine . . . Hum-hum. No, sir. I drink herbal tea. The root of a plant. I know where to find it, my mother showed me and I know how to prepare it. I'm never ill. Except for a touch of scabies, an ulcer on my leg, the odd infection or blisters. I'm hardy, I'm a beast of the jungle.

Hum, don't bother searching any more . . . The animals are far away. Your friend shouldn't have let them go. Your friend's no good. No, sir. They bolted in a hurry, as you'd expect. The world's a big place: nothing but grassy plains out there, nothing but scrub, all Indian territory . . . Tomorrow your friend will be back with more animals. Hum, hum, a horse in the middle of the jungle. I know how to find them, I can hear them moving. I listen with my ear to the ground. A horse running, popóre . . . I can follow its trail. . . . Right now I can't, it's no good, too many trails here. They've gone far away. A jaguar's eating them . . . Does that make you sad? It's not my fault; what have I done? Don't be sad. You're rich, you've plenty of horses. But you can forget those ones, the jaguar's already eaten them, atiúca! Any horse that wanders into the jungle is as good as eaten . . . The monkeys have been screeching . . . that means the jaguar's on the prowl . . .

Eh, some more, yes, sir. I like it. Terrific rum. Have you some tobacco as well? That's right, tobacco for chewing, for smoking. Have you any more, have you a lot? Ha-há. It's good. Nice tobacco, nice and strong. Yes, sir, with pleasure. If you're giving it to me, I won't say no. I like it. It's a nice smoke. Is this tobacco chico-silva? A fine day today, wouldn't you say?

Do you feel like eating something? There's meat and cassava. Eh, oh, paçoca. Lots of pepper. I've no salt. There's no more. The meat smells really good. It's an anteater I caught. Won't you have some? Anteater's very tasty. There's some cornmeal and brown sugar. You can finish it off, tomorrow I'll do some more hunting, kill a deer. No, I won't kill a deer: there's no need. The jaguar has already caught your horse, jumped on it, bled it dry . . . The big beast couldn't be more dead and she still won't leave it alone, she's on top of it . . . She's broken the horse's head, torn its neck . . . Broken its head! Broken it! . . . She's sucked all its blood, chewed a big lump of flesh. Then she grabbed the carcass, dragged it to the edge of the jungle, dragged it with her teeth. She covered it with leaves. Now she's sleeping in the bush . . . The spotted jaguar eats the rump first, then the haunch. The suaçurana starts with the breast. If it's a tapir, the two of them start with the belly, the skin is thick . . . Would you believe it? The pinima jaguar kills; the pinima is my relation! . . .

Nhem? Tomorrow morning she'll be back there, she'll eat a little and go off to drink some water. I'll get there, together with the vultures . . . Filthy creatures those vultures, they nest in the Lapa do Baú . . . I'll go there and cut myself a piece of meat. Now then, you don't need to tell me: the jaguar hunts for me whenever she can. Jaguars are my relations. My relations, my relations, ai, ai, ai . . . I'm not laughing at you. I'm munhamunhando to myself. The horse's flesh will keep until tomorrow. Horse meat is very tasty, very good. I don't eat rotten meat, axe! The jaguar don't eat it either. When the animal's been killed by a suaçurana, I don't enjoy the meat so much: she buries the horse in sand, even in the soil . . .

There isn't any coffee. Hum, the black man used to drink coffee, he really enjoyed his coffee. I don't want to live with a black man any more, never again . . . nothing but a big gorilla. The black man smells something awful . . . But the black man used to say that I smell just as much: a different smell, a sour smell. Nhem? No, the shack isn't mine, the shack doesn't have an owner. No, it didn't belong to the black man either. The thatched roof has rotted away but the rain doesn't come in, only the odd leak here and there. Ixe, when I move away from this place, I'll set fire to the shack so that nobody else can live here. Nobody's going to live on top of my smell . . .

Eat up, this isn't anteater's flesh. It's good meat, it's armadillo. I killed it myself. I didn't steal it from a jaguar. They don't keep small animals: they eat the lot. There's plenty of pepper, . . . Nhem? A-hã, yeah, it's dark. The moon isn't up yet. The moon's taking its time but it'll soon be up. Hum, there isn't any. There's no oil-lamp, no light of any kind. I'll blow on the fire. It won't do any harm, the shack won't catch fire, I'm watching; my eyes are wide open. It's nice to feel a warm fire under your hammock, it lights the place up and keeps you warm. There's firewood here, twigs, they burn nicely. When I'm on my own, I don't need any light. I can manage in the dark. I can see in the middle of the jungle. Ei, there's a light shining in the bushes: you'll see, no, it's not an eye—it's moisture from the cassava, a drop of water, resin from the tree, a grasshopper, a big spider . . . Are you frightened? Well, you can't be a jaguar then . . . You can't understand a jaguar. Can you? Speak! I can stand the heat, I can put up with the cold. The black man used to grumble about the cold. The black man worked hard, he really did, and he enjoyed his work. He used to gather firewood, do the cooking. He planted cassava. When the cassava runs out, I'll move from here. Eh, this is really nice rum!

Nhenhem? I've hunted so many jaguars. I'm always hunting them. I came here to hunt jaguars, to do nothing but hunt jaguars. Nhô Nhuão Guede brought me here. He paid me. I was given the skins, paid money for every jaguar I killed. Good money: clink-clink . . . I'm the only one who knew how to hunt jaguars. That's why Nhô Nhuão Guede made me stay here to rid the whole place of jaguars. Anhum, all on my own, it's true . . . I sold the skin, earned some more money. I bought lead bullets, gunpowder. I bought salt, I bought ammunition. Eh, I travelled a long way from here to buy everything. Even brown sugar. . . . a long way off. I can walk for miles, walk for ages, I can go fast, I know how to walk and not get tired, I travel in a straight line and I can keep on walking all night. Once I even got as far as Boi do Urucúia . . . That's right. On foot. I don't need a horse, I don't want one. I once had a horse, it died, done for, gone, had an abscess on its back. It died from the infection. Honestly. I'm telling the truth . . . I don't want a dog either. Dogs make a terrible noise, jaguars kill them. Jaguars like killing everything in sight . . .

Atiê! Atimbora! Don't you say I killed a jaguar, you mustn't. Yes I can. But not you. I no longer kill jaguars, not any more. It's wicked—that I killed. Jaguars are my relations. I killed, I killed lots of them. Can you count? Count four ten times, that's about right: then take that amount four times. So many? For every one I killed, I put a small stone in the gourd. I'm now going to throw the gourd full of stones into the river. I wish I hadn't killed any jaguars. If you tell anyone I killed a jaguar, I'll turn nasty. Don't ever say I killed them, tá-há? Were you saying something?. Good, fine, it's true. You're my friend!

Yes sir, I'm helping myself to another drink. Good rum, really special. Why not join me: the rum's yours; a swig of rum's like medicine . . . You're looking at me. What about giving me that watch? Ah, you can't, you don't want to. Okay then . . . that's okay, forget it! I don't want your watch. Forget it. I thought you wanted to be my friend . . . Hum-hum. Yeah. Hum. lá axi. Nope, I don't want a flick-knife. I don't want your money. I'm going outside. Don't you go thinking the jaguar won't come near the shack or eat this lame horse of yours. She'll be coming all right. Putting out her great big paw. The grass moves, you can hear it rustling, softly, slowly, gently: that's her. She's getting close. Her jaguar's claws—

jaguar's paw—jaguar's tail . . . She's creeping up, she wants something to eat. You ought to be scared! Are you? If she starts roaring, eh, mocan-hemo, you'll be scared all right. She snarls—she roars until her throat swells and takes in all the air . . . Urrurrú—rrrurrú . . . Almost like thunder. Everything shakes. You can get a lot into that big mouth, her mouth's the size of two! Apê! Feeling scared? Come on, I know you're not frightened. I know you like a bit of adventure, you're so good, so fine, so brave. But now you can give me your flick-knife and some money, just a little. No, I don't want your watch, forget it, I was only joking. What do I want a watch for? I don't need one . . .

Ei, I'm no fool either. Would you like a jaguar's skin? Hã—hã, look at this. Pretty skin, don't you think? I hunted it myself a long time ago. Those ones I stopped selling. I didn't want to any more. These ones here? A male cangussú I killed on the bank of the River Sorongo. I killed it after stabbing it once with my spear so as not to spoil the skin. Ooh, witch doctor! A monster of a beast. He bit the tip of the spear, left the mark of his teeth. That big jaguar then rolled up into a ball, turning over slowly, suddenly turned into an enormous snake, thrashing about with rage under my spear. He twisted and turned, furious, clawing and growling, snarling something awful, even tried to drag me into the bushes with all those thorns . . . He had me worried for a bit!

That other one, also covered with great big spots, a pinima jaguar, a big beast with a loud roar. I shot her while she was sitting up in a tree. Perched on one of the branches. She sat there, her head crouched down. She seemed to be asleep. But she was watching me . . . She looked at me almost as if she couldn't have cared less. I didn't even give her time to prick up her ears: so there, so there, boom!—I fired a shot . . . straight into her mouth so as not to spoil the skin. A-hã, she was still trying to get her claws round the branch below—where did she get the strength? She ended up hanging head down then fell, broke off two branches . . . Landed with a thud on the ground.

Nhem? Black jaguars? Here there are lots of them and lots of pixuna jaguars, as well, I used to kill. Hum, hum, the black jaguar crossbreeds with the spotted jaguar. They come swimming one behind the other, their heads and shoulder-blades sticking out of the water. I climbed up a tree on the riverbank, killed each with one shot. But first the male, the pinima jaguar that swam in front. Can jaguars swim? Sure, it's an animal that swims! It can cross a wide river, can swim in a straight line, come out where it wants . . . The suaçurana also swims but she doesn't like crossing rivers. The pair I'm talking about, that was on the stretch

below, on the other river, doesn't have a name, a mucky river . . . The
female was a pixuna but she wasn't exactly black: more the color of coffee. I dragged the two dead jaguars onto the embankment, I didn't want
to lose the skins . . . But don't you go saying I killed a jaguar. Just listen
and say nothing. Not a word. Hã? Really? Hué! Oi, do I like rum! You
already know that . . .

Good, I'll have another drink. Uai, I drink till I start sweating, till I
feel as if my tongue's on fire . . . Cã uinhuãora! I need a drink to cheer
me up. I need one to get me talking. Unless I have a good drink, I can't
talk, don't know why, I feel so tired . . . Never mind, tomorrow you'll be
gone. I'll be left here on my own, anhum. What do I care? Yeah, that's a
good skin, taken from a small jaguar with a big head. Do you want that
one? Take it. Are you going to leave me the rest of the rum? Stretch out
on the bunk, wrap yourself in your cape, cover yourself with the skin,
get some sleep. Why don't you? Take your clothes off, put your watch in
the armadillo skull, your revolver as well, nobody'll touch them. You
won't find me touching your things. I'll put some more wood on the fire,
look after things, keep the fire going, you try and get some sleep.
There's nothing but a bit of soap in the armadillo skull. No, it isn't
mine, it belonged to the black man. I don't use soap. Why don't you try
to get some sleep? Okay, okay, I didn't say a word, not a word . . .

You want to know about the jaguars? Uh-huh, they've got such a
temper, they don't talk like other people . . . I hunted as many as three
in one day. Yeah, that was a suaçurana, red like a fox, a big cat all one
color. She would sleep by day, hidden in the long grass. The suaçurana
isn't easy to hunt: she can run fast, climb trees. She wanders quite a bit,
but lives in the bush on the plateau. The pinima doesn't let the suaçurana settle on the edge of the marshes, the pinima chases the suaçurana
away . . . I've eaten her meat. It's good, tasty and tender. I cooked it
with vegetables and peppers. Lots of salt and strong pepper. As for the
pinima, I've only eaten her heart, fried and preserved in lard, I've eaten
it roasted, dried, all sorts of ways. And I used to rub the fat all over my
body. So that I'd never get frightened!

Sir? Yes, sir. For years and years, I've been wiping out jaguars in three
different places. Over there is the river Sucuriú that runs into the River
Sorongo. Over there is a wilderness. But on this side is the River
Ururáu, then twenty leagues further on you come to the Barra do Frade,
there you'll find a ranch and cattle. I've killed off all the jaguars . . .
Yeah, nobody can last out here unless he's somebody like me. Eh,
nhem? Ahã-hã . . . There aren't any houses here. The only house you'll

find is behind those palm trees, six leagues away and in the middle of
the bush. A farmer lived there, Seo Rauremiro. He died, and his wife,
his daughters and little boy. Disease killed them all off. That's the truth.
Believe me . . . Nobody comes around here, it's very hard. It's too far for
people to come. The only people who come here are wealthy hunters,
men who hunt jaguars as well as pumas and who come every year in the
month of August. They come from far away, it takes them a week.

They bring their dogs, big dogs for hunting jaguars. Each man carries
a good rifle, a shot-gun, I'd love to have one myself . . . Hum, hum, the
jaguars aren't stupid, they flee from the dogs, climb up trees. The dogs
bark their heads off, pick up the scent again . . . If the jaguar can find a
way, it makes for the wild forest where the undergrowth is dense, eh,
there it's not easy for a man to see where the jaguar's hiding. The dogs
corner her: then she goes wild, she hisses, rages, strikes out, attacks
every dog in sight, sure, she can move whatever way she likes. . . . She
lies in wait and that's when she's at her most dangerous: she wants to
kill or die once and for all . . . Yeah, she grunts like a pig, the dogs don't
get near her. Nowhere near her. One blow with her paw and that's that.
She strikes out and gives a vicious slap . . . She turns and jumps to one
side, you can't see where she comes from . . . Paff! Even when she's
injured and dying, she can still attack and kill a big dog. And how she
roars and grunts. She can rip off a dog's head. Are you frightened? Let
me show you, eh; you can see from this side where there's no wind
blowing—keep watching over there for that's where the jaguar can suddenly appear and jump on you . . . She leaps sideways, changes direction in mid-air. She jumps crosswise. It's worth knowing. She jumps, yet
holds back. Her ears tingle, there's a drumming sound like stones raining down. She zig-zags. Have you ever seen a snake? That's right, Apê!
Posanga, suú, suú, jucá-iucá . . . Sometimes there are little noises, the
rustling of dry leaves, as she comes creeping over twigs, eh, eh—a tiny
bird flies away. A guinea-pig gives a cry, from a distance you can hear:
yowl!—and it jumps into the water, the jaguar's getting close. When the
pinima is about to jump and eat you, her tail curls up with the end
sticking out, then she comes to a halt. When she stretches her neck,
the head looks bigger. When she bares her fangs, her spots seem to get
bigger, her eyes move further apart, her face screws up. Oi: what a
mouth!—ói: her whiskers look as if they're about to drop off . . . her
tongue rolls sideways . . . she stretches her paws, she's getting ready to
jump: she rests for a moment on her legs . . . ei, ei—her back legs—If
the jaguar knows she's being followed, she turns nasty, she gets down

on the ground, tears at wood, claws at everything. She gets to her feet, stands there. Anybody who tries following her, gets torn to pieces. Yeah, a cuff from a jaguar's paw is worse than being hit with a club . . . Did you see a shadow? Then you're as good as dead. Ah, ah, ah . . . Don't be frightened, I'm here.

Well, I'll just have another drink, if you don't mind. Now I'm beginning to feel good! I'm no miser, you should eat and drink what you've got while you still feel like it . . . There's nothing nicer than a full belly. This rum's terrific, just what I needed. Bah! this is lousy firewood, makes your eyes run, all this smoke . . . Nhem? You were saying? No, I don't hate it. I don't like it either. The place is what it is, much like any other place. The hunting's good, there's a nice pool to swim in. No place is all good or all bad, you have to make the best of it. I came here to earn money killing jaguars. But I don't kill any more, no more. I hunt guinea-pigs and otters and sell the skins. Yes, sir, I like people, I do. I walk a lot, sometimes I walk for ages before I meet a living soul. I can run like a wild deer . . .

A married woman lived on the side of the hill, at the bottom of the creek at Veredinha do Xunxúm. A path goes along there, a path leading to a farm. She was a good-hearted woman, called Maria Quirinéia. Her husband, Seo Siruvéio, was crazy and tied up with heavy chains. He talked nothing but rubbish, on nights when there was a pale moon he would ramble on in a loud voice, he would rant and rave, nheengava . . . They didn't die. Didn't die all from disease. Eh, man . . .

I'm enjoying this rum! I like holding it in my mouth, then letting it go down. Hum-hum. Around here, there's only me and the jaguar. We can eat the rest of the food. Jaguars also know about a lot of things. The jaguar sees things people don't see, can't see. Lots and lots of things . . . I don't like knowing too much, I only end up with a sore head. All I know is what the jaguar knows. And that's what I really do know. I've had to learn. When I first came here, I found myself on my own. Being on your own's no good, nothing but trouble. Nhô Nhuão Guede, a real swine, dumped me here all on my own. Atié! How I wished my old mother was alive, çacyara. Araa . . . all alone . . . no one around to help me . . .

I learned the hard way. I had to get by just like the jaguar. The good thing about the jaguar is that it's never in a hurry: it lies on the ground, makes use of some nice deep hole, finds a grassy spot, looks for a hiding-place behind every tree, creeps along the ground, moves quietly in and out, treading softly, pô-pu, pô-pu, even when she comes up against a trap set to catch her. She comes closer, stares, stands there staring, she's preparing to jump. Hã, hã . . . She takes a jump, sometimes two. If she gets it wrong she'll go hungry, the worst of it is that she almost dies of shame . . . Wait, she's going to jump: she looks fierce, she's out to scare everybody, shows no pity . . . She trembles from head to foot, steadies herself on her legs and, quick as a whiplash, takes one mighty leap!—she's beautiful . . .

Ei, when she's on top of the poor deer, as she's tearing it apart, every muscle in her trembling body stands out, even the spots seem brighter, those legs of hers help, eh, crouched on those fat legs she looks just like a toad, her tail curled up: she'll pounce on anything that comes within reach, her neck craned forward . . . Apê! She goes on clawing and eating, she goes . . . the deer's flesh torn to bits. The jaguar gives a loud roar, tarará, that awful tail up in the air, those strong claws, âi, her claws out, she gives another roar, that's enough. A feast of eating and drinking. If it's a rabbit, a small animal, she'll even eat the joints, swallowing the lot, mucunando, leaving scarcely any bones. The guts and entrails she won't eat . . .

The jaguar's a fine beast. Have you ever seen one? When the reeds tremble a little, rustle ever so little: that's a jaguar, that's a jaguar, eh, you can be sure . . . Have you ever seen her—when she comes padding along with her belly full? A-hã! She comes with her head down, prowling slowly: she arches her back, straightens up, raises one shoulder, then the other, and you should see her shoulder-blades, those round haunches . . . The prettiest jaguar is Maria-Maria . . . Eh, you want me to tell you about her? No, that's something I won't talk about. No, I won't tell you that . . . you want to know too much!

They left me here alone, I nhum. They left me here to work, hunting and killing jaguars. They had no right. Nhô Nhuão Guede had no right. They should have known I was related to the jaguars. Oh ho! Oh ho! I could curse myself for having killed so many jaguars, why did I do it? I know how to curse, you bet I do. I'm cursing right now! Tiss, n't, n't! . . . When my belly's full I don't like seeing people, not one little bit. I don't want to be reminded about people: I get really mad. It's as if I were being forced to talk to their ghosts. I don't like it. I'm being good, I'm saying nothing. At first, I used to like people. Now I only like jaguars. I like to feel their breath . . . Maria-Maria—pretty jaguar, congussú, fine, pretty.

She's young, Look, look—she's finished eating, she's coughing, she's licking her whiskers, oh, her whiskers are hard, white, the hairs of her whiskers tickle my face, muquirica so nicely. She goes off to drink water. There's nothing nicer than to see the jaguar Maria-Maria sprawling on the ground, drinking water. When I call, she comes running. Do you want to see? You're shaking, I know you are. Don't be scared, she's not really coming, she only comes when I call her. She's also frightened of me, just like you . . .

Eh, these grassy plains are where I belong, eh, all this land around here is mine. My mother would have liked it . . . I make sure everybody's afraid of me. Not you, you're my friend . . . and I haven't any other friend. Have I? Hum, hum. Not far from here, on the edge of the plateau, lived three men on their own who belonged to these parts. Three bandits on the run jababoras, they were in hiding here. Nhem? What were their names? Why do you need to know? Were they relations of yours? Axi! They were from Minas Gerais, one was called Gugué, a bit on the fat side; another was called Antunias—he had money stashed away! The third one was Seo Riopôro, a cruel man, a bad one: I didn't care for him at all . . .

What did they do? A-hã . . . the Jababora tribesmen fish, hunt, plant cassava: they sell skins, buy gunpowder, rifle ammunition, explosives, supplies . . . Eh, they stick to the plateau, to the prairie. The land over there's no good. Further away from here in Cachorro Prêto there are lots of Jababora tribesmen—you can go there and see for yourself. They draw off milk from the mangaba tree. Poor people! They don't even have any clothes to wear . . . Eh, some of them even go about with nothing on. Ixe . . . I've got clothes, bedding, my bowl.

Nhem? The three highlanders? No, they didn't know how to hunt jaguars, they were far too scared. They couldn't hunt jaguars with a spear like me. I used to trade tobacco for salt, have a chat with them, lend them some brown sugar. Those three died, everything died, everything—cuéra. They died of disease, eh, eh. Honestly. I'm telling you the truth, you'd better believe me or else!

With my spear? I don't kill jaguars any more. Haven't I already told you? But I know how it's done. If I wanted, I could kill all right! You want to know how? I lie in wait. The jaguar comes Heeé! She comes creeping along softly, you wouldn't even spot her with those eyes of yours. Eh, she growls but don't jump. She comes stretching her paws just like a cat. But she don't jump, no she don't. Eh—she comes up to my feet and I touch her with my spear. Erê. I touch her breast with the blade of my spear, right in the middle. The minute you touch her with anything, she lies down on the ground. She tries to strike out or catch at things, she wants to grab at everything. Sometimes she gets onto her feet. The jaguar herself pulls the tip of the spear towards her. Eh, I stick it in . . .

she lets out a gasp. The blood comes out red, at other times it comes out almost black ... Shit, poor jaguar, poor thing, the spearhead is going right into her ... Teité ... How would you like to be stabbed to death? Hum-hum, God help me ... To feel the iron sink into your flesh ... Atiúca! Are you afraid? I'm not. I don't feel pain ...

Hã-hã, don't imagine it's all that slow or gentle. Eh, heé ... The jaguar chokes with anger. Under the spear, she twists and turns, ciririca, struggles. A jaguar's a jaguar—like a snake ... she squirms all over the place, you would think there was more than one there, that she'd turned into more than one jaguar. Eh, even her tail is swishing from side to side. She coils up, rolls into a ball, turns over, eh, she's all doubled up, twisting and curling up ... You're not used to this, you don't see her, you can't, she's slipping ... You've no idea how strong she is! She opens her mouth wide, spits like mad, she's hoarse, so hoarse. She's as quick as lightning. She could pull you under her ... Ai, ai, ai ... Sometimes she even manages to escape, disappear among the bamboos, raging. She's almost done for, yet she can still kill, she savages everything in sight ... She can kill more quickly than any other animal. She once caught a dog off its guard, caught it from behind with one paw, tore the skin from its back ... Apê! Fine and pretty. I'm a jaguar ... I'm—a jaguar!

Do you think I look like a jaguar? But there are times when I really look like one. You haven't seen me. Give me that thing you've got— what's it called—a little mirror? I'd like to see my face ... Tiss, n't, n't ... I've got a fierce look. Eh, this is how I look at the jaguar, straight in the eye, without being frightened: Hã then she respects you. If you show her you're scared, you're as good as dead. You mustn't show you're frightened. The jaguar can tell, she knows how you feel inside. That's my advice and you take it from me. Hum. She hears everything, watches the tiniest movement. And when it comes to following a trail, the jaguar doesn't trail anything. She doesn't have a good sense of smell, she's not a dog. She hunts with her hearing. If an ox snores in its sleep, if there's the least sound of anything moving in the bush, the jaguar can tell from half a league away ... but I'll bet you couldn't. The jaguar doesn't sit up a tree waiting to pounce. It's only the suaçurana that goes from tree to tree catching monkeys. The suaçurana jumps to the top of the tree, but the spotted jaguar don't jump: the spotted jaguar clambers straight up like a cat. Have you ever seen it? Eh, eh, I climb trees, lie there waiting to pounce. Yes, me. It's easier to spy from up there. Nobody can see me watching. What the jaguar taught me best was how to creep along the ground to get near to your prey. She moves so slowly that you don't see her coming . . . You have to learn every move when you're hunting. I can tell how you move your hand, how you move your head up and down, I know how long it would take you to jump if you had to. I even know which leg you'd move first . . .

You want to go out? Go ahead. See how the moon has risen: with all this moonlight the jaguars are sure to be hunting. It's a clear night. When it's dark they don't hunt: only when the light is going down and around dawn . . . They spend the day sleeping in the bamboo groves on the edge of the marshes, or hidden in the bush, among the copses in the middle of the bush . . . No, sir, you don't often hear the jaguar mewing at this hour. They hunt without making any noise. Days could pass before you would hear a single mew . . . What you heard just now was the crested screamer . . . Hum. Come in. Sit on the bunk. Would you like to stretch out in the hammock? The hammock's mine, but you can use it. I have some cassava. I'll make you something to eat. You'll enjoy it. Then I'll have another drop of rum. If you don't watch me, I'll drink the bottle dry. N't, m'p aah . . .

Where did I learn to hunt? I learned a long way from here, where there are other brave men, almost as fearless as me. They taught me how to throw a spear. Uarentin Maria and Gugué Maria—two brothers. A spear just like this with a head a meter and a half long, a good shaft, easy to throw. Nhô Inácio had one just like it, old Nhuão Inácio, he was black but you couldn't have wished for a nicer man, abaeté, abaúna. Nhô Inácio knew everything when it came to using a spear. Unarmed, with nothing but his old spear, he would play with the jaguar as if he were its brother. Rei Inácio with his crossbow . . .

Nha-hem? Ha-ha. Because one jaguar didn't tell the other, they didn't know I'd come here to finish them off. They didn't suspect anything, sniffed at me as if I were their relation . . . Eh, the jaguar's my uncle, the jaguaretê, all of them. They didn't run away from me. Then I went and killed them . . . They only found out afterwards, when it was too late, and they were furious . . . Believe me, I've given up killing jaguars. I do no more killing. I can't, I should never have done it. I was punished: my luck changed, there was a jinx on me . . . I don't like to think I've killed my own relations, how could I have done that? Ai, ai, ai, my own relations . . . I ought to weep for they'll never forgive me.

Yes, sir, sometimes the jaguars caught me. They bit into my flesh, take a look. No, it didn't happen here on the prairie. It was over on the other side of the river. The other fellows with me misfired, lost their nerve at the last minute. And the big-spotted pinima attacked and rolled with us on the ground. She went wild. She clawed one man on the chest, tore at his flesh until you could see his heart inside beating away among all that blood. She ripped the skin from another man's face—Antonho Fonseca. She scratched this cross on my forehead, made a deep gash on my leg with her claws, tore the skin to shreds, mucuruça, left me with a festering wound. Her claws are not pointed or sharp, but poisonous which is why they do so much damage and cause infection. Her teeth as well. Pa! lá, iá, eh, a blow from a jaguar can knock the spear from your hand . . . They stabbed her some thirty to forty times! Hum, if you'd been there you'd be dead by now . . . She almost killed five men. She tore all the flesh from one hunter's arm, all that was left was bone and nerve and the veins sticking out . . . I hid behind a palm-tree, with a knife in my hand. The pinima saw me, grabbed me, I was under her, the two of us hugging each other. Hum, it was hard trying to get hold of her, her skin is as slippery as soap, as smooth as quiabo, she squirms left and right, just like a snake, eh, a snake . . . She was trying to rip me apart but she was getting tired, she'd lost a lot of blood. I held her mouth so that she couldn't bite. She clawed at my chest and I've no nipple left on this side. She scratched with three paws! She tore open my arm, clawed my back, she died holding on to me, she had so many stab wounds that she shed all her blood . . . she was some jaguar that Manhuãoçá! She had slobbered all over my head and for days on end I couldn't get that awful smell out of my hair . . .

Hum, hum. Yes, sir. Those jaguars know I'm one of them. The first jaguar I ever saw and didn't kill was Maria-Maria. I was sleeping in the bush not far from here, beside a little fire I'd lit. At daybreak I was asleep. She came up to me. Woke me up, started sniffing at me. I looked into those pretty eyes, yellow eyes with little black flecks flickering in the light . . . I pretended I was dead, I couldn't do anything else. She sniffed me, went on sniffing me all over, one paw in the air, I thought she was aiming for my throat. An urucuera chirped, a toad croaked and croaked, there I lay listening to the animals in the bush for what seemed like ages . . . I didn't move. I was lying in a nice, comfortable spot among the rosemary. The fire had gone out but the ashes were still warm. Maria-Maria started rubbing up against me, she was watching me. Her eyes met mine, her eyes were flashing—ping, ping: she stared at me angrily, with a sharp look in her eye, she wants to munguitar: she wouldn't let go of me. For some time she didn't do anything. Then she put her big paw onto my chest very gently. I thought—I'm as good as dead, for she knew that was where she'd find my heart. But she only pressed me very gently with one paw and patted me with the other, she was trying to wake me up with a sossoca. Eh, eh, eh, I soon got to know . . . she was some girl that jaguar—that she liked me, I soon got to know . . . I opened my eyes, looked into hers. I said in a whisper:—"Ei, Maria-Maria . . . Be a good girl, Maria-Maria . . . " Eh, she growled and seemed pleased, she started rubbing up against me once more, mião-miã. She was talking to me, jaguanhém, jaguanhém . . . Her tail had gone hard, was flicking, sacê-sacemo, a jaguar's tail is almost never still. Off she went, moved back to take a good look at me from a distance, she crouched down. I didn't move from where I was, lying on my back, I carried on talking to her, looking at her as I spoke, coaxing her to be good. When I stopped speaking, she gave a little miaow—jaguanhém . . . her belly was full, she licked her paws, she licked her neck. She had tiny spots on her forehead, drops of moisture round her nostrils . . . Then she lay down leaning against me, slapping me playfully on the face with her tail . . . She settled down to sleep beside me. She screwed up her eyes as she dozed. Sleeping on and off with her head down, her nose resting on one paw . . . I saw that her milk was drying up, I could see the nipples of her teats. Her cubs had died, who knows what killed them? Now she'll have no more cubs, not one, never, ara!—no, she won't . . .

Nhem? After that? After that she slept, uê. She snored with her head leaning to one side, showing those terrible fangs of hers, her ears folded back. That was because she could hear a suaçurana coming. A light-brown suaçurana, the color of maize. The suaçurana stopped in her tracks. She's vicious, a wicked, bloodthirsty creature. I saw those big green eyes of hers shining, so round they looked as if they were going to drop off. Hum-hum, Maria-Maria snored, the suaçurana turned tail, went away.

Eh, catú, fine and pretty, porã-poranga!—the best of all. Maria-Maria sat up at once, cocked her ears. Eh, she started walking slowly, watching her going through her daily routine you'd think she was heavy, but she can be fast and light on her feet when she wants to or needs to move in a hurry. She sways nicely when she walks, sways so much you couldn't ride her, she has a lot of hair and soft paws . . . She came to the trunk of a peroba tree, reared up, dug her claws in, ripped it from top to bottom, she was sharpening her claws scratching at the peroba. Then she had a go at the calabash. She left her claw marks and you can go and see for yourself how much damage she can do.

Ah, if I'd wanted to, I could have killed her. But I didn't want to. How could I ever have wanted to kill Maria-Maria? Besides, at that time I was

feeling sad, left here all on my own, nhum, and I was feeling even sadder
and unlucky because I'd killed jaguars, I'd had enough. From that day, I
killed no more jaguars. The last one I killed was that suaçurana which
I'd tracked down. But the suaçurana isn't my relation, I'm only related to
the black jaguar and the spotted one . . . I killed the suaçurana as the
sun came up. The suaçurana had eaten a wild deer. I finished her off in
a rage because she'd left her dirt right at the spot where I was sleeping
and there among the bamboos there was nothing but droppings. Yeah,
they cover them up, unlike the males who leave a bigger mess . . .

A-hã Maria-Maria is pretty, you should see her! Prettier than any
woman. She smells of guararema blossom after the rain. She's not all
that big. She's a cangussú with a tiny head and except for the spots,
she's yellow, bright, bright yellow. As for her spots, none of them are
black, really black: they're red, darkish, reddish-brown. She doesn't
have any? She has everything. Have you ever compared the spots and
markings on her? Count them and you'll see: they're so different that
you won't find two the same . . . Maria-Maria has lots of tiny spots. A
white face, very small, pretty, all freckled, like that, just like that. A tiny
spot in each corner of her mouth, others behind her little ears . . . The
inside of her ears is all white, like cotton. Her belly as well. Her belly
and below the neck, and on the inside of her legs. I can play with her
for hours, she loves it—She licks my hand, she licks it very gently, the
way jaguars do when they lick their cubs clean; just as well for nobody
could stand being scratched by that thick tongue of hers, thick, rough,
rougher than the leaf of the sambaíba; who knows how she manages to
go on licking her cubs with that tongue of hers without scratching
them?

Nhem? Does Maria-Maria have a mate? No, she hasn't any mate.
Xô! Pa! Atimbora! If any mate turns up, I'll kill him, finish him off, even
if he's my relation!

So there, but you'd better get some sleep. Me too. Oi: it's getting
late. Sejuçu is way up in the sky, look at its little stars . . . No sleep for
me, it's nearly time to get out there, I rise early every morning, long
before daybreak. You try and get to sleep. Why don't you lie down?—
looks as if you're only staying awake to keep asking me questions. I
answer you, then you ask me something else. What is this? And what
happens, I finish up drinking all your rum. Hum, hum, don't worry, I
won't get drunk. I only get drunk when I drink lots and lots of blood . . .
you can sleep in peace, I'll take care of things, I know how to keep an
eye on everything. I can see you're sleepy. Oi, I can draw two circles on

the ground if you want me to—those are your eyes—then if I step on
them, you'll go to sleep at once . . . Ei, but you're brave as well and can
stand up to any man. You've got a fierce look. You could even hunt
jaguars . . . steady on. You're my friend.

Nhem? No, sir, I don't know anything about that. I only know about
jaguars. I know nothing about cattle. Cattle are only for eating. Ox, cow,
bullock. My father knew. My father was no wild Indian, my father was a
white man, white like you, my father was Chico Pedro, mimbauaman-
hanaçara, a cowboy like any other, a violent man. He died in Tungo-
Tungo, on the plains of Goiás, on the estate of Cachoeira Brava. He
was murdered. That's all I can tell you. He was everybody's father. A
stupid man.

Sir? Hã, hã, yes, sir. She might get close, she might start prowling
round the shack. The jaguars hang out in these parts, each jaguar keeps
to itself for most of the year. You never get a pair of them living together
all the time, only for a month or so. It's only the jaguatiricas, the big wild-
cats who live in pairs. Ih, there are lots of them, any number. Yeah, right
here, but I don't kill any more: this is jaguaretama, the land of the
jaguars, nothing but jaguars . . . you can take it from me, I know all of
them. No more jaguars are allowed in—the ones that live here won't let
them come because there isn't much food left to hunt. I do no more
killing, now all the jaguars have a name. Did I give them their names?
Axi! No, not on my own, I just happen to know their names. Atié
. . . Well, if that's not it, how come you want to know? Why are you asking me? Are you hoping to buy a jaguar? Are you keen on having a conversation with a jaguar? . . . Teité . . . Axe . . . you needn't tell me. You just
want to know so that you can be even more frightened of them, tá-há?

Ha, good, Oi: in a cave over on the other side, nearby, lives the
jaguar Mopoca, a female cangussú. She was late in giving birth, she has
a young cub, jaguaraím. Mopoca is a good mother, she has always
moved around with her cubs, carrying the baby jaguar in her mouth.
Now she's settled down there, it's a good spot. She scarcely ever leaves
the place, never gets enough to eat. She almost never leaves the place.
Only to drink water. Now that she's given birth, she's thin, really thin,
she's always thirsty, always. The cub, jaguaraím, a jaguar cub, the baby
jaguar, there are two of them like two little balls, two funny little things
and scarcely able to move. The mopoca has a lot of milk and her young
never stop sucking . . .

Nhá-em? Eh, are there any others? Oi, further on in the same direction, about five leagues from here, is Maramonhangara, the worst jaguar

of all, she rules, fights with the others, takes them on. On the other side, on the edge of the marshes, there's spotted Porreteira, she's enormous, you should see the size of her paws, her claws, her flat paws . . . Then even further on there's Tatacica, black, really black, a jaguaretê-pixuna; she has long legs and she's pretty savage. This one catches lots of fish . . . Hem, any more black ones? There's Uinhúa, she's got a nice den, a hole on the slope of the ravine, beneath a fig-tree . . . Then there's Rapa-Rapa an old spotted pinima-jaguar and very cunning: she travels far from here, hunts up to twenty leagues away, wanders all over the place. Rapa-Rapa lives in a tiny cave—jaguars love caves, they enjoy being in there. Mpú as well as Nhá-á were chased well away from here, the others drove them out because there wasn't enough food . . . Yeah, they're always changing their den because of this . . . I don't know any more about them for they're no longer here. Tibitaba is a wild cangussú—she's a jaguar with eyebrows: look for yourself, she's over there, stretched out on top of the ravine, right on the edge, her paws hanging over the side, I'm telling you . . . There were others but not any more: Coema-Piranga, a big red cat, she met her death when she choked on a bone . . . The jaguar Putuca, old and decrepit with her ribs sticking out, she's always hungry, starving, wandering through the bush . . . Hum, hum, Maria-Maria, no, I won't tell you where she lives. How can I be sure you don't want to kill her? What do I know . . . ? Hã-hã. And the tom-cats? There are lots of them, ih, plenty of them. You should see Papa-Gente, an enormous spotted tom-cat, so big you'd die of fright. His fangs are like a butcher's knife, a dirty yellow as if he'd chewed tobacco! There's one called Puxuêra, also very old, his big molars at the back for biting into flesh have already rotted away. Suú-Suú is a jaguaretê-pixuna as black as night, he snarls something awful, if you heard it you would shake from head to foot . . . He likes the jaguar Mopoca. Apiponga isn't a pixuna at all, he's the nicest spotted male jaguar you've ever seen, and he has a big nose. Not only does he always look well-fed, but he's the best hunter of all. Then there's a male cangussú Peteçara who's half crazy, wrong in the head, he only goes about by day, prowls around, looks as if his mouth is twisted . . . then there's one called Uitauêra, Uatauêra is the other, and they're brothers, eh, but it's me who knows because they don't know . . .

Well, enough of that. No more chat. For it'll soon be daybreak and you won't have slept, your friend will be turning up with the horses and you won't be fit to travel because you're too tired. Get some rest now. Are you going to sleep? Would you like me to move out so that you can sleep here on your own? I'm off. You want me to stay? All right, but I'll keep quiet. I'll keep my mouth shut, shut tight. The shack belongs to me. Hum-hum. Why do you keep asking questions instead of going to sleep? I don't know. No, the suaçurana hasn't got a name. The suaçurana isn't my relation, she's a coward. Only the one with the black patch on her back is savage. Suaçurana plays with her cubs. Yeah, her coat is red but the cubs are spotted . . . Hum, I've done enough talking, I'm going to keep quiet, leave you in peace. Forget it! You try to get some sleep now, okay? That's right. Hum-hum. No, sir. Hum-hum . . .

Nhem? Any chance of another bottle of rum? Will you give it to me? Hã-hã . . . Apê! You want to know? I'll tell you. You're a decent fellow, nice, you're my friend. When do the jaguars marry? Ixe, is that what you call it? Filth . . . You should come here when the cold weather's nearly over and the calabash tree is in bloom, then you'd see for yourself. They go mad. They're in heat; they roar and howl, never stop mewing and grunting; they almost give up hunting for food, they get thin, wander into the jungle, go crazy, piss all over the place, at night the stink is awful, enough to knock you out . . . The female jaguar in heat mews even more, it's a different mew, sounds funny. She turns up with the hair on her back bristling, she rubs herself against the trees, lies on the ground with her belly in the air, aruê! Nothing but arrú-arrú . . . arrar-rúuuu . . . You have to run for your life or she'll eat you alive . . .

The male chases after her, he travels for league after league. If two males come? Or three? Eh, you'd get a fright if you saw the way they fight, you really would . . . The fur starts flying. Until there's only one male left with the female. Then the fun begins. They explode. They start wailing and mewing again the whole night long, they roll on the ground and start fighting. The grass gets all trampled, bamboos are broken, shrubs are flattened to the ground, they tear up bushes, break off branches. The male goes berserk, his body goes stiff, he stretches his jaws, hi, bares his fangs. Oi: his tail gets hard and lashes the air like a whip. You would run, flee. Are you listening? Me—I follow the trail. Great big paw marks, no trace of any claws . . . I'm off. One day I won't come back.

Eh, no, the male and female don't go hunting together. They go off on their own. But they keep each other company during the day, stretch out together and sleep. Put their heads together. The male facing one side, the female the other . . . Oi: I'm going to bring the jaguar Maria-Maria here, I'm not leaving her with any male. Would you like to see her? You won't try to shoot her with that revolver of yours, will you? Ei, who knows, that revolver of yours could be unlucky, hã? Let me see if there's a jinx on it, maybe I could put it right . . . Ah, you don't want me to? You won't let me touch your revolver? Your eyes have closed three times, you've already opened your mouth and yawned. If I go on counting for a bit more, do you think you might fall asleep?

Eh, whenever they breed, I can always find the lair. Their den is always hidden away where the forest is at its thickest, a great big hole inside a cave. In the middle of the jungle. The mother jaguar turns into a she-devil. When I first used to kill jaguars, I would wait for six months to make sure the cubs didn't go without food. Then I killed the mother and left the cubs to grow up. Nhem? Nope, I didn't feel sorry for them, I had to make money and sell the skins . . . Sure, I can miaow just like any cub that brings its mother running in desperation. There was one jaguar with her litter, a great big jaguaretê-pixuna, a real beauty and very nasty. I miaowed and miaowed, jaguarainhém, jaguaranhinhenhém . . . She came rushing like a wild thing, hissing with anger, not knowing where to turn. I was miaowing here inside the shack, the mother pixuna came up to the door begging me to go back to the den. She opened her paw to me . . . No, not because she wanted to kill, because she didn't want to lose her cubs, to see them scattered. I stopped miaowing, fired in the air. The pixuna ran away, fled at once, moved her young half a league from here, found another lair in the jungle swamp. Her cubs weren't pixunas, they were spotted jaguars, pinimas . . . She picks up each cub by the scruff of the neck, carries it off, jumps the ravine, leaps over any bushes . . . Eh, stupid beast! But don't you go saying she's stupid. That's for me to say. Yes, sir. I'm drinking all your rum. Yeah, burns your throat, makes you feel warm inside. I feel happy, really happy . . . Nhem? Don't know. I like going around without any clothes on, except for an old pair of pants and a belt round my waist. There's nothing soft about my skin. Ã-hã, not that I haven't got clothes to wear, I've plenty of good clothes, a shirt, a nice hat. I wear them on Sundays. I don't wear boots, I don't want them! I don't like having anything on my feet, I like going around in my bare feet, ixe, lá. Na, there are no feast-days here. Nhem? No, you won't find mass being said around here! I want to go to heaven all right, but no priests or missionaries, I don't trust them, don't want anything to do with them. I wear a little medal round my neck, I like saints. What saints? Well, there's São Bento who keeps away the snakes . . . but snake poison can't do me any harm—I've got a deer's horn, I hold it to the snakebite and it heals up. There aren't any dead souls, tagoaíbas or ghosts, you don't find them in these parts, at least

I've never seen any. There's the devil, but I've never seen him either. Hum-hum . . .

Nhenhém? What about me? You're the one who's asking. But I know why you're asking. A-hã, because I've got this hair, these tiny eyes . . . Sure. No, not from my father. He was white, he wasn't an Indian. No, not from the Caraó tribe. My mother was Péua from the Tacunapéua tribe, far away from here. But not Caraó, the Carão are cowards. The whole tribe are afraid of jaguars. My mother was called Mar'lara Maria, she was Indian. Then I lived with the Caraó tribe, I lived with them. My good, pretty mother gave me food, gave me the best of food, plenty of food, all the food I wanted . . . I travelled a lot, travelled long distances. The Caraó tribe used spears, only the Caraó hunters know how to kill jaguars with spears. Auá? Nhoa-quim Pereira Xapudo, sometimes called Quim Crênhe, was afraid of nothing. My friend! A bow, an arrow, a long arrow. Nhem? Ah, I've got more than one name. My mother named me Bacuriquirepa. Breó Bero as well. My father took me to the missionary. He baptized me, yeah, he baptized me. Gave me the name Tonico; do you think that's a nice name? Antonho de Eiesús . . . Then they started calling me Macuncôzo . . . it was the name of a farm that belonged to somebody else, it's a place they call Macuncôzo . . . Now I don't have any name at all, I don't need one. Nhô Nhuão Guede brought me here, me nhum, all on my own. He had no right! Now I haven't got a name . . .

No that's not a jaguar making that noise. It's a tapir teaching her young to swim. There are lots of tapirs around here. Tapir meat tastes good. On a hot day the tapir does all its thinking and knowing in the water. Eh, no, the pinima jaguar eats tapirs, every one of them. The tapir doesn't fight, the tapir runs, escapes. When the jaguar has jumped on her, she can't run with the jaguar on her back, not a chance, she hasn't got the strength. When the pinima jaguar jumps on the tapir, she kills it right away, the tapir's as good as dead. The jaguaretê bleeds the tapir dry. Oi, it's a clear night, good for hunting jaguars!

No, sir, that's the noise of other animals, the night-swallow, the nightjar, the wood-owl, twittering away. That animal you heard crying out was the otter saying she's hungry. She cried:—Irra! The otter goes swimming upstream. Eh, she comes out of any water with her coat dry . . . The guinea-pigs? You can hear them from a distance feeding, half in and half out of the water . . . When the jaguar roars, I'll let you know. Eh, there's no need. If she roars or yowls, you'll know at once . . . She yowls as if she were suffocating, the noise comes from the back of the throat, and what a throat . . . Heeé . . . Apê! Are you frightened? You're not frightened, are you? But you will be. The whole jungle's afraid. The jaguar can be vicious. Tomorrow you'll see, I'll show you its trail, pipura . . . One day when there's a full moon, you come here, you come and see my trail, just like a jaguar's trail, eh, I'm a jaguar! Hum, you don't believe me, do you?

Hey, crazy man . . . Hey, crazy man . . . Me . . . jaguar! Nhum? No, I'm no devil. You're the devil with that twisted mouth of yours. You're bad, evil, ugly. Am I the devil? I could be . . . I live in a shack without walls . . . I'm always swimming. I've even caught a bladder infection. Noaquim Caraó wore a cap with a hawk's feather. The feather of a macaw and flamingo as well. And ostrich feathers round his knees, ankles and waist. But I'm a jaguar. The jaguaretê is my uncle, my mother's brother, tutira . . . My relations! My relations! . . . Oi, stretch out your hand . . . Give me your hand, let me hold it . . . Just for a second . . .

Eh, you're holding a revolver? Hum-hum. No need to reach for your revolver . . . Are you afraid the jaguar is coming to the shack? Hã-hã, the jaguar Uinhúa has crossed the marshes, I can tell she's coming to hunt a guinea-pig, she's creeping through the long grass. She crawls along on her belly with her ears pricked up—her ears pop, quaquave . . . the jaguar Uinhúa is black, a black devil that shines in the moonlight. She stretches out on the ground. The blades of grass tickle inside her nostrils, annoy her, make her sneeze. She eats fish, water-fowl, herons, crakes. Listen to the uêuê of the snipe flying away, the snipe flies left and right . . . A little bird flies off in fright without making a sound. The jaguar Uinhúa isn't the least bit interested. But the guinea-pig has been frightened, has taken a jump. Have you ever heard water splashing? The jaguar Uinhúa must be in a rage. Soaking wet after being in the grass, covered in the white mud from the river bank. Here she comes . . . She knows you're here, it's that horse of yours. Here she comes . . . tuxa morubixa. Here she comes . . . sweating, she's so hot! Oi, your horse is stamping with fear. Eh, there's no need. Uinhúa has stopped in her tracks. Is she coming? No, she's not coming, that was the tataca or some toad . . . Don't be frightened. Don't be frightened, if she comes I'll shoo her away, chase her out, drive her away. I'm keeping very quiet, I mustn't move; she can't see me. Let the horse neigh, it must be trembling, its ears are pricked up. Is the hobble any good? Is the rope strong enough? It won't escape. Anyhow, that horse of yours has seen better days. Wait . . . turn your revolver away, ih!

She won't come now. The Uinhúa wasn't brave enough to come today. Don't worry, let her be: she won't die of hunger—she can catch any guinea-pig that happens to be around, a rat, some tiny animal. She even eats porcupine ... Tomorrow morning you'll see her trail. The jaguar leaves a stink behind that you can easily pick up when she goes by. First thing in the morning we can go for a bathe. Would you like that? Nhem? The smell is at its worst where they've given birth and brought up their young, there it stinks like anything. I like the smell myself ... You can settle down now, stop worrying, put your revolver away. The jaguar Uinhúa won't come now. She doesn't even belong on this side. She must have crossed the marshes, unless Maramonhangara has invaded her territory and Uinhúa got annoyed and moved away ... Everything has its own place: take the place for drinking water—the Tibitaba goes into the little pool where there's a buriti palm-tree; Papa-Gente drinks in the same place along with Suú-Suú in the stream Veredinha ... In the middle of the wide river there's a boulder: Papa-Gente swims there, climbs onto the boulder, looks as if he's standing up on the water, looks really fierce. He shakes one paw, then the other, shakes his body dry. Stares at everything, stares at the moon ... Papa-Gente likes living on an island, being capoama of the island, a-hé. Nhem? Not Papa? Axi! The jaguar stuck her paw through a hole in a hut, grabbed a small child from his bunk, ripped open his little belly ...

No, it wasn't here, it happened on the plains of Chapada Nova, eh. She was an old jaguar, the mate of a well-known jaguar jaguarpinima, a really big beast people had nicknamed Pé-de-Panela. The little boy's father worked on the land, he took his rifle and went after the jaguar, sacaquera, sacaquera. The jaguar Pé-de-Panela had killed the little boy, had killed a mule. Any jaguar that comes close to where people are living isn't scared of being chased away, an old jaguar, a jaguar chief eats people, it's a dangerous beast, almost as wicked as a cruel man. The farmer followed her trail, sacaquera, sacaquera. The pinima can walk for hours, cover long distances, travel all through the night. But Pé-de-Panela had eaten and eaten, she had drunk the mule's blood, drunk water, left her trail, gone off to sleep in the heart of the jungle, in a hole, all sprawled out. I picked up her trail, said nothing, told nobody. Didn't the farmer say the jaguar was his? The farmer went to fetch his dogs, the dogs picked up the scent and found the jaguar. They followed her. The farmer arrived, shouted with rage, the rifle wouldn't fire. Pé-de-Panela mauled the farmer, tore his head open, stuffed his hair into his brains. They buried what was left of the farmer along with the corpse of his little boy. I went there, I went to watch. They gave me food, rum, good food; I also wept with the others.

Eh, they were offering money to anyone who could kill Pé-de-Panela. I felt like having a go. They talked about tracking her down. Hum-hum . . . How can they track her down, find her by following her trail? She was far away . . . How can it be done? Hum, it can't. But I know how. I didn't do any searching. I lay down on the spot, sniffed out her scent. I turn into a jaguar. Then I actually turn into a jaguar, hã. I mew . . . And all at once I know. I headed towards the mill on the weir. And there she was: Pé-de-Panela had arrived early that morning, eaten a pig, the man who owned the pig was Rima Toruquato, a farmer in Saó. The farmer also offered me money if I'd kill Pé-de-Panela. I agreed. I asked for another pig, just on loan, tied it to the foot of the pepper-tree. As night fell, Pé-de-Panela didn't suspect I was there, so she set out to look for the other pig. But she didn't appear. She only arrived early next morning as it was getting light. She grunted, opened her mouth as she came up to me, I fired into her throat and shouted— "Eat this, uncle!. . . " Then I collected my money from everybody, was given lots of food, enough to last me for days. They lent me a horse and saddle. Then Nhô Nhuão Guede sent me here to hunt jaguars. A real swine!. A horrible man! But I came.

I shouldn't have done it? Aã, I know, I should never have come here in the first place. The jaguars are my people, my relations. They didn't know. Eh, I'm smart, cunning. I'm not frightened. They didn't know that I was a cruel relation, ready to betray them. I was only afraid of one day coming across a big jaguar walking with its paws turned in, coming out of the jungle . . . Could that happen? Hum-hum. No, no jaguar appeared, I'm not frightened any more. There's no jaguar there. The jaguar Maneta also used to break into huts just like Pé-de-Panela. People were frightened to stay in their own homes. Until one day the jaguar got her paw stuck and they were able to go out and kill her from the outside. Everybody was terrified and they only managed to cut her paw with their scythe. The jaguar roared. They hacked her wrist. She was a black jaguar. I didn't know her. They hacked her paw off and she was able to escape. Then she began terrorizing the people, she started eating humans, livestock, would leave a trail of piss three feet long, crawled around lame. And nobody could manage to catch her. They promised good money: but she couldn't be found. I didn't know her. All I knew was that she was a jaguar called Maneta. Until one day she disappeared off the face of the earth. It's really weird.

Oi, did you hear that? That sound, something yowling. Listen. Yowling way in the distance. It's the male Apiponga. He must have caught a big animal, a wild pig. He's filling his belly. He's killed it on the edge of the forest, down in the ravine where he's ripped it apart. I'll go there tomorrow. Eh. No, you don't know Apiponga: He's the one that makes the most awful noise, gives the loudest roar you've ever heard. Eh—How he can jump . . . He goes on hunting and killing all night. He can kill without leaving any mess! He eats and off he goes; and soon comes back. He sleeps during the day, lying in the sun, sleeps all sprawled out. If a mosquito bothers him, eh, he gets very annoyed. Go and see Apiponga for yourself . . . during the day he sleeps near a spring in the bush where the shrubs are really thick and there's a quarry . . .

Nhem? You want to know where Maria-Maria sleeps during the day, hã? What do you want to know for? What for? Her lair is among the rosemary in a clearing in the bush, not far from here, so there! So what? You still don't know where it is, eh-eh-eh . . . If you were to meet Maria-Maria, you would die of fright—even if she is the prettiest jaguar around. Oi: open your eyes: here she comes, she's coming, she's coming, with her mouth half-open, rolling her tongue . . . She gives little gasps when the weather's hot, rolls her tongue backwards and forwards, but it never leaves the roof of her mouth. She taps the ground with her paw, very gently, then she stretches out, flat out, closes her eyes. Eh, she puts her paws in front of her, spreads her claws—each claw's bigger than your little finger. Aí, she's looking at me, she's looking at me . . . She likes me. If I were to let her eat you, she'd gobble you up . . .

Take a look outside. The moon's so round. I'm not saying anything. The moon's not my godfather. Rubbish. You're not drinking, I'm offended, drinking here all on my own, I'm finishing off your rum. Is the moon the godfather of the caraó? The caraó was talking nonsense. Auá? The caraó called Curiua wanted to marry a white woman. He brought her things, gave them to her: a pretty mat, a bunch of bananas, a tame toucan with a yellow beak, the skin of a jabuti reptile, a white stone with a blue stone inside. The woman had a husband. A-hã, it was like this: the white woman liked the things the caraó Curiua brought her. But she didn't want to marry him for that would be a sin. The caraó Curiua burst out laughing, said he was sick, that he would only get better if the white woman joined him in the hammock. She didn't have to marry him, just to sleep with him once. He put up his hammock nearby, got in, didn't eat anything. The woman's husband arrived, the woman told him what had happened. The white man flew into a rage. He pointed his rifle at the caraó Curiua aiming for his heart. The caraó started crying but the white man shot him he was so angry . . .

Hum-hum. Oi: I was there, I never killed anyone. I didn't kill anyone in the Socó-Boi either. I've never killed people, I couldn't, my mother warned me never to kill. I was afraid of soldiers. I can't stand being locked up, if they were to lock me up, I'd die—for I was born during the cold season, at an hour when the sejuçu was right in the middle of the sky. Take a look, the sejuçu has four little stars, and two more. Good: now can you see the one that's missing? You can't see it? That other one—is me . . . My mother told me. My mother belonged to an Indian tribe, she was good to me, so good, just like a jaguar with her cubs, jaguaraím. Have you ever seen a jaguar with her cubs? You haven't? The mother licks them and licks them, takes care of them. The mother jaguar is ready to die for them, she won't let anybody get near them, no she won't . . . It's only the suaçurana that's cowardly, she runs away, leaves her young to the mercy of anybody who wants them . . .

Eh, the jaguar's my relation, the jaguaretê are my people. My mother used to say, my mother knew how to call uê-uê . . . The jaguaretê my uncle, an uncle of mine. A-hã. Nhem? You want to know if I killed any jaguars? I killed them, okay, so I killed them. But I don't kill them any more, no I don't! In Socó-Boi that Pedro Pampolino asked me, hired me to kill the other fellow to settle old scores. I didn't want to. Eu, not me. So that some soldiers can arrest me? But Tiaguim agreed and earned the money that was meant for me, he waited for the man at the side of the road . . . Nhem, what happened? I don't know, I can't remember. I didn't have anything to do with it, I didn't give him any help. I wanted nothing to do with it . . . Tiaguim along with Missiano killed lots of people. Then he went for an old man. The old man in a rage swore he'd drink the young man's blood. I heard everything. They tied up the young man, the old man cut his throat with a knife, drained the blood into a basin . . . I dropped everything, took myself off, ended up in the Chapada Nova . . .

That Nhô Nhuão Guede, the father of the fat girl, the worst man that ever was, dumped me here. He told me:—"Kill all the jaguars!" He left me here on my own, nhem, on my own so that all I could do was listen to my own voice . . . On my own the whole time, a parakeet flies past squawking, a cricket chirps all night long, can't stop chirping. The rain comes and it goes on raining and raining. I've neither father nor mother. I only killed jaguars. I shouldn't have done it. The jaguar's so pretty and my relation. That Pedro Pampolino said I was useless.

Tiaguim said I was a coward, that I'd no guts. I killed a lot of jaguars. Nhô Nhuão Guede brought me here, nobody would hire me to work with other people . . . For they said I was no good. Only fit to stay here all on my own all the time. I was really useless, couldn't do any other work, didn't want to . . . The only thing I knew was how to kill jaguars. Ah, how I wish I hadn't done it! Nobody wanted to have anything to do with me, they didn't like me, everybody pushed me around. Maria-Maria came, she came. Did they expect me to kill Maria-Maria? How could I? I couldn't kill any more jaguars, the jaguars are my relations, I felt sorry I'd ever killed them . . . I was terrified because I'd killed them. Nhem, not one? Ai, ai, man . . .

At night I tossed and turned, can't explain it, tossing and turning just for the hell of it, I couldn't get to sleep, couldn't tell whether the night was starting or ending. I felt a sudden urge . . . a desperate urge to turn into a jaguar, me, me, a great big jaguar. To go roaming like a jaguar in the shadows before daybreak . . . I was quietly roaring inside . . . Suddenly I had claws . . . I had the empty den that once belonged to a jaguaretê-pinima I myself had killed; I went there. Her smell was still strong. I lay down on the ground . . . Eh, I felt cold, cold, so cold. The cold was coming from all the woods around, coming from the fields . . . I was shivering all over. I'd never known such cold, it was colder than it had ever been. I was shivering so badly I thought I'd fall apart . . . Then I got a cramp in my whole body, I started shaking from head to foot; I couldn't help it. When I got over it, I was down on the ground on all fours, desperately trying to walk. What a relief! There I was, master of everything, alone and happy, I felt really good, the whole world needed me . . . I was afraid of nothing! At that moment I knew what everybody was thinking. If you'd been here, I'd have known what you were thinking . . . I even knew what the jaguar was thinking. Do you know what jaguars think about? You don't know? Eh, then you'd better find out: the jaguar only thinks about one thing—that everything's pretty, really pretty, for ever and ever. That's all she thinks about the whole time, all day long, always the same thing and nothing else, and she goes on thinking about this as she goes on the prowl, eating, sleeping, doing whatever she's doing . . . When something upsets her, she suddenly bares her fangs, roars, gets furious, even without thinking: for at this very moment she's stopped thinking. Only when everything calms down again does she go back to thinking as before . . .

Eh, now you know; don't you? Hã-hã. Nhem? Then I left walking on all fours. I was in such a rage, felt like killing everything, tearing at everything with my claws and teeth . . . I roared. Eh, I—snarled! The other day, my white horse that I brought, which they gave me, the horse was torn to bits, half-eaten, dead, I woke up, all covered in dry blood . . . Nhem? It didn't matter, I don't like horses . . . The horse had a bad leg, it was finished . . .

Now I wanted to go and see Maria-Maria. Nhem? I don't like women . . . Sometimes I like them . . . I start walking like a jaguar, amidst the brambles, slowly, very slowly, I don't make a sound. But the brambles don't prick, well not very much. When they prick your foot, they do a lot of damage, you feel sick for days, you can't hunt, you have to go hungry . . . Yeah, but if Maria-Maria is in that state, I take her something to eat, hã, hã.

Hum, hum. That's not the noise a jaguar makes. An urucuéra chirped, and a little animal scuttled off. Eh, how do I know? It could be a deer, a hog, a guinea-pig, near the fields . . . The other noises are made by toads, wood-crickets. Little birds as well, that chirp while they're sleeping . . . ói, if I fall asleep first, will you try and sleep as well? Rest your head on this knapsack. The knapsack don't belong to anyone, it belonged to the black man. There's nothing inside that's worth having, nothing except some old clothes, not worth anything. There was a picture of the black man's wife, the black man was married. The black man died, I took the picture, I turned it over so that I wouldn't have to look at it, carried it far away, hid it in the hollow of a tree. Far, far away; I don't like keeping the picture here beside me . . .

Eh, a jaguar roared and you didn't hear it. It roared very quietly . . . Are you frightened? You're not frightened, are you? You're not really frightened, I can see you aren't. Hum-hum. Eh, if you were near her, you would know what fear is! When the jaguar roars, a man shakes from head to foot. The hunter with a spear isn't afraid, never. Eh, it's not easy finding a hunter with a spear, there aren't many of them around. Your spear-thrower—he doesn't bat an eyelid . . . All the others are scared out of their wits. The black man more than anybody . . .

Eh, the jaguar likes eating the flesh of blacks. Whenever there's a black man with the hunting party, the jaguar goes after him. She keeps under cover, following hidden paths, behind, behind, behind, never taking her eye off him. The black man was praying, held on to the others, shook all over. He wasn't the same one that lived here in the shack; the black man who lived here was called Tiodoro. The other was a black man called Bijibo with the party coming round the edge of the river Urucúia, passing the Riacho Morto then . . . The old man with the white beard wore boots, boots made from snake-skin. The old man with the boots carried a cross-bow. He was heading with his sons and the drunken woodsman for the other side towards the Serra Bonita, they were passing through on this side to get there . . . Black Bijibo was a coward; he didn't like to travel alone, he was returning to some place—who knows where—far away . . . The black man was scared, he knew the jaguar was lying in wait: the jaguar came, a sacaquera, all that night I knew it was prowling around, uauaca, near the camp-fire, near the huts . . .

Then I spoke to the black man, told him that I was going to go with him as far as Formoso. He didn't need any weapon, I had a pistol, a rifle, I had a flick-knife, a dagger and my spear. I was lying: what I was doing was coming back here, I'd had a row with Nhô Nhuão Guede and told him to his face that I was killing no more jaguars, that I'd made up my mind and that was final. I was coming back here and took such a roundabout way just because of the black man. But black Bijibo didn't know, he was going to travel with me . . .

Oi: I had nothing much to complain about, I wasn't annoyed, I liked black Bijibo, I took pity on him and wanted to help him, for he had a lot of good food and supplies, besides, I felt sorry for him having to travel on his own . . . Black Bijibo was harmless, with that foolish fear of his, he didn't let me out of his sight for a minute . . . We walked for three days. The black man never stopped talking. I liked him. Black Bijibo had flour, cheese, salt, brown sugar, beans, dried meat, he had a hook for catching fish, salt pork . . . Holy Mother of God!—the black man was carrying all that on his back, I didn't give him a hand, I wasn't in the mood, I don't know where he got the strength . . . I went hunting: I killed deer, guan, quail . . . Could that black man eat! Atié! Atié! the amount of food he could eat was unbelievable, all he wanted to do was eat, I've never seen anything like it, never. All he did was eat or talk about food, and I would watch him eating and then eat even more myself, I stuffed myself until I was ready to burst.

We sheltered under a tree and lit a fire. I watched black Bijibo eating, there he was happily stuffing himself all day long, all day long, pushing the food inside his mouth, filling his belly. I got angry watching him, really angry . . . Axe, axi! Black Bijibo eating to his heart's content, eating everything he fancied, there was the poor jaguar searching for something to eat, ready to eat black Bijibo . . . I got even more angry. Don't you ever feel really angry? I didn't say a word. A-hã. Afterwards, all I said to black Bijibo was, we couldn't have been in a more dangerous spot, all around us were dens of spotted jaguars. Ih, the black man stopped eating at once, the black man took a long time to get to sleep.

Eh, now I wasn't angry any more, all I wanted to do was to play a trick on the black man. I went out, didn't make any noise, not a sound, moved as quietly as could be. I threw the jaguar something to eat, the lot, everything I was carrying, and hid up a tree some distance away. Eh, I crept back, covered my tracks, eh, ready for some fun . . . I went all round along one side, then the other and turned back, climbed up a tall tree, hid there . . . That she-devil, that she-devil of a jaguar didn't appear! Early next morning it was fun to see black Bijibo waking up and finding I wasn't there . . .

He cried all day and searched and searched, couldn't believe I'd gone. Eh, he opened his eyes wide. He was going round in circles, dazed out of his mind. He even looked for me inside an ant-hole . . . But he was too afraid to shout in case he disturbed the jaguars, so he called out my name in a low voice . . . Black Bijibo was trembling and I could hear his teeth chattering as I listened. He was quivering like a piece of meat roasting on a spit . . . Then he got really scared, went down on the ground, bent over, covering his ears. Then he covered his eyes . . . I waited the whole day, perched up on the tree, I was also feeling hungry and thirsty, but now I wanted, how can I put it, I wanted to see the jaguaretê eating the black man . . .

Nhem? The black man hadn't done me any harm. Black Bijibo is a decent fellow, gives no trouble. I wasn't annoyed with him any more. Nhem? It wasn't true? How do you know? You weren't there. A-hã, the black man wasn't my relation, he shouldn't have wanted to come with me. I took the black man to the jaguar. It was the black man who asked to come with me, uê. I wasn't doing anything unusual . . . Hum, why are you reaching for your revolver? Is it a good weapon? Hã-hã, a good revolver. Erê! Let me hold it in my hand, let me have a good look . . . you won't let me, you won't let me? Don't you like to see me holding it? Don't be afraid! I don't want to hold a weapon that brings bad luck. I don't let people touch my weapons, certainly not women, I don't even let them see them, that's not allowed. That brings bad luck, one bad thing after another . . . Hum, hum. No, sir. Yeah. That's up to you . . .

Hum. Hum. Yeah. No. No, sir, I don't know. Hum-hum. No sir, I'm not offended, the revolver's yours, it belongs to you. I only asked to see it, it's a fine weapon, a nice revolver . . . But my hand don't bring bad luck, pa!—I'm not a woman. There's no jinx on me. I'm . . . lucky when it comes to hunting. You won't let me hold it, you don't believe me. I'm not lying . . . That's okay, I'll just have another drop. Why don't you join me? I'm not offended. Apê, this rum's great stuff . . .

Oi: so you want to hear the rest. I'll tell you later. What happened to black Bijibo? I came back, uai. I arrived, found another black man, living right here in the shack. At first I thought: this is the other fellow's brother, he's come to get his revenge, ói, ói . . . But it wasn't that. He was a black man called Tiodoro: Nhô Nhuão Guede had settled him here for good so he could kill all the jaguars because I didn't want to kill them any more. He said the shack was his, Nhô Nhuão Guede had told him so, had given the shack to black Tiodoro for the rest of his life. But I could live with him, although I'd have to fetch firewood and go and look for water. Me? Hum, not me, not a chance.

I made myself a hammock with palm-leaves near the den of Maria-Maria. Ahã, black Tiodoro's sure to come hunting around here . . . good, very good. Black Tiodoro wasn't hunting any jaguars—he had lied to Nhô Nhuão Guede. Black Tiodoro wasn't a bad fellow, but he was scared, really scared. He had four big dogs—dogs that barked. Apiponga killed two of them, one disappeared into the forest, Maramonhangara ate the other one. Eh-eh-he . . . Those dogs didn't hunt any jaguars. Even black Tiodoro only lasted in the shack for a month: for he soon died there.

Black Tiodoro missed seeing other people, he wanted to be able to get out and go around. He used to give me food, would call me to go out with him. Eh, I know: he was frightened to go out alone in that place. He got as far as the edge of the river, began to feel scared of the anaconda. Me, eh, I've got this old club of mine, strung with tough fibre, I would put the cord round my neck, walk about with the club hanging down: I wasn't scared of anything. So there, black man . . . We walked for league after league among the marshes, good soil for planting. The farmer Seo Rauremiro was a decent man, but he always whistled at you as if you were a dog. I don't look like a dog, do I? Seo Rauremiro would say:—"You're not to come inside, stay out there, you're Indian . . . " Seo Rauremiro was chatting to black Tiodoro, passing the time of day. He gave me food, but wouldn't talk to me. I left in a rage, furious with the lot of them: with Seo Rauremiro, his wife, his daughters and his little boy . . .

I called black Tiodoro: after eating something we came away. All black Tiodoro could think about was getting across the marshes—getting onto the mat with the half-wit's wife, a fine woman that Maria Quirinéia. We called there. Then uê, they asked me to step outside, I stayed out there for a long while watching the bush, keeping an eye on the road, aruê, watching to see if anyone was coming. Lots of men were used to calling there. Lots of men: jababoras, highlanders, those three who have already met their death. Nearby, I saw the trail. It went round in a circle, the droppings of the jaguar Porreteira where she'd been out hunting. There was a light shower of rain, little more than a drizzle. I hid beneath a tree. Still no sign of black Tiodoro coming out of Maria Quirinéia's hut. That crazy husband of hers wasn't even shouting, he had been asleep, all chained up in there . . .

Uai, then I saw a highlander coming, that Seo Riopôro, the most cruel man you ever met, always in a foul temper. He wore a great big cape made from palm leaves so as not to get his clothes wet, he splashed dirt all over the place as he tramped into the mud. I came out from under the tree, walked towards him to hold him back, keep him away, as black Tiodoro had told me.

"What are you doing here, you shameless jaguar hunter?"—he asked me, shouting and bullying me.

"I'm watching the rain coming to an end . . . " I told him—"Why don't you go and get lost, you good-for-nothing?"—he shouted at me, his voice getting louder and louder. What a man he was for working himself into a rage.

Ugh, he shouted. Let him shout, Pa! So I was to get lost? Ah, I didn't care. Pa! That's fine, fine. Then I told him that the jaguar Porreteira was hiding in the cave at the bottom of the gully.

"Let me see, let me see this minute . . . " he said. And "Txi, you're lying aren't you? You're lying, you devil, because you've no shame!"

But he approached, reached the edge of the gully, stood right on the edge and leaned over, peering down at the bottom. I pushed him! I gave him the tiniest push, used scarcely any force: the highlander Seo Riopôro went flying through the air to the bottom . . . Apê! Nhem-nhem what? Did I kill him, me? No I didn't kill him. He was still alive when he hit the ground, when the jaguar Porreteira started eating him . . . Good, fine! Erê! Try eating this, uncle . . .

I didn't say a word to the black man: ói . . . The woman Maria Quirinéia gave me coffee, said I was a good-looking Indian. We came away. Black Tiodoro was mad at me, wouldn't speak to me. Because I knew how to hunt jaguars and he didn't. Me, I'm a real guide, able to find trails and pick up the scent, to find animals, trees, plants in the forest, everything, but he couldn't find a thing. I had all these skins but I wasn't interested in selling them any more. He looked at me like a dog on the scrounge. I'm sure he wanted all those skins for himself, to sell, to earn a lot of money . . . Ah, black Tiodoro lied about me to the other highlanders.

That jababora Gugué, a good man, really kind, never abused me, never. I liked getting out and about, he hated having to walk: all he wanted to do was to stretch out in his hammock on the grass all day long, from morning to night. He even asked me to fetch water in a gourd for him to drink. He did nothing. He slept, he chewed tobacco, he lay around, sprawled out, chatted. So did I. I enjoyed listening to Gugué when he got talking! Eh, he did nothing, never went hunting, didn't work the soil or grow cassava, even refused to go for a walk. Then I got tired of keeping watch for him. No, I wasn't mad at him, just fed up. You know what I mean? Have you seen him? That slouching, lazy fellow, playing the coward because it suits him, a hopeless fellow, ixe! I couldn't have cared less . . . I didn't want to get mad at him, no I didn't, I really didn't, honestly I didn't. He was a decent enough fellow. I told him I was going away.

"Don't go away . . . " was what he said. "Let's have a chat . . . " But he was the one who was sleeping, sleeping the whole day long. Suddenly, eh, I turned into a jaguar . . . lá. I couldn't stand it any longer. I got some creeper, twisted it into a really good, strong fibre. I tied that Gugué inside his hammock. I tied him up, I bound his legs and arms. When he wanted to shout, hum, xô! Axi, I didn't let him: I stuffed his mouth with a pile of leaves. There was nobody about. I lifted that Gugué with his hammock rolled round him. What a weight, eh. I carried him to Papa-Gente. Papa-Gente the king of the jaguars, and he ate the jababora Gugué . . . Papa-Gente, a great big jaguar, he grunts as he eats, grunts to his heart's content just like a jaguar cub . . . Afterwards I began to feel sad, to feel sorry for that Gugué, such a decent fellow, teitê . . .

That same night I went to have a chat with another highlander who was still around, called Antunias, a jabobora uê. What a funny looking man with that yellow face of his! He never gave anyone anything, kept everything for himself, would only lend you a lead bullet if you gave him the money for two. Ixe! Ueh . . . I arrived there, he was eating, eating something as he lay under a wicker basket, but I saw him. So I asked him if I could sleep in the shack, "Sure, you can sleep here. But you'll have to fetch wood for the fire . . . " that annoyed me "Eh, it's already night, it's dark outside, I'll gather some good wood first thing in the morning . . . " was what I told him. But then he ordered me to mend an old sandal. He told me that he was going off in the morning to see

Maria Quirinéia and that I couldn't stay in the shack on my own for I might start interfering with his things. Then I told him: I think the jaguar's caught Gugué . . .

Ei, Tunia!—for that was how Gugué used to speak. He opened his eyes wide. He asked me how did I know? I told him I had heard Gugué cry out and the grunts of the jaguar gobbling him up. He asked me if I'd seen anything. Then, do you know what he told me? Axi. So, if the jaguar had caught Gugué then everything that belonged to Gugué was now his. He was moving on to another serra and if I liked I could go with him and help to carry his hammock and belongings. "Yeah, I'll come . . ." I told him.

Ah, that's something I'm not telling you, I'm saying nothing, not a word! What do you want to know for? Do you have to know everything? You'd think you were a soldier . . . Okay, okay, I'll tell you, you're my friend. I touched him with my spear . . . Shall I show you what happened? Ah, you don't want me to? You're afraid I'll stick my spear into your chest, is that it, nhem? Why do you want to know then? Axe, you're a soft fellow . . . always scared . . . So, there was nothing for it but keep on walking and he cried all the time, sacêmo, in the dark he kept falling and getting up again . . . "You mustn't shout, you mustn't shout . . ." I told him, warned him, as I pushed him with the point of my spear. I took him to Maria-Maria . . .

Early next morning, I felt like a drink of coffee. I thought: I'll call on Maria Quirinéia and ask her for some. I started making my way there, began seeing droppings! Everywhere, all along the slope of the plateau, the trail of a jaguar . . . Ei, my jaguars . . . But they all must know about me, eh, I'm their relation—eh, if not, I'll start a fire in the fields, in the bush, in a clearing in the bush, in their den, I'll start a fire everywhere, when the drought comes to an end . . .

That woman Maria Quirinéia has a kind heart. She gave me coffee and something to eat. That crazy husband of hers Seô Suruvéio kept fairly quiet, it wasn't his moon, all he did was laugh his head off, but he didn't shout. Eh, but Maria Quirinéia started staring at me in a funny way, she was somehow different: her eyes were shining, she was laughing, started twitching her nostrils, gripped me by the hand, began stroking my hair. She told me I was good-looking, really good-looking. I—felt pleased. But then she tried to pull me down onto the mat beside her, eh, uê, uê . . . I got furious, really furious, went into a rage, such a rage that I wanted to kill Maria Quirinéia, hand her over to the jaguar Tatacia, give her to all the jaguars!

Eh, I jumped to my feet, was just about to grab Maria Quirinéia by the throat. But she spoke first: "Oi, your mother must have been very pretty, very nice, very good, am I right?" That woman Maria Quirinéia was very good, very pretty, I remember I liked her a lot. I told her that everybody had died, that the jaguar had eaten them and that she'd better move away, take herself off somewhere else, leave at once, at once, at once, not waste a minute, I meant it . . . Go anywhere, but she must get away. Maria Quirinéia got scared, really scared, said she couldn't leave her half-witted husband. I told her I'd help her, go with her. Take her to the Vereda da Conceição. There she knew people. Yeah, I went with her. Her crazy husband gave us no trouble, well, not much. I asked him, "Shall we walk further on, Seo Nhô Suruvéia?" He replied:—"Let's go, let's go then, let's . . . " The river was high, this was the rainy season, which made things more difficult. But we made it, Maria Quirinéia said goodbye:—"You're a good man, a brave man, a good-looking man. But you don't like women . . . " Then I told her:—"I can't stand them. I've got . . . big claws." She laughed and laughed and laughed, I returned alone, skirting all these paths along the edge of the river.

Uê, uê, I went all the way round, then found a path behind the marshes: the last thing I wanted was to meet farmer Seo Rauremiro. I felt hungry but I didn't want his food—he was such a proud man. I ate a custard-apple and some sweet beans under the hedge where I was resting. After an hour it turned cold, so cold I felt cramp in my leg . . . Eh, I don't know what happened after that, I woke up and found myself in the farmer's house. It was early in the morning. I was lying in a pool of blood, my nails all stained with blood. The farmer was dead, bitten to death, the farmer's wife, his daughters, his little boy . . . Eh, juca-jucá, atiê, atiuca! I began to feel sorry, to feel angry. Hum, nhem? You're saying I killed them? I bit them but I didn't kill them . . . I don't want to be locked up . . . I could taste their blood in my mouth, feel it on my face. Hum, I went outside, went alone into the forest, dazed after climbing all those trees, eh, there's so much forest . . . I walked and walked, couldn't tell you for how long. But when I started to come round, I was wearing no clothes and dying of hunger. Covered in dirt, in earth, with a bitter taste in my mouth, atiê, as bitter as the bark of the Peroba tree . . . I was sprawled out among the rosemary, at the very spot Maria-Maria came up to me . . .

Are you listening, nhem? Has it sunk in . . . I'm a jaguar . . . didn't I tell you? Axi. Didn't I tell you—I turn into a jaguar? A big jaguar, tubix-aba. Oi, my claws, take a good look—big, black claws, hard claws . . .

Get nearer, smell me: don't I stink like a jaguar? Black Tiodoro said I did, ei, ei . . . I wash my body in the river every day . . . But you can go to sleep, hum, hum, don't stay up waiting for your friend. You're sick, you ought to lie on the bunk. The jaguar won't come here, you can put your revolver away . . .

Aaã! You've already shot people with it? You've killed, so you've killed? Why didn't you say so right away? A-ha, so you've actually killed people. How many have you killed? Have you killed a lot of people? Hã-hã, you're a brave fellow, my friend . . . Sure, let's drink rum until our tongues sting as if we'd eaten sand . . . I'm thinking about something good, something nice: the people we're going to kill tomorrow, what about it, my friend? Are we going to kill a comrade, a bad comrade, who wasn't up to any good, let his horse bolt into the forest . . . are we going to kill him? Uh, uh, atimbora, keep still! You're very sleepy . . . Oi: haven't you seen Maria-Maria, ah, so you haven't seen her. You ought to. She'll be coming any minute, she'll come when I call her, she'll come and munguitar, milk you until you're dry . . .

Nhem? Steady on, take it easy . . . When I was with her there in the rosemary, you should have seen us. Maria-Maria makes faces, scratches the ground with her claws, jumps sideways, a light jump the way jaguars do, pretty, very pretty. She bristles, her tail goes stiff, she opens and closes her mouth, quickly, like someone who's sleepy . . . Just like you, eh, eh . . . she paces up and down, swaying, slowly, she's frightened of nothing, moving her haunches up and down, that shiny coat of hers, she creeps up quietly, the prettiest jaguar of all, full of life . . . She grunted at me gently, she wanted to come with me to catch black Tiodoro. Ai, I suddenly felt that cold, that cooooold, shivered all over . . . Eh, eh, I'm skinny, I can easily slip through anywhere, the black man was on the fat side . . . I moved closer, down on all fours . . . black Tiodoro's eyes were wild with fear. His eyes got bigger and bigger . . . , I start roaring . . .

Did you like that? The black man was hopeless, Oi: you're different, you're my friend . . . Oi: let me take a good look at you, let me touch you just for a minute, put my hand on you . . .

Ei, ei, what are you doing? Turn that revolver away! Don't fool around, stop pointing that revolver . . . I haven't moved, I'm standing still, very still . . . Oi: Do you want to kill me? Stop pointing that revolver, point it over there! You're sick, you're out of your mind . . . Have you come to arrest me? Oi: I'm putting my hands on the ground, just for the hell of it, because I want to . . . Oi, this damn cold . . . Are you crazy? Atié. Get out, the shack's mine. Atimbora! If you kill me, your friend'll arrest you when he comes . . . The jaguar's coming, Maria-Maria, she'll eat you . . . The jaguar's my relation . . . Ei, what about the black man? I didn't kill the black man, I was only joking . . . Oi, the jaguar! Ui, ui, you're a decent fellow, why do you want to do this to me, don't kill me . . . I . . . Macuncôzo . . . Don't do this, don't . . . Nhenhenhém . . . Heeé! . . . Hé . . . Aar-rrã . . . Aaâh . . . you arrhoôu me . . . Remuaci . . . Rêiucàanacê . . . Arraã . . . Uhm . . . Ui . . . Ui . . . êeêê . . . êê . . . ê . . .

THE DAISY DOLLS

by Felisberto Hernández

translated by Luis Harss

To María Luisa

I

NEXT TO A GARDEN WAS A FACTORY, AND THE NOISE OF THE MACHINES seeped through the plants and trees. And deep in the garden was a dark weathered house. The owner of the "black house" was a tall man. At dusk his slow steps came up the street into the garden, where—in spite of the noise of the machines—they could be heard chewing on the gravel. One autumn evening, as he opened the front door, squinting in the strong light of the hall, he saw his wife standing halfway up the grand staircase, which widened out into the middle of the courtyard, and it seemed to him she was wearing a stately marble gown, gathered up in the same hand that held on to the balustrade. She realized he was tired and would head straight up to the bedroom and she waited for him with a smile. They kissed and she said:

"Today the boys finished setting up the scenes . . ."

"I know, but don't tell me anything."

She saw him up to the bedroom door, ran an affectionate finger down his nose and left him to himself. He was going to try to get some sleep before dinner: the dark room would divide the day's worries from the pleasures he expected of the night. He listened fondly, as he had since childhood, to the muffled sound of the machines, and fell asleep. In a dream he saw a spot of lamplight on a table. Around the table stood several men. One of them wore tails and was saying: "We have to turn the blood around so it will go out the veins and back through the arteries, instead of out the arteries and back through the veins." They all clapped and cheered, and the man in tails jumped on a horse in the courtyard and galloped off, through the applause, on clattering hooves that drew sparks from the flagstones. Remembering the dream when he woke up, the man in the black house recognized it as an echo of something he had heard that same day—that the traffic, all over the country, was changing from left- to right-hand driving—and smiled to himself. Then he put on his tail coat, once more remembering the man in the dream, and went down into the dining room. Approaching his wife, he sank his open hands in her hair and said:

"I always forget to bring a lens to have a good look at the plants in the green of your eyes. I know how you get your complexion, though: by rubbing olives in your skin."

She ran her forefinger down his nose again, then poked his cheek, until her finger bent like a spider leg, and answered:

"And I always forget to bring scissors to trim your eyebrows!"

As she sat down at the table he left the room, and she asked:

"Did you forget something?"

"Could be . . ."

He came right back and she decided he had not had time to use the phone.

"Won't you tell me where you went?"

"No."

"Then I won't tell you what the men did today."

He had already started to answer.

"No, my dear olive, don't tell me anything until after dinner."

And he poured himself a glass of the wine he imported from France.

But his wife's words had dropped like pebbles into the pond where his obsessions grew, and he could not get his mind off what he expected to see later that night. He collected dolls that were a bit taller than real women. He had had three glass cases built in a large room. In the biggest one were all the dolls waiting to be chosen to compose scenes in the other cases. The arrangements were in the hands of a number of people: first of all, the caption writers (who had to express the meaning of each scene in a few words). Other artists handled settings, costumes, music, and so on. Tonight was the second show. He would watch while a pianist, seated with his back to him, across the room, played programmed works. Suddenly the owner of the black house remembered he must not think of all this during dinner. So he took a pair of opera glasses out of his pocket and tried to focus them on his wife's face.

"I'd love to know if the shadows under your eyes are also plants."

She realized he had been to his desk to fetch the opera glasses, and decided to humor him. He saw a glass dome, which turned out to be a bottle. So he put down the opera glasses and poured himself some more wine from France. She watched it gurgle into his glass, splashing black tears that ran down the crystal walls to meet the wine on its way up. At that moment, Alex—a White Russian with a pointed beard—came in, bowing at her, and served her a plate of ham and beans. She used to say she had never heard of a servant with a beard, and he would answer that it was the one condition Alex had set for accepting the job. Now she shifted her eyes from the glass of wine to the man's wrist, where a tuft of hair grew out of his sleeve, crawling all the way down his hand to his fingers. As he waited on the master of the house, Alex said:

"Walter" (the pianist) "is here."

After dinner, Alex removed the wineglasses on a tray. They rang against each other, as if happy to meet again. The master, half-asleep—in a sort of quiet glow—was pleasantly roused by the sound and called out after him:

"Tell Walter to go to the piano. He mustn't talk to me as I come in. Is the piano far from the glass cases?"

"Yes, sir, on the other side of the room."

"Good. Tell Walter to sit with his back to me, to start on the first piece in the program and keep repeating it without stopping until I flash the light at him."

His wife was smiling. He went up to kiss her and for a moment rested his flushed face on her cheek. Then he headed for the little parlor off the big show room. There he started to smoke and sip his coffee, collecting himself: he had to feel completely isolated before going in to see the dolls. He listened for the hum of the machines and the sounds of the piano. At first they reached him in what seemed like watery murmurs, as if he were wearing a diver's helmet. Then he woke up and realized some of the sounds were trying to tell him something, as if he were being singled out from among a number of persons snoring in the room. But when he tried to concentrate on the sounds, they scattered like frightened mice. He sat there puzzled for a moment, then decided to ignore them. But suddenly he realized he was not in his chair any more: he had gotten up without noticing it. He remembered having just opened the door, and now he felt his steps taking him toward the first glass case. He switched on the light in the case and through the green curtain he saw a doll sprawled on a bed. He opened the curtain and mounted the podium, which was actually a small rolling platform on rubber casters, with a railing. From there, seated in an armchair at a little table, he had a better view of the scene. The doll was dressed as a bride and her wide open eyes stared at the ceiling. It was impossible to tell whether she was dead or dreaming. Her arms were spread in an attitude of what could be either despair or blissful abandon. Before opening the drawer of the little table to read the caption, he wanted to see what his imagination could come up with. Perhaps she was a bride waiting for the groom, who would never arrive, having jilted her just before the wedding. Or perhaps she was a widow remembering her wedding day, or just a girl dressed up to feel like a bride. He opened the drawer and read: "A moment before marrying the man she doesn't love, she locks herself up, wearing the dress she was to have worn to her wedding with the man she loved, who is gone forever, and poisons herself. She dies with her eyes open and no one has come in yet to shut them." Then the owner of the black house thought, "She really was a lovely bride." And after a moment he savored the feeling of being alive when she was not. Then he opened the glass door and entered the scene to have a closer look. At the same time, through the noise of the machines and the music, he thought he heard a door slam. He left the case and, caught in the door to the little parlor, he saw a piece of his wife's dress. As he tiptoed over to the door, he wondered whether she had been spying on him—or maybe it was one of her jokes. He snatched the door open and her body fell on him. But when he caught it in his arms it seemed very light . . . and he recognized Daisy, the doll who resembled her. Meantime his wife, who was crouching behind an armchair, straightened up and said:

"I wanted to give you a surprise, too. I just managed to get her into my dress."

She went on talking, but he did not listen. Although he was pale, he thanked her for the surprise: he did not want to discourage her, because he enjoyed the jokes she made up with Daisy. But this time he had felt uneasy. So he handed Daisy back to her, saying he did not want too long an intermission. Then he returned to the show room, closing the door behind him, and walked toward Walter. But he stopped halfway and opened another door, which gave onto his study, where he shut himself in, took a notebook from a drawer, and proceeded to make a note of the joke his wife had just played on him with Daisy, and the date. First he read the previous entry, which said: "July 21. Today, Mary"—his wife's name was Daisy Mary, but she liked to be called Mary, so when he'd had a doll made to look like her they had dusted off the name Daisy for the doll—"was in the balcony, looking out over the garden. I wanted to put my hands over her eyes and surprise her. But before I reached her I saw it was Daisy. Mary had seen me go to the balcony—she was right behind me, laughing her head off." Although he was the only one to read the notebook, he signed each entry with his name, Horace, in large letters and heavy ink. The entry before last said: "July 18. Today I opened the wardrobe to get my suit and found Daisy hanging there. She was wearing my tail coat, which looked comically large on her."

Having entered the latest surprise, he was back in the show room, heading for the second glass case. He flashed a light at Walter for him to go on to the next piece in the program and started to roll up the podium. In the pause Walter made before taking up the new piece, he felt the machines pounding harder, and as the podium moved the casters seemed to rumble like distant thunder.

The second case showed a doll seated at the head of a table. Her head was tilted back and she had a hand on each side of her plate, on a long row of silverware. Her posture and the way her hands rested on the silverware made her look as if she were at a keyboard. Horace looked at Walter, saw him bowed over the piano with his tails dangling over the edge of the bench, and thought of him as a bird of ill omen. Then he stared at the doll and had the sudden feeling—it had happened to him before—that she was moving. The movements did not always begin right away, nor did he expect them when the doll was dead or lying down, but this time they started too soon, possibly because of her uncomfortable position. She was straining too hard to look up at the ceiling, nodding slightly, with almost imperceptible little jerks that showed the effort she was making, and the minute he shifted his gaze from her face to her hands, her head drooped noticeably. He in turn quickly raised his eyes to her face again—but she had already recovered her stillness. He then began to imagine her story. Her dress and surrounding objects suggested luxury, but the furniture was coarse and the walls were of stone. On the far wall there was a small window, and behind her a low, half-open door, like a false smile. She might be in a dungeon in a castle. The piano was imitating a storm and every now and then lightning flashed in the window. Then he remembered that a minute ago the rolling casters had reminded him of distant thunder and the coincidence unsettled him. Also, while collecting himself in the little parlor, he had heard those sounds that had been trying to tell him something. But he returned to the doll's story: maybe she was praying, asking God to liberate her. Finally, he opened the drawer and read: "Second scene. This woman is expecting a child soon. She is now living in a lighthouse by the sea. She has withdrawn from the world, which has blamed her for loving a sailor. She keeps thinking, 'I want my child to be alone with himself and listen only to the sea.'" He thought, "This doll has found her true story." Then he got up, opened the glass door, and slowly went over her things. He felt he was defiling something as solemn as death. He decided to concentrate on the doll and tried to find an angle from which their eyes could meet. After a moment he bent over the unhappy girl, and as he kissed her on the forehead it gave him the same cool, pleasant sensation as Mary's face. He had hardly taken his lips off her forehead when he saw her move. He was paralyzed. She started to slip to one side, losing her balance, until she fell off the edge of the chair, dragging a spoon and a fork with her. The piano was still making sea noises, and the windows were still flashing and the machines rumbling. He did not want to pick her up and he blundered out of the case and the room, through the little parlor, into the courtyard. There he saw Alex and said:

"Tell Walter that's enough for today. And have the boys come in tomorrow to rearrange the doll in the second case."

At that moment Mary appeared:

"What's the matter?"

"Nothing: a doll fell—the one in the lighthouse . . ."

"How did it happen? Is she hurt?"

"I must have bumped into the table when I went in to look at her things . . ."

"Now let's not get upset, Horace!"

"On the contrary, I'm very happy with the scenes. But where's Daisy? I loved the way she looked in your dress!"

"You'd better go to bed, dear," answered Mary.

But instead they sat on a sofa, where he put his arms around her and asked her to rest her cheek on his for a moment, in silence. As their heads touched, his instantly lit up with memories of the two fallen dolls, Daisy and the girl in the lighthouse. He knew what this meant: the death of Mary. And, afraid his thoughts might pass into her head, he started to kiss her ears.

When he was alone again in the darkness of the bedroom, his mind throbbing with the noise of the machines, he thought of the warning signs he had been receiving. He was like a tangled wire that kept intercepting calls and portents meant for others. But this time all the signals had been aimed at him. Under the hum of the machines and the sound of the piano he had detected those other hidden noises scattering like mice. Then there had been Daisy falling into his arms when he opened the door to the little parlor, as if to say: "Hold me, for Mary is dying." And it was Mary herself who had prepared the warning, as innocently as if she were showing him a disease she did not yet know she had. Just before, there had been the dead doll in the first case. Then, when he was on his way to the second case, the unprogrammed rumble of the podium, like distant thunder, announcing the sea and the woman in the lighthouse. Finally, the woman slipping out from under him, falling off her chair, condemned to be childless, like Mary. And, meantime, Walter, like a bird of ill omen, with his flapping coattails, pecking away at the edge of his black box.

II

Mary was not ill and there was no reason to think she was going to die. But for some time now he had been afraid of losing her and dreading what he imagined would be his unhappiness without her. So one day he had decided to have a doll made to resemble her. At first the result had been disappointing: he had felt only dislike for Daisy, as for a poor substitute. She was made of kidskin that attempted to imitate Mary's coloring and had been perfumed with Mary's favorite scents, yet whenever Mary asked him to kiss her he expected to taste leather and had the feeling he was about to kiss a shoe. But in time he had begun to notice a strange relationship developing between Daisy and Mary. One morning he saw Mary singing while she dressed Daisy: she was like a girl playing with a doll. Another time, when he got home in the evening, he found Mary and Daisy seated at a table with a book in front of them. He had the feeling Mary was teaching a sister to read, and said:

"It must be such a relief to confide in someone who can keep a secret!"

"What do you mean?" said Mary, springing up and storming out of the room.

But Daisy, left behind, held firmly in place, tipped over the book, like a friend maintaining a tactful silence.

That same night, after dinner, to prevent him from joining her on their customary sofa, Mary sat the doll next to her. He examined Daisy's face and disliked it once more. It was cold and haughty, as if to punish him for his hateful thoughts about her skin.

A bit later, he went into the show room. At first he strolled back and forth among the glass cases. Then, after a while, he opened the big piano top, removed the bench, replaced it with a chair—so he could lean back—and started to walk his fingers over the cool expanse of black and white keys. He had trouble combining the sounds, like a drunk trying to unscramble his words. But meantime he was remembering many of the things he had learned about the dolls. Slowly he had been getting to know them, almost without trying. Until recently, Horace had kept the store that had been making his fortune. Alone, after closing time every day, he liked to wander through the shadowy rooms, reviewing the dolls in the show windows. He went over their dresses, with an occasional sidelong glance at their faces. He observed the lighted windows from various angles, like a stage manager watching his actors from the wings. Gradually he started finding expressions in the dolls' faces similar to those of his salesgirls. Some inspired the same distrust in him, others the certainty that they were against him. There was one with a turned-up nose that seemed to say, "See if I care." Another, which he found appealing, had an inscrutable face: just as she looked good in either a summer or a winter dress, she could also be thinking almost anything, accepting or rejecting him, depending on her mood. One way or another, the dolls had their secrets. Although the window dresser knew how to display each of them to her best advantage, at the last moment she always added a touch of her own. It was then that he started to think the dolls were full of portents. Day and night they basked in covetous looks and those looks nested and hatched in the air. Sometimes they settled on the doll's faces like clouds over a landscape, shadowing and blurring their expressions, and at other times they reflected back on some poor girl innocently happening by, who was tainted by their original covetousness. Then the dolls were like creatures in a trance, on unknown missions, or lending themselves to evil designs. On the night of his quarrel with Mary, Horace had reached the conclusion that Daisy was one of those changeable dolls who could transmit warnings or receive signals from other dolls. Since she lived in the house, Mary had been showing increasing signs of jealousy. If he complimented one of his salesgirls, he felt Mary's suspicion and reproach in Daisy's brooding look. That was when Mary had started nagging him until she got him to give up the store. But soon her fits of jealousy, after an evening in mixed company, had reached the point where he had also had to give up visiting friends with her.

On the morning after the quarrel he had made up with both of them. His dark thoughts bloomed at night and faded in the daytime. As usual, the three of them had gone for a walk in the garden. He and Mary carried Daisy between them—in a long skirt, to disguise her missing steps—as if gently supporting a sick friend. (Which had not prevented the neighbors from concocting a story about how they had let a sister of Mary's die so as to inherit her money, and then, to atone for the sin, had taken in a doll who resembled her, as a constant reminder of their crime.)

After a period of happiness, during which Mary prepared surprises for him with Daisy and he hastened to enter them in his notebook, had come the night of the second show, with its announcement of Mary's death.

Horace had then hit on the idea of buying his wife a number of dresses made of durable material—he intended these memories of her to last a long time—and asking her to try them on Daisy.

Mary was delighted, and he also pretended to be, when, at her urging—but in response to his subtle hints—they had some of their closest friends to dinner one night. It was stormy out, but they sat down to eat in a good mood. He kept thinking of all the memories the evening was going to leave him with and tried to provoke some unusual situations. First he twirled his knife and fork—like a cowboy with a pair of six-shooters—and aimed them at a girl next to him. She went along with the joke and raised her arms, and he tickled her shaved armpits with the knife. It was too much for Mary, who burst out:

"Horace, you're being a brat!"

He apologized all around and soon everyone was having fun again. But when he was serving his wine from France, over dessert, Mary saw a black stain—the wine he was pouring outside the glass—growing on the tablecloth, and, trying to rise, clutching at her throat, she fainted. They carried her into the bedroom, and, when she recovered, she said she had not been feeling well for days. He sent at once for the doctor, who said it was nothing serious but she had to watch her nerves. She got up and saw off her guests as if nothing had happened. But, as soon as they were alone, she said:

"I can't stand this life any more. You were messing with that girl right under my nose."

"But, my dear . . . "

"And I don't just mean the wine you spilled gaping at her. What were you up to in the yard afterward when she said, 'Horace, stop it'?"

"But, darling, all she said was 'a boring topic.'"

They made up in bed and she fell asleep with her cheek next to his. But, after a while, he turned away to think about her illness. And the next morning, when he touched her arm, it was cold. He lay still, gazing at the ceiling for several grueling minutes before he managed to shout: "Alex!" At that moment the door opened and Mary stuck her head in—

and he realized it was Daisy he had touched and that Mary had put her there, next to him, while he slept.

After much reflection, he decided to call his friend, Frank, the doll manufacturer, and ask him to find a way to give Daisy some human warmth.

Frank said:

"I'm afraid it's not so easy, dear boy. The warmth would last about as long as a hot-water bottle."

"All right, I don't care. Do what you want, just don't tell me. I'd also like her to be softer, nicer to touch, not so stiff . . . "

"I don't know about that, either. Think of the dent you'd make every time you sank a finger in her."

"Well, all the same, she could be more pliant. And, as for the dent— that might not be such a bad idea."

The day Frank took Daisy away, Horace and Mary were sad.

"God knows what they'll do to her," Mary kept saying.

"Now then, darling, let's not lose touch with reality. After all, she was only a doll."

"Was! You sound as if she were dead. Anyway, you're a fine one to talk about losing touch with reality!"

"I was just trying to comfort you . . . "

"And you think dismissing her like that is the way to do it? She was more mine than yours. I dressed her and told her things I've never told anyone, do you realize? And how she brought us together—have you ever thought of that?"

He was heading for his study, but she went on, raising her voice:

"Weren't you getting what you wanted with our surprises? Wasn't that enough, without asking for 'human warmth'?"

By then he had reached the study and slammed the door behind him. The way she pronounced "human warmth" not only made him feel ridiculous but soured all the pleasures he was looking forward to when Daisy returned. He decided to go for a walk.

When he got back, Mary was out, and when she returned they spent a while hiding the fact that they were unexpectedly glad to see each other.

That night he did not visit his dolls. The next morning he was busy. After lunch he and Mary strolled in the garden. They agreed that Daisy's absence was temporary and should not be made too much of. He even thought it was easier and more natural to have his arm around Mary instead of Daisy. They both felt light and gay and enjoyed being together.

But later, at dinnertime, when he went up to the bedroom for her, he was surprised to find her there alone. He had forgotten for a moment that Daisy was gone, and now her absence made him strangely uneasy. Mary might well be a woman without a doll again, but his idea of her was no longer complete without Daisy, and the fact that neither she nor the house seemed to miss Daisy was like a kind of madness. Also, the way Mary drifted back and forth in the room, apparently not thinking of Daisy, and the blankness for her expression, reminded him of a mad-woman forgetting to dress and wandering naked. They went down to dinner, and there, sipping his wine from France, he stared at her in silence, until finally it seemed he caught her with Daisy on her mind. Then he began to go over what the two women meant to each other. Whenever he thought of Mary, he remembered her fussing over Daisy, worrying about how to get her to sit straight without sagging, and plan-ning to surprise him with her. If Mary did not play the piano—as Frank's girlfriend did—it was because she expressed herself in her own original manner through Daisy. To strip her of Daisy would be like stripping an artist of his art. Daisy was not only part of her being but her most charm-ing self, so that he wondered how he ever could have loved her before she had Daisy. Perhaps in those days she had found other means or ways to express that side of her personality. Alone in the bedroom, a while back, without Daisy, she had seemed insignificant. Yet—Horace took another sip of his wine from France—there was something disquieting about her insignificance, as if Daisy had still been there, but only as an obstacle she had put up for him to trip over on his way to her.

After dinner he kissed Mary's cool cheek and went in to look at his glass cases. One of them showed a Carnival scene. Two masked dolls, a blonde and a brunette, in Spanish costumes, leaned over a marble balustrade. To the left was a staircase with masks, hoods, paper stream-ers and other objects scattered on the steps with artful neglect. The scene was dimly lit—and suddenly, watching the brunette, Horace thought he recognized Daisy. He wondered whether she had been ready sooner than expected and Mary had sent for her as a surprise. Without looking again, he opened the glass door. On his way up the staircase he stepped on a mask, which he picked up and threw over the balustrade. The gesture gave the objects around him physical reality and he felt let down. He moved to the podium, irritated because the noise of the machines and the sound of the piano did not blend. But after a few sec-onds he turned to the dolls again and decided they were probably two women who loved the same man. He opened the drawer and read the caption: "The blonde has a boyfriend. He discovered, some time ago, that he preferred her friend, the brunette, and declared his love to her. She was also secretly in love with him but tried to talk him out of it. He persisted, and, earlier on this Carnival night, he has told the blonde about her rival. Now the two girls have just met for the first time since they both learned the truth. They haven't spoken yet as they stand there in a long silence, wearing their disguises." At last he had guessed the meaning of one of the scenes: the two girls in love with the same man. But then he wondered whether the coincidence was not a portent or sign of something that was already going on in his own life and whether he might not really be in love with Daisy. His mind flitted around the question, touching down on other questions: What was it about Daisy that could have made him fall in love with her? Did the dolls perhaps give him something more than a purely artistic pleasure? Was Daisy really just a consolation in case his wife died? And for how long would she lend herself to a misunderstanding that was always in Mary's favor? The time had come to reconsider their roles and personalities. He did not want to take these worries up to the bedroom where Mary would be waiting for him, so he called Alex, had him dismiss Walter, then sent him for a bottle of wine from France and sat for a while, alone with the noise of the machines. Then he walked up and down the room, smoking. Each time he came to the glass case he drank some wine and set out again, thinking: "If there are spirits that inhabit empty houses, why wouldn't they also inhabit the bodies of dolls?" He thought of haunted castles full of spooked objects and furnishings joined in a heavy sleep, under thick cobwebs, where only ghosts and spirits roam, in concert with whistling bats and sighing marshes . . . At that moment he was struck by the noise of the machines and he dropped his glass. His hair stood on end as it dawned on him that disembodied souls caught the stray sounds of the world, which spoke through them, and that the soul inhabiting Daisy's body was in touch with the machines. To shake off these thoughts he concentrated on the chills going up and down his spine. But, when he had settled in his armchair, his thoughts ran on: no wonder such strange things had happened on a recent moonlit night. They were out in the garden, all three of them, and suddenly he started chasing his wife. She ran, laughing, to hide behind Daisy—which, as he well realized, was not the same as hiding behind a tree—and when he tried to kiss her over Daisy's shoulder he felt a sharp pinprick. Almost at once he heard the machines pounding, no doubt to warn him against kissing Mary through Daisy. Mary had no idea how she could have left a pin in the doll's dress. And how—he asked himself—could he have been so foolish as to think Daisy was there to grace and adorn Mary, when in fact they were meant to grace and adorn each other? Now, coming back to the noise of the machines, he confirmed what he had been suspecting all along: that it had a life of its own, like the sound of the piano, although they belonged to different families. The noise of the machines was of a noble family, which was perhaps why Daisy had chosen it to express her true love. On that thought he phoned Frank to ask after Daisy. Frank said she was nearly ready, that the girls in the workshop had found a way to . . . But at this point Horace cut him off, saying he was not interested in technical details. And, hanging up, he felt secretly pleased at the thought of girls working on Daisy, putting something of themselves into her.

The next day, at lunchtime, Mary was waiting for him with an arm around Daisy's waist. After kissing his wife, he took the doll in his arms, and for a moment her soft warm body gave him the happiness he had been hoping for, although when he pressed his lips to hers, she seemed feverish. But he soon grew accustomed to this new sensation and found it comforting.

That same night, over dinner, he wondered: "Why must the transmigration of souls take place only between people and animals? Aren't there cases of people on their deathbed who have handed their souls over to some beloved object? And why assume it's a mistake when a spirit hides in a doll who looks like a beautiful woman? Couldn't it be that, looking for a new body to inhabit, it guided the hands that made the doll? When someone pursues an idea, doesn't he come up with unexpected discoveries, as if someone else were helping him?" Then he thought of Daisy and wondered whose spirit could be living in her body.

Mary had been in a vile mood since early evening. She had scolded Daisy while dressing her, because she would not hold still but kept tipping forward—and now that she was full of water, she was a lot heavier than before. Horace thought of the relationship between his wife and the doll and of the strange shades of enmity he had noticed between women who were such close friends that they could not get along without one another. He remembered observing that the same thing often happened between mother and daughter . . . A minute later, he raised his eyes from his plate and said:

"Tell me something, Mary. What was your mother like?"

"May I ask the reason for your question? Do you want to trace my defects to her?"

"Of course not, darling. I wouldn't think of it!"

He had spoken in a soothing voice, and she said:

"Well, I'll tell you. She was my complete opposite. Calm as a clear day. She could spend hours just sitting in a chair, staring into space."

"Perfect," he said to himself. Although, after pouring himself a glass of wine, he thought: "On the other hand, I can't very well have an affair with the spirit of my mother-in-law in Daisy's body."

"And what were her ideas on love?"

"Do you find mine inadequate?"

"Mary, please!"

"She had none, lucky for her. Which was why she was able to marry my father to please my grandparents. He was wealthy. And she made him a fine wife."

Horace, relieved, thought: "Well, that's that. One thing less to worry about."

Although it was spring, the night turned cold. Mary refilled Daisy, dressed her in a silk nightie and took her to bed with them, like a hot water bottle. As he dropped off to sleep, Horace felt himself sinking into a warm pond where all their legs tangled, like the roots of trees planted so close together he was too lazy to find out which ones belonged to him.

III

Horace and Mary were planning a birthday party for Daisy. She was going to be two years old. Horace wanted to present her on a tricycle. He told Mary he had seen one at the Transportation Day fair and he was sure they would let him have it. He did not tell her the reason for using this particular device was that he had seen a bride elope with her lover on a tricycle in a film years ago. The rehearsals were a success. At first he had trouble getting the tricycle going, but as soon as the big front wheel turned it grew wings.

The party opened with a buffet dinner. Soon the sounds from human throats and necks of bottles mixed in an increasingly loud murmur. When it was time to present Daisy, Horace rang a school bell in the courtyard and the guests went out holding their glasses. They saw him come tearing down a long carpeted hallway, struggling with the front wheel. At first the tricycle was almost invisible beneath him. Of Daisy, mounted behind him, only her flowing white dress showed. He seemed to be riding the air, on a cloud. Daisy was propped over the axle that joined the small back wheels, with her arms thrust forward and her hands in his trouser pockets. The tricycle came to a stop in the center of the courtyard, and, acknowledging the cheers and applause, he reached over with one hand and stroked her hair. Then he began pedaling hard again, and as the tricycle sailed back up the carpeted hallway, gathering speed, everyone watched in breathless silence, as if it were about to take flight. The performance was such a success that Horace tried to repeat it, and the laughter and applause were starting up again when suddenly, just as he reached the yard, he lost a back wheel. There were cries of alarm, but when he showed he was not hurt there was more laughter and applause. He had fallen on his back, on top of Daisy, and was kicking his legs in the air like an insect. The guests laughed until they cried. Frank gasped and spluttered:

"Boy, you looked like one of those wind-up toys that go on walking upside down!"

Then they all went back into the dining room. The men who arranged the scenes in the glass cases surrounded Horace, asking to borrow Daisy and the tricycle to make up a story with them. He turned them down, but he was so pleased with himself that he invited everybody into the show room for a glass of wine from France.

"If you wouldn't mind telling us what you feel watching the scenes," said one of the boys, "I think we could all learn something."

He had started to rock back and forth on his heels, staring at his guests' shoes. Finally he made up his mind and said:

"It's very difficult to put into words, but I'll try . . . if you promise meantime to ask no more questions and to be satisfied with anything I care to say."

"Promised!" said one who was a bit hard of hearing, cupping a hand to his ear.

Still, Horace took his time, clasping and unclasping his hands. To quiet the hands, he crossed his arms and began:

"When I look at a scene . . . " Here he stopped, then took up the speech again, with a digression: "(It's very important to see the dolls through a glass, because that gives them the quality of memories. Before, when I could stand mirrors—now they're bad for me, but it would take too long to explain why—I liked to see the rooms that appeared in them.) So . . . when I look at a scene, it's like catching a woman in the act of remembering an important moment in her life, a bit—if you'll forgive the expression—as if I were opening a crack in her skull. When I get hold of the memory, it's like stealing one of her undergarments: I can use it to imagine the most intimate things and I might even say it feels like a defilement. In a way, it's as if the memory were in a dead person and I were picking a corpse, hoping the memory will stir

in it . . . " He let his voice trail off, not daring to describe the weird stirring he had seen.

The boys were also silent. One of them thought of emptying his glass
of wine at a swallow and the others imitated him. Then another said:

"Tell us something more about yourself—your personal tastes,
habits, whatever."

"Ah, as for that," said Horace, "I don't think it would be of any help
to you in making up your scenes. For instance, I like to walk on a
wooden floor sprinkled with sugar. It's that neat little sound . . . "

Just then Mary came in to ask them all out into the garden. It was a
dark night and the guests were requested to form couples and carry
torches. Mary took Horace's arm and together they showed the way. At the
door that led into the garden, each guest picked a small torch from a table
and lit it at a flaming bowl on another table. The torchlight attracted the
neighbors, who gathered at the low hedge, their faces like shiny fruit with
watchful eyes among the bushes, glinting with distrust. Suddenly Mary
crossed a flowerbed, flicked a switch, and Daisy appeared, lit up in the
high branches of a tall tree. It was one of Mary's surprises and was greeted
with cheers and exclamations. Daisy was holding a white fan spread on
her breast. A light behind the fan gave her face a theatrical glow. Horace
kissed Mary and thanked her for the surprise. Then, as the guests scattered, he saw Daisy staring out toward the street he took on his way home
every day. Mary was leading him along the hedge when they heard one of
the neighbors shout at others still some distance away, "Hurry! The dead
woman's appeared in a tree!" They staggered back to the house, where
everyone was toasting the surprise. Mary had the twins—her maids, who
were sisters—get Daisy down from the tree and change her water for bed.

About an hour had gone by since their return from the garden when
Mary started looking around for Horace and found him back in the
show room with the boys. She was pale, and everyone realized something serious had happened. She had the boys excuse Horace and led
him up to the bedroom. There he found Daisy with a knife stuck under
one breast. The wound was leaking hot water down her dress, which
was soaked, and dripping on the floor. She was in her usual chair, with
big open eyes. But when Mary touched her arm she felt it going cold.

Collapsing into Horace's arms, Mary burst out crying:

"Who could have dared to come up here and do such a thing?"

After a while she calmed down and sat in a chair to think what was
to be done. Then she said:

"I'm going to call the police."

"You're out of your mind," he said. "We can't offend all our guests just because one of them misbehaved. And what will you tell the police? That someone stuck a knife in a doll and that she's leaking? Let's keep this to ourselves. One has to accept setbacks with dignity. We'll send her in for repairs and forget about it."

"Not if I can help it," said Mary. "I'm going to call a private detective. Don't let anyone touch her—the fingerprints must be on the knife."

Horace tried to reason with her, reminding her the guests were waiting downstairs. They agreed to lock the doll in, as she was. But, the moment Mary had left the room, he took out his handkerchief, soaked it in bleach, and wiped off the handle of the knife.

IV

Horace had managed to convince Mary to say nothing about the wounded doll. The day Frank came for her, he brought his mistress, Louise. She and Mary went into the dining room, where their voices soon mixed like twittering birds in connecting cages: they were used to talking and listening at the same time.

Meantime, Horace and Frank shut themselves in the study. They spoke one at a time, in undertones, as if taking turns at drinking from a jug.

Horace said, "I was the one who stuck the knife in her so I'd have an excuse to send her in to you . . . without going into explanations." And they stood there in silence, with their heads bowed.

Mary was curious to know what they were discussing. Deserting Louise for a minute, she went to put her ear to the study door. She thought he recognized her husband's voice, but it sounded hoarse and blurred. (At that moment, still mumbling into his chin, Horace was saying, "It may be crazy, but I've heard of sculptors falling in love with their statues.") In a while, Mary went back to listen again, but she could only make out the word "possible," pronounced first by her husband, then by Frank. (In fact, Horace had just said: "It must be possible," and Frank had answered, "If it's possible, I'll do it.")

One afternoon, a few days later, Mary realized Horace was acting strangely. He would linger over her, with fond eyes, then abruptly draw back, looking worried. As he crossed the courtyard at one point, she called after him, went out to meet him and, putting her arms around his neck, said:

"Horace, you can't fool me. I know what's on your mind."

"What?" he said, staring wildly.

"It's Daisy."

He turned pale:

"Whatever gave you that idea?"

He was surprised that she did not laugh at his odd tone.

"Oh, come on, darling . . . After all, she's like a daughter to us by now," Mary insisted.

He let his eyes dwell on her face, and with them his thoughts, going over each of her features as if reviewing every corner of a place he had visited daily through many long happy years. Then, breaking away, he went and sat in the little parlor to think about what had just happened. His first reaction, when he suspected his wife had found him out, had been to assume she would forgive him. But then, observing her smile, he had realized it was madness to suppose she could imagine, let alone forgive, such a sin. Her face had been like a peaceful landscape, with a bit of golden evening glow on one cheek, the other shaded by the small mound of her nose. He had thought of all the good left in the innocence of the world and the habit of love, and the tenderness with which he always came back to her face after his adventures with the dolls. But in time, when she discovered not only the abysmal nature of his more than fatherly affection for Daisy but also the care with which he had gone about organizing his betrayal, her face and all its features would be devastated. She would never be able to understand the sudden evil in the world and in the habit of love, or feel anything but horror at the sight of him.

So he had stood there, gazing at a spot of sun on his coat sleeve. As he withdrew his arm, the spot had shifted, like a taint, to her dress. Then, heading for the little parlor, he had felt his twisted insides lump and sag, like dead weights. Now he sat on a small bench, thinking he was unworthy of being received into the lap of a family armchair, and he felt as uncomfortable as if he had sat on a child. He hardly recognized the stranger in himself, disillusioned at being made of such base metal. But, to his surprise, a bit later, in bed with the covers pulled up over his ears, he went straight to sleep.

Mary was on the phone to Frank, saying:

"Listen, Frank, you'd better hurry with Daisy. Horace is worrying himself sick."

Frank said:

"I have to tell you, Mary, it's a bad wound, right in the middle of the circulatory system. We can't rush it. But I'll do my best, I promise."

In a while, Horace woke up under his pile of blankets. He found himself blinking down a kind of slope, toward the foot of the bed, and saw a picture of his parents on the far wall. They had died in an epidemic when he was a child. He felt they had cheated him: he was like a chest they had left full of dirty rags instead of riches, fleeing like thieves in the dark before he could grow up and expose the fraud. But then he was ashamed of these monstrous thoughts.

At dinner, he tried to be on his best behavior.

Mary said:

"I called Frank about hurrying Daisy."

If only she had known the madness and betrayal she was contributing to by hastening his pleasure! he thought, blindly casting right and left, like a horse trying to butt its way out.

"Looking for something?" asked Mary.

"No, here it is," he said, reaching for the mustard.

She decided that if he had not seen it standing there in front of him, he must not be well.

Afterward he got up and slowly bent over her, until his lips grazed her cheek. The kiss seemed to have dropped by parachute, onto a plain not yet touched by grief.

That night, in the first glass case, there was a doll seated on a lawn, surrounded by huge sponges, which she seemed to think were flowers. He did not feel like guessing her fate, so he opened the drawer with the captions and read: "This woman is sick in the head. No one has been able to find out why she loves sponges." "That's what I pay them for, to find out," he said to himself, and then, bitterly: "The sponges must be to wipe away her guilt."

In the morning he woke up rolled into a ball and remembered the person he had become. It seemed to him even his name had changed, and if he signed a check it would bounce. His body was sad, as it had been once before, when a doctor told him he had thin blood and a small heart. But that other time he had gotten over the sadness. Now he stretched his legs and thought: "Formerly, when I was young, I had far stronger defenses against guilt: I cared much less about hurting others. Am I getting weak with age? No, it's more like a late flowering of love and shame." He got up, feeling better. But he knew the dark clouds of guilt were just over the horizon, and that they would be back with night.

V

The next days, Mary took Horace for long walks. She wanted to get his mind off Daisy. Yet she was convinced it was not Daisy he missed but the real daughter she could never have.

The afternoon Daisy was returned, Horace did not show any particular affection for her, and again Mary feared she was not the reason for his sadness. But, just before dinner, she noticed him lingering over Daisy with restrained emotion, and felt relieved.

After that, for several nights, as he kissed his wife before going in to see his dolls, he watched her face intently, with searching eyes, as if to make sure there was nothing strange hidden anywhere. He had not yet been alone with Daisy.

Then came a memorable afternoon when, in spite of the mild weather, Mary replenished Daisy's hot water, packed Horace comfortably into bed with her for his nap, and went out.

That evening he kept scanning every inch of her face, watching for the enemy she would soon become. She noticed his fidgety gestures, his stilted walk. He was waiting for the sign that he had been found out.

Finally, one morning, it happened.

Once, some time ago, when Mary had been complaining of Alex's beard, Horace had said: "At least he's not like one of those twin maids of yours that you can't tell apart."

She had answered: "Why, do you have anything special to say to either of them? Has there been some mix-up that has . . . inconvenienced you?"

"Yes, I was calling you once—and who do you think turned up? The one who has the honor to bear your name."

After which the twins had been ordered to stay out of sight when he was home. But, seeing one vanish through a door once at his approach, he had plunged after her, thinking she was an intruder, and run into his wife. Since then Mary had them come in only a few hours in the morning and never took her eyes off them.

The day he was found out, Mary had caught the twins raising Daisy's nightie when it was not time to dress her or change her water. As soon as they had left the bedroom, she went in. In a little while the twins saw the lady of the house rush across the courtyard into the kitchen. On her way back she was carrying a carving knife. They were terrified and tried to follow her, but she slammed the door on them. When they peeped through the keyhole her back blocked their view, so they moved to another door. She had Daisy flat on a table, as if to operate on her, and was in a frenzy, stabbing her all over. She looked completely disheveled: a jet of water had caught her in the face. Two thin spurts rose in an arc from one of Daisy's shoulders, mixing in the air, like the water from the fountain in the garden, and her belly gushed through a rip in her nightgown. One of the twins had knelt on a cushion, with a hand over one eye, the other eye stuck, unblinking, to the keyhole. When the draft that blew through the hole made her eye run, her sister took her place. Mary also had tears in her eyes when she finally dropped the knife on Daisy and slumped into an armchair, sobbing, with her face buried in her hands. The twins lost interest in the scene and returned to the kitchen. But soon the lady called them back up to help her pack. She had decided to handle the situation with the wounded dignity of a fallen queen. Determined to punish Horace and, meantime, to adopt the appropriate attitude in case he showed up, she instructed the twins to say she could not receive him. She began making arrangements for a long trip and gave the twins some of her dresses. They followed her out into the garden, and when she drove off in the family car they finally realized what was happening and started to howl over the lady's misfortune. But, back in the house with their new dresses, they were gleeful. They drew open the curtains that covered the mirrors—to spare Horace the unpleasantness of seeing himself in them—and held the dresses up to their bodies for effect. One of them saw Daisy's mangled shape in a mirror and said: "What a beast!" She meant Horace, who had just appeared in a door and was wondering how to ask them to explain the dresses and the bare mirrors. But, suddenly catching sight of Daisy sprawled on the table in her torn nightie, he directed his steps toward her. The twins were trying to sneak out of the room, but he stopped them:

"Where's my wife?"

The one who had said "What a beast!" stared him full in the face and answered:

"She left on a long trip. And she gave us these dresses."

He dismissed them and the thought came to him: "The worst is over." He glanced at Daisy again: the carving knife still lay across her belly. He was not too unhappy and for a moment even imagined having her repaired. But he pictured her all stitched up and remembered a rag horse he had owned as a child, with a hole ripped in it. His mother had wanted to patch it up, but it had lost its appeal and he had preferred to throw it away.

As for Mary, he was convinced she would come back. He kept telling himself: "I have to take things calmly." He welcomed the return of the bold and callous self he had been in his prime. Looking back over the morning's events, he could easily see himself betraying Daisy as well. A few days ago Frank had shown him another doll: a gorgeous blonde with a shady past. Frank had been spreading word of a manufacturer in a northern country who made these new dolls. He had imported the designs and—after some experimenting—found them workable. Soon a little shy man had come by, with big pouchy eyes gleaming under heavy lids, to inquire about the dolls. Frank had brought out pictures of the available models, saying: "Their generic name is Daisy, but then each owner gives them whatever pet name he wants. These are the models we have designs for." After seeing only three of them the little shy man had picked one almost at random and put in an order for her, cash in hand. Frank had quoted a stiff sum, and the buyer had batted his heavy lids once or twice, but then he had signed the order, with a pen shaped like a submarine. Horace had seen the finished blonde and asked Frank to hold her for him, and Frank, who had others on the way, had agreed. At first Horace had considered setting her up in an apartment, but now he had a better idea: he would bring her home and leave her in the glass case where he kept the dolls waiting to be assigned their roles. As soon as everyone was asleep he would carry her up to the bedroom, and before anyone was up in the morning he would put her back in the glass case. He was counting on Mary not returning in the middle of the night. From the moment Frank had set the doll apart for him, he had felt himself riding a lucky streak he had not known since adolescence. Just happening to have been out until it was all over with Daisy meant a higher power was on his side. With this assurance, in addition to his new youthful vigor, he felt in command of events. Having decided to exchange one doll for another, he could not stop to shed tears over Daisy's mutilated body. Mary was certain to be back, now that he no longer cared about her, and she could dispose of the corpse.

Suddenly Horace started to edge along the wall like a thief. Sidling up to a wardrobe, he drew the curtain across the mirror. He repeated the gesture at the other wardrobe. He had had the curtains hung years ago. Mary was always careful to shield him from the mirrors: she dressed behind closed doors and made sure the curtains were in place before leaving the room. Now he was annoyed to think the twins had not only been wearing Mary's clothes but had left the mirrors uncovered. It was not that he disliked seeing things in mirrors, but his sallow face reminded him of some wax dolls he had seen in a museum one afternoon. A shopkeeper had been murdered that day, as had many of the people whose bodies the dolls represented, and the bloodstains on the wax were as unpleasant to him as if, after being stabbed to death, he had been able to see the wounds that had killed him. The only mirror in the bedroom without a curtain was the one over the dresser: a low mirror before which he bent just far enough for a quick glimpse at the knot of his tie as he went by absently each day. Because he combed and shaved by touch, from the mirror's point of view he had always been a man with no head. So now, after covering the other mirrors, he went by it as blithely as usual. But when it reflected his hand against his dark suit he had the same queasy sensation as when he caught sight of his face. He realized then that his hands were also the color of wax. At the same time, he remembered some loose arms he had seen in Frank's office that morning. They were pleasantly colored and as shapely as those of the blonde doll, and, like a child asking a carpenter for scraps, he had told Frank:

"I could use some arms and legs, if you have any left over."

"Whatever for, dear boy?"

"I'd like the men to make up some scenes with loose arms and legs. For instance, an arm hanging from a mirror, a leg sticking out from under a bed, and so on."

Frank, wiping his face, had watched him askance.

At lunch that day, Horace drank his wine and ate as calmly as if Mary were out spending the day with relatives. He kept congratulating himself over his good luck. He got up feeling elated, sat at the piano for a while, letting his fingers wander over the keys, and finally went up for his nap. On his way past the dresser he thought: "One of these days I'll get over my dread of mirrors and face them." He had always enjoyed being surprised and confused by the people and objects reflected in mirrors. With another glance at Daisy, who would simply have to wait until Mary got back, he lay down. As he stretched out under the covers, he touched a strange object with the tip of his foot, and he jumped out of bed. For a moment he just stood there, then he pulled back the covers. It was a note from Mary that said: "Horace, here's what's left of your mistress. I've stabbed her, too. But I can admit it—not like a certain hypocrite I know who only wanted a pretext to send her in and have those sinful things done to her. You've sickened my life and I'll thank you not to look for me. Mary."

He went back to bed but could not sleep and got up again. He avoided looking at Mary's things on the dresser as he avoided her face when they were angry at each other. He went out to a movie. There he shook hands with an old enemy, without realizing it. He kept thinking of Mary.

When he got back to the black house, there was still a bit of sunlight shining in the bedroom. As he went by one of the covered mirrors, he saw his face in it, through the wispy curtain, lit by a glint of sun, bright as an apparition. With a shiver, he closed the shutters and lay down. If the luck he used to have was coming back, at his age it would not last long, nor would it come alone but accompanied by the sorts of strange events that had been taking place since Daisy's arrival. She still lay there, a few feet away. At least, he thought, her body would not rot. And then he wondered about the spirit that had once inhabited that body like a stranger and whether it might not have provoked Mary's destructive fury so that Daisy's corpse, placed between him and Mary, would keep him away from her. The ghostly shapes of the room disturbed his sleep: they seemed to be in touch with the noise of the machines. He got up, went down to dinner and began to drink his wine. He had not known until then how much he missed Mary—and there was no after-dinner kiss before he headed for the little parlor. Alone there with his coffee, he decided he ought to avoid the bedroom and dinner table while Mary was gone. When he went out for a walk a bit later he remembered seeing a student hotel in a neighborhood nearby, and found his way there. It had a potted palm in the doorway and parallel mirrors all the way up the stairs, and he walked on. The sight of so many mirrors in a single day was a dangerous sign. He remembered what he had told Frank that morning, before encountering the ones in the bedroom: that he wanted to see an arm hanging from a mirror. But he also remembered the blonde doll and decided, once again, to overcome his dread. He made his way back to the hotel, brushed past the potted palm, and tried to climb the stairs without looking at himself in the mirrors. It was a long time since he had seen so many at once, wherever he turned, right and left, with their confusion of images. He even thought there might be someone hidden among the reflections. The lady who ran the place met him upstairs and showed him the vacant rooms: they all had huge mirrors. He chose the best and promised to return in an hour. In his dark house he packed a small suitcase, and on his way back to the hotel he remembered that it had once been a brothel—which explained the mirrors. There were three in the room he had chosen, the largest one next to the bed, and since the room that appeared there was prettier than the real one, he kept his eyes on the one in the mirror, which must have been tired of showing the same mock-Chinese scenery over the years, because the gaudy red wallpaper looked faded, as if sunk in the bottom of a misty lake with its yellowish bridges and cherry trees. He got into bed and put out the light, but he went on seeing the room in the glow that came in from the street. He had the feeling he had been taken into the bosom of a poor family, where all the household objects were friends and had aged together. But the windows were still young and looked out: they were twins, like Mary's maids, and dressed alike, in clinging lace curtains and velvet drapes gathered at the sides. It was all a bit as if he were living in someone else's body, borrowing well-being from it. The loud silence made his ears hum, and he realized he was missing the noise of the machines and wondered whether it might not be a good idea to move out of the black house and never hear its sounds again. If only Mary had been lying next to him now, he would have been perfectly happy. As soon as she came back he would invite her to spend a night with him in the hotel. But then he dozed off thinking of the blonde doll he had seen that morning. He dreamed of a white arm floating in a dark haze. The sound of steps in a neighboring room woke him up. He got out of bed, barefoot, and started across the rug. He saw a white spot following him and recognized his face, reflected in the mirror over the fireplace. He wished someone would invent a mirror that showed objects but not people, although he immediately realized the absurdity of the idea, not to mention the fact that a man without an image in the mirror would not be of this world. He lay down again, just as someone turned on a light in a room across the street. The light fell on the mirror by the bed, and he thought of his childhood and of other mirrors he remembered, and went to sleep.

VI

Several days had gone by. Horace now slept in the hotel and the same pattern of events repeated itself every night: windows went on across the street and the light fell on his mirrors, or else he woke up and found the windows asleep.

One night he heard screams and saw flames in his mirror. At first he watched them as if they were flickers on a movie screen, but then he realized that if they showed in the mirror they must be somewhere in reality, and, springing up and swinging around, all at once, he saw them dancing out a window across the street, like devils in a puppet show. He scrambled out of bed, threw on his robe and put his face to one of his windows. As it caught flashes in its glass, his window seemed frightened at what was happening to the one across the street. There was a crowd below—he was on the second floor—and the firetruck was com-

ing. Just then, he saw Mary leaning out another window of the hotel.
She had already noticed him and was staring as if she did not quite recognize him. He waved, shut his window and went up the hall to rap on
what he figured was her door. She burst right out saying:

"You're wasting your time following me."

And she slammed the door in his face.

He stayed there quietly until he heard her sobbing inside, then he
answered:

"I wasn't following you. But since we've met, why don't we go
home?"

"You go on if you want," she said.

He thought he had sensed a note of longing in her voice, in spite of
everything, and the next day he moved back happily into the black
house. There he basked in the luxury of his surroundings, wandering
like a sleepwalker among his riches. The familiar objects all seemed full
of peaceful memories, the high ceilings braced against death, if it
struck from above.

But when he went into the show room after dinner that evening, the
piano reminded him of a big coffin, the silence of a wake. It was a resonant silence, as if it were mourning the death of a musician. He raised
the top of the piano, and, suddenly, terrified, let it fall with a bang. For
a moment he stood there with his arms in the air, as if someone were
pointing a gun at him, but then he rushed out into the courtyard shouting:

"Who put Daisy in the piano?"

As his shouts echoed, he went on seeing her hair tangled in the
strings, her face flattened by the weight of the lid. One of the twins
answered his call but could not get a word out. Finally Alex appeared:

"The lady was in this afternoon. She came to get some clothes."

"These surprises of hers are killing me," Horace shouted, beside
himself. But suddenly he calmed down: "Take Daisy to your room and
have Frank come for her first thing in the morning. Wait!" he shouted
again. "Something else." And—after he had made sure the twins were
out of earshot—lowering his voice to a whisper: "Tell Frank he can
bring the other doll when he comes for her."

That night he moved to another hotel. He was given a room with a
single mirror. The yellow wallpaper had red flowers and green leaves
woven in a pattern that suggested a trellis. The bedspread was also yellow and irritated him with its glare: it would be like sleeping outdoors.

The next morning he went home and had some large mirrors brought into the showroom to multiply the scenes in the glass cases. The day passed with no word from Frank. That evening, as Alex came into the showroom with the wine, he dropped the bottle . . .

"Anything wrong?" Horace said.

He was wearing a mask and yellow gloves.

"I thought you were a bandit," said Alex as Horace's laugh blew billows in the black silk mask.

"It's hot behind this thing, and it won't let me drink my wine. But before I remove it I want you to take down the mirrors and stand them on the floor, leaning on chairs—like this," said Horace, taking one down and showing him.

"They'd be safer if you leaned the glass on the wall," Alex objected.

"No, because I still want them to reflect things."

"You could lean their backs on the wall then."

"No, because then they'd reflect upward and I have no interest in seeing my face."

When Alex had done as he was told, Horace removed his mask and began to sip his wine, pacing up and down a carpeted aisle in the center of the room. The way the mirrors tipped forward slightly, toward him, leaning on the chairs that separated them from him, made him think of them as bowing servants watching him from under their raised eyelids. They also reflected the floor through the legs of the chairs, making it seem crooked. After a couple of drinks he was bothered by this effect and decided to go to bed.

The following morning—he had slept at home that night—the chauffeur came, on Mary's behalf, to ask for money. He gave him the money without asking where she was, but assumed it meant she would not be back any time soon. So when the blonde arrived, he had her taken straight up to the bedroom. At dinnertime he had the twins dress her in an evening gown and bring her to the table. He ate with her sitting across from him. Afterward, in front of one of the twins, he asked Alex:

"Well, what do you think of this one?"

"A beauty, sir—very much like a spy I met during the war."

"A lovely thought, Alex."

The next day he told the twins:

"From now on you're to call her Miss Eulalie."

At dinnertime he asked the twins (who no longer hid from him):

"Can you tell me who's in the dining room?"

"Miss Eulalie," both twins said at once.

But, between themselves, making fun of Alex, they kept saying: "It's time to give the spy her hot water."

VII

Mary was waiting in the student hotel, hoping he would return there. She went out only long enough for her room to be made. She carried her head high around the neighborhood, but walked in a haze, oblivious to her surroundings, thinking, "I am a woman who has lost her man to a doll. But if he could see me now he would be drawn to me." Back in her room, she would open a book of poems bound in blue oilcloth and start to read aloud, in a rapt voice, waiting for Horace again. When he failed to show up, she would try to see into the poems, and if their meaning escaped her she abandoned herself to the thought that she was a martyr and that suffering would add to her charm. One afternoon she was able to understand a poem: it was as if someone had left a door open by chance, suddenly revealing what was inside. Then, for a moment, it seemed to her the wallpaper, the folding screen, even the washbowl with its nickel-plated taps also understood the poems, impelled by something in their nature to reach out toward the lofty rhythms and noble images. Often, in the middle of the night, she switched on her lamp and chose a poem as if she could choose a dream. Out walking again the next day in the neighborhood, she imagined her steps were poetry. And one morning she decided, "I would like Horace to know I'm walking alone among trees with a book in my hand."

Accordingly, she packed again, sent for her chauffeur and had him drive her out to a place belonging to a cousin of her mother's: it was in the outskirts and had trees. The cousin was an old maid who lived in an ancient house. When her huge bulk came heaving through the dim rooms, making the floor creak, a parrot squawked: "Hello, milksops!" Mary told Prairie of her troubles without shedding a tear. The fat cousin was horrified, then indignant, and finally tearful. But Mary calmly dispatched the chauffeur with instructions to get money from Horace. In case Horace asked after her, he was to say, as if on his own, that she was walking among trees with a book in her hand. If he wanted to know where she was, he should tell him. Finally, he was to report back at the same time the next day. Then she went and sat under a tree with her book, and the poems started to float out and spread through the countryside as if taking on the shapes of trees and drifting clouds.

At lunch Prairie was silent, but afterward she asked:

"What are you going to do with the monster?"

"Wait for him and forgive him."

"Not at all like you, my dear. This man has turned your head and has you on a string like one of his dolls."

Mary shut her eyes in beatific peace. But later that afternoon the cleaning woman came in with the previous day's evening paper and Mary's eyes strayed over a headline that said: "Frank's Daisy Dolls." She could not help reading the item: "Springwear, out smartest department store, will be presenting a new collection on its top floor. We understand some of the models sporting the latest fashions will be Daisy Dolls. And that Frank, the manufacturer of the famous line of dolls, has just become a partner in Springwear Enterprises. One more example of the alarming rate at which this new version of Original Sin—to which we have already referred in our columns—is spreading among us. Here is an example of a propaganda leaflet found at one of our main clubs: 'Are you homely? Don't worry. Shy? Forget it. No more quarrels. No budget-breaking expenses. No more gossip. There's a Daisy Doll for you, offering her silent love.'"

Mary had awakened in fits and starts:

"The nerve! To think he could use the name of our . . . !"

Still grasping for words, her eyes wide with outrage, she took aim and pointed at the offending spot in the paper:

"Prairie, look at this!"

The fat cousin blinked and rummaged in her sewing basket, searching for her glasses.

"Have you ever heard anything like it?" Mary said, reading her the item. "I'm not only going to get a divorce but kick up the biggest row this country has ever seen."

"Good for you, at last you've come down out of your cloud!" shouted Prairie, extricating her hands, which were raw from scrubbing pans. And, at the first chance she had, while Mary strode frantically up and down, tripping over innocent plants and flowerpots, she hid the book of poems from her.

The next day the chauffeur drove up wondering how to evade Mary's questions about Horace, but she only asked him for the money and then sent him back to the black house to fetch the twin called Mary. Mary—the twin—arrived in the afternoon and told her all about the spy they had to call Miss Eulalie. At first Mary—Horace's wife—was aghast. In a faint voice, she asked:

"Does she look like me?"

"No, Madam—she's blonde and she dresses differently."

Mary—Horace's wife—jumped up, but then dropped back into her armchair, crying at the top of her lungs. The fat cousin appeared and the twin repeated the story. Prairie's huge breasts heaved as she broke into pitiful moans, and the parrot joined the racket screeching:

"Hello, milksops!"

VIII

Walter was back from a vacation and Horace was having his nightly showings again. The first night, he had taken Eulalie into the show room with him, sat her next to him on the podium and kept his arms around her while he watched the other dolls. The boys had made up scenes with more important characters than usual. There were five in the second glass case, representing the board of a society for the protection of unwed mothers. One of them had just been elected president of the board; another, her beaten rival, was moping over her defeat. He liked the beaten rival best and left Eulalie for a moment to go and plant a kiss on her cool forehead. When he got back to the podium he listened for the buzz of the machines through the gaps in the music and recalled what Alex had told him about Eulalie's resemblance to a war spy. Nevertheless, he feasted his eyes greedily on the varied spectacle of the dolls that night. But the next day he woke up exhausted and toward evening he had dark thoughts of death. He dreaded not knowing when he would die, or what part of his body would go first. Every day it was harder for him to be alone. The dolls were no company but seemed to say, "Don't count on us—we're just dolls." Sometimes he whistled a tune, but only to hang from the thread of sound as if it were a thin rope that snapped the moment his attention wandered. Other times, he talked to himself aloud, stupidly commenting on what he was doing, "Now I'm in my study. I've come to get my inkpot." Or he described his actions as if he were watching someone else: "Look at him, poor idiot—there he is, opening a drawer, unstopping the inkpot. Let's see how long he has left." When his fear caught up with him, he went out.

Then, one day, he received a box from Frank. He had it pried open: it was full of arms and legs. He remembered asking Frank for discards and hoped the box did not include any loose heads, which would have unsettled him. He had it carried in to the glass cases where he kept the dolls waiting to be assigned their roles, and called the boys on the phone to explain how he wanted the arms and legs incorporated into the scenes. But the first trial angered him: it was a disaster. The moment he drew the curtain, he saw a doll dressed in mourning, seated at the foot of what looked like the steps of a church. She was staring straight ahead, with an incredible number of legs—at least ten or twelve—sticking out from under her skirt. On each step above her lay an arm with the palm of the hand turned up. "The clumsy fools," he said to himself. "They didn't have to use all the arms and legs at once." Without trying to figure out the meaning of the scene, he opened the drawer with the captions and read, "This is a poor widow who has nothing to eat. She spends her day begging and has laid out hands like traps to catch alms." "What a dumb idea," he went on mumbling to himself. "And what an undecipherable mess they've made of it." He went to bed in a bad mood. On the point of falling asleep, he saw the widow walking with all her legs, like a spider.

After this setback Horace felt very disappointed in the boys, the dolls, and even Eulalie. But a few days later Frank took him out for a drive. Suddenly, on the highway, Frank said:

"See that small two-story house by the river? That's where that little shy man—you remember, the one who bought your blonde's sister— lives with your—uh—sister-in-law." He slapped Horace on the leg and they both laughed. "He only comes at night. Afraid his mother will find out."

The next morning, toward noon, Horace returned to the spot alone. A dirt road led down to the shy man's house by the river. At the entrance to the road stood a closed gate, and next to it a gatehouse probably belonging to the forest ranger. He clapped, and an unshaven man in a torn hat came out chewing on a mouthful of something:

"Yeah—what is it?"

"I've been told the owner of that house over there has a doll . . . "

The man, now leaning back on a tree, cut him short:

"The owner's out."

Horace drew several bills from his wallet, and the man, eyeing the money, began to chew more slowly. Horace stood there thoughtfully rippling the bills as if they were a hand of cards. The man swallowed his mouthful and watched. After giving him time to imagine what he could do with the money, Horace said:

"I might just want to have a quick look at that doll . . . "

"The boss'll be back at seven."

"Is the house open?"

"No, but here's the key," said the man, reaching for the loot and pocketing it. "Remember, if anyone finds out, I ain't seen you . . . Give the key two turns . . . The doll's upstairs . . . And, mind you, don't leave nothing out of place."

Horace strode with brisk steps down the road, once again full of youthful excitement. The small front door was as dirty as a slovenly old hag, and the key seemed to squirm in the lock. He went into a dingy room with fishing poles leaning against a wall. He picked his way through the litter and up a recently varnished staircase. The bedroom was comfortable—but there was no doll in sight. He looked every-where, even under the bed, until he found her in a wardrobe. At first it was like running into one of Mary's surprises. The doll was in a black evening gown dotted with tiny rhinestones like drops of glass. If she had been in one of his showcases he would have thought of her as a widow sprinkled with tears. Suddenly he heard a blast, like a gunshot. He ran to look over the edge of the staircase and saw a fishing pole lying on the floor below, in a small cloud of dust. Then he decided to wrap the doll in a blanket and carry her down to the river. She was light and cold, and while he looked for a hidden spot under the trees, he caught a scent that did not seem to come from the forest and traced it to her. He found a soft patch of grass, spread out the blanket, holding her by the legs, slung over his shoulder, and laid her down as gently as if she had fainted in his arms. In spite of the seclusion, he was uneasy. A frog jumped and landed nearby. As it sat there for a long moment, panting, he wondered which way it was going to leap next and finally threw a stone at it. But, to his disappointment, he still could not devote his full attention to this new Daisy Doll. He dared not look her in the face for fear of her lifeless scorn. Instead, he heard a strange murmur mixed with the sound of water. It came from the river, where he saw a boy in a boat, rowing toward him with horrible grimaces. He had a big head, gripped the oars with tiny hands, and seemed to move only his mouth, which was like a piece of gut hideously twisted in its strange murmur. Horace grabbed the doll and ran back to the shy man's house.

On his way home, after this adventure with a Daisy belonging to someone else, he thought of moving to some other country and never looking at another doll. He hurried into the black house and up to the bedroom, grimly determined to get rid of Eulalie—and found Mary sprawled face down on the bed, crying. He went up and stroked her hair, but realized Eulalie was on the bed with them. So he called in one of the twins and ordered her to remove the doll and to have Frank come for her. He stretched out next to Mary and they both lay there in silence waiting for night to fall. And then, taking her hand and searching painfully for words, as if struggling with a foreign language, he confessed how disappointed he was in the dolls and how miserable his life had been without her.

IX

Mary thought Horace's disappointment in the dolls was final, and for a while they both acted as if happier times were back. The first few days, the memories of Daisy were bearable. But then they began to fall into unexpected silences—and each knew who the other was thinking of. One morning, strolling in the garden, Mary stopped by the tree where she had put Daisy to surprise Horace. There, remembering the story made up by the neighbors and the fact that she had actually killed Daisy, she burst into tears. When Horace came out to ask her what was wrong, she met him with a bleak silence, refusing to explain. He realized she had lost much of her appeal, standing there with folded arms, without Daisy. Then, one evening, he was seated in the little parlor, blaming himself for Daisy's death, brooding over his guilt, when suddenly he noticed a black cat in the room. He got up, annoyed, intending to rebuke Alex for letting it in, when Mary appeared saying she had brought it. She was in such a gay mood, hugging him as she told him about it, that he did not want to upset her by throwing it out, but he hated it for the way it had taken advantage of his guilty feelings to sneak up on him. And soon it became a source of further discord as she trained it to sleep on the bed. He would wait for her to fall asleep, then start an earthquake under the covers until he dislodged it. One night she woke up in the middle of the earthquake:

"Was that you kicking the cat, Horace?"

"I don't know."

She kept coming to the defense of the cat, scolding him when he was mean to it. One night, after dinner, he went into the show room to play the piano. For some days now he had called off the scenes in the glass cases and, against his habit, left the dolls in the dark, alone with only the drone of the machines. He lit a footlamp by the piano, and there, on the lid, indistinguishable from the piano except for its eyes, was the cat. Startled, he brushed it off roughly and chased it into the little parlor. There, jumping and clawing to get out, it ripped a curtain off the door to the courtyard. Mary was watching from the dining room. She saw the curtain come down and rushed in with strong words. The last he heard was:

"You made me stab Daisy and now I suppose you want me to kill the cat."

He put on his hat and went out for a walk. He was thinking that, if she had forgiven him—at one point, when they were making up, she had even said, "I love you because you're a bit mad"—Mary had no right now to blame him for Daisy's death. In any case, seeing her lose her attraction without Daisy was punishment enough. The cat, instead of adding to her appeal, cheapened her. She had been crying when he left and he had thought, "Well, it's her cat—so it's her guilt." At the same time, he had the uneasy feeling that her guilt was nothing compared to his, and that, while it was true that she no longer inspired him, it was also true that he was falling back into his old habit of letting her wash his sins away. And so it would always be, even on his deathbed. He imagined her at his side still, on his predictably cowardly last days or minutes, sharing his unholy dread. Perhaps, worse still—he hadn't made up his mind on that point—he would not know she was there.

At the corner he stopped to gather his wits so he could cross without being run over. For a long time he wandered in the dark streets, lost in thought. Suddenly he found himself in Acacia Park. He sat on a bench, still thinking about his life, resting his eyes on a spot under the trees. Then he followed the long shadows of the trees down to a lake, where he stopped to wonder vaguely about his soul, which was like a gloomy silence over the dark water: a silence with a memory of its own, in which he recognized the noise of the machines, as if it were another form of silence. Perhaps the noise had been a steamboat sailing by, and the silence was the memories of dolls left in the wreck as it sank in the night. Suddenly coming back to reality, he saw a young couple get up out of the shadows. As they approached, he remembered kissing Mary for the first time in a fig tree, nearly falling out of the tree, after picking the first figs. The couple walked by a few feet away, crossed a narrow street and went into a small house. He noticed a row of similar houses, some with "for rent" signs. When he got home, he made up again with Mary. But, later that night, alone for a moment in the show room, he thought of renting one of the small houses on the park with a Daisy Doll.

The next day at breakfast something about the cat caught his attention: it had green bows in its ears. Mary explained that all newborn kittens had the tips of their ears pierced by the druggist with one of those machines used for punching holes in file paper. He found this amusing and decided it was a good sign. From a street phone he called Frank to ask him how he could distinguish the Daisy Dolls from the others in the Springwear collection. Frank said that at the moment there was only one, near the cash register, wearing a single long earring. The fact that there was only one left seemed providential to Horace: she was meant for him. And he began to relish the idea of returning to his vice as to a voluptuous fate. He could have taken a trolley, but he did not want to break his mood, so he walked, thinking about how he was going to tell his doll apart in the throng of other dolls. Now he was also part of a throng, pleasantly lost—it was the day before Carnival—in the holiday crowd. The store was farther away than he had anticipated. He began to feel tired—and anxious to meet the doll. A child aimed a horn at him and let out an awful blast in his face. He started to have horrible misgivings and wondered whether he should not put things off until afternoon. But when he reached the store and saw costumed dolls in the show windows he decided to go in. The Daisy Doll was wearing a wine-colored Renaissance costume. A tiny mask added to her proud bearing and he felt like humbling her. But a salesgirl he knew came up with a crooked smile and he withdrew.

In a matter of days he had installed the doll in one of the small houses by the park. Twice a week, at nine in the evening, Frank sent a girl from his shop over with a cleaning woman. At ten o'clock the girl filled the doll with hot water and left. Horace had kept the doll's mask on. He was delighted with her and called her Hermione. One night when they were sitting in front of a picture he saw her eyes reflected in the glass: they shone through the black mask and looked thoughtful. From then on he always sat in the same place, cheek to cheek with her, and whenever he thought the eyes in the glass—it was a picture of a waterfall—took on an expression of humbled pride he kissed her passionately. Some nights he crossed the park with her—he seemed to be walking a ghost—and they sat on a bench near a fountain. But suddenly he would realize her water was getting cold and hurry her back into the house.

Not long after that there was a big fashion show in the Springwear store. A huge glass case filled the whole of the top floor: it was in the center of the room, leaving just enough space on all four sides for the spectators to move around it. Because people came not only for the fashions but also to pick out the Daisy Dolls, the show was a tremendous success. The showcase was divided into two sections by a mirror that extended to the ceiling. In the section facing the entrance, the scene—arranged and interpreted by Horace's boys—represented an old folk tale, "The Woman of the Lake." A young woman lived in the depths of a forest, near a lake. Every morning she left her tent and went down to the lake to comb her hair. She had a mirror which some said she held up behind her, facing the water, in order to see the back of her head. One morning, after a late party, some high-society ladies decided to pay the lonely woman a visit. They were to arrive at dawn, ask her why she lived alone, and offer their help. When they came up on her, the woman of the lake was combing. She saw their elegant gowns through her hair, and curtsied humbly before them. But at their first question she straightened up and set out along the edge of the lake. The ladies, thinking she was going to answer the question or show them some secret, followed her. But the lonely woman only went round and round the lake, trailed by the ladies, without saying or showing them anything. So the ladies left in disgust, and from then on she was known as "the madwoman of the lake." Which is why, in that part of the country, a person lost in silent thought is said to be "going round the lake."

In the showcase, the woman of the lake appeared seated at a dressing table on the edge of the water. She wore a frilly white robe embroidered with yellow leaves. On the dresser stood a number of vials of perfume and other objects. It was the moment in the story when the ladies arrived in their evening gowns. All sorts of faces enthralled by the scene went by outside the glass, looking the dolls up and down, and not only for their fashions. There were glinting eyes that jumped suspiciously from a skirt to a neckline, from one doll to the next, distrusting even the virtuous ones like the woman of the lake. Other wary eyes seemed to tiptoe over the dresses as if afraid of slipping and landing on bare flesh. A young girl bowed her head in Cinderella-like awe at the worldly splendors that she imagined went with the beautiful gowns. A man knit his brows and averted his eyes from his wife, hiding his urge to own a Daisy Doll. The dolls, in general, did not seem to care whether they were being dressed or undressed. They were like mad dreamers oblivious to everything but their poses.

The other section of the showcase was subdivided into two parts—a beach and a forest. The dolls on the beach wore bathing suits. Horace had stopped to observe two in a "conversational" pose: one with concentric circles drawn on her belly, like a shooting target (the circles were red), the other with fish painted on her shoulderblades. Carrying his small head stiffly, like another doll head, among the spectators, Horace moved on to the forest. The dolls in that scene were natives and half-naked. Instead of hair, some grew plants with small leaves from their heads, like vines that trailed down their backs; they had flowers or stripes on their dark skins, like cannibals. Others were painted all over with very bright human eyes. He took an immediately liking to a negress, who looked normal except for a cute little black face with red button lips painted on each breast. He went on circling the showcase until he located Frank and asked him:

"Which of the dolls in the forest are Daisies?"

"Why, dear boy, in that section they're all Daisies."

"I want the negress sent to the house by the park."

"I'm sold out right now. It'll take at least a week."

In fact, no less than twenty days went by before Horace and the negress could meet in the house by the park. She was in bed, with the covers drawn up to her chin.

He found her less interesting than expected, and when he pulled back the covers she let out a fiendish cackle in his face. It was Mary, who proceeded to vent her spite on him with bitter words. She explained how she had learned of his latest escapade: it turned out his cleaning woman also worked for her cousin Prairie. Noticing his strange calm—he seemed distraught—she stopped short. But then, trying to hide her amazement, she asked:

"So now what do you have to say for yourself?"

He went on staring blankly, like a man sunk into a stupor after an exhaustion of years. Then he started to turn himself around with a funny little shuffle. Mary said, "Wait for me," and got up to wash off the black paint in the bathroom. She was frightened and had started to cry and sneeze at the same time. When she got back he had vanished. But she found him at home, locked in a guest room, refusing to talk to anyone.

X

Mary kept asking Horace to forgive her for her latest surprise. But he remained as silent and unyielding as a wooden statue that neither represented a saint nor was able to grant anything. Most of the time he was shuttered in the guest room, almost motionless (they knew he was alive only because he kept emptying bottles of wine from France). Sometimes he went out for a while in the evening. When he returned he had a bite to eat and then lay flat on the bed again, with open eyes. Often Mary went in to look at him, late at night, and found him rigid as a doll, always with the same glassy stare. One night she was stunned to see the cat curled up next to him. She decided to call the doctor, who began giving him injections. He was terrified of the injections but seemed to take more of an interest in life. So, with the help of the boys who worked on the glass cases, she convinced him to let them set up a new show for him.

That night they had dinner in the dining room. He asked for the mustard and drank a considerable amount of wine from France. He took his coffee in the little parlor, then went straight into the show room. The first scene had no caption: among plants and soft lights, in a large rippling pool, he made out a number of loose arms and legs. He saw the sole of a foot stick out through some branches, like a face, followed by the entire leg, which reminded him of a beast in search of prey. As it glanced off the glass wall, it hesitated before veering in the opposite direction. Then came another leg, followed by a hand with its arm, slowly winding and unwinding around each other like bored animals in a cage. He stood there for a while, dreamily watching their different combinations, until there was a meeting of toes and fingers. Suddenly the leg began to straighten out in the commonplace gesture of standing on its foot. He was dismayed and flashed his light at Walter, as he moved the podium to the next scene. There he saw a doll on a bed, wearing a queen's crown. Curled up next to her was Mary's cat. This distressed him and he was angry at the boys for letting it in. At the foot of the bed were three nuns kneeling on prayer stools. The caption read, "The queen died giving alms. She had no time to confess, but her whole country is praying for her." When he looked again, the cat was gone. But he had the uneasy feeling it would turn up again somewhere. He decided to enter the scene—gingerly, watching for the unpleasant surprise the cat was about to spring on him. Bending to peer into the queen's face, he rested a hand on the foot of the bed. Almost at once, a hand belonging to one of the nuns settled on his. He must not have heard Mary's voice pleading with him, because the minute he felt her hand he straightened up, stiff as death, stretching his neck and gasping like a captive bird trying to flap its wings and caw. Mary took hold of his arm, but he pulled away in terror and began turning himself around with a little shuffle, as he had done the day she had painted her face black and laughed in his face. She was rattled and frightened again and let out a scream. He tripped on a nun, knocking her over. Then, on his way out of the case, he missed the small door and walked into the glass wall. There he stood pounding on the glass with his hands, which were like birds beating against a closed window. Mary did not dare take hold of his arm again. She ran to call Alex, who was nowhere to be found. Finally he appeared, and, thinking she was a nun, asked politely what he could do for her. Crying, she said that Horace was mad. They went into the show room but could not find him. They were still looking for him when they heard his steps in the gravel of the garden. They saw him cut straight through the flowerbeds. And when they caught up with him, he was going toward the noise of the machines.

About the Authors

Gabriel García Márquez was born in 1928 in Aracataca, Colombia. As a child he lived with his grandparents near a banana plantation. He studied law in Bogotá and Cartagena, then became a journalist and a writer. *No One Writes to the Colonel and Other Stories* (1968) was his first book published in an English translation. It was followed by *One Hundred Years of Solitude* (1970), *Leaf Storm and Other Stories* (1972), *The Autumn of the Patriarch* (1976), *Innocent Eréndira and Other Stories* (1978), *In Evil Hour* (1979), *Chronicle of a Death Foretold* (1982), *Collected Stories* (1984), *The Story of a Shipwrecked Sailor* (1986), *Clandestine in Chile: The Adventures of Miguel Littín* (1987), *Love in the Time of Cholera* (1988), *Collected Novellas* (1990), *The General in His Labyrinth* (1990), *Of Love and Other Demons* (1995). In 1982 García Márquez was awarded the Nobel Prize for Literature.

Ana Lydia Vega was born in Santurie, Puerto Rico, in 1946. She has published in Spanish four collections of short stories—*Virgins and Martyrs* (1981), *Encancaranublado and Other Tales of Shipwreck* (1982), *Passion for History and Other Tales of Passion* (1987), and *False Chronicles of the South* (1991). In 1994 an English translation of her short fiction was published under the title *True and False Romances.* Ana Lydia Vega is a professor of French and Caribbean Literature at the University of Puerto Rico, Rio Piedras.

Guillermo Cabrera Infante was born in 1929 in Gibara, Cuba, a small town in Oriente Province. His parents, who were founders of the Cuban communist party, moved to Havana in 1941. Cabrera Infante published his first short story when he was seventeen and in 1952 he was jailed briefly for publishing a story entitled "English Profanities." In 1954 he became a film critic and founded the first film library in Cuba.

He then became editor of the cultural weekly *Lunes de Revolucion* until it was banned by Castro in 1961. From 1962 to 1965 he was cultural attaché with the Cuban Embassy in Brussels and in 1966 he immigrated to England, became a British citizen, and now lives in London. His books published in English are *Three Trapped Tigers* (1971), *A View of Dawn in the Tropics* (1978), *Holy Smoke* (1982), *Infante's Inferno* (1984), *A Twentieth-Century Job* (1991), *Writes of Passage* (1994), and *Mea Cuba* (1995). Cabrera Infante has also written screenplays and film and literary criticism.

ALVARO MUTIS was born in Bogotá, Colombia, in 1923. As a child he lived in Brussels, returning to Bogotá to complete his education. Since 1956 he has lived in Mexico. The author of poetry, short stories, and novels, his first poetry was published in 1948, his first short stories in 1978, and his first novella, *The Snow of the Admiral*, the initial volume in the Maqroll series for which he received the Prix Medicis, in 1989. In English his books are *Maqroll: Three Novellas* (1992) and *The Adventures of Maqroll: Four Novellas* (1995). His poetry has appeared in *The New Yorker*.

ALEJO CARPENTIER (1904–1980) was born in Havana, the son of a French father and a Russian mother who moved to Cuba. He became a journalist and in 1924 was editor of the magazine *Carteles*. Imprisoned for signing a manifesto against the dictator Machado, he moved to Paris when released and lived there for eleven years, becoming friendly with the Surrealists. He returned to Cuba in 1939 and worked in radio. He lived in Venezuela from 1945 to 1950, and after returning to Cuba he entered the diplomatic service and served in France. His novels translated into English are *The Lost Steps* (1956), *The Kingdom of This World* (1957), *Explosion in the Cathedral* (1963), *Reasons of State* (1976), *Concert Baroque* (1988), *The Harp and the Shadow* (1990), *The Chase* (1990), and a collection of short works, *War of Time* (1970).

JULIO CORTÁZAR (1914–1984) was born in Brussels. His parents were from Argentina and he returned there as a young boy, living outside Buenos Aires. At twenty he began to write short stories and his first story was published in 1946 by Jorge Luis Borges. In 1951 he moved to France, where he lived until his death. His short stories have been published in English in several volumes: *The End of the Game* (1967), *Cronopios and Famas* (1969), *All Fires the Fire* (1973), *A Change of*

Light (1980), *We Love Glenda So Much* (1983), and *Unreasonable Hours* (1995). Among his novels published in English are *The Winners* (1965), *Hopscotch* (1966), *62: A Model Kit* (1972), and *A Manual for Manuel* (1978). Cortázar also published essays, poetry, literary criticism, and translations.

João Guimarães Rosa (1908–1967) was born in Cordisburgo in Minas Gerais, bordering Brazil's sertão, the vast and isolated plateau of plain and jungle covering nearly a third of the country. He studied and practiced medicine but in 1934 entered the diplomatic service, serving in Hamburg, Colombia, Paris, and as a delegate to UNESCO before returning to Rio in 1953. As head of the Department of Frontier Demarcation he frequently visited Minas Gerais and the backlands, which were the source of his fiction. His first collection of stories, *Sagarana,* was published in English in 1938 and in 1963 his epic novel *The Devil to Pay in the Backlands* (*Grande Sertão: Veredas*) appeared in an English translation. Two additional short story collections were published in English: *The Third Bank of the River* in 1962 and *Tutameia* in 1967, three months before his death. Guimarães Rosa also wrote two volumes of short novels published in Brazil in 1956 and 1969.

Felisberto Hernández (1902–1964) was born in Montevideo, Uruguay. When he was nine years old, he began to play the piano; at twelve he was playing in movie houses, accompanying silent movies, and at twenty he was touring small-town concert halls of Uruguay and Argentina. He paid for the publication of his first four books of short prose pieces. His three later story collections were published in Spanish: *No One Had Lit a Lamp* (1947), *The Daisy Dolls* (1949), and *The Flooded House* (1960). He lived in Paris for two years and died impoverished and unknown. In 1993 a collection of his short fiction was published in English entitled *Piano Stories*.

●

Cass Canfield, Jr. is a Senior Editor at HarperCollins who has published numerous Latin American authors over the years.

Ilan Stavans teaches at Amherst and is the author of *The Hispanic Condition, Bandido, The One-Handed Pianist and Other Stories,* and other works. He is also co-editor of *Growing Up Latino.* He has contributed articles and reviews to the *Nation,* the *Washington Post,* the *Boston Globe,* the *Miami Herald, Bloomsbury Review, Commonweal,* and other media.